# THE DEVIL'S REBIRTH:

## The Terror Triangle of Ikhwan, IRGC and Hezbollah

# THE DEVIL'S REBIRTH:

## The Terror Triangle of Ikhwan, IRGC and Hezbollah

*Edited By*

# Noor Dahri

Vij Books India Pvt Ltd
New Delhi (India)

*Published by*

**Vij Books India Pvt Ltd**
(Publishers, Distributors & Importers)
2/19, Ansari Road
Delhi – 110 002
Phones: 91-11-43596460, 91-11-47340674
Mob: 98110 94883
E-mail: contact@vijpublishing.com
Web : www.vijbooks.in

Copyright © 2021, *Author*

ISBN: 978-93-90439-62-1 (Hardback)

ISBN: 978-93-90439-64-5 (Paperback)

ISBN: 978-93-90439-65-2 (ebook)

# CONTENTS

## PART 3

## HEZBOLLAH

# Acknowledgement

The edited volume is a collaborative project and I am fortunate to have been able to edit the comprehensive and deep research of leading academics and analysts from different countries to provide a global spotlight on the growing security and national threat of Islamist organisations such as Ikhwan ul Muslimeen, IRGC and Hezbollah in the Middle East as well as across the globe. I would like to thank sincerely the participating authors who consented to give me the permission to publish their research and rich contributions that undoubtably make this a more authoritative volume.

My final and greatest thanks to my family, who understood and supported me throughout the entire process; and in particular, my wife, Farah, and my children Barirah and Bayyinah, who had to give up a great deal of "quality time" with their father while this book was being written.

My special appreciation to my best friend Musa Khan Jalalzai for his unwavering support and help in editing and publishing this book.

# INTRODUCTION

## Muslim Brotherhood

The first modern political Islamic movement *Jam iyyat al-Ikhwan al-Muslimin* (Muslim Brotherhood) was born in Egypt in 1928 by its founder Hasan al-Banna (1906-1949). The main objectives of Ikhwan were based on spiritual reformation as well as social welfare in youth within a society such as physical training, sports, religious and ideological indoctrination, national pride, resistance against foreign domination and establishing a state under the Sharia rule.[1] The leadership of Ikhwan was well learned and talented, they were shortly able to open its branches all over Egypt by visiting the branches, writing, speaking and providing assistance to people of Egypt in need. For example: Ikhwan had only five branches in 1930 but by 1949, they dramatically increased to two thousand branches and by 1941 the Ikhwan was so powerful and influential movement in the society so that when Hasan al Banna (HB) was arrested by the order of Egyptian Prime Minister under the pressure generated by the British Empire but, he soon released him due to the fear of revolt that would topple his government.[2] MB established the structure of welfare throughout the country and it was Hassan al Bana's ideology to bring an education reformation in the country, therefore in the initial stage organisation's focus was on the welfare of an ordinary citizen of the country. They established welfare centres, Islamic education institutions, separate schools for boys and girls and also involved deeply in community services, this was the reason MB got massive popularity in public and within a short period of twenty years, Ikhwan gained estimated three hundred thousand members by 1946.[3]

### Ikhwan Administrative Structure

The MB established a network of the social and religious centres in approximately every city and village of the country and this was the basic push for their organisation's support and establishing public support. Members of the organisation showed their great loyalty to the branches

1

as well as to the organisation.[4] The Ikhwan had a proper organised administrative structure from top to bottom and it seemed like a state within the state. The organisation had different administrative departments such as General guide which was operated under General Guide Bureau and General Consultative Council. The organisation had a very efficient system of recruiting, training and multiplying youth over the time and had several levels of sub departments. For instance, the Rover scouting movement, athletic training, prayers, Qur'anic study, and charitable work. The structure of "The Battalions" was added in 1937 and was categorised from one to four subgroups of ten members, each subgroup was being supervised by a deputy, to whom the local members pledged an oath of strict obedience, discipline, and secrecy. Later, al-Banna replaced "the battalions" with the "Cooperative Family".[5]

**Ikhwan Milestones**

The pressure mounted from hardcore militant members of the organisation upon Hasan al Banna to start a military campaign against the Egyptian regime to overthrow the government. In 1939 dissenters broke off within the organisation to from the militant branch, named as "Mohammad's Youth". In around 1940, Hasan al Banna formed a secret department within the organisation, "Tanfidah" which means "Execution" as a secret military branch of the organisation. The militant members of the organisation forced al Banna to form such special apparatus earlier than he might have chosen to form later when he kept its profile exceptionally low during the period of the Second World War.[6]

**The Role & Ideology of Qutb in Ikhwan**

Sayyid Qutb was born in 1906 to his father who was a landowner as well as a political activist, holding a weekly meeting to discuss the political matters. When Qutb was at the age of 23, he moved to Cairo for his further education in a British style institution before starting his new job as a teacher in the ministry of Public Instruction. He was a highly intelligent young man and was keen to learn everything he had interest in. He devoted himself with literature and became a critic author that motivated him to write novels. He then started encountering the work of many famous scholars, including the word of Nobel Prize winner French Eugenicist Alexis Carrel. For his criticism, he soon became famous around his entire circle as he has a charismatic character to attract people through his writings and speeches.[7]

The latest wave of political Islamist terrorism that wrapped the world with the blood of innocents which started in 20th century to onwards actually is an ideology of Qutbism. The leading member of 20th century's political Islamic ideologue was Sayyid Qutb of Egypt, who joined the Muslim Brotherhood (Ikhwan ul Muslimoon) in the 60s after completing his educational tour in the USA arranged by the Egyptian Government being an employee.

The deeper study of the ideology of Sayed Qutb finds that he was a more revolutionist than a Jihadist. He struggled all his second phase of life against the sinful (according to his thoughts) and corrupt Muslim regimes such as the tyranny Egyptian government. He did not advocate terrorism directly, according to his speeches and writings that seems that he was interested in to wage a non-violent Jihad against the cruel and corrupt Muslim states. It is claimed by some academic scholars that today's Jihadist ideology is far different than the ideology that Qutb introduced in the 20th century. He was an Islamic theorist who introduced the revolutionary theory in his movement which unfortunately later turned into the revolutionist ideology of Islamist Jihadism.

*According to a PhD scholar, El-Sayed el-Aswad:*

> "Despite the existence of common and shared components between Qutb's views and the ideology of present Islamists, and despite the impact of Qutb's thought on the latter's ideology, there are fundamental differences between them. This implies that despite the radical trend of Qutb's writings and teachings portraying Islam as a force opposing Western secular imperialism, Qutb did not support the wide-ranging and indiscriminate violence advocated locally by the Egyptian jihadist groups of the 1970s and 1980s, and globally by the extreme Islamists of global jihad like Bin Laden and Ayman al-Zawahiri operating through al-Qaeda. For Qutb, jihad must be directed toward sinful and corrupt Muslim regimes."[8]

But the question is this that how would a certain group wage a Jihad against the sinful and corrupt Muslim regimes? The only answer would come in a mind is "armed struggle" and, in this struggle, terrorists would indiscriminately target civilians by calling them "Taghut" tyranny or the followers of tyrant regimes. In this case, his writings intentionally or unintentionally promoted terrorism under the banner of just Jihad.

In the early stage of his practical life, he was a government servant and worked with various government departments. He was a pro state at that time but had a deep eye on the core principles of Ikhwan ul Muslimoon (Muslim Brotherhood). His philosophy suddenly changed when he returned from the USA and decided to join the Brotherhood in relations to introduce an awakening model for the young supporters. He introduced a West-inspired model of revolution into the Ikhwan movement which practiced the concept of Sufism at the time.[9]

Sayyid Qutb was an intellectual individual who was already known for his writings well before joining the Ikhwan movement. He authored a book named "Social Justice in Islam" in 1940s. During these years Qutb visited the USA for his further training where he expressed his hateful and negative thoughts towards the American materialistic culture, as opposed to the spiritual and moral culture of Islam. His political and religious struggle was changed from an Islamic scholar to a social revolutionist after returning from the US where he spent nearly two years and, in those years,, he transformed himself from a religious scholar to a radical revolutioanist.[10]

In 1953, the year after the revolution of the Egyptian Free Officer, he joined the Ikhwan ul Muslimoon (Muslim Brotherhood). In the beginning, he and his members of the Ikhwan movement supported Egyptian ruler Gamal Abdel Naser but later his relations with Gamal Naser deteriorated when he did not accept the Islamic Political Orientation. After a year of Qutb's joining the Ikhwan, Gamal Naser survived from the bloodied attempt of his assassination in 1954, that blamed on Ikhwan which forced them to go underground and that was the time when the journey from the ideological conflict to a social revolution between the Ikhwan and Egyptian government started. The period from 1954 to 1960 was an era that changed the political arena of Egypt from political and social reform to a bloodiest revolution.[11]

The continuous conflict between the Egyptian regime and Ikhwan ul Muslimoon ended when the Ikhwan leadership was persecuted and imprisoned, including Al-Hudaybi, then Supreme Guide of the Muslim Brotherhood and Sayyid Qutb. In prison, Sayyid Qutb wrote a masterpiece of Ikhwan "The Milestones" that discussed the notion of God's sovereignty (Hakimiyaa) as well the notion of Jihad, which was originally developed by an Indian intellectual Abu Al-Hassan Nadwi and a Pakistani Muslim scholar Abu Al-A'la Maududi. When Qutb released from the prison in

1964, he changed his peaceful and democratic revolutionary thoughts into the militant Islamist revolutionary ideology that's prime objective was to overthrow the Egyptian government and to form a Muslim state based on the principles of the first era of Islam.[12]

He joined the secret organisation within Muslim Brotherhood seeking to revive the Islamist movement and to establish an Islamist system in order to replace the socialist government. This was the step when the actual war of conflict between Gamal Naser and Ikhwan movement began and in retaliation, Egyptian authorities arrested Qutb again along with two other Ikhwan leaders and he was finally executed in 1966. The revolutionary movement did not end here but the ideological struggle that turned into the violent Islamist movement has rapidly risen because the death of Qutb by Egyptian regime gave a final breath to the resistance movement of Qutb that spread all over Egypt and across borders. Mohammad Qutb, a brother of Sayyid Qutb left Egypt for Saudi Arabia and joined a Saudi university as a lecturer.[13] He was the main ideologue of Qutbism who induced the political Islamist violent ideology into the minds of Saudi generations. It was the peak time in 1980s when his ideology got a new birth through the Afghan Jihad. There were many prominent students among the circle of Mohammad Qutb who later joined the Afghan war that were Usama bin Laden and Dr Ayman Al Zawahiri who later created a global terrorist network titled Al-Qaeda.[14]

The claim of international media that Usama Bin Laden and Dr Ayman al Zawahiri were Salafists is completely a wrong and bias claim. These both Jihadists figures were influenced by Ikhwanic ideology, not Salafists or Wahabis. There are also some Salafist political parties in Egypt that gained a great victory in a 2011 revolution, such as Al-Asalah (The Authenticity), Al Fadilah (The Virtue) and Al-Nur (The Light) that have dominated Egyptian political arena after the 2011 revolution. There are huge political, religious and ideological differences between the Salafist movements and Ikhwan ul Muslimoon that created a huge space between both opposite ideologies.[15]

John Calvert, the author of "Sayyid Qutb and the Origins of Radical Islamism" noted in his book:

*"If Qutb were alive, he would have been terrified by the extremist trends of the post-Qutb Islamists".*[16]

## Muslim Brotherhood and Iran Connection

Qutb was an influential figure for Iranian, even though the Muslim Brotherhood never mentioned Iranian revolution as their ideological model but some academic researchers' asses Iranian revolution as an example model of the revolutionist ideology of Muslim Brotherhood. However, because of the sectarian difference of Sunni and Shia, Ikhwan did not want to give a credit of their revolutionist ideology to Iranian revolutionists but Qutb's work was being translated and disseminated in Iran.[17]

Yusuf Anal successfully connected the ideological link of Qutb with Iran:

> "In 1984, the postal service of the Islamic Republic of Iran issued a stamp depicting a man behind bars who appears to be deep in thought".[18]

It was a scene from the 1966 trial of the Egyptian MB ideologues, Sayyid Qutb. However, Shahid Hamid argued that MB did not want to introduce a complete Iranian type revolution to overthrow governments but to change the peoples' minds.

"The distance with Iran would only grow as Sunni Islamists learned a strategic lesson from the 1990s and 2000s: Winning elections was not enough to assume power. Just as important was reassuring the West that they would not follow the Iranian model or pursue "one man, one vote, one time."[19]

Iran was one the first country to celebrate the victory of the MB winning the election in Egypt and its leader Mohammad Morsi became the first MB president in 2012 and paid homage to the martyrs of the Egyptian revolution of 2011. The Egyptian government under Morsi had bilateral relations with Iran and he would not disappoint Iranian expectations; he became the first Egyptian President to visit the Islamic Republic of Iran in August 2012.[20] No only this, but in February 2015, a conference on Sayyid Qutb "Reading and Re-reviewing the Views of Sayyid Qutb" was held in Tehran which was attended by many prominent Iranian intellectuals,[21] who revealed that Sayyid Qutb has been read and studied in Iran for many years in his life. At the conference they also discussed how re-evaluate Qutb's views.

Some of the ideological opinions of Sayed Qutb were same as Shia belief about first Islamic caliphs as he agreed with Shia Muslims by accusing the

Islam's third caliph 'Uthman b. Affan' (d. 656 CE), of nepotism and considers his years in office as an unfortunate turning point in Islamic history, which resulted in the rise of the worldly corrupt Umayyad dynasty.[22]

## IRGC

Iran is a Shia country that has developed a mass militia networks around the Middle East in order to gain its political, religious and ideological influence in Arab countries. Iran has hundreds of private militias to control the region through violence and to step down the elected governments. Islamic Revolutionary Guards Corps (IRGC) is a main Iranian official and governmental organisation that has established the empire of mafia and militia networks across the world particularly in the Arab world. Al- Quds Force is an Iranian semi government organisation that operates openly and freely in Syria, Iraq, Yamen, Bahrain, Lebanon, Libya, Afghanistan, Lebanon and in many other states. Many commentators have claimed that the IRGC, Quds Force and their Lebanese proxy, Hezbollah, have been successful in account of their doctrine.

There are reports that Iran has spent $30 billion since 2011 in the war of Syria in order to support Asad regime and the reports have also indicated that an estimated 80,000 Shia foreign fighter that were recruited and trained by the IRGC have travelled to fight in Syria to defend Asad forces.[23] There are more than 121 violent Islamist inspired and perpetrated attacks around the world and only in 2017, at least 84,000 people died because of the Islamist Terrorism.[24] In 2018, it was announced that the IRGC has a total 9,000 ideological coaches, 40 percent of whom are clerics, who teach the training modules to newly join recruiters and that the IRGC's aim to increase this number by 50 every year.[25]

## Al-Quds

The IRGC has the special equivalent of one Special Forces division, plus additional smaller formations and these forces are given special priority IN terms of training and equipment. In addition, the IRGC has a special Quds force that plays a major role in giving Iran the ability to conduct unconventional warfare overseas using various foreign movements' proxies.[26]

In January 2006, Iran's Supreme National Security Council (SNSC) decided to place all Iranian operations in Iraq under the command of the Quds forces. At the same time, the SNSC decided to increase the personnel strength of the Quds to 15,000.[27] The exact data for the Quds are not available but according to some reports their current manpower increased from 15,000 to 50,000 in the Middle East region. The al-Quds forces are under the command of Brigadier General Esmail Qaani and have supported nonstate actors in many foreign countries. These including Hezbollah in Lebanon, Hamas and the Palestinian Islamic Jihad in the Gaza strip and the West Bank, the Shi'ites militias in Iraq, the Shi'ites in Afghanistan. Links to Sunni extremist groups like Al-Qaeda and ISIS have been reported.[28]

## Hezbollah

Hezbollah is a Shia militant Islamist organisation based in Lebanon which was founded in 1985 after the Lebanon war with Israel in 1982. Hezbollah's has many political and Jihadist wigs as the Jihad council[29] which is a paramilitary wing of the organisation and its political wing is "The Loyalty", the Resistance Bloc party[30] which represent Hezbollah in the Lebanese parliament. Since the death of Abbas al-Musawi in 1992, the group has been led by Hassan Nasrallah, its Secretary-General. The organisation's political or the military wings are considered terrorist organisations in 21st countries, as well as by the Arab League and the European Union.[31]

The idea of Hezbollah arose among Lebanese clerics who had studied in Najaf, and adopted the model set out by Ayatollah Khomeini after the Iranian Revolution in 1979. The organisation was established as part of an Iranian effort, through funding and the dispatch of a core group of pasdaran instructors, to aggregate a variety of Lebanese Shia groups into a unified organisation in order to resist the Israeli invasion[32] and as well as to improve the standing and status of the long marginalised and underrepresented Shi'ite community in the country.[33] A contingent of 1,500 pasdaran instructors arrived in the midst of the Syrian government, which occupied Lebanon's eastern highlands, permitted their transit to a base in the Bekaa valley.[34]

Iran and its Islamic Revolutionary Guard Corps (IRGC) provided funds and training to the budding militia, which adopted the name Hezbollah, meaning "The Party of God." It earned a reputation for extremist militancy due to its frequent clashes with rival Shiite militias, such as the Amal Movement, and attacked on foreign targets, including the 1983 suicide bombing of barracks housing U.S. as well as against the French troops in Beirut, in which more than three hundred people died. Hezbollah became a vital asset to Iran, bridging the Shiite Arab-Persian divides as Tehran established proxies throughout the Middle East.[35]

The book consists of three parts; the first part is about Ikhwan ul Muslimeen and its revolutionary ideology, the second part of the book highlighted the IRGC and its command and structure and the last part of the book discussed the Hezbollah and its operational military wings as well as its collaboration with drug cartel in the region and across the world. Each part has different chapters written by well experienced academics and famous researchers in the field of above topics. They deeply analysed the roots of those terrorist organisations and how these movements sustained and nurtured for many decades in the regions. They have also disclosed many secrets of the organisations hidden from the world such as their involvements in secretly supporting Al-Qaeda leadership and also providing assistance to ISIS as well as their connection with the killings of diplomats in foreign countries and networking with cross border drug cartels and international mafias.

Dr Nawaf Obaid's insightful analysis of the role of the Muslim Brotherhood in Arab societies and the political process is a "must read" for understanding the basis for the intractable conflicts that plague the Middle East. Dr. Obaid offers a concise history of the Muslim Brotherhood country-by-country as a foundation for his incisive analysis on the principal reasons the group failed to achieve their political ambitions. Today, as the Muslim Brotherhood's influence continues to wane, this report raises important questions on the future of the Middle East. Is the Arab Spring a thing of the past? Will the "old order" resume its role in ruling the Middle East? What is the future of political Islam? These questions and others reverberate through the pages of this penetrating review of the Muslim Brotherhood's legacy and how it continues to shape events that are unfolding, today.

Dr Zuhdi Jasser introduced the ideological terms and ideas in order to understand the mechanism of the Muslim Brotherhood. He described them that our founding fathers were able to navigate a war of ideas against theocracy. We can do it again in the 21st century with Islam. It is absurd to assert that just because the Muslim Brotherhood is an Islamist group which uses its interpretation of the faith of Islam as a basis for its rule, that the United States cannot wage a battle against Islamist theocrats while cherishing Muslim liberals, modernists and critical thinkers. We have for too long been playing a "whack-a-mole" program against by-products of Muslim Brotherhood ideologues rather than directly countering the primary cancer cells of the Muslim Brotherhood operations.

In order to understand the Muslim Brotherhood, the following terms and ideas must become part of the fair domain of our national security agencies. Our agency analysts and government experts are both smart and fair enough to know that each of these terms carries with it a diverse set of interpretations from within the 'House of Islam' and that suppressing this essential debate hands the debate to our Islamist enemies. I submit the following terms and proposed definitions for the record in hopes that other government agencies follow suit and rather than engaging Islamist apologists who obstruct and deny, that they instead begin engaging honest Muslims who are ready to confront the global radical movements that use them:

**A.** Islam: the faith tradition, its practice, and scriptures identified by over 1.6 billion Muslims in the world.

**B.** Islamism and Islamists: the theo-political movement (Islamism) or party and its adherents (Islamists) who seek to establish Islamic states governed by shar'ia law in Muslim majority nations and institutions. Muslim Brotherhood members are Islamists.

**C.** Shar'ia: Islamic theological jurisprudence as interpreted by Muslim jurists and clerics and practiced by Muslims. The legal instrument of Islamist theocrats.

**D.** Jihad: a holy war or armed struggle against unbelievers or enemies of an Islamic state. It can also mean spiritual struggle within oneself against sin.

**E.** Wahhabism: a Sunni Islamist movement based in a puritanical literalism and intolerance of any other interpretations or faith. A revivalist movement originated in the Najd of Arabia in the mid-19th century by Ibn Abdul Wahhab. It is the dominant strain of thought empowered by the Kingdom of Saudi Arabia. Its ideas are central to the Salafi jihadism of groups like the Islamic State in Iraq and Syria (ISIS).

**F.** Salafism: Sunni Islamic fundamentalism, which attempts to return normative Muslim practices to the literal ways of the Prophet Muhammad in the 7th century. Salaf literally means "companions of the Prophet". It is often synonymous with Wahhabism but is far more ubiquitous. Salafism, like Wahhabism, deplores invention.

**G.** Salafi jihadism: The expansionist ideology (a combination of Salafism with militant jihadism) of groups like the Muslim Brotherhood that seek to create Islamic states and a global caliphate.

**H.** Caliphate and Caliphism: the theo-political ideology or desire by Islamists to re-establish the caliphate, a globally unified Islamic governance of Islamic states which are led by a single caliph.

**I.** Ummah: the entire Muslim Faith community, but it can also mean the Islamic state

**J.** Islamic reform, Ijtihad: critical interpretation of scripture (exegesis) and Islamic jurisprudence in the light of modernity.

**K.** Takfir: the rejection ('excommunication') of another Muslim from the faith community. The declaration of another Muslim as an apostate.

Dr Lorenzo Vidino analysed the aims and methods of Europe's Muslim Brotherhood by exposing them how they gained influence in the European countries. He described that in 1990 Yusuf al-Qaradawi, an influential Sunni scholar and the unofficial theological leader of the international Muslim Brotherhood (al Ikhwan al Muslimoun), published a book called Priorities of the Islamic Movement in the Coming Phase. This treatise can be considered the most recent manifesto of the Islamist revivalist movement. As Qaradawi explains in the introduction, the "Islamic Movement" is meant to be the "organised, collective work, undertaken by the people, to restore Islam to the leadership of society" and to reinstate "the Islamic caliphate system to the leadership anew as required by sharia"

Qaradawi's treatise introduces a new agenda and modus operandi for the movement, signalling a clear break with many Salafi groups and even with some past ideological elements of the Muslim Brotherhood. While the book does not rule out the use of violence to defend Muslim lands, it generally advocates the use of Dawah, dialogue, and other peaceful means to achieve the movement's goals. This doctrine is commonly referred to as "Wassatiyya," a sort of "middle way" between violent extremism and secularism, and Qaradawi is one of its key proponents.

After examining the situation of the "Islamic Movement" throughout the Muslim world, the dissertation devotes significant attention to the situation of Muslims living in the West. Qaradawi explains how Muslim expatriates living in Europe, Australia and North America "are no longer few in numbers," and that their presence is both permanent and destined to grow with new waves of immigration. While Qaradawi says that their presence is "necessary" for several reasons such as spreading the word of Allah globally and defending the Muslim Nation "against the antagonism and misinformation of anti-Islamic forces and trends" it is also problematic. Because the Muslim Nation, and there- fore Muslim minorities "scattered throughout the world," do not have a centralized leadership, "melting" poses a serious risk. Qaradawi warns, in other words, that a Muslim minority could lose its Islamic identity and be absorbed by the non-Muslim majority.

Qaradawi sees the lack of Muslim leadership not only as a problem, however. He also views it as an unprecedented opportunity for the Islamist movement to "play the role of the missing leadership of the Muslim Nation with all its trends and groups." While the revivalist movement can exercise only limited influence in Muslim countries, where hostile regimes keep it in check, Qaradawi realises that it is able to operate freely in the democratic West. Muslim expatriates disoriented by life in non-Muslim communities and often lacking the most basic knowledge about Islam, moreover, represent an ideally receptive audience for the movement's propaganda. Qaradawi asserts that revivalists need to take on an activist role in the West, claiming that "it is the duty of [the] Islamic Movement not to leave these expatriates to be swept by the whirlpool of the materialistic trend that prevails in the West."

What Qaradawi outlines in his treatise might, at first glance, appear to be nothing more than a fantasy. In reality, it corresponds to what the international network of the Muslim Brotherhood has been doing in the West for the past fifty years. Since the end of World War II, in fact, members of al Ikhwan al Muslimoon have settled in Europe and worked relentlessly to implement the goals stated by Qaradawi. In almost every European country, they founded student organizations that, having evolved into nationwide umbrella organisations, have become thanks to their activism and to the financial support from Arab Gulf countries the most prominent representatives of local Muslim communities. They established a web of mosques, research centres, think tanks, charities and schools that have been successful in spreading their heavily politicised interpretation of Islam. Finally, today, with the creation of a supranational jurisprudential body called the European Council for Fatwa and Research, the Ikhwan is taking its first, cautious steps toward Qaradawi's final goal: the introduction of sharia law within the Muslim communities of Europe.

Alma Keshavarz presented his review about IRGC and Al-Quds activities in the region. He has researched about the different units of the organisations such as UNIT 400 and he described it that both the IRGC and Quds Force have been secretive and Iran keeps most, if not all, of their activities and resources well-guarded. However, given the military unit's expansive operations, they developed another section within the organisation for more specialised operations. This section is known as Unit 400, which is believed to be a clandestine unit of the Quds Force under the direct command of the Supreme Leader of Iran. Specifically, this Unit is employed to seek out Western targets across the world. A 2012 report investigated the botched Bangkok plot to assassinate Israeli diplomats in Thailand, revealing that Majid Alavi, a former deputy Iranian intelligence minister, "shifted to the Quds Force [2012] and along with [Hamed] Abdollahi, a commander accused in the Washington plot," operates Unit 400, which is "known as the Special Operations Unit."

According to State Department cables, Alavi also spied on dissidents living in London and Los Angeles. Additionally, the 2012 report obtained information from U.S. officials that Unit 400 "conducts sensitive covert operations abroad [that] include terrorist attacks, assassinations, kidnappings and sabotage." They have also supplied Iraqi Shiite militants, as well as "weapons, equipment, training and money to Afghan insurgents… and also arrange the delivery of lethal aid into Syria and Lebanon and military training for Hezbollah and Palestinian militants."

Hence, the Quds Force has expanded its network to include a tight unit for the sole purpose of targeting westerners. The Arbabsiar plot as well as those afterwards continues to show the IRGC and Quds Force ambitions, though also indicative of their limits.

Udit Banerjea has written a very deep research about the intelligence role of the IRGC and how deeply analysed the comparison of its Intel capability with the US CIA. He wrote that prior to the Iranian Revolution in 1979, Iran's primary intelligence apparatus was an organisation known as SAVAK, an acronym for Sazman-e-Ettela'atva Amniat-e-Keshvar (National Security and Intelligence Organisation). The pre-revolutionary government of Iran, under the Shah Mohammad Reza Pahlavi, had been installed with the help of the U.S. Central Intelligence Agency (CIA) and the British, and had aligned with the West in the Cold War.

Mohsen Hamidi has brought a well analysed report about the Afghan Shia organisation of male fighters' calls "Fatemiyun". He said in his report that Over the last eight years, thousands of Afghan men and some boys have fought on the side of the Iran supported Assad government in Syria as members of the Fatemiyun group. Although they are sent to Syria from Iran and supported by the Iranian government, Tehran describes the group as "self-motivated." This dispatch, which is the first in a two-part series, explores why so many Afghan men decided to join the group and what the consequences of this might be for Afghan society at large. Given the recent drawdown of Syria's armed conflict, many of these men are now returning home, either to Iran or Afghanistan. This return is fraught with complexities. Mohsen Hamidi also examines the reports that warn of a Fatemiyun threat in Afghanistan and notes how the Syrian war has become a way of life for some of these men, for better or for worse.

Dr. Magnus Norell has examined the international community's long series of failures in Lebanon between the May 2000 Israeli withdrawal and the 2006 war with Hezbollah failures caused primarily by an inability to confront Lebanon's truly divisive issues. These problems had repeatedly led to new crises and posed a danger to the entire region. The conflict between Lebanon and Israel was no longer a conflict between two states. Since the end of Lebanon's fifteen-year civil war, Hezbollah has remained strong enough to drag the country into war against the will of the sovereign government. In tandem with its military operations, Hezbollah, or the "Party of God," has provided legal, social, and political services to many Lebanese. Hezbollah is thereby able to keep its conflict with Israel alive, making any attempt at a peaceful solution impossible.

At the same time, Syria and Iran are working both regionally and internationally to interfere with the various initiatives intended to strengthen the Lebanese government. This situation is an embarrassment to the international community. In the face of threats from Damascus and Tehran, the United Nations and, to some extent, the European Union have allowed themselves to be run over. The best example of this trend is the UN Interim Force in Lebanon (UNIFIL), whose presence in the South was supposedly bolstered with the passage of UN Security Council Resolution (UNSCR) 1701 near the end of the 2006 war. Shortly afterward, Syria made it clear that any attempt to patrol the Lebanese-Syrian frontier, the main access route for arms from Iran to Hezbollah, would be seen as a hostile act and met by force and closure of the border. The threat had its intended effect. Even before the ink had dried on UNSCR 1701, the UN declared that it had no intention of patrolling the border it had been empowered to control. Today, three years after UNSCR 1701 expanded UNIFIL's authority and increased its size from 2,000 to 15,000 personnel, the force is still incomplete. This reluctance to seriously confront the basic problems of Lebanon and its neighbourhood is rooted in a fear of placing the UN in conflict with Hezbollah, even if such a move would benefit the Lebanese government.

Ioan Pop & Mitchell D. Siberia have presented a deep latest research about how Iran and Hezbollah adopted new tactics and modus operandi in the west in order to target diplomats, Iranian opposition leaders, dump the ammunition as well as commit terrorist activities in the western countries. In their report, the readers will find how the Tensions between the United States and Iran/Hezbollah have been on the rise since 2018 when the U.S. administration withdrew from the 2015 nuclear deal. These tensions spiked in January 2020 when U.S. strikes killed Qassem Soleimani, the leader of Iran's IRGC-Quds Force. Furthermore, there is mounting evidence that in recent years, Iran and Hezbollah have sought to create a sleeper network in the U.S. and Western Europe, which could be activated to launch attacks as part of a retaliatory attack. This report assesses Iran and Hezbollah pre-operational modus operandi in the West derived from court documents and open source reporting of the recent arrest of Hezbollah and Iranian agents in the US and abroad. It sheds light on the recruitment, training, and placement of these agents and the intricacies of their past operations. While it is impossible to predict when, where or how Iran/ Hezbollah might retaliate as retribution for Soleimani's killing, this article argues that there is growing number of indicators and warning signs for a possible attacking the U.S. or against U.S. interests abroad.

Noor Dahri
Founder & Executive Director
Islamic Theology of Counter Terrorism (ITCT)
November 2020, United Kingdom

# PART 1

# IKHWAN UL MUSLIMEEN (MB)

## Chapter 1

# The Muslim Brotherhood: A Failure in Political Evolution

## *Dr. Nawaf Obaid*

### Foreword

Nawaf Obaid's insightful analysis of the role of the Muslim Brotherhood in Arab societies and the political process is a "must read" for understanding the basis for the intractable conflicts that plague the Middle East. Dr. Obaid offers a concise history of the Muslim Brotherhood country-by-country as a foundation for his incisive analysis on the principal reasons the group failed to achieve their political ambitions. Today, as the Muslim Brotherhood's influence continues to wane, this report raises important questions on the future of the Middle East. Is the Arab Spring a thing of the past? Will the "old order" resume its role in ruling the Middle East? What is the future of political Islam? These questions and others reverberate through the pages of this penetrating review of the Muslim Brotherhood's legacy and how it continues to shape events that are unfolding, today.

-Rolf Mowatt-Larssen, Director, Intelligence and Defense Project

### Introduction

While the Muslim Brotherhood (MB) started as a movement centered on resistance to what it saw as the Westernization, or de-Islamization of Muslim culture, it soon realized that resistance was only as effective as its access to power. Thus, began the group's long attempt to infiltrate the halls of governance. As this report will show, these attempts have failed. In essence, the tree of the Muslim Brotherhood has been unable to flower into a viable governmental structure for the Arab world because it is still fed by its oppositionist roots. Three core elements of the MB have kept it from being able to mature into and be accepted by the Arab public as a preferred political entity. First, the MB's primary objective was defined in its early years in educational terms: "to raise a new generation of Muslims who will understand Islam correctly."[1] It was a return to Islam, "din wadawla." Islam was viewed not only as a guide to private belief and ritual but also as a comprehensive system of values and governance intrinsically different from (and superior to) the political systems of the West.

As one can see from the group's nearly nine decades of history, this emphasis on religious ideology has not served it well when it comes to securing votes or being accepted into roles in governmental systems that, even in the relatively religious MENA region, inherently crave and reward more religiously neutral technocrats. Despite its extensive social efforts in many countries it has filled large social gaps left open by inept bureaucracies by providing services such as food handouts, education, health information, and community-building campaigns again and again, one finds MB representatives, and the organization itself, struggling to convince the larger public and government officials that its intentions are not tainted by an ideology bent on inserting more religion including sharia into politics and the legal system. And as this report will show, the Arab populace seems to have grown increasingly inimical to such insertion over the lifetime of the organization.

The second aspect of the MB that has kept it from being able to gain access to governance is the fact that the organization has frequently been unable to keep its members in step. The Brothers have split over various issues: the degree to which the organization should seek to implement sharia, the means by which that should be done, the methods proper to responding to the group's suppression, the organization's view on jihadist violence, and the types of candidates and positions to put forth during elections and in parliaments. This lack of ideological coherency has resulted in a sense among the Arab populace that the group is too riddled by infighting to be trusted with governance.

For example, under President Nasser, the Brotherhood was suppressed and dissolved in 1954, spurring the creation of the "secret apparatus."[2] This group attempted to assassinate Nasser, who retaliated by putting on trial, exiling, and hanging members of the Brotherhood a purge that lasted until

1970. The imminent threat of the Nasser regime caused a split within the organization, resulting in the ideological radicalization of many members and inspiring Sayyid Qutb's call for holy war against the system and its supporters. Once again, Nasser harshly punished Brotherhood members and executed Qutb. The period of ease between the Brotherhood and the later-elected Sadat then wore thin and some Brotherhood members called again for holy war, while others urged a more conservative, institutional response. Constant pressures like these have incessantly tested the group, forcing members to continually alter their thinking and redirect their message, with the result that the overall position of the group has become muddled.

This example hints at the third innate MB feature that has prevented it from developing into a viable form of governance: its connection with and/ or failure to refute connections to jihadist terror and political violence. The Brotherhood has been designated as a terrorist organization by Saudi Arabia, Egypt, the United Arab Emirates, and Russia (Kredo, 2015). In December 2015, a report made by British Prime Minister David Cameron pointed out that although the Brotherhood has been vocal about its opposition to al-Qaeda, "it has never credibly denounced the use made by terrorist organisations of the work of Sayyid Qutb, one of the Brotherhood's most prominent ideologues."[3] This contrasts with the U.S.'s approach, which still acknowledges the organization as being overall non- violent.

In a National Security Council email, the argument is made that "the de-legitimization of non-violent political groups does not promote stability," but rather "advances the very outcomes that such measures are intended to prevent."[4] Whether or not the MB is officially designated as a terrorist group, its actions have led many to link it with al-Qaeda, Hamas, and ISIS and other acts of politically or religiously motivated violence. The group's support for violence in Egypt is well documented and discussed briefly below. In the 1970s and 80s in Syria, the MB consistently engaged in violent interchanges with the Baathist government.[5] These confrontations culminated in February 1982 with the killing of 30,000 civilians by Alawites and some Kurds.[6]

The IAF in Jordan has maintained that it has "consistently refrained from violent political action in Jordan and remained committed to nonviolent change."[7] And yet, four IAF members attended a funeral tent erected by Abu Musab al-Zarqawi leader of al-Tawhid and member of al-Qaeda on June 11,

2006.[8] The IAF has also expressed support for Hamas.[9] There have recently been reports that the senior official of the IAF "called for support of ISIS and condemned the Western air strikes in Syria and Iraq."[10] The Palestinian Islamic Jihad (PIJ) was an offshoot of the Brotherhood that vehemently opposed Israel's existence, designating Israel "as a manifestation of Western imperialism in the Islamic lands."[11] In attempts to distract from the Oslo Peace Accords, the PIJ bombed a military bus by Netanya in January 1995 and set off a suicide nail bomb in Tel Aviv in March 1996 (BBC, 2003). And then there is Hamas, the Palestine branch of the Muslim Brotherhood, which is responsible for numerous acts of violence via its intifadas.

Finally, in Tunisia, the trend has largely been a failure of the Brotherhood to clearly and swiftly distant itself from jihadist terror. In August 2013, Ennahda declared Ansar al-Sharia a terrorist organization, but for many Tunisians, this response was "too little, too late." Then came the assassination of secular human rights activist Chokri Belaid and, five months later, his fellow leftist Mohamed Brahmi.[12] These assassinations created a rallying cry throughout Tunisia for change and led to Ennahda surrendering the interior ministry. The sense was that the group had been lax on fighting terrorists as countless cells had been allowed to form along the Algerian border in the mountainous areas.[13] In short, as an oppositionist movement that has had a difficult time keeping its members united and that also has myriad links to terrorism and/or a failure to address terrorism, the MB has struggled to gain legitimacy as a viable form of governance. This report will trace why. It begins, in Chapter 1, with a history of the group from its origins in Egypt and its central ideological underpinnings to its links to political violence and its engagement in the elections following the so-called Arab Spring. In Chapter 2, the major MB affiliates in other countries Syria, Jordan, Palestine, Morocco, and Tunisia are profiled. Then, Chapter 3 provides a more in-depth look at why the group failed in its objectives.

Finally, in the Conclusion, the claim is made that the Muslim Brotherhood is doomed to stay stuck in its past. Yes, it will most likely continue to offer social services, make religious assertions, and seek political offices. However, its history is far too riddled with infighting, violence, and resistance to give way to a cohesive organization that will ever gain widespread support as a source of respectable political leadership in the Arab world.

## What Is The Muslim Brotherhood?

The Muslim Brotherhood is an organization founded in 1928 by Hassan Al Banna in Ismailia, Egypt, following the abolition of the Islamic caliphate in Istanbul in 1924. Al Banna believed that moral decadence, economic bankruptcy, and anti-religious education were all part of the deliberate design of European powers to weaken and dominate the Muslim world, and his thinking greatly influenced the Brotherhood's early trajectory. From an unusually young age, Al Banna was preoccupied with the moral laxity he saw around him. He felt that there was a decrease in the respect for tradition and religion and a widespread enthusiasm for Western secular culture.

There were other similar groups, but what distinguished the Muslim Brotherhood was its religious interpretation of the country's malaise and the prescribed framework for its solution. The Brotherhood sponsored local social services and community projects that demonstrated the group's concern with public welfare and created new avenues for recruitment, which captured the hearts and minds of Egyptians. From 1928 to 1932, the primary goal of the Muslim Brotherhood was enlargement of its membership around Ismailia. Within four years, the organization had branches along the eastern and western edges of the Delta. The establishment of each headquarter was followed by the creation of a project (mosque/school) that came to serve as the focus for the activities of the community. In 1932, the first branch of the Muslim Brotherhood was established in Cairo. By 1949, there were two thousand branches and 300-600, 00 members.

In Ismailia, the Brotherhood contained both the middle and the lower-class elements although it was unclear which group dominated. Eventually, persons from the lower echelons of the educated middle class occupied the leading positions, giving the Brotherhood the popular and non-elitist character that it retained even after it had become an influential political force. Protecting the organization's financial independence became a major concern for Al Banna. He advocated a policy of non-reliance on local authorities for financial aid to welfare projects and relied on bene-factors who were not in a position to dominate the movement. Thus, the Brotherhood's professed nonalignment with the dominant political forces, underpinned by its relative financial independence, added much credibility to its ideological program.

The Muslim Brotherhood never offered a detailed and coherent vision of the Islamic order it sought to create. It stemmed from the group's emphasis on Amal (action) and Tanziim (organization) over Fikra (ideology).[14] This rendered the political thought of the group susceptible to conflicting interpretations. Some see its rejection of partisan conflict and calls for the establishment of a comprehensive Islamic order as evidence of a coercive project to gain state power and impose its agenda by force. But viewing the group this way misses many important nuances.

In its formative years, the Brotherhood was mostly devoted to a bottom-up approach of incremental societal reform. Yet it still embraced jihad in regards to Western imperialists and Zionists. In the 1930s, it invoked the principle of jihad against rival opposition groups and the Egyptian government, establishing paramilitary organizations like the Jawala (Rovers) and the Kata'ib (Battalions) that drew inspiration from the fascist youth organizations of interwar Europe. Late in 1942, the Brotherhood established a separate unit that came to be known as the "secret apparatus," a group that was responsible for the assassination of a prominent judge.[15] Nevertheless, the Brotherhood's most significant strategy has been its willingness to work within the existing political system for the advancement of its goals.

As early as 1941, the Brothers advocated participation in the system through contesting elections, aware they would need to do so if they were to have any real influence. Unsurprisingly, the Muslim Brotherhood set up an international organization. The Brotherhood was formed largely in response to the fall of the last Caliphate, and the movement stressed the universal nature of Islam and the Ummah.[16] Although Al Banna was focused on local issues, he also sought to spread his ideology and movement beyond Egypt, and he sent members to spread Da'wa. However, for Al Banna, Egypt was always the center and soul of the movement. Still, the Brotherhood was not averse to creating alternative centers of power whenever Cairo found itself under pressure (for example, the 1954 crackdown).

As the Brotherhood continued to develop internationally, Cairo came to act as a natural arbiter and leader, and intervened to resolve local issues. However, these interventions were spontaneous and lacked any real organizational formality until the 1970s, when a group of hawkish Brotherhood leaders sought to amplify Cairo's role. They emerged from prison to find that the Egyptian Brotherhood was dwindling, while others in the region were flourishing. The international environment was offering distinct opportunities that they could use to strengthen their clique and the Egyptian branch. This was the driving force behind the international Tanzeem.[17]

New insistence was placed on the obedience that other Brotherhood groups should display toward the Egyptian Murshid in order to strengthen control over existing branches in the Arab world. They began to harness opportunities in other countries where the Brotherhood had a presence. For example, Ramadan's opening of Islamic centers in Europe was seen by Egyptian leaders as an opportunity to harness media freedom. These activities were financed by Saudi Arabia and its Arab Gulf allies, who wanted to use the Brotherhood to shore themselves up against nationalist regimes in the region. The Brotherhood in Egypt wanted to bring all this activism in the Gulf, along with the petrodollars, under its control. The Muslim Brotherhood's support flourished throughout the Arab world for most of the 1950s through the 1970s, primarily due to external political tensions and transitions. From 1954 to 1970, the group remained the target of Nasser, who either imprisoned its members or exiled them. This provoked the rise of new schisms within the organization by encouraging the ideological radicalization of some of its members, who reached the conclusion that any regime that could inflict such suffering was irredeemably corrupt and could only, be combated by arms.

One of these men was Sayyid Qutb, a leader of the Brotherhood, who often wrote from his prison cell. He developed the concepts of Jahiliyya (all systems based on man made laws) and Hakimiyya (imposition of Islamic laws), exhorting youth to form a vanguard ready to launch a holy war against the modern Jahili system and all those who supported it, with the ultimate objective of developing a system based on the laws of God. Many of his thoughts and ideas spurred the emergence of several militant Islamic groups in the 1970s.[18] By the early 1980s, the Brotherhood was under pressure to establish an international body because of Sadat and Mubarak's crackdown on the movement in Egypt. To that end, it published a document called La Iha al-Dakhiliya (The Internal Statute).[19] This document, which marked the official establishment of the international Tanzeem, formalized the existing relationships between Cairo and other branches.

It also contained new international leadership structures comprising a General Guidance Office and General Shura Council, headed by the Murshid. Consequently, it put in place a system whereby national branches were formally bound by decisions made by the center. It created a highly centralized system that gave the Egyptians access to control and finances, which would feed their local and international ambitions. However, they discovered that doing so would be a greater challenge than anticipated. Cairo's insistence on running the show lost the Brotherhood some key thinkers who might have pushed the movement forward in a more creative way.

## The Arab Spring

When the so-called Arab Spring struck, new conditions arose for the Muslim Brotherhood. The Islamists did not initiate the Arab Spring, nor did it directly evoke Islam. Rather, it occurred across religious, political, and social lines. Many Islamists, in fact, stood on the sidelines of the uprisings. However, the MB was quick to take advantage of the unrest. In fact, Egypt's parliamentary elections of November 2011 and January 2012 found two-thirds of the popular vote going to Islamists 37.5 percent went to the Freedom and Justice Party, while the Islamist Bloc received 27.8 percent. The Islamist parties made little mention of religious topics in their platforms during the Arab Spring elections. In the Al-Nour Party's 8,876-word platform, "Sharia" was mentioned five times; "Islam" was mentioned 25 times and "economy" 58 times. The Muslim Brotherhood's 12,639-word platform contained "Sharia" 14 times and "economy" 35 times. Finally, Morsi's presidential campaign platform of 15,000 words consisted of "Islam" 36 times, "Sharia" eight times, "economy" 158 times and "development" 178 times.

As Olivier Roy stated in his article, "The Transformation of the Arab World" in the Journal of Democracy, "Islam as a theological corpus has not changed, but religiosity has."[20] For many more than fifty percent jobs and economic development was the top priorities. Because Egypt was relatively underdeveloped, its voting bloc of the poor did not look at long-term promises but instead looked at the short-term—i.e., the social services offered by Islamists that might make their day-to-day lives easier. It would seem that another force at play is that the demographics of those following Islam have changed. Younger generations of Muslims throughout countries that partook in the Arab Spring were not focused on Islam or religion, per se; rather, they were concerned with getting jobs that they had believed would be attainable once they graduated from higher education schools. For example, 54 percent of college graduates in Cairo were jobless at the time of the Arab Spring.[21]

Religiosity is also on the wane in younger generations. Social media has made them much more lenient in regards to dress, sex, and sexuality. According to a poll executed in Algeria, Jordan, Lebanon, Morocco, Palestine, Kuwait, and Yemen, less than 60 percent of people between the ages of 18 and 24 identified as religious, versus the roughly 80 percent of people 55 and up.[22]

Even so, while Islamism in its purest form is not necessarily as popular, its core values which could be seen as fundamental human rights, essentially remain intact. As political scientist Bassam Tibi has said, Islamism is a political ideology that is distinct from Islam and its teachings. It is more about core values than specific religious aspects. Because of this sense of Islamism being about basic human rights, Islamist parties have seen some success despite the fact that the majority of their constituents are younger men who are less pious than older generations and feel that religion should be kept separate from the social and political spheres. In fact, according to an Arab Barometer report, about 80 percent of the support for Islamist parties comes from the young; yet, nearly two-thirds feel that men of religion shouldn't have an influence on the decisions of the government, and less than 50 percent felt that Egypt would be better off with public office leaders who had strong religious beliefs.

According to Majzoub, "opinions regarding the political parties in Egypt do not seem to be linked to their religious platforms."[23] Furthermore, she says, "it would appear that religion is instrumental to the success of the Islamist parties only in as much as it is a required predisposition among the population. It is a necessary but not sufficient factor, making possible the existence and success of Islamist parties, but not guaranteeing it."[24] The Pew Research Center's Global Attitudes & Trends found that there was a generally positive attitude toward the Brotherhood; more than 70 percent gave them a favorable rating. Adding to the Islamist parties' appeal is what Majzoub calls social alienation. Such alienation has come at the hands of Western and colonialist influences, creating major class differences within societies. The petite bourgeoisie is made up of educated youth, who have found that a high level of education doesn't improve job opportunities or income. This petite bourgeoisie has thus become disillusioned with the status quo. "As a result," Majzoub says, "economic hardships were politicized, as they were seen to be grounded in the deliberate actions of the regimes rather than created by demographic changes."[25]

Generally, Islamists, rather than governments, were big on social changes bringing forth services like schools, health clinics, business enterprises, mosques, and community centers. Further, the increase in Western consumption, as well as the social and cultural ways of the West, directed people toward the more modest, attractive alternative of Islamism. Interestingly enough, countries that have not withstood a Western influence are not particularly strong breeding grounds for Islamism; i.e., the draw toward Islamism is often stronger when fostered by a move away from something less traditional.

Overall, its organizational capacity played strongly into the MB's hands. Islamism was seen as a familiar, deeply entrenched element of society. It is hypothesized that Islamists are more disciplined, competent, and cohesive than their secular counterparts. They are thought to run better election campaigns, or at least that they expend more effort to purchase the loyalties of voters with social services and other goods. Thus, it could be presumed that Muslims aren't necessarily voting for Islam, but responding to Islamist effectiveness or expressing gratitude for services. On the other hand, secular parties weren't properly organized and were therefore not a viable alternative. They lacked the message, even if the alter- native offered by the Islamists lacked structure.

The secular leaders were unfamiliar and untested, whereas the Islamists had already established reputations for themselves via television, pamphlets, and other modes of communication. Particularly in Tunisia, secular parties also lacked a common goal; votes were often scattered among their parties, denying any one party a victory. Similarly, the leftists were considered somewhat less organized than the Islamists, whose organizational head start was much easier to accept. Following the removal of Mubarak, it was believed that a leftist group would fill the void in Egypt, particularly since Egyptians sought a redistribution of wealth. Left-leaning parties like the Egyptian Social Democratic Party and the Popular Socialist Alliance emerged. But the Islamists dominated, not because people were prioritising religious and moral concerns, but because they thought the Brotherhood would mend the sins of Mubarak.

In short, although full of contradictions and sometimes unfulfilled promises, the Islamists were considered more dependable, demonstrating an unwavering commitment to social change. As Majzoub has said, "deconstructing the success of the Islamist parties in the post-revolution Arab world has shed light on the political demands of the Arab populations: freedom, justice and equality. There is nothing Muslim about these demands."[26] As long as there is economic unrest and there is an attractive, willing party that pledges to address this unrest, it is quite likely that this party will be at least somewhat successful.

## Ties to Terrorism

No overview of the Muslim Brotherhood would be complete without discussing its links to Islamic extremist terror. Much of the Muslim Brotherhood's reputation as an extremist group has come from the influence and writings of Sayyid Qutb in the 1950s and 1960s. Following the overthrow of King Farouk's pro-Western rule in 1952, Qutb was initially on good terms with Gamal Abdel Nasser and supported his Free Officers Movement. However, Qutb and the MB quickly realized that Nasser's pan-Arab nationalist and secular views did not align with their idea of an Islamic society. Tensions developed between Nasser and the Brotherhood, and in 1954 Nasser dissolved the group and imprisoned Qutb for several years. His imprisonment and torture are said to have radicalized him and resulted in his extremist publications.

Qutb's radical views invoked global jihad and stressed the difference between "jahiliyya," or the ignorance that is at the heart of man made laws, and "hakimiyya," or the imposition of Islamic laws in order to realize God's sovereignty. He urged the youth to be vanguards against the modern jahili system and its supporters, maintaining the ultimate goal of establishing a legal system that revolved around Sharia. From Qutb stemmed Qutbism, which, along with other youth-led movements, divided those who belonged to and supported the Islamist cause from those who did not. One of these youth-led movements included Organization 65, which was accused of conspiring to overthrow the government. This incident led to a concentrated extermination of Muslim Brotherhood members through various trials and executions. Inevitably, Qutbist thought also influenced al-Qaeda, which employed his ideas of waging holy war against secular government as a way of achieving their ends.

Qutb was executed in 1966 by the government. The 1970s saw a resurgence of Qutbist thought under Anwar Sadat, although not without contest. Hassan Al Hudaybi, Supreme Guide of the Muslim Brotherhood until his death in 1973, took issue with the turn away from the gradual reformist approach in the Islamist movement, with his arguments being outlined in his 1971 book Preachers, Not Judges. For obvious reasons, the increased militant presence of members of the Brotherhood who favored a more aggressive stance resulted in a crackdown by Anwar Sadat and subsequently culminated in Sadat's assassination at the hands of Egyptian Islamic Jihad in 1981.

The 1980s and 1990s saw something of an improvement in relations, with the Brotherhood entering Parliament and attempting to solve problems from within the establishment. However, the existing divisions grew even deeper among its members between those who thought they should work within Egypt's system and those who believed that cooperating with non-Islamists was compromising Islamic values. The small number of reformists those who followed the "moderate Muslim Brotherhood narrative" of the West was shut out of the Brotherhood by the radicals, who were inclined to maintain a more aggressive political approach.[27] The Egyptian government has banned the Muslim Brotherhood and its Palestinian offshoot, Hamas, claiming they are terrorists. The Egyptian president, Abdel Fattah el-Sisi, has criticized the U.S. for primarily looking at ISIS and al-Qaeda rather than focusing on the Muslim Brotherhood in Syria.[28]

As a result, nationalist media has seen el-Sisi's onslaught of the Brotherhood, "imprisoning thousands and killing hundreds during street protests," as "the rescuer of Egypt from Islamic militancy."[29] Egypt's President of the Supreme Council for Islamic Affairs, Dr. Mohamed Mokhtar Gomaa, has called the Brotherhood "harmful to Islam," claiming that it is "the progenitor of the Islamic State and similar terrorist groups" and is "disrupting education at Egyptian universities."[30] Gomaa has also made the case that religion should be separate from politics, stating that Egypt "should advocate a centrist form of Islam, especially that of Al Azahr, which is the center of Islamic learning in Egypt and across the Islamic world."[31]

## Origins of the Main Muslim Brotherhood Affiliates in the Arab World

The Muslim Brotherhood believed that a necessary prelude to a truly Islamic renaissance was not only the liberation of each Muslim land, but also the unification of the Arab world, starting with Egypt, Syria, Jordan, Palestine, Tunisia, and Morocco. In serving their definition of Arabism, the Muslim Brotherhood believed they were serving Islam.

### Syria

There are pronounced differences between the Muslim Brotherhood of Syria and that of Egypt. First, unlike some other Muslim Brotherhood sister organizations, the Syrian organization was on all points independent from the Egyptian center.[32] Second, the Syrian Brotherhood was formed by the Ulama class, rather than against the religious establishment as in Egypt. Further, it remained a small, elite organization that never reached the same level of mass appeal that its counterparts in some other Arab countries did. Finally, up until 1958, the Syrian Brotherhood was a parliamentary body that participated in Syrian politics. This stands in contrast to the Egyptian Brotherhood, which remained divorced from parliamentary politics until the 1980s.

### The Syrian Brotherhood does, however, have an Egyptian connection

The mother movement in Egypt provided Syrian Islamic activists with inspiration and an organizational model. When the Egyptian Brotherhood delegation visited Syria, it found associations there to be similar to what existed in Egypt. Furthermore, many of the Syrian Brotherhood's founders had studied at al-Azhar and were acquainted with the Egyptian Brothers. The group rose indigenously in the wake of the failed Great Syrian Revolt of 1925-1927.[33] A loose network of religious associations, referred to as the "Jamiyyat al-Gharra," sprang up to counter the French Mandate's secularizing influences. Islamist youth movements also emerged alongside the Jamiyyat, which organized a series of all Syrian conferences that brought about the formation in 1945-1946 of the Muslim Brotherhood with Dr. Mustafa Sibai as Secretary General. The Egyptian Ikhwan provided ideological and organizational inspiration to Dr. Sibai. However, although the Syrian Brothers considered Hassan al-Banna to be the spiritual leader of the movement, the group retained its operational independence, unlike the affiliate in Jordan.

Syria witnessed rapid socioeconomic change post-independence. The rates of urbanization increased, leading to sectarian and ethnic mixing in the cities. This provided fertile ground for the development of ideologically based political parties, such as the Baath, Communists, and the Brotherhood.[34] Further, the increased availability of education without the economy to handle it led to the rise of a disgruntled proletariat. In this context, socialism became an attractive ideology. In order to compete with other ideologically based parties, the Syrian Brotherhood adopted Socialism in the early stages of its formation. For example, in 1959, it participated in elections as the "Islamic Socialist Front," seeking to emphasize the socialist elements of Islam.

The MB competed with the Baath and Communists for the same urban lower- and middle-class constituencies, but the traditional Sunni middle class, including Ulama, were also attracted to it. Because leaders were competing heavily with the Communist Party for sentiment among the populace, they focused a great deal on workers. For instance, they did well with unions, sports clubs, and social welfare groups. They also established a number of workers' schools that helped provide schooling for both workers and their children, thus combating illiteracy. When the neo-Ba'athists seized power in 1966, they began a process of secularization.[35] The aim was to replace Islam with Arab nationalism. The main losers in this purge were the urban populations in which the MB had its roots. Hafez al-Assad attempted to open a new page in relations with Islamic forces to widen his coalition's base, so he actively tried to gain religious sanction and affiliation. These efforts led to prominent Lebanese Shia Cleric Musa Sadr handing down fatwa saying that Alawis were Shias. But this was too little, too late.

In 1976, militant Muslims who had broken away from the MB mounted a violent struggle against the government. The rank-and-file MB had to decide whether or not to join. From 1976 to 1982, it waged a violent campaign against the Baath regime, and they succeeded in mobilizing significant backing. In 1979 the Ikhwan launched an attack on the Aleppo Artillery School and massacred 33 Alawis. The MB then took partial control of several Syrian cities in 1980. In June of that year, it attempted to assassinate Assad. This resulted in a major punitive campaign against the movement that included the murder of one thousand inmates who had been members of the MB. Emergency Law 49 was passed in late 1980, which enacted the death penalty for any member of the MB. Then, in February 1982, the government attacked the city of Hama in order to quell an MB uprising, and while figures differ many thousands of Syrians were killed.[36]

With the Hama massacre, the violent uprising ended. In retrospect, the rebellion was not an organized movement but instead a number of inter- connected acts of popular protest that lacked a guiding hand and were not accompanied by any kind of political or propaganda activity that might have moved Syrian public opinion to the side of the rebels. A new opposition coalition was formed called the National Alliance for the Liberation of Syria, which then became the National Front for Saving Syria in 1990. Its main objective was toppling the government.

Throughout the 1990s, there was a recognizable improvement in relations between the MB, other Islamic circles, and the government, much of it due to the latter's responding more positively to Islamic groups in the post-violent uprising phase of 1982-1990. For example, the government began demonstrating more openness to manifestations of religious faith among its citizens (scarf, preaching, religious schools, Islamic textbooks, etc.). It released most members of the MB who had been in prison since the early 1980s and continued to Islamize the Alawite community by establishing a relationship with Iranian Shia clerics.[37] It also permitted, and even encouraged, moderate clerics, including those outside the official religious establishment, to stand for elections as independents (indeed, several were elected to the People's Assembly). Finally, it allowed many of the leaders of the Ikhwan who were exiled in the early 1980s to return.

When Bashar al-Assad came to power in 2000, it was unclear what his stance toward the Islamists would be. On the one hand, he showed signs of reconciliation with Islam. On the other, his actions stressed his secular outlook. For example, he did not say the customary Bismillah (in the name of God) at the beginning of his inaugural speech, but he did repeal his father's law against the wearing of head scarves in educational institutions. The Syrian media stressed Bashar's Islamic credentials and he passed a law that allowed MB members to return to Syria as individuals. This seemed to indicate that Bashar was willing to reach a compromise between the government and the MB.

The MB exploited the death of Hafez Al Assad to try to forge a new beginning in its relations with the government.[38] This was partly due to the need to make peace with Bashar in the face of their irrelevance to current Syrian realities, but they also hoped to exploit Bashar's inexperience to establish a new status for themselves in Syria. However, Bashar rejected the Brotherhood's advances, and relations with them remained fraught. Despite the MB failing to reconcile with the Ba'athists, the government did improve its ties in the 1990s to radical Islamic movements throughout the Arab world. Damascus became a site of pilgrimage for the leaders of these groups, largely due to the misleading perception that Syria was the only state still committed to the struggle against Israel. The government's closeness to other Islamist groups was a harsh blow to the Ikhwan, and they lost the support of other Arab Islamist movements. Nevertheless, the closeness between the government and these radical Islamist movements backfired when many of them became implicated in terror attacks around the world (including 9/11).

## Jordan

Like its Egyptian parent organization, the Jordanian Brotherhood began as a socially oriented organization that subsequently shifted to politics and international affairs especially with the conflict in Palestine. This political involvement resulted in the running of candidates in the 1950s and 1960s, a twenty-year hiatus, then again in 1989. Since its formation, the IAF has built impressive structures internally by way of electing party leaders, having free regular turnover in top positions, and selecting its candidates through a process that begins with its branches holding primaries before forwarding names to the party leadership.[39] The Jordanian Monarchy's relationship with the Muslim Brotherhood is an uneasy one. Periods of accommodation and co-optation are occasionally punctuated by periods of open conflict. Unlike in Egypt, the Jordanian Monarchy never sought to suppress the MB. As a result, some have seen the relationship between the government and the Muslim Brotherhood as a sign of tacit cooperation. However, others believe their relationship to be guarded but not overtly hostile.[40]

The Muslim Brotherhood has largely operated within the framework of Jordanian law. The government has shifted that framework to contain the MN, often merely steering it toward new fields of activity rather than suppressing it altogether. When the government confronted its most severe challenges during the 1950s and 1960s in regards to Palestine, the Muslim Brotherhood stood aloof, a position that allowed it to retain its operations in many social spheres and even run for Parliament. Mindful of its limited ability to affect the composition of government or pass legislation, the IAF has been active in using Parliament as a platform to raise issues regarding Palestine, the economy, corruption and waste,political reform, and social, cultural, and religious issues. The chief reward of parliamentary participation has been the ability to raise concerns and gain visibility.

Shortly before the 1993 election date, King Hussain changed the electoral law to disadvantage Islamists.[41] After the liberalized political party law was passed, the Islamic movement did not try to repackage the Muslim Brotherhood as a political party but rather formed what is now known as the Islamic Action Front (IAF) and ran under that banner. A few years later, in 1997, it assembled a coalition of opposition parties to threaten to boycott elections if the law was not changed. Though no change came, the party ran again in 2003.

In its early years, the IAF placed great stress on internal reform and political freedoms. However, more recently, it has lagged behind other Islamist movements in focusing on internal issues and has instead concentrated on external issues, such as Palestine and Iraq. Overall, however, the ideology of the IAF is remarkably restrained for an Islamist organization. For instance, it modified its law to be consistent with the Islamic Sharia but used gentle terminology, pointing to the "supreme goals" of Sharia. This terminology is a common tool for Islamist movements to emphasize ways in which the pursuit of the Sharia is consistent with public welfare and not an imposition of a set of burdensome restrictions.

Two major international developments have conspired to sharpen the contest between the Jordanian Monarchy and its Islamic opposition, trans- forming a source of domestic tension into a potential crisis. One is the rise of Hamas, which Jordan has been concerned might draw on its sympathizers in the country for support, pulling it back into conflict with Israel and potentially threatening to damage its ties with the U.S. The second international development was the U.S. invasion of Iraq in 2003; the Brotherhood opposed Jordan's cooperation with the U.S. By 2006, in the wake of the Amman hotel bombings and the Hamas electoral victory, the IAF and the authorities were engaged in open confrontation.[42] The assumed popularity of the IAF lies in the Muslim Brotherhood's ability to mobilize its supporters and get them to the voting booths, something that was done greatly by means of patronage especially from the Islamic Center Charity Society (ICCS).[43] Further, their success reflects the weakness of the Jordanian opposition, as well as low voter turnout, to a greater degree than it does the inherent popularity of the IAF.

While the IAF can present the Islamic movement with many accomplishments, it may have trouble moving beyond what it has already achieved in the current Jordanian environment. The IAF's freedom to maneuver continues to be circumscribed by its institutional links to the Muslim Brotherhood, preventing it from pursuing its platform purely on an electoral calculus. The Jordanian government seems to have realized that the alternative to a legitimate Islamist opposition might be the emergence of a splintered movement, but one that is also much less restrained.[44] In short, the Jordanian MB is currently undergoing a critical transitional phase because of regional challenges, including ISIS and being designated as a terrorist organization by Saudi Arabia, Egypt, and the UAE. It faces four prominent challenges: overlap between the political party and the MB; female membership; ongoing ideological shifts and reorientation of the movement's political discourse; and tensions between younger and older generations. There has been limited success in addressing these four areas, which has contributed to the current crisis and the overall restrictive nature of the organizational structure of the Brotherhood.

## Palestine

In Palestine, the rising tide of Islamism as a framework of national liberation remained a particularly powerful political option in the absence of a sovereign and independent state.[45] The Egyptian Muslim Brotherhood's connection to Palestine dates back to 1935, when Hassan Al Banna sent his brother to establish contacts there. In 1945, the group inaugurated its first branch in Jerusalem and subsequently established several more offices. Sheikh Ahmad Yasin, who moved the group increasingly toward confrontation, maintained an ideology that points to the distinctive history of the Brotherhood in Gaza. From 1948 until 1967, Egypt administered the Gaza Strip. Nasser's crackdown on Egypt's Islamists extended to Gaza, where the organization was outlawed and many Brotherhood members, including Yasin, were persecuted and arrested. The experience of the Gaza Brothers would later bring to Hamas the radicalizing experience of incarceration, along with an expertise in building decentralized and clandestine organizations.[46]

In the West Bank, on the other hand, the MB was legal.[47] After the creation of Israel, relations between the Muslim Brotherhood and Hashemite Kingdom in Jordan which had annexed the West Bank in 1950 were generally smooth and cordial despite periodic tensions. Jordan did not permit cross-border violence against Israeli targets, so there was no tradition of armed militancy against Israel. The MB in the West Bank and the MB in Gaza never formed a common organizational link, even under a common occupation after 1967. The activity of the Brotherhood in the West Bank was social and religious, not political. In the eyes of the Brotherhood, the loss of Palestine was God's punishment for turning away from Islam, so the natural first step was the re-Islamization of society. But that meant that the Brotherhood was on the defensive from attacks by the nationalist groups.

In the years following the Israeli occupation of the West Bank and Gaza, the Brotherhood continued to operate as a social organization seeking to establish an Islamic generation, which had little relevance for a population seeking liberation from foreign occupation. Thus, the emerging Palestinian nationalist resistance movement had greater appeal. However, Israel's victory in the Six-Day War (1967) was a severe blow to the stature of secular nationalist and Arab socialist governments, as well as the popular appeal of ideas they claimed to embody, and encouraged a return to Islam.

Influential to the Brotherhood's strength were the Iranian Revolution in 1979, the 1981 assassination of Egyptian President Anwar Sadat by Isla-mists, and the emergence of Hezbollah as a major force in Lebanon.[48] The 1982 Israeli invasion of Lebanon forced the Palestine Liberation Organization (PLO) to move its headquarters to Tunis, placing even greater physical distance between the organization and the Palestinians. All of the afore mentioned domestic, regional, and international shifts lent an increasingly religious cast to the conflict, laying the groundwork for a decisive turn in Palestinian politics toward Islamism and influencing the creation of the Islamic Jihad and Hamas.

The Islamic Jihad was founded in 1980. It advocates an armed struggle against Israel and rejects coexistence with Arab countries, especially those that have strong ties to the West. Because of its focus on liberating

Palestine, the group shares a common objective with the PLO factions. It has launched military operations against Israel with the participation of certain Fatah elements. It opposes the gradualism of the Brotherhood and the PLO's strategy of "occupation management." It weds Islamism to patriotism, insisting that the restoration of Palestine requires the annihilation of Israel. It also performs high profile attacks against Israeli targets. Arguably, the Islamic Jihad set the stage for the 1987 Intifada. The Islamic Jihad's prominence, however, did not last; it remained small and never commanded nearly the following of the Brotherhood, which criticized Jihad for concentrating on political issues at the expense of Islamic education.

With the eruption of the Intifada, the Brotherhood was confronted with an ideological dilemma. Given the unprecedented events, it could not remain on the sidelines; however, it was difficult to justify joining the Intifada when its previous positions regarding violence were well known. To avoid this dilemma, it created an ostensibly separate organization to take responsibility for its participation in the Intifada. A Hamas Charter was drawn up in August 1988, proclaiming Hamas to be a wing of the Brotherhood and calling on the people to stand up against Israeli occupation. As Hamas became more popular, the Brotherhood began to deliberately equate the two organizations.[49]

Hamas's charter contains the philosophy of the movement, its rationale, and its positions on central issues, such as social welfare, the role of women, and other Islamic movements like the PLO. Its position on most of these questions does not differ from that of the Brotherhood, but it pays less attention to transforming society and much more to the Palestinian cause and jihad. With regards to Palestine, Hamas believes the land of Palestine is a Waqf upon all Muslims until the Day of Resurrection; therefore, it is not right to give up any part of it. According to Hamas, there is no solution to any amount of enemy occupation on Muslim land but jihad. It seeks to uproot Israel from lands that have been occupied since 1967 and establish an Islamic state in its place. Since the 1990s, it has depicted the struggle as a form of resistance to an occupying power.

Hamas refers to the PLO as a "father, brother, relative, or friend" of the movement, and stresses the fact that both have a common plight and destiny and face the same enemy.[50] At the same time, Hamas criticizes the PLO's secular course and its leadership, as well as its political program calling for the establishment of a Palestinian state that would coexist with the State of Israel and its acceptance of UN SC resolutions 242 and 338. Hamas makes no explicit claims to being an alternative to the PLO, but its repeated references to Islam as the alternative to the failed nationalist and secular ideologies would seem to imply a certain projection of itself as an alternative to an organization embracing such failed ideologies. Hamas has remained relatively simple and lacks the complex bureaucracy of the PLO. The leadership of the movement is entrusted to a Majlis Shura whose members live inside and outside the occupied territories.[51]

From the beginning, the leadership has been plagued by repeated losses in their ranks through deportations and imprisonment, necessitating periodic reorganizations both at the central leadership and committee or branch levels. The mass deportations of 1992 removed most of the frontline leaders. However, the devastating effect of this event was mitigated by the fact that the leadership has always relied on strategic decisions to come from its extended leadership abroad, especially the Brotherhood in Jordan and Egypt. As a branch of the Brotherhood, Hamas has been able to build on the mother organization's extensive infrastructure in expanding its public base of operations, facilitating useful vehicles for spreading Hamas's ideas and influence, and enlisting supporters. Hamas's non-participation in the political process has led it to concentrate its efforts on Intifada activity. It has become the party most engaged in armed actions against Israeli targets. Hamas's military strikes are also intended to embarrass the negotiating factions and bolster its own position as a major Palestinian force that cannot be ignored and without which no agreement can be reached.[52]

## Tunisia

One of the most important issues in post-revolution Tunisia concerned the relationship between Islam and politics. Should Tunisia allow religious political parties, or should the country maintain its long standing practice of separation of religion and politics? The Six-Day War heavily influenced Sheikh Rachid Al Ghannouchi while he was studying in Damascus. He believed that the nationalist way was wrong; even though his heart was perfectly reassured of Islam, he realized that what "[he] had been following was not the right Islam but a traditional and primitive version of it. The traditional model was not ideological, nor did it represent a comprehensive system. It was a conventional and religious sentiment, a set of traditions, customs, and rituals that fell short of representing a civilization or a way of life."[53]

In 1970, Al Ghannouchi returned to Tunisia and formed a small grass roots Islamic movement with Abdel Fattah Mourou. They initially concentrated on social and cultural issues instead of explicit political messages. "Our work focused on the development of ideological conscience and consisted essentially of a critique of the Western concepts which dominate the spirit of youth," Al Ghannouchi said.[54] They brought together conservative Tunisians who felt disillusioned by and excluded from the secular authoritarianism of Presidents Bourguiba and Ben Ali. During the 1970s, the Islamic movement developed in Tunisia because of internal and external factors. Internally, Tunisia witnessed a crisis within the ruling party and a conflict between its liberal and conservative wings. In 1978, there was a violent clash between the leftist trade union and the government. The Islamic movement, which had previously only talked about social issues, started writing about politics—in particular the conflict between the government and the union. It backed the government, as Islamists regarded the left to be the traditional enemy of the Islamist movement.[55]

Externally, the confluence of two factors, namely the decline in the appeal of nationalism throughout the Arab world and the 1979 Iranian Revolution, created the conditions that enabled the rise of Islamism in Tunisia. Al-Ghannouchi went to great lengths to associate the Muslim Brotherhood with the Islamic Movement in Iran. The Tunisian Islamists benefited from siding with the government during the conflict with the union. They found that they were granted more space for political activism. Their writings, influenced by the ideas of the Muslim Brotherhood in Egypt, began focusing on the West and its attendant evils. As the organization grew, they decided that it was necessary to organize a founding congress.

In 1980, the congress decided it would openly apply for official registration as a political party, and in 1981 it became the Islamic Tendency Movement (MTI).[56] The group's program opposed modernization, secularism, and the Western world. This ushered in a period of confrontation with the government, which, fearing an Islamic Revolution a la Iran, immediately cracked down on the party. Bourguiba imprisoned many members and rejected MTI's directing of the mosques, believing that they were set on seizing power. The crackdown quickly degenerated into a full-blown attack on Islamists and against expressions of religion in the public square. Praying, mosques, veils, and beards were all banned.

However, Al Ghannouchi had a political ideology distinct from his Iranian counterparts. He held an open commitment to democracy as a viable "method of preventing those who govern from permanently appropriating power for their own ends." It was a "system of governance in which rulers are held accountable for their actions in the public realm by citizens, acting indirectly through the competition and cooperation of their elected representatives." He also believed that if "by democracy, one means the liberal model of government that prevails in the West, a system under which the people freely choose their representatives and leaders, and in which there is an alteration of power as well as freedoms and human rights for the public, then the Muslims will find nothing in their religion to oppose democracy, and it is not in their interest to do so anyway."[57]

Al Ghannouchi asserted that a violent, Iranian-style revolution was not the answer. Rather, change would be most successful if it came from the bottom up a slow process that gradually transformed society and used increased political participation and democratic principles to bring about a desired goal: a state that was both democratic and Islamic in nature. The government's stance on Islamists changed in the second half of the 80s as conflict with the labor union resurfaced. The Bread Uprising of January 1984 caused Prime Minister Muhammad Mzali to fire the minister of interior and engage in a hostile confrontation with the union. To counter-balance, he tried to re-establish relations with the Islamists. In a gesture of goodwill, the government began releasing imprisoned members from jail. Mzali and Abdel Fattah Mourou held several public meetings, and the Islamic movement was allowed to re-enter discussions regarding politics.

Mzali tried to include the Islamists, though President Bourguiba was hesitant. However, the radical wing of the MTI severed their newly formed relations with the government, opting for a confrontation strategy. They believed that the end of the Bourguiba government was coming. There- fore, when Prime Minister Mzali's government fell in 1986, a new wave of Islamist persecution emerged, culminating in a death sentence for Al Ghannouchi in 1987. President Bourguiba was deposed shortly afterwards. However, Ben Ali's accession to power ushered in a new period of participation. The initial months of the Ben Ali presidency looked promising. Ben Ali tried to reposition himself as a reformer and released political prisoners. Until late 1989, the Islamists played their cards carefully, intent on maintaining their dialogue with the government. Further, in response to Ben Ali's requirement that no party try to monopolize Islam, MTI agreed to change its name to Ennahda.

The Islamist independents failed to win any seats in Parliament, yet they still won 17 percent of the vote, displacing the secular left their main opposition. However, Ennahda's participation in the parliamentary elections spelled the end of the period of participation. It put forward a few extremist proposals denouncing women's rights and exploiting religion in political life. President Ben Ali deemed Ennahda too dangerous for public order, reversed his strategy and reneged on promises to initiate a democratic "changement" in Tunisia.[58] Many Ennahda members fled. Some split to form a moderate group, while others formed a radical branch. The 1990 Gulf War particularly pitted the Islamists against the government, resulting in more imprisonments and exiles of Ennahda leaders. It was not until 1996, when Ennahda held its first Congress in Belgium that it finally decided to adopt a more moderate stance.

In 2003 in France, representatives from four of Tunisia's major non-government parties (Ennahda, Congress for the Republic (CPR), Ettakatol, and the Progressive Democratic Party (PDP)[59] met to negotiate and sign a "call from Tunis." They endorsed two fundamental principles: any future elected government would have to be founded on the sovereignty of the people as the sole source of legitimacy; and the state while showing respect for the people's identity and its Arab-Muslim values would provide guarantee of liberty of beliefs to all and the political neutralization of places of worship. In 2005, the same parties reaffirmed the "18 October Coalition for Rights and Freedoms in Tunisia," which included an existing liberal family code, a civic state, and no compulsion in religion.[60]

Following Tunisia's 2011 Arab Spring revolution, Ennahda re-entered Tunisian politics after a long hiatus. Al Ghannouchi and Ennahda had a history as the primary opposition to Bourguiba and Ben Ali. They bore the battle scars that gave them popular legitimacy, despite returning to politics amidst deep suspicions that their democratic claims were not credible. Ennahda's electoral platform reflected Al Ghannouchi's long-held progressive views about reform, democracy, equality, the civil state, pluralism, and human rights. The 2011 political transition gave the group the opportunity to test this commitment, creating a tension between the theoretical combination of Islam and democracy and the practice of democracy (which had to be the same for all opposition parties). Overall, in interaction with other groups, the leaders of Ennahda insisted on democratic commitment.

## Morocco

Though the Justice and Development Party (PJD) was founded in 1967 by Abdelkrim Al Khatib, it did not participate in elections until 1997, when it gained nine seats. From 1997 to 2002, it focused on corruption and ethical and religious issues. There has been a great deal of antagonism between the PJD and the leftist and secular parties in Parliament, with the latter scrutinizing the party's relationship with the al-Tawhid movement and orchestrating an anti-PJD media campaign following the 2003 terrorist attacks. The party participated in politics according to the dictates of the constitution and at the same time-maintained links with al-Tawhid. Some al-Tawhid members felt their political participation compromised the religious and social character of the movement. Other members felt that Islam was all- encompassing, but this functional separation made sense.[61]

In the early 2000s, the PJD refashioned itself into a party less concerned with purely theological issues and more involved in social and economic problems. The party made a breakthrough with its 2005 endorsement of a new, more liberal Mudawwana (the code regulating marriage and family life), which indicated that, "the PJD was looking to become a pragmatic player committed to political participation."[62] It made tremendous efforts to present itself as an exemplary bloc in Parliament (i.e., implementing attendance, questions, training, and legislative initiatives). It also fiercely opposed the 2006 election law, demanded accountability, and complained about unconstitutional activity. The pillars for its vision of constitutional reform included the institution of necessary mechanisms to secure independence of the judiciary; the expansion of supervisory and legislative prerogatives of House of Representatives and review of those of the House of Councilors; and the guarantee that the executive branch was accountable to Parliament.[63]

In 2007, the party's platform, called "Together to Build a Just Morocco," addressed additional economic and social policies. Instead of referring to the Sharia, it mentioned "the protection of Morocco's Islamic identity" as its main religious-based priority. It promoted a healthy, competitive, and open economy, as well as a generous redistribution of wealth to combat poverty, deal with the negative consequences of unemployment, and cover the costs of a universal health care system. There was a strong positive relation between education and the PJD votes in the 2002 and 2007 elections, thus concluding that support for Moroccan Islamists was not driven by a clientelist rationale in either election. The 2003-2009 municipal mandates thus constituted a phase of political apprenticeship. The PJD modelled themselves as "the good men" pragmatic managers of local issues fostering good neoliberal governance.[64] The religious references became less marked, and instead the needs of the local population were emphasized. They promoted the "politics of doing" in a context of competitive clientelism through management discourse, euphemization of the relationship with Islam, and moral clientelism. This accommodation and integration strategy, however, turned out to be politically costly for the party and led to the disappointment and disaffection of its supporters. It lost a lot of votes in the 2007 legislative elections.

From 2007 to 2012, the PJD's concerns were similar to those of the previous few years. They mostly opposed the 2008 budget law, believing that it showed the government's lack of concrete strategic plans to resolve the country's economic ills, and suggested that the influence of big business over the parliament had pushed legislation in the wrong direction. The fact that the PJD only added four seats (but lost 100,000 votes) surprised many. This was due to the appeal of the Independence Party to traditionally religious constituencies in Morocco (so the religiously minded did not necessarily vote for the PJD). Though the party has always preached democratic principles, the 2008 Sixth National Convention of the PJD concretely demonstrates the democratic character of the party. The convention displayed the PJD's commitment to the representation of women and youth, as well as collective decision-making. It introduced its future political platform, which was centered around questions of democratization of governance, institutional and constitutional reforms, and integration of the masses within the national developmental plans. This was the most sophisticated program to be presented by any Islamic movement to date.[65]

The Arab Spring worked in favor of the PJD, as the Monarchy learned that it needed to broaden its democracy to include the Islamists. The PJD's official statement depicted Moroccan politics as displaying worrisome signs of an entrenched authoritarianism that employed the judiciary, bureaucracy, and the Sahara Cause. But, the PJD did not participate in the February 20, 2011 protests, rather choosing to support them from a distance. This approach resulted in the PJD winning a plurality in the elections and obtaining the prime ministership, making Morocco the first Arab country to have an Islamist head of government. PJD won a plurality and was elevated from an opposition party to a key partner in national political decision-making. In essence, the PJD succeeded because it played it smart. It displayed similar behavior as other Islamist actors in neighboring countries; however, while it benefitted from the indispensable angry streets, it was not controlled by them. It pressured the key political actor in the country (the Monarchy), yet refrained from clashing with it by making alliances with other opposition movements to facilitate such pressures and avoid isolation.[66]

The Moroccan model of political Islamism is one that is "characterized by molding specific state religious policy, deploying Islam selectively and strategically, resetting the power relationship between political party and allied religious wings, and proactively navigating domestic and international competition."[67] Morocco's Islamists have carved their own path and countered the predictions that mainstream political Islam is on the wane. In certain ways, the Egyptian coup and rise of ISIS have given Morocco's Isla- mists "a new lease on life," as it has changed expectations and vindicated their accommodationist approach.[68] The PJD is intent on showing that it represents its own unique mode, but it does not seem to have a long-term vision beyond survival. In essence, it works well within the existing system, so it has an interest in retaining it.

Because they emerged from the Egyptian Muslim Brotherhood, the Islamist movements of Syria, Jordan, Palestine, Tunisia, and Morocco all share similar issues with regards to their struggles to gain footholds in their respective countries and combat outside influences. Many of these governments, such as those of Egypt, Jordan, and Morocco, have expressed interest in incorporating some form of Islamic democracy. Each sister organization has also faced the difficult decision of working either within or against the system and focusing on either a social reform of society (bottom-up) or a politically-oriented approach (top-down), yet each has often sought both. Finally, all of these parties have faced tensions and conflict within their own cadres, oftentimes resulting in the splintering off into smaller, more charged movements. In the case of Syria, its MB was not much different from the Egyptian one ideologically. Like the Egyptian MB, the Syrian Brotherhood resisted opposing Western influence particularly, France's secular education policies. However, unlike the Egyptian MB, which formed in opposition to the established religious clerical establishment, the Syrian MB included members of the Ulama. Therefore, the Syrian MB and Ulama maintained a relatively symbiotic relationship, each body supporting the other. This changed with the rise of the Baath regime in the 1960s, whose attempts to abolish Islam from Syrian society and replace it with Arab nationalism was logically not welcomed by many Syrian MB members. The IAF of Jordan, similarly, had a relatively easy relationship with the Jordanian Monarchy in the beginning. The IAF did not fight with the royal authority and was not suppressed by it because of its inclination toward operating within the established framework. The IAF was a complicit and relatively gentle organization. Even so, the relationship between the IAF and the Jordanian state has become steadily more adversarial since the party's founding at the height of Jordan's experiment with political liberalization in the early 1990s. Jordan currently faces the challenge of not knowing whether to treat the Islamic movement as a security threat or a political party.

The relationship between the Islamic movement in Palestine and the central authority, on the other hand, has been filled to the brim almost solely with conflict, particularly in Gaza. The loss of the Six-Day War to Israel sparked a renewed interest in Islam. Prior to this, Egypt's administering of the Gaza Strip meant the outlawing of many Brotherhood members, whose experience would later influence those of Hamas. Hamas's pushback against the political process has led it instead to focus on Intifada and armed actions against Israeli targets. The success of Tunisia's Islamist movement has also fluctuated and declined throughout the years. Like Egypt and Syria, it dismissed the effects of colonization on the part of the French, whose presence severely fractured the role of Islam in Tunisian life. In the 1978 clash between the leftist trade union and the government, it picked the government side. It moved from talking about social issues and started writing about politics—in particular the conflict between the government and the labor union. Al-Ghannouchi wanted to work within the system rather than toppling it, dismissing the idea of violent revolution.

In the case of the PJD in Morocco, they have found a way to operate within the system. The group has secured a foothold in government through an accommodationist posture toward the Moroccan Monarchy. When the PJD assumed office, it did so under the King's auspices. The new constitution mandated that the party that won the majority of votes would be guaranteed the prime ministry position, but it also gave the Monarch a significant veto and other powers. PJD officials still evoke religion but almost never do so when in opposition with the state. The PJD also abided by a 2013 state edict that prohibited religious leaders from running for office.

Islamic movements have also faced internal disagreements, which were often the result and cause of splinter groups. In Syria, the change in tactics represented by the move to armed struggle against the Baath regime was partly due to a generational shift. The younger generation, which was influenced by Sayyid Qutb, was willing to act independently once it became clear that the older leadership of the MB was not willing to adopt their notions of the importance of violent confrontation to bring about change. In Jordan, tensions arose between old and young generations following the success of the protests in Egypt and Tunisia. A project called "Political Memoirs" began, which consisted of events during which older members of the MB wrote about their experiences. A Student and Youth Congress also developed in order to better integrate young people into their structures.

Hamas in Palestine was initially created as a wing of the MB in the 1980s in order to address social problems and focus on jihad without compromising the Brotherhood's own message; however, many MB affiliated members who support the Palestinian cause, such as Jordan's IAF, are divided over their willingness to identify with Hamas. Members of the IAF are also torn on how large a role Islam should play in one's life. While they have had a relatively stable relationship with the government and many seek member-ship in the loyal opposition, numerous members oppose conceding their principles. Inevitably, all of the Muslim Brotherhood sister organizations in Syria, Jordan, Palestine, Tunisia, and Morocco had to either compromise or take more forceful action against their respective governments to promote their social and political causes.

Why Did The MB Ultimately Fail in Achieving Its Objectives?

## Egypt

When Hassan Al Banna's Muslim Brotherhood first started, it was poised to be a highly adaptive political creature, weathering the permutations of ordinary parties and surviving the usual crises. Countless party organisms will modulate their organizational and ideological features to align with changing environmental cues and incentives, regardless of ideology. Islamist parties are no exception. In fact, given the sensitivity of politics in the Middle East, it can almost be expected that Islamist movements will alter their methods in some fashion even if they risk compromising their original intent.

One of the driving forces motivating political parties is the institutional rule of participation, rather than the commandments of ideology. Even the most ideologically committed and organizationally stalwart are transformed in the process of interacting with competitors, citizens, and the state. Setting out to win the Egyptian hearts and minds for an austere Islamic state and society, the Brotherhood has always been a flexible political party that is highly responsive to the unforgiving calculus of electoral politics. The Brotherhood's most significant strategy has been its willing- ness to work within the existing political system for the advancement of its goals; as early as 1941, the MB advocated participation in the system through contesting elections, knowing they had to do so if they were going to have any real influence. Yet this often had the effect of compromising Brotherhood values.[69]

The group's oft-times conflicted internal dialogue suggests that its stress on Amal (action) and Tandhiim (organization) over Fikra (ideology) muddled the vision of the Islamic order it sought to create, subsequently denying any interpretation as the sole "correct" one.[70] This led to fragmentation within the party, affecting the Brotherhood's overall coherency and instead portraying it as an in-between entity constantly in suspension: not enough for some, and too much for others. Such lack of coherency caused the formation of the breakaway of party as well as Qutbist thought, which in turn influenced al-Qaeda's organizational and theological underpinnings. Likewise, over the years, the Brotherhood's flexibility on certain matters has driven members of its target audience to look to other opposition groups whose positions have been a bit more solid. One such group is the Salafis. The Salafis were able to gain ground because the Brotherhood made compromise after compromise, diluting the purity of the Islamic components of its message in the process, while the Salafis claimed to be the true and pure purveyors of God's word and, just as importantly, God's law. In other words, the rise of the Salafis coincided with the Brotherhood's moderation on Islamic issues.

The factions and differences in opinion among the Egyptian Brotherhood are quite likely the result of a discourse that exhibited a number of unresolved contradictions and ambiguities, which stretch all the way back to the group's formation. The absence of literature on the Brotherhood's relationship with Sharia reflects the vacillation of its ideology with regard to Sharia and its followers. For one, there was tension between the ultimate authority of God as expressed by Sharia and the authority of the nation's elected representatives in Parliament or local councils in accordance with the popular will. In the early days, the Brotherhood was not concerned with the precise nature of how the Islamic state was organized, save for the fact that it was built on Sharia. Its position on the rights of those who did not subscribe to its agenda was also unclear for example, its stance on the right of the private citizen to choose his or her own values and lifestyle. Following Hassan al-Banna's death in 1949, it was deemed necessary by many to formalize specific characteristics that would realize the Muslim state, but the Muslim Brotherhood still limited itself to generalities.

Contributing to the Brotherhood's incoherency was its ambivalence toward formal political institutions such as Parliament and political parties. Its indecisive policy toward participating in elections led to charges of political duplicity. The Brotherhood tried participating in electoral politics as early as 1941, but because of disappointing election results, its members decided to stay away from politics for the time being. This would change in the years to come, particularly in the 1970s, when President Anwar Sadat held power and many Brotherhood members were elected to Parliament.

However, throughout its years, the Brotherhood has had a mostly adversarial relationship with the Egyptian regime. Under President Nasser, the Brotherhood was suppressed and dissolved in 1954, spurring the creation of the "secret apparatus."[71] This group attempted to assassinate Nasser, who retaliated by putting on trial, exiling, and hanging members of the Brotherhood a purge that lasted until 1970. The imminent threat of the Nasser reign caused a split within the organization, resulting in the ideological radicalization of many members and inspiring Sayyid Qutb's call for holy war against the system and its supporters. Once again, Nasser harshly punished Brotherhood members and executed Qutb. The period of ease between the Brotherhood and the later elected Sadat, too, would wear thin, and again the Brotherhood would call for holy war. These constant pressures tested the group, forcing members to alter their thinking and redirect their message.

The Brotherhood sought to survive Presidents Sadat and Mubarak's attacks in the 1980s through the creation of an international body and the publication of La Iha al-Dakhiliya (The Internal Statute). This document formalized ties between Cairo and other Brotherhood branches across the Arab world. Even though this formalization allowed the Egyptian Brotherhood more control and access to finances, it also meant that the international branches were formally bound to the center and had to answer to Cairo. The document, which is considered to have put in place the international organization, "Tanzeem al Dawli,"[72] consisted of new international leadership structures comprised of a General Guidance Office and General Shura Council. This cost the Brotherhood many members, as those who did not wish to be at the mercy of Cairo decided to exit the movement.

Iraq's invasion of Kuwait in 1990 plunged the Brotherhood into disarray, challenging its administrative and ideological unity. Some members' loyalties lay with Iraq; others, Kuwait. The Brotherhood ended up condemning the invasion, but rather mildly. It very strongly objected to the presence of U.S. troops in the region and Arab troops working alongside the West. The Kuwaiti Ikhwan split from the international Tanzeem in 1991 was a major blow and caused serious financial implications given Kuwait having been an important source of funds.

This episode demonstrated the difficulties of being an international movement. While the Ikhwan could broadly agree on theological issues, politics were a different matter. In spite of the dream of the Ummah, nationalist priorities and interests ultimately continued to dominate. Transnational Islamism proved to be just as flimsy a concept as Arab nationalism before it; many Islamist movements have been uninterested in linking with the international Tanzeem. For instance, the Sudanese Muslim Brotherhood, under Turabi, refused to have its independence circumscribed by the inter- national Tanzeem; the Libyan Brotherhood, found only in exile in the UK and the US, followed suit. The inflexibility of the Egyptian Muslim Brotherhood leadership and their unwillingness to accept anyone with a different political or intellectual approach has meant that they never allowed any space for personalities to develop inside the movement.[73]

In short, the story of the international Tanzeem highlights the Ikhwan's never-ending difficulties of reconciling its role as both a local organization with local branches and priorities on the one hand, and an international body and school of thought on the other. The decline of the international Tanzeem may have started in 1991, but 9/11 was its death. Post-9/11, the Brotherhood wanted to downplay its global Islamist image, actively trying to give the impression that the Tanzeem was simply a coordinating body with no power in decisions over the local level. Nevertheless, there is still an informal hierarchy, and Cairo is still considered the movement's spiritual home.[74] These facts will always provide it with some moral authority.

In the end, regardless of moral valuations, the rules of political engagement hold powerful sway over the behavior and make-up of political actors who must answer to cultural and moral issues of importance. The Egyptian Muslim Brotherhood was no exception. As it sought to impress a theological agenda, which itself was never fully agreed to, on a variety of local and national actors, it experienced near-crippling paradoxes that seriously compromised most of its major objectives.

## Syria

Problems for the Syrian Brotherhood arguably began in the 1960s in the face of ideological opposition from a substantial segment of the Syrian people. While the quickly moving socioeconomic change occurring in the country influenced the popularity of the Muslim Brotherhood's ideology, it also fanned the fire of other movements that were not necessarily in the same ideological category as the Brotherhood Communists and the Ba'athists, for example. When the latter acquired power, the Ba'athists refused to allow Islam to play a role in Syrian society, repressing the Islamist movement and replacing it with Arab nationalism. Most affected by the Ba'athists' erasure of Islam were the urban populations in which the Brotherhood originated.

The Ba'athists' authoritarian tendencies forced the Brotherhood to emphasize the importance of a staunchly opposing view: democracy. By necessity it has had to espouse the advantage of the rule of the people, representative government, and free elections. Yet this vision of democracy was to differ from the Western version in the sense that it appointed men of religion as the supervisors of the election process and state legislators; this, in a sense, was its Achilles heel. Unfortunately, the plan as envisioned by the Syrian MB leaders was that there would be no supervising system put in place to monitor the men of religion who were supervising everyone else. So, while the MB sought to differentiate itself from the Ba'athists' tyrannical methods, it still delegated a tremendous amount of power to a particular group of people, with little accountability.

The presidency of Alawite Hafez Al Assad, which started in 1971, made the situation even more difficult for the Syrian Brotherhood. At first, Al Assad led the regime in attempts to open a new page in relations with Islamic forces in the country.[75] Al-Assad wanted to widen his coalition's base, so he actively tried to gain religious sanction and affiliation. Religious minorities were tolerated more than they had been previously; however, political dissidents like the Brotherhood—mostly because the Sunnis represented the overwhelming majority of Brothers were not. In 1974, under heavy pressure from Al Assad, Lebanese leading Shia clergy Musa as-Sadr handed down a very controversial Fatwa saying that Alawis were Shiites, thereby linking al-Assad more directly to a recognized denomination in Islam, but this was too little, too late, and the above-mentioned period of violence occurred.[76]

Following this phase, the MB knew it had to placate the Alawi regime or be exterminated.[77] Thus, in March of 1982, the National Alliance for the Liberation of Syria, which later became the National Front for Saving Syria in 1990, was formed with the goal of toppling the Al Assad government. According to the Ikhwan's narrative, the government rested on a narrow sectarian basis and acted on behalf of an external conspiracy to destroy Syria from within by instigating a civil war and oppressing "true" Muslims. Therefore, it believed that overthrowing the government and saving the nation was imperative. In fact, the Ikhwan has long accused the government of compromising the Islamic nature of the Syrian people from within through a policy of erosion and disintegration.

Despite this, the Ikhwan scaled back its attacks in the 1990s because of the prospect of conducting talks with governmental representatives. But an examination of Ikhwan publications shows that engagement in talks was merely a tactical response to changing circumstances, rather than an abandonment of their cause. At the same time, adversarial relations with the government lessened as it developed ties to other Islamist movements throughout the Arab world. Members of the Brotherhood who had been imprisoned years earlier were released. Leaders of the Ikhwan who left in the 1980s were allowed to return, and the open practice of Islam head scarves, religious schools, and preaching was permitted. As noted earlier, Damascus became a site of pilgrimage for the leaders of radical Islamic groups, largely due to the perception that Syria was the only state still committed to the struggle against Israel. This closeness between the government and these Islamist groups was a harsh blow to the Ikhwan, as they lost the support of other Arab Islamist movements.

Still, the Brotherhood's unwillingness to compromise on its principles rendered the government's changes relatively insignificant. In the end, it became clear that the government's absurd conditions for reconciliation with the Brotherhood leaders repenting, confessing guilt, and refraining from any MB activity were impossible for them to accept. The efforts thus fell through. As was also noted earlier, when Hafez Al Assad's son, Bashar Al Assad, came to power in 2000, he did not say Bismillah at the beginning of his inaugural speech, but he did repeal his father's law against the wearing of head scarves in educational institutions.[78] The Syrian media also stressed Al Assad's Islamic credentials, and he passed a law that allowed MB members to return to Syria as individuals. This seemed to indicate that Al Assad was willing to reach a compromise between the government and the Ikhwan.

In 2001, the Brotherhood published the "Covenant of National Honor for Political Activity," which outlined the basis for joint activity with other opposition groups in Syria. But it was unsuccessful, as Bashar al-Assad rejected it. Once again, the Brotherhood's hope of turning over a new leaf with a Bashar-led government proved over-reaching. The failure of the Islamic rebellion in Syria bears witness to several limitations of political Islam in the Arab world today. The radical religious groups failed to break out of the traditional circles of support and gain it from other sectors of the population. Further, the government was able to create the image of positive state-religion relations, with a Syrianethnic-Alawite secular state dressed up in Islamic symbols and gestures of cooperation.

In April 2009, then-leader of the Syrian MB, Ali Sad al-Din Al Bayanuni, announced an end to the Brotherhood's participation in the National Salvation Front (NSF), a coalition of various opposition groups founded by former Syrian president Abdul Halim Khaddam committed to overthrowing the Baath government. Some viewed the announcement as a decision on the part of the MB to cease actively opposing the government.[79]

Other Muslim Brotherhood experts had a different view. The withdrawal from the NSF did not represent a fundamental shift in the Brotherhood's long-standing stance against Assad. Rather, the Brotherhood had always said that it would not be able to reach any fundamental understanding with Assad unless the latter accepted the basic conditions for a true reconciliation: the allowance of leaders to return to Syria and operate in the MB movement. Al Bayanuni's announcement of the Brotherhood's separating itself from the NSF, therefore, was a continuation rather than a rupture in the Ikhwan's history in Syria.

## Jordan

As mentioned in an earlier chapter, the Islamic Action Front, Jordan's branch of the Muslim Brotherhood, has built exceptional internal structures by electing party leaders, having free regular turnover in top positions, and selecting its candidates through a process that begins with its branches holding primaries before forwarding names to the party leadership. Yet while it has developed such structures, the IAF has also developed its own internal faults, which have led to the decline of the Islamist movement in Jordan. Many of these faults have come as a price the group paid for shifting its focus from social issues to political affairs, particularly Palestine. The Egyptian Muslim Brotherhood also made this transition, which undoubtedly affected the vagueness of its precise policies.

Overall, the IAF's very loose embrace of Islamist ways has led it to be considerably timid for an Islamic organization. It used gentle, non-radical terminology that would not alienate too many people.[80] As with the Brotherhood in Egypt, the issue of Sharia became a pivotal one. Some members of the IAF felt that Sharia law should have a much greater role in society; others did not. The IAF altered its message in order to comply with the Islamic Sharia. But instead of being direct, it employed soft terminology that is often a common tool for Islamist movements seeking to emphasize the ways in which the pursuit of the Sharia is consistent with public welfare. This message was seen as much more palatable compared with imposing a set of burdensome restrictions.

In earlier years, the IAF placed great stress on internal reform and political freedoms, but it now lags behind other Islamist movements in focusing on internal issues (Palestine and Iraq, for example, in the 2005 reform program).[81] Complicating the IAF's success is its platforms. It has developed a series of platforms that have stood little chance of implementation and are instead indicative of the state of disagreement within the party, as well as its willingness to test the limits of loyal opposition.[82] There are various areas of division first and foremost, its attitudes toward the Jordanian system. Some wish to be members of the loyal opposition, while others admonish the concession of principles. There are also divisions in opinion regarding the role Islam should play in one's life—some believe Sharia law should play a greater role in Jordanian law than it does. Finally, many members of the IAF support the Palestinian cause but are divided over their willingness to identify with Hamas. Because of the significance of these topics, the IAF's inability to have an internal consensus has resulted in a weakness and incoherence that has muddled its message.

There are four prominent challenges and areas for reform where the IAF has been lacking. These include overlap between the political party and Muslim Brotherhood, female membership, ongoing ideological shifts and reorientation of the movement's political discourse, and tensions between younger and older generations. As mentioned previously, the lack of clarity on the legal status of the Muslim Brotherhood led to confusion regarding the political role of the IAF and the preaching role of the Muslim Brotherhood, causing it to be difficult to differentiate between the Muslim Brotherhood and the IAF. It has sought to address the problem of female membership by reserving 11 of 80 seats within the IAF Consultative Council for women; the Muslim Brotherhood has yet to formalize this arrangement.

There have been accusations that the party members are not the sole decision-makers, as the IAF has made critical decisions after consulting and deferring to sister organizations in Egypt and Palestine. Its deferential attitude toward these two countries proves that it has not quite established a separate identity from the Muslim Brotherhood a particularly important part of the IAF's ability to be independent and have Jordan's best interests at heart rather than juggling other priorities. Also splitting the party is its participation in elections; each round of parliamentary elections has set off divisive debates over whether the party should participate in a skewed process.

In 2006, the Muslim Brotherhood again found itself divided upon the death of Abu Musab Al Zarqawi.[83] Even though the Brotherhood refused to apologize for the visitation of four of its members to Al Zarqawi's funeral tent, it did issue two statements clarifying its positions. Some saw this as an attempt to pacify the government, and this led to 18 out of the 40 of the Muslim Brotherhood's consultative council members submitting their resignations. Deeply divided internally, the IAF held a poll of its members before its leaders decided against withdrawing from Parliament.

## Palestine

Much of the failure of the Muslim Brotherhood in Palestine rests in its unsettled ideology and the controversial trajectory of its splinter group, Hamas. Hamas's radical Islamist approach has not only divided Palestinians but also many other members of the movement throughout the Arab world, like the IAF in Jordan.[84] In the years following the Israeli occupation of the West Bank and Gaza, the Brotherhood continued to maintain its role as a social organization that hoped to found an Islamic generation. But its social message was not enough for those who sought liberation from the foreign occupation. Since the Brotherhood never quite resisted the occupation in the way that the emerging Palestinian nationalist resistance movement did, it never became a mass movement. Thus, the more forceful Palestinian movement had greater appeal to the masses.

In the 1980s, a fissure developed along class and ideological lines within the Brotherhood.[85] It was the old elite of the Brotherhood urban, upper middle-class merchants versus the activist middle stratum, who were lower middle class and university-educated. This latter group was mostly based in refugee camps, domains that were formerly bastions of Arab nationalism. The ideological fissure regarded tactics: should one seek to free the soul or the nation first? The overlapping class and ideological fissures, in addition to mounting social pressures, finally resulted in a palace coup by the middle stratum of the Brotherhood against its leaders, leading to the establishment of Hamas.

Hamas was established as a more attractive alternative to the Islamic Jihad, and a more effective, more forceful alternative to the Brotherhood. The Islamic Jihad had emerged in opposition to the Brotherhood's gradualist ways in 1980, yet they did not catch on the way its members would have liked; it remained small and could not garner a following resembling the likes of the Brotherhood. So, to address the criticisms that the Brotherhood was not doing enough to resist Israeli occupation, Hamas was established.

With the eruption of the First Intifada in 1987, the Brotherhood was con- fronted with an ideological dilemma much like the Brotherhood in Egypt, when a faction of members decided to violently retaliate against Israel.[86] Just like the Egyptian Brotherhood, members of the Palestinian Brotherhood could not simply sit back and watch as Palestinians rose against the Israeli occupation in Gaza and the West Bank. Still, it was not easy to justify joining the Intifada when its previous positions were well known. Therefore, the Brotherhood created Hamas to join the resistance in its stead.

Unlike the Jordanian Brotherhood, which was much more accommodating to its authorities, Hamas has stood by jihad as being the only solution to enemy occupation. Hamas felt that the supposed "peaceful solutions"[87] that sought to solve the Palestinian question conflicted with the doctrine of the Islamic Resistance Movement, because giving up any part of the homeland would be the same as giving up part of the religious faith itself. It opposed the Madrid peace talks that occurred in 1991 and subsequent Arab-Israeli negotiations.

During the 1993 Oslo Accords, the political and military wings of the Islamic movement which Hamas predominated were substantively weakened by a combination of factors. One was the intense pressure that was imposed by both Israel and the Palestinian Authority. Another was the end of Intifada, which was critical to Hamas's thinking and action, and undermined the resistance component of the Palestinian struggle.

Further damaging to the Islamic movement's political and military wings in Palestine was the Palestinian population itself. Among Palestinians, there was a growing alienation from politics in favor of cultural and religious practices. After some time, the economic costs of Hamas's military operations and terrorist attacks became too high in an eroding socioeconomic environment, and widespread popular opposition to such attacks played an important role in ending them. At the same time, the younger of the Hamas cadres were disillusioned by Hamas's failure to achieve any change and decided to desert the organization altogether.[88]

Finally, the Palestinian Authority succeeded in co-opting some parts of the military in newly established Islamic parties or groups. In response, Hamas steadily shifted its emphasis to the social sector, effectively providing a range of important services. It redirected its approach, searching for accommodation within the status quo. In the period before the Second Intifada in 2000, Hamas was no longer predominantly calling for political or military action against Israel, but instead shifting its attention to social works and the propagation of Islamic values and religious practice. The definition of threats facing Palestinian society also changed. Threats were no longer confined to political and military attacks, but went so far as cultural aggression against Palestinian values, beliefs, and practices. Defeating the occupier became a matter of cultural preservation, the building of a moral consensus, and the development of an Islamic value system.[89] The Islamic movement was creating a discourse of empowerment despite the retreat of its long-dominant political sector.

On the one hand, in the five years preceding the unrest, the Islamists particularly Hamas, were undergoing a process of de-radicalization and searching for political and social accommodation within the status quo of Palestinian society. It represented a pronounced shift away from emphasis on political-military action to social-cultural reform. Hamas slowly but steadily abandoned political violence as a form of resistance and a strategy for defeating the occupier. But on the other hand, the Intifada and Fateh's militarization of the conflict sidelined the role of civil society and supported re-ascendance of the political military wing as the defining and authoritative component within the Islamic movement. This has proved problematic to the Brotherhood's success in Palestine. In 2006, elections in Palestine led to a major victory for Hamas over Fateh. 74 of the 132 Palestinian Legislative Council seats went to Hamas, with Hamas winning 44.45 percent of the vote and Fateh winning 41.43 percent.[90] The Near East Consulting firm conducted exit polls at the elections and found some two-thirds to three-quarters of the respondents felt that security, anti-corruption, and economic prosperity would greatly improve under Hamas, but also around three-quarters wanted Hamas to change its stance toward opposing Israel's right to exist.

Following the election, the Palestinian government split, with a Fateh government in the West Bank and a Hamas government in Gaza. While Gaza had long been a site for the Intifada and attacks against Israel had been common, they escalated with the ascendancy of Hamas. This has become known as the Gaza-Israeli conflict. Israel's response to Hamas taking control, and the subsequent escalation in violence that ensued, was to seal its border with the Gaza Strip, which prevented the flow of people and goods. When internal fighting broke out between Hamas and Fateh, and Hamas effectively took control of the Gaza Strip, Israel clamped down even harder, leading to further conflict and a marked increase in poverty due to a lack of economic trade.

The Gaza War, which involved everything from small skirmishes to full-scale battles, lasted up until August 2014 (its worst year), and left the entire area devastated. For this reason, Hamas has become intensely unpopular in Gaza. In fact, according to Nader Said-Foqahaa, director of the Arab Center for Research & Development, a public opinion survey firm based in Ramallah, if Fateh and Hamas were to face off in elections now, Fateh would garner 45 percent of the vote in the Gaza Strip. The Hamas leader, Ahmad Youssef, has himself recognized the need for change: "The Islamic movement in Palestine in particular needs to undertake intellectual and practical revisions regarding its role in the local and the international changes in the world."[91]

## Morocco

Morocco's Islamist movement is comprised of the political group Al Tawhid (which formed the Justice and Development Party, or PJD) and the non-political group al-Adl Wal Ihsan. PJD's desire to remain valid within the Moroccan political sphere has led to the stripping away of any overtly religious aspects. It has pressured the key political actor in the country the Monarchy but it has refrained from clashing with it by making alliances with other opposition movements to facilitate such pressures and avoid isolation. The PJD has secured a foothold in government through an accommodationist posture toward the Monarchy, while the anti-Monarchical al-Adl Wal Ihsan has sustained its appeal and access through non-violent activism.[92]

Like many Islamic parties, Morocco's PJD is still working to find a sustainable balance between the practical requirements it needs to fulfill in order to participate in elections and its own ideological Islamist values despite its electoral success. The very strict Moroccan governing body has forced it to adopt moderate political and social stances while also still trying to speak to those attracted to its Islamist framework. As a result, the Islamist movement has found itself remaining flexible arguably, capitulating to reach the mainstream.

In 2003, the terrorist attacks in Casablanca caused a great deal of antagonism between the PJD and the leftist and secular parties in Parliament.[93] The PJD was slammed with an anti-PJD media campaign; it adjusted its message to start focusing on management and administration decisions. It dropped unconditional support of Islamic identity themes, subsequently losing the blessing of the Movement of Unity and Reform (MUR), which ceased to lend a hand in the party's 2007 campaign. After the PJD split from the MUR, the PJD signaled that it would separate proselytizing from politics. The party would only be responsible for governance and administration, a somewhat shocking claim for an Islamist party.

The election of Abdelilah Benkirane as Secretary-General of the PJD in 2004 sealed the party's identity as an accomodationist group, as he was known to advocate gradual reform and compromise.[94] In order to promote constitutional and legal reforms, the PJD had to form coalitions with other opposition forces. It also took to a mild approach in its platform. For example, instead of referring to the Sharia, the 2007 electoral platform mentioned "the protection of Morocco's Islamic identity" as its main religious-based priority. In 2007, its platform, which was "Together to Build a Just Morocco," detailed economic and public policy proposals without any mention of Sharia. It is important to note, however, that this shift away from religion actually caused it to lose votes between 2002 and 2007.

Overall, the PJD was instrumental in coordinating a unified opposition front that compelled the government to respond favorably to political pressure and change the constitution, though the new constitution didn't reduce the power of the Monarch. The party still supported the government's legitimacy, but it would not tolerate authoritarianism and political exclusion.

## Tunisia

Tunisia is alone in being a bit of a success story for the MB, though it should be remembered that after they recently won power, accusations that they were lax on terrorism forced them to give it up again. Ennahda's overall success can be attributed to its partly unselfish, partly observational nature. It compared itself with models that worked and those that didn't, and vocalized its opinions about global events. It condemned the treatment of Morsi supporters who were killed in the Raaba Massacre of 2013 by the Egyptian government, professing solidarity with them and their struggle. It dismissed violence as a solution, aware that this was often the reason why other movements failed or became fractured. When various Ennahda leaders, members, and supporters were asked what kind of Islamist party Ennahda aspired to emulate after the Arab Spring, none said the Egyptian Muslim Brotherhood. In fact, the majority said Turkey's AK party; Ghannouchi, particularly, believed that the "AK Party will gradually make Turkey a more Muslim country through education, building the economy, and diversifying the media. That's our model not law. Make people love Islam. Convince, don't coerce them."[95] According to Hamadi Jebali, former Secretary General of Ennahda and former head of Tunisian government from 2011-2013, Ennahda was "much closer to the AKP than to the Muslim Brotherhood. We are a civic party emanating from the reality of Tunisia, not a religious state." Most obviously, as exemplified by other movements in other countries, "internal fighting" was seen as a weakness, "a failure at its prime."[96]

Others said Tunisia would carve its own model following its independence, possibly taking inspiration from the German Christian Democrats. In making the case to share power, Ghannouchi and Ennahda leaders frequently invoked the example of Algeria and the civil war. Its lesson was that the long-term politics of gradualism was advisable, especially at moments of democratic transition. According to Al Ghannouchi, "our priority is to participate...one party should not govern alone. A party alone cannot face these [transitional, post-authoritarian] challenges."[97]

In Tunisia, various political parties worked together to prevent internal violence from occurring. Ennahda compromised, giving up its democratically earned power peacefully. It valued the end goal over preserving the party's power, wishing to "lay the foundations for freedom with a constitution based on consensus, opening the way to make Tunisian political life democratic and then to build a democratic system."[98] Had Ennahda refused to give up its power, as the Brotherhood in Egypt did, this may have led to a bloody civil war. Instead, the movement prioritized a democratic future for Tunisia rather than its own success. Ennahda's concept of the relationship between state and religion did not differ much from the way in which previous post-colonial regimes had organized it. However, at the level of its strategic and political behavior as a party, it strived to behave democratically, in accordance with its official declarations of commitment to democracy. Ennahda sought a peaceful rotation of power for the Tunisian government, protecting everyone from the temptation to hold onto the power. "At the same time," Al Ghannouchi said, "power-sharing protects us from the threat of being subjected in the future to exclusion, marginalization, and torture."[99]

According to Al Ghannouchi, "the human genius lies in its ability to manage this difference and politics gives it the ability to manage it in a sound, peaceful, and civilized way, without using any brutality to enable the people to coexist despite their differences. This difference can enrich the diversity of life, not an element of destruction, and this is the difference between the civilized and backward people."[100] Ennahda also wished to forge relations between Islamic thought and Western thought by taking part in academic and scientific settings at Western universities. However, this proved unfruitful because the West had been influenced by Ben Ali's rejection of Ennahda's political and institutional status.

Al Ghannouchi's resistance to a violent revolution produced favorable results. During the uprisings, Tunisians did not represent the future as secular or Islamist, just as reconfigurable. The sudden absence of institutionalized politics made it ripe for radical change, allowing unification around the demand for a total rupture with the past. Once the president fled, this momentary exception ended and with it came "fugitive democracy,"[101] a free society consisting of diversities that can nonetheless enjoy moments of commonality when through public deliberations collective power is used to promote or protect the wellbeing of the collectively.

In mid-May 2016, Ennahda held a three-day congress, the first of its kind since 2012, and emerged with the announcement that it would separate the religious (al-da'awi) from the political (al-siyasi).[102] There appear to be three reasons for this new development. First, the group is attempting to synchronize itself with the "deep state," or the political establishment created by Bourguiba that is modeled on French secularism. Second, the move professionalizes Ennahda, marking an important turn toward its goal of being a fully legitimate political party. Finally, the group is becoming more democratic and less factional as it allows members to discuss its internal organization and positions. This has led to a broader and shrewder view of democracy as the inevitable forum in which Ennahda will succeed or perish.[103]

## Conclusion

The Muslim Brotherhood has witnessed numerous ups and downs since Al Banna's inception of the organization. Over the years, the group has been transformed from a highly secretive hierarchical organization led by anointed elders into a fragmented, multi-vocal political association. The group's moments of success have largely resulted from its attempts to remain relevant to changing political conditions. What is clear is that the Brotherhood is struggling to find a place in Arab political scenes due to its extensive history of blending religion with politics, infighting, and links to terrorism.

When comparing today's Islamist movement with Al Banna's Egyptian Brotherhood, it is difficult to say that it has ultimately succeeded in realizing the goals that the MB's founder set out to achieve. Yet it can also be said that the Muslim Brotherhood, from which the other organizations sprouted, was itself ideology based, not fully practical and therefore unsustainable. Although Al Banna realized that political organization of the Islamic states demonstrated a move toward a united religio-political community, its definition of the powers that the modern nation-state would possess were not spelled out. However, Al Banna was clear about his intolerance of the notion of a separation between Islam and the state, a concession both the IAF in Jordan and the JPD in Morocco made in order to maintain a foothold in politics.

Ultimately, the Brotherhood is an oppositionist movement that has failed to transform itself into a system that can govern. Some claim its ideology has been at the heart of its problems, which have been exacerbated by its inescapable habit of fostering multiple and often contradictory beliefs. The timeless arguments of old versus young and conservative versus modern have consistently caused the Brotherhood to undergo numerous identity crises. Such crises, Khalil Al Anani says in "The Muslim Brotherhood After Morsi," have had a hand in the Brotherhood's inability to maintain power. As the Brotherhood was transitioning into ruling, it "ought to have made the transition from its world of ideas and ideological and organizational prejudices to the world of politics and realistic programs that come with a need for political, social, and economic adaptation and balance."[104]

63

However, the Brotherhood has too often failed to follow this advice. The group now appears to be shifting toward a more conservative approach, assuming the classic tunnel vision that has prevented it from seeing the issues at hand. As Al Anani reports, "When I asked Dr. Mahmoud Hussein, Brotherhood general-secretary, what he thought of June 30 [2013], he answered that it would be a normal day and that the people would defend them…At that point, I realized that the Brotherhood leadership was living in another world with no connection to what was happening."[105] In another article, Khaled Matei, a member of the Freedom Justice Party, says, "We don't accept this government. This election, if they do it, is not legal because all of them are not legal."[106] Arguably, this rigid refusal to accept the government as legal could hurt the Brotherhood's image and any chance of it getting back into the political sphere.

In recent affairs, El Sisi has made it clear that he does not wish to stamp out Islam; rather, he opposes those who abuse it for their own best interests. His insistence on claiming Islam and redefining it has sent a positive message to many others who have grown tired of watching Islamists kill in the name of their religion. For instance, after the Charlie Hebdo shooting, El Sisi called for a "religious revolution," suggesting that the "contemporary understanding of [Islam] is infected with justifications for violence, requiring the government and its official clerics to correct the teaching of Islam."[107] El-Sisi has even exerted his control over the dissemination of Islam in Egypt by establishing imams in mosques who are aligned with the will of the government, and by dictating sermons.[108]

El Sisi's rhetoric has been aptly applied—much more aptly than the Brotherhood is generally able to do and has been enhanced by convenient timing. From 1993 to 2008, Islamist militants were behind 60 percent of the terrorist bombings with the highest casualties.[109] For years, headlines have presented the Islamist extremists of the Taliban and al-Qaeda as the enemy, and the ties between the Brotherhood and such groups, even if tenuous, have been enough to create pushback against them. The Brotherhood has become a scapegoat for many of the violent attacks that occur in the country, notably the assassination of the Egyptian prosecutor Hisham Barakat who "oversaw a number of high-profile cases against officials and supporters of the Muslim Brotherhood."[110] Although the Brotherhood condemned these attacks on Twitter and pointed the finger at the government for "provoking bloodshed," there is hardly any denying the power that El-Sisi's anti-Muslim Brotherhood narrative has over the main political conversation.[111]

The July 3 deposition of Morsi demonstrates the Brotherhood's unpreparedness to rule the people with set guidelines, despite the fact that it had waited years over eighty—to put someone in power. But it also demonstrates the ease with which such a government could become corrupt. While Mubarak's role as a puppet for the United States was widely accepted by Egyptians tired of the ruler's abuse of power, Morsi and his ties to the Brotherhood did not present itself as enough of a contrast. The acquisition of power by the Brotherhood simply resulted in a continuance of the "systematic subversion" that Egyptians had endured for years, oppressing them with even more hegemony.[112]

Thus, when Morsi came into power, his consulting with the Brotherhood appeared to be questionable, and his later declaration of absolute rule affirmed the perception of the Brotherhood as overbearing. Had the group developed a less hegemonic approach, it could have perhaps maintained a more serious stance in the public's eye. Further undermining its seriousness was the Brotherhood's constant reconstruction of its viewpoints. For example, during his oath of office in Tahrir Square in 2012, Morsi promised to work toward the freeing of Sheikh Omar Abdel Rahman, an Islamist convicted of planning to bomb various NYC landmarks. "I see signs for Omar Abdel Rahman and detainees' pictures," he said. "It is my duty and I will make all efforts to have them free, including Omar Abdel Rahman" (Kirkpatrick, 2012). Following this, however, a Brotherhood spokesman said that Morsi "intended to ask federal officials in the United States to have Mr. Abdel Rahman extradited to Egypt on humanitarian grounds. He was not seeking to have Mr. Abdel Rahman's contradictions overturned or calling him a political prisoner."[113]

The verbal redaction made by the Brotherhood member was just one more representation of an Egyptian ruler being inconsistent. As Al Anani has said, "the Brotherhood interfered in the presidency, issuing statements and adopting positions that conflicted with it."[114] This was harmful to the image of Morsi, and rendered him, in the people's eyes, as "subordinate to the Brotherhood. In a country where the office of president has historically enjoyed considerable prestige, the Brotherhood made many political and strategic errors that helped to prematurely bring their rule to an end."[115]

Clearly, the range in its opinions on acts committed by radical groups is eclipsing its overall function. Shadi Hamid says part of the problem is generational: "If you're a 60-year-old Brother, you've had the nonviolence doctrine drilled into you for decades, but if you're 22 and have only been in the Brotherhood for three years, you feel less bonded to it."[116] Obviously the Brotherhood needs to be much more vocal in its stance against extremism, picking a side and following through. And picking the radical side of ISIS and even Hamas would be problematic, considering this is the narrative that El-Sisi has constructed since his acquisition of power following Morsi's deposition. This would merely confirm the widely growing reputation of Islamists as a violent, staunch oppositional force that ignores the government and even, in some cases, the will of the majority.

Al Anani has argued that it is this mentality that cost the Brotherhood Morsi's presidency; that "vicious campaigns of incitement and distortion significantly contributed to turning public opinion against the Brother-hood, and led to a large turnout for the demonstrations of June 30, 2013 demanding an end to the Morsi's rule."[117] In short, there is little room for ambiguity in a political sphere whose stakes are raised higher and higher with each passing day. The inability of the Muslim Brotherhood and its sister organizations to have a truly successful run throughout the Arab world is reflective of both external and internal factors, many of which have been mentioned in the previous chapters. At the same time, externally, the MB and its sister organizations were receiving conflicted messages from dominating rule. Relations with republican governments and monarchies have proved crucial to the Islamist movement's reach. The sensitive, ever-changing political climate of the Arab world meant governments could be friends to the Islamic movement in one season and imprisoning it members in the next. Chaotic forces coming from without and within severely damaged the movement's chances of thriving. Although many Arab dictatorships have allowed opposition parties to function, this leniency has mainly fed those leaders' own self-interests. They have managed to keep tight control of the political spectrum.

For all Islamist groups, no matter how progressive or conservative, the fundamental problem is that they are neither movements nor parties, but an often-confusing mixture of both. On the one hand, a reason for joining the movement may be to get into heaven. On the other, the temptation of power, the distortion of Islamist priorities, and the undermining of the delicate balance between preaching and partisan politics have persisted for decades, degrading the essence of the very project that the Islamist groups have set out for themselves.

In conclusion, the rise of Islamic extremism in the media has been particularly damaging to the Brotherhood's image, causing it to be furtively stamped out in Egypt, although in some places other than Tunisia Islamism has managed to hang onto a modicum of legitimacy like the IAF in Jordan and the JPD in Morocco. Still, if history is any guide, the expectation that the MB will think realistically seems facile in the face of a litany of perpetual "ifs." If it can indoctrinate its youth members against violence. If it can convince its members to patiently overcome the frustration that the Egyptian government might incite within them. If it can convince the public that it is not engaged in or supporting terror. If it can return to its roots and win people over through peaceful social programs. With so many "ifs" that never seem to fully come to resolutions acceptable to populations increasingly demanding of democracy, the Muslim Brotherhood appears stuck, and is, in the opinion of this author, likely to continue to dwindle in power as the Arab world transforms itself into a region intolerant of, and working in international collaboration to destroy, those who engage in politically motivated violence.

*Dr. Nawaf Obaid is currently a Commissioner at the Commission on International Justice & Accountability (CIJA).He currently serves as the CEO of the Essam&Dalal OBAID Foundation (EDOF) in Geneva, Switzerland. Dr. Obaid has a Bachelors Degree in Foreign Service from Georgetown University's Walsh School of Foreign Service and a Masters Degree in Public Policy from Harvard University's Kennedy School of Government. He began his doctoral coursework at the Massachusetts Institute of Technology's Political Science Department and completed an MPhil & DPhil in the Department of War Studies at King's College, London University. Intelligence and Defense Project. BelferCenter for Science and International Affairs Harvard Kennedy School Intelligence and Defense Project Belfer Center for Science and International Affairs Harvard Kennedy School 79 JFK Street Cambridge, MA 02138. www.belfercenter.org. Statements and views expressed in this report are solely those of the author and do not imply endorsement by Harvard University, Harvard Kennedy School, or the Belfer Center for Science and International Affairs. Design & Layout by Andrew Facini. Copyright 2017, President and Fellows of Harvard College Printed in the United States of America. The Muslim Brotherhood. A Failure*

## CHAPTER 2

# THE MUSLIM BROTHERHOOD, SAYYID QUTB AND ISLAMIST EXTREMISM

*Sako Abou Bakr*

## Introduction

"We are the umma of the believers, living within a Jahili society. As a community of believers, we should see ourselves in a state of war with the state and the society. The territory we dwell in is the House of War."[1] These were the words of Sayyid Qutb in an Egyptian military court in April, 1966 before he and two of his companions were sentenced to death by hanging. The offense; conspiring against the government and plotting its overthrow, the evidence used by the state prosecutors in the trial, besides 'confessions,' a book, Qutb's final piece of literature, Ma'alim fi al-Turuq, Signposts.[2]

This study does not set out to be a thorough analysis of the political and religious ideology of Sayyid Qutb. Rather it is an attempt to identify the political and social climate in Egypt as the primary motivation which led to the development of Qutb's radical interpretations of Islam. Notions of Arab nationalism and Arab socialism dominated the political discourse of Qutb's Egypt and hearts and minds were enraptured by promises of its populist leader, Gamal Abdel Nasser. This chapter in Arab history from the early 1950's until the late 1960's is etched in historical memory as the era of pan-Arabism. However, it was also a vital period in the evolution of fundamentalist Islam into its more radical form which first expressed itself in the 1970's and is until today at the base of radical fundamentalist Islamic thought worldwide. This piece will demonstrate the principal role played by Sayyid Qutb in this transformation and reveal that radical interpretations of Islam were given impetus to develop in Egypt during this period due to the nature of Nasser's regime.

## The Brotherhood, Nasser and the New Tyranny

In the desert prisons and political detention centers of Nasser's republic, enmity towards the regime and the society that supported it was nurtured within the minds of those victims forgotten by the Republic, al-Ikhwan al-Muslimun, the Muslim Brotherhood. One particularly brutal commander of a military prison in Cairo told his prisoners in 1966, all of whom were members in the Brotherhood, "You know my opinion of you…you deserve to be annihilated…for you constitute a worse danger to this country than the Jews."[3] The hostility of the Brotherhood towards Nasser's regime revealed itself unabashedly in the final manifesto of its most prolific ideologue in that generation, Sayyid Qutb, in Ma'alim fi al-Turuq, Signposts.

Composed in prison and first published in 1964, the book was reportedly read by Nasser himself and allowed to circulate initially but was then banned a year later. The regime came to recognize that Qutb's book offered a scathing criticism of Nasserist Egypt and directly challenged the official state identity of pan-Arabism. By 1965, Nasser and pan-Arabism as an Egyptian state and national identity had endured a series of defeats at the regional level, no doubt this reverberated domestically and Nasser was looking to reaffirm his power in Egypt by making an example of the Brotherhood.

Nasser, as a charismatic leader, had developed strong connections with the masses and often identified for them the "enemies of the people," whether they were external threats emanating from the West, imperialists, or Israel or if they were regional or domestic threats such as reactionary Arab governments or 'merchants of religion,' like the Brotherhood.[4] Proponents of Signposts within the Brotherhood who had managed to begin re-organizing after years of disarray were hunted down, the book's author and his closest companions were sentenced to death. The Egyptian secret police charged with combing Signposts for subversive material found it to be "a rejection of pan-Arab nationalism," among calling for other actions potentially threatening to the regime.[5]

This was not the first altercation the Brotherhood had experienced with the regime. Years prior, in 1954, Nasser used a failed attempt on his life in Alexandria by a Brotherhood member as a pretext to crush what had become the largest domestic political obstacle to solidifying his control in the years immediately after the July 23 Revolution of 1952. The Brotherhood had largely been caught unawares by the decisiveness and scope of Nasser's action against them. Immediately following the attempt on Nasser's life mobs were organized with the help of government run transport-unions. They were raucous in their denouncements of the Brotherhood, chanting slogans as they descended on Brotherhood headquarters where they succeeded in burning it to the ground. On October 29, two days after Mahmud Abd al-Latif, Nasser's would-be assassin, fired and missed several shots, Nasser proclaimed, "The revolution shall not be crippled: if it is not able to proceed white, then we will make it red."[6]

## The regime followed with a concerted effort to vilify the Brotherhood in the press

Brotherhood plots to destroy the young government along with Egyptian infrastructure emerged, plans for hundreds of assassinations were revealed, but most insulting of all was the accusation that the Brotherhood and their leaders were 'merchants of religion' using Islam to attain their fantastic political goals. Mass arrests of the Brotherhood ensued, farcical trials were held, hangings and prison sentences were meted out, and with both public opinion and the government working against them the Brotherhood's internal organization and leadership was thrown into peril.[7]

The year 1954 presented a unique quandary for the Brotherhood. The organization was still reeling from the assassination of their founder, spiritual guide and political tactician, Hassan al-Banna, in 1949. Al-Banna had founded the organization in 1928 in a quest to lead modern Muslim society back to the 'true' Islam as embodied by the initial generations of Muslims, the Salaf. Al-Banna argued that modern Muslims were culturally, politically and economically subordinate to European powers because they had deviated from the practices and teachings of their religion. He was exceptionally disillusioned with the state of the highest Islamic authority in Egypt, al-Azhar. He claimed the institution did not effectively defend Islam from the onslaught of foreign concepts and ideas from the West and charged that the officials of al-Azhar failed in their duties to be a "spokesman for a living and dynamic Islam."[8] The Brotherhood's main objective was to rectify this state of weakness by re-inculcating society with the teachings of 'true' Islam and striving for a society in which Islam would govern all aspects of everyday life.

Al-Banna considered a Muslim one who professed the tawhid, the confession that 'there is no God but God and Muhammad is his Prophet,' and whose life conduct reflected that confession. He stressed the importance of understanding the scripture of the Quran and the sunnah, the tradition, on an individual basis rather than relying on religious experts for interpretations.[9] The Brotherhood was dedicated to the establishment of an Islamic order, one that emphasized the role of shariah in everyday life. However, al-Banna was careful not to make the issue a divisive one by calling for the state to adopt and implement shariah, rather the government should be inspired by religion and the shari'ah, hence the call for an Islamic order and not an Islamicstate.[10]

Al-Banna, then, did not advocate radical action to overthrow the government, though he was a proponent of activism and a branch of the Brotherhood would carry out political assassinations in the 1940's, he sought only reform of the established system. Moreover, he advocated that Islam validated parliamentary democracy and the two could be reconciled.[11] From the Brotherhood's theoretical base as established by Hassan al-Banna, Sayyid Qutb would formulate radical new interpretations of what constitutes a Muslim the Islamic state, and its governance, and methods of ushering it in.

By 1954 al-Banna was five years departed, the Brotherhood's internal weakness made them susceptible targets for the regime. Their organizational and ideological platform had lost its bearings. The Brotherhood had often accused "the military-political- ethical-social invasion" represented by the British imperialist presence in Egypt as the primary cause of the country's decrepit state. This menace had ceased to exist when Nasser concluded a treaty with the British leading to the withdrawal of British forces in October of 1954. The organization was ideologically ill-prepared when the onslaught of Nasser's foray against them began.[12]

Action against the Brotherhood on such a wide scale was unprecedented in Egypt. Exceptionally puzzling to the Brotherhood was Nasser, he and most of his clique, the Free Officers, had either been members of the organization in years prior, or, at a minimum maintained amiable contact. The Brotherhood was supportive of the Free Officers takeover of the government and took steps to coordinate their efforts with the revolutionaries during the coup of July 23, 1952. Among those sentenced to prison in the initial wave of arrests was Sayyid Qutb, having only years before been a close associate of the Free Officers. He was reported to have been the only civilian who attended private meetings of the Revolutionary Command Council. He delivered a key note speech at the officers' club in August, 1952 and even declined a position as the Minister of Education in the new regime. But cordial relations had gone by the wayside by 1954, Qutb was the head of the Propagation of Islam section within the Brotherhood, and as such he spearheaded advocacy for Islamic reform and criticized the new government for failing to live up to the expectations of the revolution.[13] However enigmatic Nasser's actions against the Brotherhood were come late 1954, many of the organizations members would have many long years in prison to contemplate the plight that befell them, most influential among them, Sayyid Qutb.

While the Brotherhood found itself debased and besieged like no time in its history, the young army colonel Gamal Abdel Nasser would use the successful suppression of the Brotherhood as a springboard to consolidate his power in Egypt. He harnessed the momentum and public sympathy from the failed attempt on his life to push the first President of the newly proclaimed Republic, Muhammad Naguib, and those loyal to him, out of the government. Nasser, now in full control, entered Egypt into Cold War and regional politics and in no discreet manner. He signed a highly touted weapons deal with the Soviet Bloc in 1955 and championed Egypt's role in the non-aligned movement. In July of 1956, he nationalized the Suez Canal under the pretext that funding was needed for the building of the Aswan high dam and Egypt's economic and agricultural advancement. With the aid of resolute U.S. diplomatic intervention, he managed to achieve a grand political victory out of a disastrous military defeat inflicted on Egypt by Britain, France and Israel. By the end of 1956, Nasser's star was rising and fast.

Throughout the region he was celebrated as a hero young, charismatic, impassioned, Nasser enraptured Egypt and the Arab world at large with promises of pan-Arab unity, socialism, and the restoration of lost honor. In 1958, Nasser would join Syria and Egypt under the banner of the United Arab Republic, seemingly fulfilling the prophecy he was unyieldingly touting.[14] Though Nasser would experience politically damaging regional setbacks beginning with the dissolution of the UAR in 1961 and involvement in a costly war to aid revolutionary army officers in Yemen beginning in late 1962 the major symbolic accomplishments of the 1950's served as the "preliminary groundwork on which future charismatic legitimacy would rest," and would help him retain popular support even in the face of blows to his regional and domestic prestige.[15]

Nasser also harbored a revolutionary vision with regard to Egypt's economic situation. He promised to strengthen state institutions and strove for sweeping social reform which led to an expansion of the public sector. Economic actions of the regime such as the 1952 Land Reform act, which redistributed 13 percent of agricultural land to poor tenant farmers and established a 200 feddan limit on land ownership, and the nationalization of virtually the entire economy from 1956 onwards, came to be major symbols of Nasserist Egypt. The National Charter of 1962 continually referred to 'Arab socialism' as a means to achieve social justice and equality and the Charter established the Arab Socialist Union as the sole representative body of the Egyptian people which included vast cross sections of the social stratum. To manage the massive nationalization of most of Egypt's rapidly expanding industrial sector and its transportation and public utilities sectors, government institutions and bureaucracy proliferated as well. In the 1960's Nasser's economic policies had almost eliminated unemployment in Egypt.[16] Nasser had "emerged in a society in crisis, confronted the challenge, had a message, and found people disposed to believe in his message and follow his lead in search of salvation in this world or in the hereafter."[17] By incorporating the entire population into the drive for social justice and appealing to notions like unity, pan-Arabism, and independence from the West, Nasserism had become a populist movement whose messianic leader managed to establish a rare and exceptional connection with the masses.

Though the veneer looked glossy, below the surface of Nasser's Egypt existed the realities of what was essentially a police state run by a dictator, albeit the regime enjoyed wide support. There was little room for competing ideologies, political parties were banned, save for one comprised of party members loyal to the regime, secret security services crushed out political dissent and the media was strongly influenced by the state. Throughout the 1950's the press was strongly infiltrated by government sympathizers but maintained some freedom, however in 1960 the institution was officially nationalized turning the media into, in the words of one critic, "a government agency exercising the only freedom available to it—the freedom to justify, support and flatter."[18]

In what is perhaps an irony of history, that during these heady days of pan-Arabism and Nasserism when the future of Egypt and the Arabs looked auspicious, Sayyid Qutb began to put pen to paper diagnosing the ills of a society and a political doctrine he felt was plagued, ultimately offering what he viewed as the only remedy, Islam. However, this call to Islam was to be injected with radical new ideas which would alter the landscape of Islamic thought, much of the virulence of his ideas coming from contempt for pervasive Nasserist symbology as manifested by strong state institutions, and the prevalence of pan-Arab and socialist principles.

## Modern Jahiliyyah: The Ideological Break with the Brotherhood's Past

"If we look at the sources and foundations of modern modes of living, it becomes clear that the whole world is steeped in jahiliyyah, and all the marvelous material comforts and advanced inventions do not diminish its ignorance. This jahiliyyahis based on rebellion against the sovereignty of Allah on earth. It attempts to transfer to man one of the greatest attributes of Allah, namely sovereignty, by making some men lords over others."[19]

Jahiliyyah, traditionally defined by Western and Islamic scholars alike as "the age, or condition, of ignorance" in pre-Islamic Arabia before Muhammad's revelation,[20] was re-interpreted by Qutb and transposed onto modern society. Though he was not the first to do this, Sayyid Abul A'la al-Mawdudi had reinvigorated the term and its modern meaning in his writings as early as 1939 in India.[21] Qutb, however, can be credited with popularizing and building on Mawdudi's notion of jahiliyyah. Qutb uses the term repeatedly in Signposts, his final and most radical piece of literature. In one chapter alone it appears 52 times whereas it is only mentioned four times in the Qur'an.[22]

Closely intertwined with Qutb's notion of jahilliyyah is that of hakimiyyah, the sovereignty of God. One of the conditions of jahilliyah is the failure of the society and its leaders to recognize the hakimiyyah of Allah. Hakimiyyah implies that Allah is the sovereign of sovereigns to which there is no human equivalent. Recognition of this fact is the necessary prerequisite to the establishment of shari'ah, Allah's law, which is also his sovereign will.[23] The tawhid is the acknowledgement that sovereignty is only Allah's, hence the only responsibility of a human leader who is a Muslim is to implement shari'ah. All matters of governance and society must be decided through consultation with shari'ah, which is essentially equivalent to consulting with Allah since his law is his will, acknowledging the sovereignty of him alone. The individual caprices and whims of a human leader outside of this sphere are considered un-Islamic and the hakimiyyah of Allah usurped. Hakimiyyah, then, is "the crossroads between Islam and jahiliyyah."[24] Perhaps, for Qutb, there could be no greater usurper than Nasser, he symbolized all the characteristics of a jahili ruler, he promised the people salvation not through Allah but through socialism and Arab unity, he denied shari'ahits function as law of the state and he was complicit in elevating pan-Arab nationalism to the status of a religion among the Arabs.

Most crucially, Qutb continues that according to shari'ah, "to obey" is "to worship," hence if one obeys the laws of humans and of governments who reject the implementation of Allah's law then that person is essentially denying the hakimiyyah of Allah by worshipping something other than him and is guilty of shirk, unbelief.[25] Such reasoning leads Qutb to his conclusion, "we may say that any society is a Jahili society if it does not dedicate itself to submission to Allah alone in its beliefs and ideas, in its observances of worship, and in its legal norms. According to this definition, all societies existing in the world today are jahili."[26] The ramifications of this conclusion, which even places Muslim states, their governments and their people in the category of jahili, is this, "the position of Islam in relation to all these Jahili societies can be described in one sentence: it considers all these societies un-Islamic and illegal."[27] No other thinker went so far, even Mawdudi always distinguished between pure-jahiliand half-jahili societies, the former rejecting Allah outright while the latter, of which Muslim societies were a part, accepted Allah but didn't follow his law.[28]

Qutb makes no such concessions. The rejection of Allah's law is the rejection of the hakimiyyah of Allah and is jahiliyyah. Al-Banna, while recognizing Muslim society in Egypt was in a perilous state and Muslims needed to be guided and inspired by the shari'ah, never declared Egypt or Egyptians to be living in a state of jahiliyyah. In fact, al-Banna recognized the Egyptian constitution of 1923 as a legitimate document because of its declaration to conform to Islamic principles, given he had disputes with particularities and certain articles of the document, he stressed reform was necessary, never did he deem society as a whole jahiliin nature.[29] Furthermore, Qutb had essentially equated abiding by the laws of the Egyptian state with committing shirk, meaning large portions of Muslim Egyptians were actually unbelievers and false Muslims.

To better understand the evolution of Qutb's theories about society, politics and the role of Islam in both and why he came to arrive at such sweepingly damning conclusions his life experiences can be telling.[30] While always considering himself a Muslim it was not until his visit to the United States in 1948, when he was thrown into a different cultural milieu, that he began to find solace in Islam and identify it as having "presented humanity with a complete cure for all of its problems."[31] Sent by the Egyptian government to investigate the American educational system, Qutb's leanings toward Islam were compounded by his abhorrent American cultural experience in which he was disgusted with most every aspect of society, most explicitly sexual promiscuity, racism, female behavior, the culture of materialism, disregard for the elderly, and the commercialization of Christianity.[32] Qutb would return to Egypt in 1950 committed to his new found passion and belief in Islam. Soon thereafter he would join the Brotherhood and rise to prominence rapidly as its chief ideologue.

While Qutb's experience in the U.S. served a catalyst for his ideological evolution, the years he spent in Nasser's prisons were to be "for him and for his followers...the crucial formative experience."[33] The brutality and injustice Qutb encountered in the prisons of Nasser's "progressive" republic conjoined with the overbearing influence the regime wielded over all aspects of the state's function came "to symbolize the relationship of the state to the society."[34] Judging by accounts of Qutb's prison experience and Signposts, Qutb most likely perceived Nasser as the worst kind of dictator, a nominal Muslim who championed ideas of pan-Arabism and socialism, imported and secular ideologies, and misled the Muslims of the Arab world down a treacherous path away from Islam. All the while, the true believers, the Brothers, sat behind bars where they were brutalized by unbelievers. Furthermore, Nasser was virtually idolized by 'the Arab street' throughout Qutb's life, he promised to be the savior of the Arab nation while Allah and his religion were diminished.

Qutb became completely convinced of the Jahili nature of the regime when in 1957 at the Liman Tura prison on the outskirts of Cairo, 23 Brothers were brutally murdered in their prison cells and another 46 were injured. The prisoners had failed to report for the day's labor, having come to believe they were to be murdered upon convening. They attempted to lock themselves in their cells but the guards were able to breech this defense and carried out a massacre. Qutb, who was chronically ill, was in the infirmary as the wounded and dead poured in and watched as the guards left the wounded for dead without a hint of remorse. This event is attributed with having unnerved and exasperated Qutb, leading him to conclude that the society in which he was born and raised was not an Islamic one.[35]

As was customary of many Islamist thinkers of the first half of the 20th century, those considered "the old Muslim Radicals," Qutb initially identified with the notion that Arab nationalism was a necessary stage in the progression toward the emergence of an Islamic state. The Arabs, it was argued, played a vital role in the establishment and perpetuation of Islam from its inception hence they were the only group capable of leading the Islamic revival. Pan-Arabism then would serve as the first and necessary phase of the more grandiose aspiration of pan-Islam. Qutb himself came out in a similar sort of conditional support for Arab nationalism in early 1953, "There is...no serious contradiction between Arab nationalism and pan-Islam as long as we understand Arabism as a mere stage."[36] However, over the course of his imprisonment he would come to reject any notion of Arabism entirely, most likely because those Arab regimes, specifically Nasser's, who trafficked in the ideology, cut Islam out of the equation entirely and worse, worked brutally to oppress the religions true practitioners. Through declarations of social revolution and marching under the banner of pan-Arabism, Nasser propelled the power of the state to unprecedented heights. Moreover, pan-Arabism provided non-Muslim Arabs the mechanism to govern over Arab Muslim states, a notion best exemplified by Michel Aflaq's prominence in Syria. The pan-Arabism of Nasser aspired to create a nation based on the European model in which land, history, ethnicity, and language played the essential role in a united national consciousness, an end in and of itself of which Islam was to be subservient and subsumed.

Qutb, harkening back to the Islamic past during the era of Muhammad and the Four Rightly Guided Caliphs, averred that Islam united peoples of varied nations, ethnicities, and classes and provided for the ultimate social equality from day one. Qutb, unlike the ideology of the Brotherhood before him, did not assign exceptional value to the Arab role in the history of Islam, rather concerning the first community of Muslims, he writes "this marvelous civilization was not an Arabic civilization, even for a single day:

It was purely an Islamic civilization. It was never a nationality but always a community of belief."[37] By contrast, the Brotherhood had always believed that since the Arabs were the first Muslims, "if the Arabs are humiliated, then so is Islam." Hence, a prerequisite to a strong worldwide Islamic community was a strong Arab Islamic community, unified as one.[38]

While the notion of mimicking the ways of the Salaf was introduced by al-Banna much earlier, Qutb expands on this and defines the Muslims nationality as only "his belief" and his nation as dar al-Islam, the house of Islam, where shari'ahis implemented. This in contrast to every other nation which resides in dar al-Harb, the house of War, where the flawed laws of humanity reign supreme and dilute or prevent God's sovereignty.[39] Al-Banna claimed Islam allowed for nationalism in the sense that, by the stipulations of Islam, one should have love for one's country and place of birth and desire to better that place through the superior devotion to the spread of God's message to serve the larger Islamic community.[40] However, Qutb, by requiring that a Muslim's nation is only one in which shari'ahis implemented, considered all Muslims to live in dar al- Harb.

## Qutb's Egypt and the Legacy of Signposts

As Qutb's disillusionment with Nasser and the society around him steadily inclined, he came to conclude that Muslim society was no longer Islamic and that just as in the time of Muhammad a minority of true believers existed in a sea of jahiliyyah, referring to the pre-Hijra period in which the first generation of Muslims lived in persecution in Mecca.[41] Except now, the forces of jahiliyyah were even more venomous and dangerous than the Quaraysh in the time of Muhammad. Qutb wrote of modern jahilliya has "a living movement," with a great deal of organization and cohesion in the practical realm.[42] The Quraysh were merely ignorant of God's call, the modern day antagonists of Islam, assumedly most conspicuously embodied by Nasser, proclaimed themselves to be Muslims and worked against the religion by spoiling and diluting it from within. They enjoyed popular support and that of compromised religious officials, like those of al-Azhar who would often issue religious rulings in favor of government policies, some even slandered the Brothers as medieval terrorists conspiring against Islam.

For Qutb, the power of the jahiliyyah forces arrayed against the umma was so great he advocated fleeing Jahili society altogether so as to be cleansed of its impure influences and anti-Islamic practices. This is predicated on the model of the Prophet Muhammad's hijra from Mecca to Medina in 622 C.E. Qutb urged that, "When a person embraced Islam during the time of the Prophet, peace be upon him, he would straightaway cut himself off from jahilliyah. When he stepped into the circle of Islam, he would start a new life, separating himself off completely from his past life under ignorance of the Divine Law."[43] Qutb's defenders, most prominently his brother Muhammad Qutb, rejected that Signposts advocated a modern day hijra, claiming it is a misinterpretation of the text and that Signposts urges a spiritual withdrawal, not a physical one.[44] However, it seems that advocacy of emulating the hijra was not a misinterpretation but rather one of the many interpretations that could be gleaned from Qutb's message which was often lacking in specifics. No example of this is more clearly discernable than Shukri Mustafa's practice of withdrawal from Egyptian society in the 1970's. Mustafa was well known to be deeply influenced by Signposts.[45] Furthermore, since Qutb tended to literally interpret the Quran, his followers would employ the same methods when approaching his work.[46]

Qutb wrote Signposts to serve two purposes, first, to critique Egyptian society from his unique Islamic worldview and second, to instruct, motivate, and guide the vanguard of the umma on their quest to re-assert hakimyyah and Islam. Qutb put forward a virulent message in order to buoy the Islamic movement in Egypt at a time when it was crippled by Nasser's popularity and government action against them. Moreover, Qutb sought to de-legitimize the Islamic support offered to Nasser's regime in the form of al- Azhar scholars and some former Brothers.[47]

Signposts is a book whose ideas have been interpreted by many radical Islamists worldwide as a comprehensive work applicable to this day, but a more accurate interpretation of Signposts would account for its authors immediate situation and goal for the future of the Brotherhood movement, especially in Egypt. Examples from Signposts are perhaps necessary to elucidate this point. "History tells us," or perhaps Qutb's own experience told him, "that the Jahili society always chooses to fight and not to make peace. It normally attacks the vanguard of Islam at its very inception, whether it be a few persons, or larger groups, or it may wait until this vanguard has become a well-established community."[48] Here, Qutb braces the movement for another onslaught from the regime, he stipulates it could happen at any juncture hence his prophecy was likely to be qualified.

Moreover, the cult of the leader that developed around Nasser perturbed Qutb, this is clear when he wrote, "Jahiliyyah is the worship of some people by others, that is, some people become dominant and make laws for others, without caring about the use or misuse of their authority, and regardless of whether these laws are against injunctions of Allah."[49] What is also discernable from this excerpt is Qutb's disenchantment with the supreme authority of the state. Nasser had little respect for the legal establishment in Egypt; in 1956 the judiciary in Egypt was purged, what resulted was a document that conferred upon the office of the Presidency unrestricted power.

Nasser's regime managed to undermine the courts and the state's legal authorities by overstepping them entirely through the establishment of 'exceptional courts' where 'critical' issues could be dealt with. The Brothers were often tried in a court presided over by a Military tribunal. Nasser's power was not genuinely accountable to any institution in Egypt, religious scholars, the judiciary or the electorate. Overall, there was a lack of the "rule of law" in Egypt, a criticism that gained credence among Islamists in Nasser's Egypt.[50] Qutb, having been sentenced to prison, and later death by these military courts, was acutely aware of this predicament and extremely embittered by the circumstances. Hence, Qutb called for the establishment of hakimiyyah which would bring the ultimate rule of law to Egypt and usher in the banishment of corrupt and contemptible human sovereigns.

Upon Qutb's release from prison in 1964, for reasons that aren't entirely clear, his ideas had gained a following among small but resurgent forces of the Brotherhood who sought to restore the organization and exact revenge. Qutb had succeeded in articulating for the organization an inspiring ideological path and re-invigorated a new generation of Muslim radicals who were prepared to depart from the "atrophied fundamentalism" of the old Brotherhood.[51] Al-Banna was the principal leader responsible for the Brotherhood's rise and success. His literary legacy however was lacking, leaving an ideological and spiritual vacuum when he died. With Signposts Qutb had filled this void and now the Brotherhood understood why Nasser sought to crush them out and when the second major wave of crackdowns against the Brotherhood took place in 1965 Signposts was essentially justified. Furthermore, Qutb's hanging fulfilled his role as a martyr, joining the likes of al-Banna, who was assassinated by the government in 1949, and other Brotherhood members killed throughout the 50's and 60's by Nasser's regime. Martyrdom proved the righteousness of the struggle, indeed "the halo of persecution suffered in defence [sic] of a faith and a social ideal confers a status of absolute truth upon Islamicist discourse."[52]

## Conclusion

Qutb's theories would have far ranging effects that was not limited to the Brotherhood in Egypt. His ideas inspired new generations of radical Islamists who were ready to transform thought into deed. However, his influential manifesto embodied in Signposts owes much of its virulence, passion, and power to the era in which it was spawned. Nasser's crushing defeat in 1967 would expose the bankruptcy of pan-Arabism and the mortality of its messianic leader. Furthermore, Egypt's long-term economic woes, some stemming from the socialist policies implemented under Nasser, provided further credence to Qutb's discourse and a path for his ideas to make inroads among wider swaths of the population desperately seeking a cure for the ailment and weakness of Arab and Islamic societies alike. Qutb's theories are potentially highly destabilizing for Muslim and non-Muslim governments in that he left behind a series of utopian thoughts penned while incarcerated under brutal conditions—he was a thinker, not the builder of a nation nor a political leader forced to deal with situations in a pragmatic manner on the practical level. There exists, then, an uneasy balance between the practical and the theoretical in his writings, those who have attempted to act on Qutb's theories have exposed the ambiguities.[53] But time will be the ultimate judge of Qutb's ideological longevity. Notions as such have the advantages and disadvantages of existing in the realm of ideas.

*Sako Abou Bakr is a Researcher for the Project for CHIIS at Islamic Theology of Counter Terrorism (ITCT), UK. He works as a Project Manager at Aid Organisation for Refugees and Asylum Seekers (ASSAF) in Israel and also worked as a Security Analyst at International Institute for Counter Terrorism (IICT) from 2015-15. Sako is also a Co-founder of African Student Organisation as well Organisation for African Communities in Israel. Mr Abou Bakr is a recent M.A graduate in Conflict resolution and Global studies from the Interdisciplinary Centre (IDC) Herzilya in Israel with a B. A in Government in Counter Terrorism and International affairs. Sako is a security analyst in the Middle Eastern studies specially Egypt and Counter terrorism researcher. Sako was born and bred in Egypt and currently resides in Israel for the last 16 years. He is a linguist fluent in Arabic, English, French and Hebrew.*

## CHAPTER 3

# THE MUSLIM BROTHERHOOD'S GLOBAL THREAT

## *Dr. M. Zuhdi Jasser*

### Introduction

As a devout Muslim who loves my faith, and loves my nation, the avoidance behavior of confronting the Muslim Brotherhood is a major obstacle to our national security and harmony. This has stemmed from a bigger policy to de-emphasize "radical Islam" and the "Islamist" root cause of global Islamist terror. There is no better place to begin an honest conversation about the Islamist threat imposed upon our nation than a focus on the Muslim Brotherhood. A denial of the truth about the Muslim Brotherhood has actually emboldened extremists on both sides of this debate: both radical Islamists and anti-Muslim fascists. In fact, nothing would be more pro-Muslim than the marginalization of the Muslim Brotherhood and its direct affiliates. Making the Muslim Brotherhood radioactive would allow the light to shine upon their most potent antagonists in Muslim communities, those who reject political Islam and believe in liberty and the separation of mosque and state.

Since 9/11 the discussion of the global security threat of the Muslim Brotherhood has sadly and noticeably demonstrated our national disfunction in addressing the depth of the real threat of radical Islam and more specifically the threat of Islamism (aka, political Islam). Our negligence, ignorance, and distraction has enabled groups like the Muslim Brotherhood to take advantage of our unprecedented freedoms and excessively thrive in a manner frankly often not possible anywhere else in the world. It seems that almost every discussion about Muslims and Islam looks at our communities, organizations, faith, and movements through a binary lens of good or bad, ally or enemy. The reality is that it is far more complicated and yes, at times, nuanced. As we take a look at the Muslim Brotherhood, I will lay out for you their origins, history, networks, ideologies, and direct connections to terrorism.

Neither Islam nor Muslims are monolithic and should not be treated as such by anyone – much less our government and media. Please understand, it is as equally foolhardy in counter-terrorism and counter-radicalization work to refuse to acknowledge the role of political Islam in the threat as it is to villainize the whole of Islam and all Muslims. The majority of Americans are smart enough to understand that truthfully identifying the Muslim Brotherhood as a radical terror organization does not demonize all or even most Muslims. In fact, identifying the primary cancer cell(s) of global radical Islamism will go a long way towards beginning to assuage the fears of concerned Americans. Any gross generalization either way is dangerous.

Stating the House of "Islam has no problems" is just as problematic as declaring that "Islam and all Muslims are the problem." I am here to tell you that our national security policy of refusing to say that "Islam currently has a problem" is dangerous. This surrender, which began just after 9-11, has chartered a course towards failure. It has hamstrung our homeland security heroes from addressing any of the most central Islamist precursors of militant Islamists. If the agency actually emphasized the central role of radical Islamism and its attendant theo-political ideologies of groups like the Muslim Brotherhood, it would shift the entire axis of our agency apparatus toward once and for all beginning to actually address the root cause of the theocratic strains of Islam (or Islamism), which would begin to make us safer. So-called Violent Extremism (VE) is simply an endpoint of a common supremacist ideology that is innately theo-political and is a radicalization process that occurs over months to years and is far easier to publicly monitor than waiting for guess work on "Violent Extremism". There is no better representative of an organization with global reach that endlessly produces Islamist terror progeny than the Brotherhood.

Almost 17 years after 9/11, it is not too late to begin correcting this wrong-headed policy. The best place to begin this course correction is in our approach towards the Muslim Brotherhood. Those who say that an honest identification of the radicalism behind membership and ideology of the

Muslim Brotherhood would enflame Brotherhood sympathizers both ignore the successes of Muslim Brotherhood's global project during the past two decades (if not the last century), and they use the very evidence that the Brotherhood are militant Islamists to argue against us identifying them as a threat. It also presumes that the United States is afraid of facing terror groups and their sympathizers due to their radicalization. It also presumes that the United States national security policy should forever remain in a posture of defense against the Muslim Brotherhood rather than one of an offense.

## Islamic ideological Framework and the Muslim Brotherhood

Our founding fathers were able to navigate a war of ideas against theocracy. We can do it again in the 21st century with Islam. It is absurd to assert that just because the Muslim Brotherhood is an Islamist group which uses its interpretation of the faith of Islam as a basis for its rule, that the United States cannot wage a battle against Islamist theocrats while cherishing Muslim liberals, modernists and critical thinkers. We have for too long been playing a "whack-a-mole" program against by products of Muslim Brotherhood ideologues rather than directly countering the primary cancer cells of the Muslim Brotherhood operations.

In order to understand the Muslim Brotherhood, the following terms and ideas must become part of the fair domain of our national security agencies. Our agency analysts and government experts are both smart and fair enough to know that each of these terms carries with it a diverse set of interpretations from within the 'House of Islam' and that suppressing this essential debate hands the debate to our Islamist enemies. I submit the following terms and proposed definitions for the record in hopes that other government agencies follow suit and rather than engaging Islamist apologists who obstruct and deny, that they instead begin engaging honest Muslims who are ready to confront the global radical movements that use them:

**A.** Islam: the faith tradition, its practice, and scriptures identified by over 1.6 billion Muslims in the world.

**B.** Islamism and Islamists: the theo-political movement (Islamism) or party and its adherents (Islamists) who seek to establish Islamic states governed by shar'ia law in Muslim majority nations and institutions. Muslim Brotherhood members are Islamists.

**C.** Shar'ia: Islamic theological jurisprudence as interpreted by Muslim jurists and clerics and practiced by Muslims. The legal instrument of Islamist theocrats.

**D.** Jihad: a holy war or armed struggle against unbelievers or enemies of an Islamic state. It can also mean spiritual struggle within oneself against sin.

**E.** Wahhabism: a Sunni Islamist movement based in a puritanical literalism and intolerance of any other interpretations or faith. A revivalist movement originated in the Najd of Arabia in the mid-19th century by Ibn Abdul Wahhab. It is the dominant strain of thought empowered by the Kingdom of Saudi Arabia. Its ideas are central to the Salafi-jihadism of groups like Islamic State in Iraq and Syria (ISIS).

**F.** Salafism: Sunni Islamic fundamentalism which attempts to return normative Muslim practices to the literal ways of the Prophet Muhammad in the 7th century. Salaf literally means "companions of the Prophet". It is often synonymous with Wahhabism but is far more ubiquitous. Salafism, like Wahhabism deplores invention.

**G.** Salafi-jihadism: The expansionist ideology (a combination of Salafism with militant jihadism) of groups like the Muslim Brotherhood that seek to create Islamic states and a global caliphate.

**H.** Caliphate and Caliphism: the theo-political ideology or desire by Islamists to re-establish the caliphate, a globally unified Islamic governance of Islamic states which are led by a single caliph.

**I.** Ummah: the entire Muslim Faith community, but it can also mean the Islamic state

**J.** Islamic reform, Ijtihad: critical interpretation of scripture (exegesis) and Islamic jurisprudence in the light of modernity.

**K.** Takfir: the rejection ('excommunication') of another Muslim from the faith community. The declaration of another Muslim as an apostate.

To think that these words and concepts, and others are off limits in the freest nation on earth, censored to our agencies, is just incredulous considering the growing threat we face today from violent Islamism. It smacks of a bizarre invocation of blasphemy laws in America. It is groups like the Muslim Brotherhood that have benefited from our refusal to discuss these elements of Islam and Islamism. Violent manifestations of each of these above ideas are a natural byproduct of the intolerant non-violent underbelly of theo-political autocratic belief systems. Any security apparatus unable or unwilling to connect the dots between the non- violent and violent manifestations of these ideologies is leaving us bare and will continue to miss the signs of radicalization. A designation of the Muslim Brotherhood as a terrorist organization will necessitate a bring about a long overdue better understanding of these concepts by our security apparatus.

The latest recommendations from the Homeland Security Advisory Council ignorantly state the exact opposite recommending that only "plain American English words" be used and these terms be avoided.[1] We cannot functionally address the global threat of the Muslim Brotherhood without understanding these concepts.

Interim Report and Recommendations of the Homeland Security Advisory Council Countering Violent Extremism (CVE) Subcommittee of the US Department of Homeland Security. June 2016.

I hope and pray that my testimony today about the Muslim Brotherhood will open your eyes to the reality our government has been dismissing when it comes to their global threat upon our national security.

Personally, I will add that we are rendered entirely unarmed in our work at AIFD and in the Muslim Reform Movement in America, Canada, and Europe if we cannot engage our own faith community within the House of Islam on these ideas and if agencies are too timid to address the threat of the Muslim Brotherhood and its influence in radicalizing Muslims across the planet into "Violent Islamism".[2] All of the Muslim leaders in our Muslim Reform Movement would agree that looking just at "Violent Extremism" (VE) is too nebulous, nonspecific and will result over and over in agency blinders to the attacks we have seen including the radical Islamist attacks at Fort Hood, Boston Marathon, Chattanooga, San Bernardino, and now Orlando. We cannot hold security agencies accountable to precursor ideologies and warning signs when those precursors and their groups like the Muslim Brotherhood are not identified as real threats.

## History of the Muslim Brotherhood

We hear many denials all over the map about the Brotherhood threat. From dismissals that the Muslim Brotherhood is disorganized, to it is normalized, to it is too weak. We hear "it is not one organization" to "it is non-existent" to "no one knows what it actually is" to "it is a legitimate peaceful political party that participates in elections in Egypt and Tunisia and elsewhere". On and on. Essentially, it is imperative that we first agree on what the facts are regarding the Muslim Brotherhood.

The Muslim Brotherhood was founded in Egypt in 1928. It expanded rapidly across Egypt upon the ideas of its founder Hassan Al-Banna on the premise the Islamic world was declining against Western hegemony. From the outset it established a secret apparatus to serve as "defender of the movement against the police and governments of Egypt." Another founding father of the Brotherhood Islamist movement, Sayyid Qutb authored the primary manifesto of the Muslim Brotherhood's ideology Milestones in 1964. This book argued for the establishment of Islamic political systems with whatever means necessary most particularly using violent jihad. Having been particularly impacted by his impression of freedom in America during his two-year stay at the University of Colorado, referred to any part of the world without an Islamic governance as corrupt and ignorant or "jahilliyah". They both called for the implementation of traditional and theocratic Islamic society.

Al-Banna and then Qutb put forth the notion that Islam is all encompassing for society and their motto became and remains until today, "Allah is our objective, the Prophet is our Leaders, the Qur'an is our constitution, jihad is our way, and death for the sake of God is our highest aspiration."[3] Al-Banna argues for Islamic liberation theology in a step-wise process from individual, to family, home, education, society, and nation to rid it of foreign domination, political, economic, and spiritual in an Islamic state and its caliphate of states in order to master the world. This process begins with the societal 'upbringing' process of children also known as Tarbiyah a program seen in the youth programs of all Muslim Brotherhood indoctrination programs including western Brotherhood organizations like the Muslim American Society (MAS).

For decades the Muslim Brotherhood cut its teeth on its own perennial victimization and repression by severely autocratic Arab regimes like the Egyptian dictatorships of Gemal Abdel Nasser, Anwar Sadat, and Husni Mubarak as well as other Arab regimes that they conveniently associated with secularism even though the distinction between Western liberal democratic secularism and Arab tyrannical secularism was intentionally dismissed by them as all being jahilli (ignorant). It is no coincidence that Qutb was not only the founding father ideologically of the Muslim Brotherhood but also inspired Osama bin Laden, Al Qaeda leaders, and radical jihadists across the planet. There have been many less frontal more supposedly democratically accommodating descendants of Qutbian ideology. However, its underlying supremacist jihadist mission of its party and secret apparatus never changes.

Their logo and motto has always been the same. Some apologists try to say that jihad is a greater jihad and not a lesser jihad of militant movements. In fact, the founder, Hassan al-Banna, rejected the greater jihad and in his tract "On Jihad" said as: "... Jihad in its literal significance means to put forth one's maximal effort in word and deed, and Benessa said in an undated speech in the sacred law it is the slaying of the unbelievers and related connotations, such as beating them, plundering their wealth, destroying their shrines and smashing their idols... It is obligatory on us to begin fighting with them after transmitting the invitation to embrace Islam, even if they do not fight against us."[4] Thus, terrorism is appropriate when it suits the MB and its affiliates. Sheikh Yusuf Qaradawi, today's contemporary Al-Banna, in his speeches and books, has enlisted the same thought process on salafi-jihadism.

## Moderating the Muslim Brotherhood?

Robert S. Leiken and Stephen Brooke of the Nixon Center tried to bizarrely argue in 2007 that the Muslim Brotherhood could somehow be moderated and be an ally against supposedly more radical groups like Al Qaeda and against other common more radical enemies like Iran.[5] They famously argued that American policy should be to find the moderates within the Muslim Brotherhood and use them rather than avoid them. As Muslim brotherhood expert, Eric Trager points out in his book, Arab Fall, Mark Lynch even "went further to say that the Muslim brotherhood could serve as a 'firewall' against Al Qaeda style radicalism." He further noted that Lynch said its organization "allows it to effectively monitor and control social space through mosques, charities, organizational networks, and widespread networks adding that the brotherhood's presence in religious institutions made it a more effective counter to jihadis than domestic intelligence agencies or non-Islamists neither of which could penetrate the religious sphere." [6, 7]

It is unfathomable that D.C. thought leaders were convincing Americans that the mothership of Sunni Muslim radicalization would be our ally only because it was positioned so centrally within the Muslim theological network of Egypt and other Muslim states and communities. It is a "bigotry of low expectations" that caters only to the existing Islamic establishment at the expense of Muslims and all the vulnerable populations under the boots of Islamists. In fact, in D.C. its very cancerous network became the reported reason for which we should tolerate and turn a blind eye to supposedly "minority radical offshoots" rather than treat the primary cancer of the Muslim Brotherhood itself. Put another way. According to voices of policy makers sympathetic to Muslim Brotherhood Islamists, the alternative to trying to defeat the Muslim Brotherhood is allying with the radical global terrorist group in the hope of somehow sharing some goals. I find that very premise deeply offensive both as an American and as a Muslim.

There was also a growing false premise that the Brotherhood had rejected violence and accepted electoral politics, political parties and nonviolence. Many in the West even wanted to believe that they had rejected Qutbism. However, none of these statements, which were façades, were joined with theological and ideological reform and rejection of core Islamism. Trager summarized that: "The Brotherhood's autocratic behavior in power (after 2011) discredited the moderate Muslim Brotherhood argument to a great extent and not because the Brotherhood's behavior or goals fundamentally changed once it became Egypt's ruling party as some have argued. Rather those who touted the Brotherhood's moderation mistakenly privileged the group's political tactics which have shifted over time in their analysis while downplaying the totalitarian and anti-Western goals that have defined the brotherhood since its founding.[8]

"In short, the Muslim Brotherhood was never a moderate organization or a democratic one in any sense of that word. It is a rigidly hierarchical, purpose driven vanguard that seeks total control over its members so that they can mobilize them for empowering Hassan al-Banna's deeply politicized interpretation of Islam as an all-embracing concept. It accepts electoral institutions as a mechanism for winning power but its ultimate goal is theocratic: it seeks to establish an Islamic state and ultimately establish a global Islamic state that will challenge the West. And following Mubarak's ouster it was the only political group in Egypt with a nationwide political machine. The brotherhood therefore had an unprecedented opportunity to finally transition from spreading its message within Egyptian society to pursuing power outright"[9]

Simply put: there is no 'moderate' Muslim brotherhood; that is a misnomer. Every arm of the organization goes towards the purpose of supporting its central primary mission of Islamist hegemony and rule.

## The Muslim Brotherhood is a terrorist organization

Prior to the Arab Awakening in 2011, the Muslim Brotherhood leadership often made no qualms about supporting the goals of Al Qaeda. In September 2010 the Supreme Guide of the Muslim Brotherhood, Mohamed Badie, delivered a weekly sermon mirroring the ideological themes of Al-Qaeda's August 1996 declaration of war against the United States. Calling on Arab and Muslim regimes to confront not just Israel, but also the U.S., he declared that "Resistance is the only solution against the Zio-American arrogance and tyranny." This "resistance" can only come from fighting and understanding "that the improvement and change that the [Muslim] nation seeks can only be attained through jihad and sacrifice and by raising a jihadi generation that pursues death just as the enemies pursue life." He also predicted the imminent downfall of the U.S., saying, "The U.S. is now experiencing the beginning of its end, and is heading towards its demise."[10] Barry Rubin remarked, "The Muslim Brotherhood's leader has endorsed anti-American jihad and a view virtually identical to al-Qaida's ideology. Since the Brotherhood is the main opposition in Egypt and Jordan and the most powerful group in Muslim communities of Europe and North America, this is serious stuff" ..."it was a declaration of war that went unnoticed. The Muslim Brotherhood recently called for jihad on the U.S. and Israel, adopting a view almost identical to Al-Qaeda's."[11]

For any naysayers over the years, the Muslim Brotherhood's recent period of rule of the Egyptian government of 17 months that came to an end in June 2013 proved that it was not a functional moderate democratic organization but rather a radical militant Islamist organization which produced and continues to produce many terrorist offshoots in their network of organizations and individuals. At some point every honest analyst will need to recognize that the fruit of the poisoned tree will never be acceptable, and it is the Brotherhood's tree which is the primary problem in the Arab Sunni world and not just its "whack a mole" byproducts.

We have learned many lessons from the revolutions of the Arab Awakening in 2011. Most significant of those is how directly related the Muslim Brotherhood is to almost every Sunni radical Islamist group in the region. There was direct communication between Pres. Mohammed Morsi and Al Qaeda leader Ayman Al-Zawahiri according to a November 22, 2013 article in Egypt's Al-Watan newspaper. Morsi allegedly agreed to grant a presidential pardon to over 20 terrorists including one of the lotteries childhood friends who was running Ansar Bayt-al-Maqdis, an ISIS branch in the Sinai.[12] Morsi's brother actually mediated the initial contacts between Al-Zawahiri and Morsi himself. In a telling confluence of ideologies and strategies, Al-Zawahiri told Morsi, "Rule by God's law for us to stand beside you, there is no so-called democracy, then get rid of your opponents," according to the El-Watan transcript.

The Al Qaeda militants also even agreed at a remote border area training camps with common personnel to defend the Brotherhood regime. For those who question the veracity of these accounts, there is no doubt that attacks in the Sinai increased following Morsi's fall from power. And Brotherhood leader Mohammed el-Beltagy following Morsi's deposition said that attacks in the Sinai would stop the second president Morsi is reinstated"[13] Ansar Beit al-Maqdis, the group responsible for most of the attacks, belonged to al-Qaida before joining the Islamic State (ISIS) in 2014. Reports indicate that Ansar Beit al-Maqdis was "structurally" tied with the MB.

On January 27, 2015, the Muslim Brotherhood published on their official Ikhwanonline.com website an announcement that the organization was entering a "new phase" and calling its followers to prepare for a "long, uncompromising jihad" against the Egyptian government. The statement also positively recalled the Muslim Brotherhood's terrorist past, including the operations of the "secret apparatus" terror wing active in the 1940s and 1950s, and the group's battalions organized by Brotherhood founder Hassan al-Banna that fought against Israel during its War of Independence in 1948.[14] Since Aug 2013, Muslim Brotherhood members in Egypt have been killed in firefights during attacks on police and military targets, and during the manufacture and placement of explosives for acts of terrorism. There were innumerable calls for violence in '14-'15 by the leadership of the Muslim Brotherhood including calling for retribution and beheadings from rotten bodies. Coptic Christians faced ongoing violence from vigilante

Muslim extremists, including members of the Muslim Brotherhood, many of whom acted with impunity.

Attacks included 70 churches and more than 1,000 homes and businesses of Coptic families torched in the ensuing violence. During the Muslim Brotherhood protests, direct incitement towards the Copts was repeatedly reported from leading Muslim Brotherhood figures, and since the protest dispersal this targeting of the Christian community continues in official statements on Muslim Brotherhood social media outlets and from its leadership. As the United States Commission on International Religious Freedom (USCIRF) has previously noted, this terror campaign by the Muslim Brotherhood is not a new development. Over the past decade violence by the Muslim Brotherhood has been directed at the Coptic community, as it observed back in its 2003 Annual Report.[14] MB Sheikh EssamTelemeh said if police detain your family you should organize and kidnap their family as hostages.[15]

A senior Egyptian Muslim Brotherhood leader, Ashraf Abdel Ghaffar, gave a July 3, 2015 interview where he defended the sabotage of power stations and high voltage pylons targeting Egyptian citizens by the Muslim Brotherhood as punishment for support of the Egyptian government.[16] Then, On May 27, 2015, a group of 159 Muslim Brotherhood- associated scholars from 35 nations announced the publication of a document endorsing violence in Egypt in response to a "war against Islam's principles." Specifically, Article 4 of the "Call to Egypt" calls for "retribution punishment" against government officials, judges, police, soldiers, religious officials, and media personalities backing the government.[17] The document was affirmed by the Muslim Brotherhood in an English-language statement published on their official website.[18]

I served on USCIRF from 2012 to 2016 and visited Egypt in 2013 when the Muslim Brotherhood was in control of government. I was not only struck by their inability to rule but by their monocular Islamist lens with which they viewed Egyptian society, government and the world. I was also struck by the number of American Muslim Brotherhood sympathizers who had gone back to help facilitate the Muslim Brotherhood's governance. Even with that, they were all quite young and not very interested in making the Constitutional process egalitarian and secular. They insisted upon keeping final authority of law with the clerics in determining its adherence to shar'iah. Last, they would have nothing with abandoning their motto, symbol and jihadism.

Furthermore, if not most importantly, the connection between the Muslim Brotherhood, Al Qaeda, ISIS, and other radical Islamist groups was noted in a series of emails between Secretary of State Hillary Clinton and confidant Sid Blumenthal on April 7, 2011. Blumenthal reported at the time that he was directly told by the highest levels that the relationship between the MB, Al Qaeda and other radical groups was "complicated".[19]

## Muslim Brotherhood's Global Threat

This relationship was also not only limited to Egypt. The Clinton emails describe definitive links between the MB and Al Qaeda in Libya as seen for example with Ali Al-Salabi, who founded the Al Qaeda linked Libya national party (LNP). Al-Sallabi is described as Qaradawi's man in Libya (Muslim Brotherhood leader Sheikh Yusuf Al-Qaradawi based in Qatar since exile from Egypt in 1961).[20] The LNP was dominated by former members of Al-Qaeda linked Libyan Islamic Fighting Group (LIFG) who maintained al-Qaeda ties during their struggle with forces of former dictator Muammar al-Qaddafi. Militias of the Libyan Muslim Brotherhood joined forces with U.S. designated terrorist organizations, particularly Ansar al-Sharia, as part of the Shura Council of Benghazi Revolutionaries and Libya Dawn forces fighting against the military forces of the internationally recognized Libyan government.[21]

Similarly, in Tunisia, Rached al-Ghannouchi, head of Tunisia's Brotherhood affiliated Ennahda Party, was allied with Ansar al-Sharia and its late leader, Abu Iyadh, a former Bin Laden ally sanctioned by the U.S. after 9/11. Abu Iyadh was responsible for al-Qaida's assassination of Northern Alliance leader Ahmed Shah Masood two days before the attacks on the Twin Towers and the Pentagon.[22]

Yemen's MB also has deep connections to Al Qaeda in the Arab Peninsula through Sheikh Abdul Majid al-Zindani. Treasury Department officials described al-Zindani as a "Bin Laden loyalist" in a 2004 press release. He also helped al-Qaida leader Anwar al-Awlaki, while serving on the board of the Brotherhood-linked Union of Good, which raises funds for Hamas.[23, 24] On February 2, 2004, the Treasury Department designated Shaykh Al-Zindani, a leader of the Yemeni Muslim Brotherhood's Al-Islah political party, a terrorist. The Treasury Department's designation states that al-Zindani has a "long history of working with Bin Laden, serving as one of his spiritual leaders," in addition to his activities in support of Al-Qaeda, including recruiting and procuring weapons. Al-Zindani was also identified in a federal lawsuit as a coordinator of the October 2000 suicide attack targeting the U.S.S. Cole in Aden, Yemen that killed 17 U.S. Navy sailors, including personally selecting the two suicide bombers. In September 2012, al-Zindani reportedly called for his supporters to kill U.S. Marines stationed at the U.S. Embassy in Sana'a, Yemen.

Zindani is the personification of the link between elements of the Muslim Brotherhood and Al-Qaeda because Zindani has been a leader of the Yemeni Brotherhood's Al-Islah Party, a member of Al-Qaradawi's International Union of Muslim Scholars, the Union of the Good Hamas fundraising syndicate, and was identified as a mentor of Osama Bin Laden and an advisor to AQAP in 2013. Additionally, Al-Qaida and the Muslim Brotherhood have also used many of the same funding mechanisms, such as the Lugano, Switzerland based Al-Taqwa Bank.[25]

And in what was a significant low point in American foreign policy Blumenthal reported to Clinton that "MB leaders were pleased with the results of the discussions with the USG and IMF both of which in the analysis of the MB leaders appear to accept the idea of Egypt as an Islamic state". This sentiment from the U.S. continued and was reinforced at the 2012 World Economic Forum in Davos. Their entire model for rule as expressed by the Supreme Guide Mohamed Badie was that they would use the Turkish model of civilian rather than clerical rule as long as it always was in line with Islamic law as the Egyptian Constitution of 2012 enumerated. This is by definition a theocracy. Gemal Al-Banna, Hassan al-Banna's brother warned prior to his death in January 2013, that shari'ah would then always prevail in such a system.

In Kuwait, the Kuwaiti Muslim Brotherhood's Lajnat al-Daawa al-Islamiya ("Islamic Call Committee") was designated by President George W. Bush on September 23, 2001 by Executive Order 13224 and by Secretary of State Colin Powell on January 9, 2003. Reasons cited for the designation included Lajnat al-Daawa being used as a financial conduit for Osama bin Laden and Al-Qaeda, and its funding of terrorist groups in Chechnya and Libya. Both Al-Qaeda operations chief Khalid Sheikh Mohammed and World Trade Center bomber Ramzi Yousef held positions with the organization.[26]

Last but not least, the designation of Muslim Brotherhood entities as terror organizations is not new. The Hamas designation is a Muslim Brotherhood designation. The United States has previously designated global elements of the Muslim Brotherhood. The terrorist group HAMAS, which self-identifies as "one of the wings of the Muslim Brotherhood in Palestine," was designated a terrorist organization by President William Clinton on January 23, 1995 by Executive Order 12947, and later by Secretary of State Madeline Albright on October 7, 1997.[27, 28]

## The Muslim Brotherhood in the United States

This all then comes full circle with many obvious connections of American Islamist leaders to the Muslim Brotherhood and its terror apparatus. One glaring example is Esam Omeish, a former president of the Muslim American Society (MAS). The MAS is a well known as the overt arm in the US of the global Muslim Brotherhood as chronicled by an extensive investigative series in the Chicago Tribune.[29] He remains a prominent figure at Dar al- Hijra mosque in Falls Church, Virginia. Last summer he was labeled by the national security committee of the Libyan House of Representatives as an enemy of the state. He has recently advocated that the U.S. support a group known variably as the "Revolutionary Shura Council," or the "Mujahideen Shura of Derna," despite ties between its officials and al-Qaida. Egypt's air force bombed the group in retaliation for terror attacks against Coptic Christians in April.[30] Omeish endorsed Libya's Muslim Brotherhood in a 2012 IRIN News article, stating that although it came in a distant second in Libya's 2012 elections, it "may be able to provide a better platform and a more coherent agenda of national action."[31] After appointment to a statewide immigration commission in 2007 by Virginia Senator Tim Kaine, Omeish was asked to resign after a revelation among others that he praised "Palestinians who chose the jihad way to liberation" during a rally in 2000. He has also congratulated Palestinians who gave "up their lives for the sake of Allah and for the sake of Al-Aqsa". The connection of the MB motto, mission, militant groups and their American affiliates could not be more obvious. There is no public information that Omeish was directly involved in any terror support. But his advocacy for jihad, the Brotherhood and its affiliates speaks volumes. The common link for many radical Islamist groups regionally and globally is the Muslim Brotherhood.

Another clinic in how American Muslim Brotherhood affiliates serve to water down or misdirect their global connections to terrorism is in the wake of the Syrian Revolution of 2011. Make no mistake. Like other revolutions in the wake of the Arab Awakening, the Syrian Revolution began as a popular attempt at shedding the yoke of Bashar Al-Assad's tyranny and his Ba'ath Party. But in the wake of the regime's genocidal approach to its own citizenry, a vacuum arose which was filled by militant Islamist groups that coalesced into ISIS in 2013. I discuss this evolution in depth at Georgetown University's Religious Freedom Institute in:" Understanding the Cauldron that Brewed ISIS."[32] However, all of that does not ameliorate the direct connection between the Syrian Muslim Brotherhood and the host of radical Islamist groups operating in the region including ISIS and Al Qaeda. Because of its Muslim Brotherhood connections and ideologies, the Syrian American Council (SAC) became a dominant force among Syrian-Americans lobbying for American influence among anti-Assad revolutionary movements in Syria.

As has been typical, despite our diversity within the Syrian Muslim community, Islamists with a strong mosque and Brotherhood network are able to marginalize the rest of us secular liberal democratic thinkers. The Syrian American Council has repeatedly represented Islamist interests in Syria. They brought Islamist members of the Free Syria Army (FSA) to D.C. to lobby for support only days prior to the FSA working with Turkey to invade the Kurdish enclave of Afrin in North-western Syria, an American ally who helped defeat ISIS in Syria and Iraq. As the Investigate Project notes, "no distinction existed between the FSA, Ahar al-Sham or Jabhat al-Nusra, Anas al-Abdeh, former president of the anti-Assad National Coalition of Syrian Revolution and Opposition Forces (ETILAF)" told the London based Al-Hayat in 2016.

The SAC's connection to the MB is apparent. Molham al-Droubi a key leader of the Syrian MB told IPT in 2013 that many of the SAC's members formerly belonged to the Syrian MB. An Arabic post in 2014 notes that its ideology is closer to ISIS that to the West. In fact, the Syrian MB stated that American attacks against ISIS and its allies are not the answer. They have openly mourned the death of Al-Qaeda leader in Ahrar Al Asham.[33] Then in Qatar, the global MB leader, Yusuf al-Qaradawi an influential spiritual guide of the Muslim Brotherhood joined in criticizing the American military campaign against ISIS since while he is anti-ISIS, he only wants movements acting in the name of Islam and jihad to fight in the region.[34] According to Kamal al-Labwani a former ETILAF member and secular democratic activist, SAC's lobbying led the U.S. to support extremists who posed as moderates.[35]

Another illustrative focal point between the Muslim Brotherhood and radical Islamist groups is Mohammed Ghanem. He openly supported MB ideologue, Sheikh Qaradawi saying in a 2012 Facebook post, "I love this appreciated scholar very much, even I adore his jurisprudence. I consider this a great honor and now I am over the moon." Ghanem is a central figure in U.S. government and State Department contacts with the Syrian opposition and was in fact was romantically involved with Khulood Kandil the former State Department Syria Opposition Outreach Desk Officer.[36] Her uncle, Hisham Kandil, was Egypt's prime minister during the Brotherhood's brief rule in Egypt. Ghanem openly minimized the threat of radical Islamist groups. He stated, "Americans never felt this insecure when Ahrar al-Sham or other 'extremist' rebels established safe havens inside Syria. This is because when Syrian rebels – whatever their political beliefs – conquer territory from Assad or ISIS, they do so to seek greater opportunity and freedoms for their homeland...contrary to some news reports, rebel fighters are not barbarians."[37] He went on to condemn the Obama administration's 2012 labeling of Jabhat al-Nusra (a known Al Qaeda affiliate) a terrorist organization because "it cooperates closely with the Free Syrian Army and because it has achieved military successes and has delivered critical civilian aid."[38]

SAC also notoriously brought Sheikh Mohammad Rateb Nabulsi, a known terror apologist, to the United States for a speaking and fund raising 17 city tour in early 2014. His website had an April 2001 fatwa fully sanctioning suicide bombing against Israeli civilians. He also is a known homophobe with long screeds against homosexuality appearing for example in April 28, 2011 on Al-Aqsa TV of HAMAS saying "Homosexuality involves a filthy place and does not generate offspring... that is why brothers, homosexuality carries the death penalty." He also directly and repeatedly connected what he described with homosexuality to his hate for western free nations. This cleric was clearly responsible for radicalizing countless Muslims. [39]

The Muslim Brotherhood's network is also bolstered by a direct support by leadership of various humanitarian organizations. Islamic Relief USA (IRUSA) is a prime example of this activity in the United States. Khaled Lamada, IRUSA board chairman has been criticized for his connections to the Egyptian Muslim Brotherhood. A Facebook picture in January 2015 shows him displaying a Muslim Brotherhood salute along with Egyptian MB luminaries like Waleed Sharaby; a leader of the MB-linked Egyptian Revolutionary Council.[40] His social media profile is rife with Egyptian MB support. He posed in 2015 with MB Shura council member Gamal Heshmat and exiled pro-Brotherhood Egyptian judge Waleed Sharaby. Heshmat and Shraby have openly supported terrorism. Heshmat met in 2014 in Qatar with Khaled Meshaal, who was a top Hamas official at the time. He has ridiculed the U.S. designation of Hamas as a terror group.

Lamada is tied closely to the Egyptian Americans for Freedom and Justice (EAFJ) who have endorsed Brotherhood linked terrorists in Egypt. EAFJ connections to MB leadership in Egypt are deep. Lamada spoke at the EAFJ 2016 Ramadan Iftar fundraiser. Lamada for his part denies any of these affiliations. But social media posts also suggest other IRUSA board members Mohamed Amr Attawiand Hamdy Radwan also have deep MB loyalties. Many of their names link back to the 1991 Muslim Brotherhood phone book founded by Palestine Committee of the MB in the U.S. The United Arab Emirates included IRW on a 2014 list of terror groups. They described IRW as 'Islamic Relief of the Global Muslim Brotherhood'. Bangladesh has barred IRW from working with Rohingya refugees from Burma due to concerns it would radicalize them. Israel did the same in Gaza since IRW had been known to employ HAMAS members. These are all claims IRW denies. A number of European banks including Credit Suisse, HSBC, and UBS, have refused to do business with IRW over concerns with their terror financing. IRW is the largest U.S. Muslim charity and provides 25 percent of its annual budget. It is a USAID partner.[41] A recent comprehensive report by the Middle East Forum lays out the detailed case for IRW's connection to the Muslim Brotherhood and its global militant Islamist network.[42]

## The Explanatory Memorandum of 1991 and the US Muslim Brotherhood

Some detractors to Muslim Brotherhood designation have stated that such a designation would be "exploited and manipulated for political gain". Some have dismissed the MB as "non-existent" and that the 1991 Memorandum presented in the Holy Land Foundation Hamas terror financing trial and convictions in 2008 as suspect and "conspiracy theories". The document's veracity has withstood multiple legal challenges during the HLF trial and multiple other circumstances. It was seized from the "archivist" Ismail Elbarasee of the Muslim Brotherhood in the

U.S. The network's existence and mission is certainly not only dependent upon this document, but now over the past 27 years since they met in Philadelphia in 1991 and plotted a "civilizational jihadist process" whereby Brotherhood members in America work toward destroying the Western civilization from within" all of the actions of these MB legacy groups in the America have towed the MB Islamist line with little deviation and certainly no open antagonism. From the previously mentioned Muslim American Society, Syrian American Council, to the larger Islamic Society of North America, North American Islamic Trust (NAIT), Islamic Circle of North America (ICNA), and CAIR (Council on American Islamic Relations) to name a few, their agendas are consistent with this global support and theocratic, theo-political activist process and network of the Muslim Brotherhood. For those of us who have grown up in Muslim communities with families from Muslim majority nations, we know who the theo-political advocates for the Muslim Brotherhood are and the leadership of these organizations typically fits that ideological pattern. It is abjectly false to state that the only evidence of the MB in the U.S. is that memorandum.

In the Holy Land Foundation prosecutions - the largest terrorism financing trial in American history - Justice Department officials successfully argued in court that the international Muslim Brotherhood and its U.S. affiliates had engaged in a wide-spread conspiracy to raise money and materially support the terrorist group HAMAS. The Holy Land Foundation (HLF) officials charged in the case were found guilty on all counts in November 2008, primarily related to millions of dollars that had been transferred to HAMAS. During the trial and in court documents federal prosecutors implicated a number of prominent U.S. Islamic organizations in this conspiracy, including the Islamic Society of North America (ISNA), the North American Islamic Trust (NAIT), and the Council on American-Islamic Relations (CAIR). These groups and their leaders, among others, were named as unindicted co-conspirators in the case. The Justice Department told the court that these U.S. Muslim Brotherhood affiliates acted at the direction of the international Muslim Brotherhood to support terrorism in a July 2008 court filing: "ISNA and NAIT, in fact, shared more with HLF than just a parent organization.

They were intimately connected with the HLF and its assigned task of providing financial support to HAMAS. Shortly after HAMAS was founded in 1987, as an outgrowth of the Muslim Brotherhood (Govt. Exh. 21-61). The International Muslim Brotherhood ordered the Muslim Brotherhood chapters throughout the world to create Palestine Committees, whose job it was to support HAMAS with "media, money and men." (Govt. Exh. 3-15). The U.S.-Muslim Brotherhood created the U.S. Palestine Committee, which documents reflect was initially comprised of three organizations: the OLF (HLF), the IAP, and the UASR. CAIR was later added to these organizations (Govt. Exh. 3-78) listing IAP, HLF, UASR and CAIR as part of the Palestine Committee, and stating that there is "[n]o doubt America is the ideal location to train the necessary resources to support the Movement worldwide..."). The mandate of these organizations, per the International Muslim Brotherhood, was to support HAMAS, and the HLF's particular role was to raise money to support HAMAS' organizations inside the Palestinian territories. Govt. Exh. 3-17 (objective of the Palestine Committee is to support HAMAS).[43]

The fact that the international Muslim Brotherhood does terrorism financing inside the U.S. was attested to by then- FBI Director Robert Mueller, who testified before the House Select Committee on Intelligence in February 2011, and responded to a question about the Muslim Brotherhood's networks and agenda in the U.S.: "I can say at the outset that elements of the Muslim Brotherhood both here and overseas have supported terrorism. To the extent that I can provide information, I would be happy to do so in closed session. But it would be difficult to do in open session."[44]

The lack of a terror designation for the Muslim Brotherhood has given them freedom to operate terror financing indirectly to the MB which then provides support to Al Qaeda. One of the examples cited by Richard Clarke in his U.S. Senate Banking Committee testimony was the case of Soliman Biheiri, who ran an investment firm specializing in Islamically permissible investments, the Secaucus, New Jersey-based BMI Inc. BMI offered a range of financial services for the Muslim community, and invested in businesses and real estate. According to federal prosecutors, among the shareholders of BMI were Al-Qaeda financier Yassin Al-Qadi and top HAMAS leader Mousa Abu Marzook - two specially designated global terrorists. Both

Qadi and Marzook operated separate businesses out of BMI's offices that also did business with BMI.

Other BMI investors included Abdullah bin Laden, nephew of Osama bin laden, and Tarek Swaidan, a Kuwaiti Muslim Brotherhood leader. In a Sept. 2003 detention hearing, federal prosecutors described Biheiri as "the U.S. banker for the Muslim Brotherhood," and stating that "the defendant came here as the Muslim Brotherhood's financial toehold in the U.S." Biheiri was convicted on federal immigration charges on October 9, 2003.[45] Even prior to that the connections have been well known. Before the U.S. Senate Banking, Housing and Urban Affairs Committee in October 2003, Richard Clarke, former National Coordinator for Security and Counterterrorism for Presidents William Clinton and George W. Bush, testified to the extent that terrorist organizations continued to operate inside the U.S. and the connection to the Muslim Brotherhood networks:

"Dating back to the 1980's, Islamist terrorist networks have developed a sophisticated and diversified financial infrastructure in the United States. In the post September 11th environment, it is now widely known that every major Islamist terrorist organization, from Hamas to Islamic Jihad to Al Qaeda, has leveraged the financial resources and institutions of the United States to build their capabilities. We face a highly developed enemy in our mission to stop terrorist financing. While the overseas operations of Islamist terrorist organizations are generally segregated and distinct, the opposite holds in the United States. The issue of terrorist financing in the United States is a fundamental example of the shared infrastructure levered by Hamas, Islamic Jihad and Al Qaeda, all of which enjoy a significant degree of cooperation and coordination within our borders. The common link here is the extremist Muslim Brotherhood - all of these organizations are descendants of the membership and ideology of the Muslim Brothers."

In court papers, federal prosecutors noted that the Holy Land Foundation trial included "numerous exhibits...establishing both ISNA's and NAIt is intimate relationship with the MB, the Palestine Committee and the defendants in the case."[46] A 1988 FBI report also identified many of these ideologically obvious Islamist groups ISNA, NAIT and IIIT as members of the "Ikhwan model" with the aim for recruiting support for an Islamic revolution in the U.S." The Saudi funded "Bridge Initiative," an arm of Georgetown University's Prince Alwaleed bin Talal Center for Muslim-Christian Understanding, argued in 2016 that the document was merely "one man's utopian vision". Their response was that if the idea "was central in a Muslim movement one would think more would have taken up the idea and spread it". As is typical of Salafi-jihadi apologists funded by the Saudis, they ignore the vast number of attacks on our soil linked to American Muslim radicalization by Muslim Brotherhood affiliated ideologies and mosques from Fort Hood in 2009 to the Boston bombing of 2013 to San Bernardino and on. Not to mention that from the beginning global MB icons had no qualms in engaging openly as endorsers of their Brothers in the United States.

For example, in 1995, global Muslim Brotherhood spiritual leader Sheikh Yusuf al-Qaradawi confirmed the connections between Muslim Student's Association and the Brotherhood, and said that the goal of the organization was to "conquer" the U.S. through dawa (Islamic proselytizing). In a 1995 speech to an Islamic conference in Ohio, al-Qaradawi, said victory will come through dawa. He said, "conquest through dawa, that is what we hope for." Qaradawi is well chronicled in fatwas justifying Hamas suicide bombings against Israeli civilians. He further said, "We will conquer Europe, we will conquer America, not through the sword but through dawa.' He has long been barred from the United States. In his speech, al-Qaradawi further said the dawa would work through Islamic groups set up by Brotherhood supporters in [the U.S.].

He praised supporters who were jailed by Arab governments in the 1950s and then came to the United States to "fight the seculars and the Westernized" by founding this country 's leading Islamic groups. He named the MSA [as one such group]. Though many Muslim youth today may reject any association with Qaradawi, good luck finding any denunciations of Qaradawi or the Muslim Brotherhood for that matter by Muslim Student's Association chapters around the United States. The civilizational argument is made by their continued denigration of western society, government, and the United States by the progeny of these programs. The Explanatory Memorandum, like Qutb's Milestones, should serve in their own words to highlight their global threat.

## The Cold War Analogy

In the Cold War, Leninist communist principles fueled the Soviet hegemonic global plan for driving communist revolutions. Similarly, Ladan and Boroumand argue in "Terror, Islam, and Democracy" that "Like Mawlana al- Mawdudi and various Western totalitarians Sayyid Qutb identified his own society (in his case, contemporary Muslim polities) as among the enemies that a virtuous, ideologically self-conscious vanguard minority would have to fight by any means necessary, including violent revolution, so that a new and perfectly just society might arise. His ideal society was a classless one where the "selfish individual" of liberal democracies will be banished in the exploitation of man by man would be abolished. God alone would govern it through the implementation of Islamic law (shar'iah). This was Leninism in Islamist dress."[47] Qutb may have railed against some aspects of the godlessness of communism and socialism within his works; however, it is clear that he was influenced by them in the formulation of some of his core ideas. Ibrahim Al-Hodaiby writes in an article four decades after Sayyid Qutb's execution: "In Milestones Qutb presents a manifesto for change, one heavily influenced by Lenin's revolutionary "What is to be Done?" with the clear Islamization of its basic notions." They even borrowed the term 'vanguard' from Lenin.

So, in essence for those of us reformists who reject socialism and communism as well as the Muslim Brotherhood's Islamism and seek liberty, there is nothing more pro-Muslim and pro-modern Islamic interpretations then supporting a Muslim Brotherhood designation as a global terrorist organization. They are today's equivalent in a liberation theology mantra of the Cold War's communist parties (Muslim Brotherhood) and communism (Islamism).

## Other states have designated the MB an FTO

Multiple states have declared the Muslim Brotherhood a terrorist organization and/or proscribed the group from operating in their countries. An Egyptian court banned the group in October 2013, and the government officially declared the Muslim Brotherhood a terrorist organization in December 2013;[48] the Kingdom of Saudi Arabia designated the group on March 7, 2014;[49] the Cabinet of the United Arab Emirates published a list of terrorist organizations, including the Muslim Brotherhood and its local affiliates;[50] on March 21, 2014, the Foreign Minister of Bahrain backed the terrorist designations of the Muslim Brotherhood by both the United Arab Emirates and Saudi Arabia. While certainly various members of the Organization of Islamic Cooperation have their own hypocrisies when it comes to terrorism and the promotion of Salafi-jihadism, their designations carry with them some admission with regards to the associated global network, funding streams and a shift, especially with petro-Islamist gulf states to some of their previous rather facilitative policies with pertaining to the Muslim Brotherhood.

While the MB is a Sunni Islamist group hatched in Egypt, the overlap with Islamist movements in Pakistan and Asia are quite central. This dates back to the relationship between Hassan al-Banna and Mawlana Al-Mawdudi. While the MB hatched groups like ISNA and NAIT, Mawdudi's Jamaat-e-Islami hatched similar groups like the Islamic Circle of North America (ICNA). There has always been major overlap between leadership and organizational ideologies, but no conversation on the MB should ignore their major cross-cultural affiliates like the Turkish AKP, the Pakistani JI, or even the Shi'a Iranian Khomeinists.

## Public Obstacles

Denial fuels bigotry rather than quelling it: If the reason for routinely publicly engaging Muslim leaders after acts of Islamist terror against Americans is simply to quell the fear of Americans, I will contend that the denial and obfuscation of the administration and the Muslims they engage does the exact opposite. Enabling the deep denial of the need for American Muslims to address the root causes of Islamist inspired terrorism and its separatism by not naming the Muslim Brotherhood a terror organization actually in the end fuels a growing fear of Muslims and Islam due to our policy choices for avoidance over transparency. Pew polling demonstrates that American feelings about Muslims is "cooler" than any other faith group scoring a 40 out of 100.[51] In fact, there is nothing that would do more to melt away anti-Muslim bigotry to the extent that it exists than for Americans to see Muslims step away from denial and actually engaging and confronting the Jihad and the Muslim Brotherhood with their own jihad for liberty and against theocracy. We should be calling for a jihad against jihad rather than shielding Muslims and Americans from the tough love that they need.

Defensive posture: the last 90 years of the Muslim Brotherhood existence has proven that a Western fear of riling up the militant Islamists by proactively identifying them as terrorists is only going to empower them through appeasement and defensiveness rather than taking them on offensively. Every day the Muslim Brotherhood militants will find an excuse to commit an act of terror or blame the west for their ills rather than their own theocracy. It is long overdue for us to take the offense against the Muslim Brotherhood.

Bipartisan blinders and false assumptions: Both the Bush administration and the Obama administration have thus far erroneously felt that giving the radical Islamists air time for their Islamic theological verbiage will lend them credibility. From the time of Attorney General Gonzales, onward there have been significant attempts by the Department of Justice to control the lexicon used to describe radical Islamists, with repeated recommendations to avoid any religiously charged terminology. The assumption that radical Islamists need our air time in order to brand themselves is false and it is more absurd to assume that their identity and branding can be defeated by ignoring groups like the Muslim Brotherhood. In fact, it requires the opposite—honest exposure, engagement, and marginalization of the Muslim Brotherhood. In fact, the suppression of the truth of their Islamist identity is an obstacle to a whole host of policies and engagements which would be the beginning of their defeat.

The problem of the Organization of Islamic Cooperation (OIC) Lobby: The OIC is the proverbial elephant in the room. On the issue of the Muslim Brotherhood there is some significant division within the Arab Sunni world. The constant refrain from the Obama administration that the United States should not "declare war against 1.6 billion Muslims and their governments" is related to global intimidation by the OIC sadly while ignoring the plight of Muslim and non-Muslim dissidents in their nations who lead the fight against Islamist movements.

First, make no mistake. Across the Middle East and Muslim majority world, many leaders, scholars, and pundits call these individuals and their acts exactly what they call themselves- Islamists and jihadists. Some of these governments like Saudi Arabia, UAE, and Egypt, have come around and perhaps in the interest of self-preservation have identified the threat of the Muslim Brotherhood and are finally beginning to defund the very Islamist groups their petro-Islam fed around the world that were berthed by the Muslim Brotherhood.

However, their approach is very schizophrenic because the Islamic states of each OIC nation is based in some form of autocratic theocracy and platforms for theo-political movements that are either directly Islamist like the Khomienists of the Islamic Republic of Iran or the shar'ia state of the Islamic Republic of Pakistan or the Wahhabism of the Kingdom of Saudi Arabia. All these states have state sponsored ideologies that are the underbelly that inspires militant movements like ISIS, Hamas, Al Qaeda, and Hezbollah and their Muslim Brotherhood common ideologies. Those Islamist governments often exploit the militancy of jihadists in order to dictate the ruling form of Islam. Only in the United States and in the West can we both identify the radicalism of the Muslim Brotherhood while also countering with an offense of secular liberal ideals of universal human rights which is far more effective than the Islamism and Salafism of OIC nation-states who are just jihadists of a different flavor. There is no country that would be more effective at beginning to eliminate the Muslim Brotherhood than the United States due to the profound safe harbor they have enjoyed in the United States.

The OIC nations hide behind the façade of "countering violent extremism" all the while their government's fuel "violent Islamism". It is heartbreaking as an American Muslim to see my own American democratic government invoke OIC-like blasphemy law behaviors preventing the antiseptic of sunlight upon the Islamist ideas which[52] How Americans Feel about Religious Groups: Jews, Catholics and Evangelicals rated warmly, Atheists and Muslims more Coldly. Pew Research Center: Religion and Public Life. July 16, 2014. Radicalize our co-religionists. With our founders' history in defeating theocracy, Americans are uniquely qualified to understand the battle against theocracy from within a faith. The best summary of the influence of the OIC upon our public discourse regarding Islam is Deborah Weiss' monograph, "The Organization of Islamic Cooperation's Jihad on Free Speech".[53]

## The Dangers of Qatar and Turkey

These divisions are beginning to bear out with countries like Qatar and Turkey which are dominated by leaders sympathetic to or directly involved in Islamist party politics. With Qatar for example, it has become the Arab national safe haven for former Egyptian Muslim Brotherhood luminaries and activists. They have provided them not only safe haven but a global perch from which to spread their ideology and hegemony. Their media arm, Al Jazeera, is reportedly staffed by upwards of 90 percent MB sympathizers. Their position on the MB has placed them squarely in the cross hairs of Saudi Arabia, the United Arab Emirates and Egypt. It is not surprising that along with Qatar's relationship with the Brotherhood it is also very sympathetic politically ideologically and economically with Iran and its Khomeinists. This schism within the Sunni region led to an embargo last year on Qatar that remains until Saudi demands are met with abandonment of the Muslim brotherhood being primary.

The Emir of Qatar has been historically close to Sheikh Yusuf al-Qaradawi who has been there since 1961. Qatar has been all in with the belief that the brotherhood represented the wave politically of the future in the Middle East. They similarly have supported Hamas and the Iranian global sponsorship of terror turning a blind eye to their support of Hezbollah and the Assad regime. They share rich natural gas fields with the Iranian regime. The Brotherhood's desire to create a global Sunni caliphate and Islamic state positioned the Qatari royal family to be part of that leadership. However, this positioning has put them not only in the advocacy of all of the terror connections of the Muslim Brotherhood globally but also at odds with the other regimes in the Middle East who see the Muslim Brotherhood as an existential threat. Make no mistake. The Muslim brotherhood would not be what it is today were it not for petro-Islam billions coming from Qatar and until a year ago the rest of the Gulf states.[54]

A designation of the Muslim brotherhood as a terror group is essential for American and global security and the containment of the Qatari royal families anti-Western and anti-democracy pro-Islamist positions. Additionally, their fealty for the Iranian theocrats and their heavy economic cooperation also demands their containment. The other global platform for the Muslim brotherhood is growing with the country of Turkey which also has an Islamist party in control--the Islamist Justice and Development Party (AKP) of Recip Erdogan. Turkey is a separate case study requiring a hearing on its own; however, its decades-old support of Hamas, It is aid to help Iran subvert the sanctions against them, and its own evangelical Dawa into the West including now the largest mosque in the United States built in Maryland by the Turkish Republic's diyanet religious authority are all consistent with and in parallel to the project of the Muslim Brotherhood.

While Erdogan's government for years was sympathetic to the Assad regime in Syria, the revolution of 2011 was viewed as an opportunity to have a neighboring Sunni Islamist power sympathetic to the AKP in place. So, Turkey along with Qatar proceeded to aid and supports the radical Islamist element of the Syrian Muslim Brotherhood and marginalizes the more liberal secular elements of the revolution. It also helped them counter their

Kurdish enemies. Qatar did the same. Nothing epitomizes the relationship between Erdogan's AKP and the global Muslim Brotherhood then the recent hosting by the Republic of Turkey of the 90th anniversary gala of the Muslim brotherhood. Speeches and rhetoric from the event and releases around the event in Turkey noted the Brotherhood's call to continue on the path of a comprehensive restoration of Islamic states around the world.[55]

Turkish groups closely allied to President Recip Erdogan have lobbied Congress to end U.S. support of the Kurdish People's Protection Units (YPG) which is the backbone of the US supported Syrian Democratic Forces (SDF) against ISIS. The Turkish American branch of Erdogan's Islamist AKP, MUSAID USA and the Turkish American National Steering Committee (TASC), were closely involved. Interestingly IPT reported that none of these groups lobbied with FARA registration (Foreign Agents Registration Act). Michael Rubin of AEI notes that "It is not just MUSAID USA. There's at least half a dozen organization and maybe twic that who have down the same rabbit hole" of influence operations. Apparently, these two organizations have also been on the FBI's radar. MUSIAD Executive Director Ibrahim Ulya sent an email to President Erdogan's son-in-law Berat Albayrak, Turkey's energy minister and thought to be Erdogan's heir apparent. In that he discussed the accusations of espionage by the FBI. Frequent communications between them expose how close these American organizations are with the Islamist AKP ruling party of the Republic of Turkey.

IPT notes that these groups have courted U.S. Islamist groups as they have the Muslim Brotherhood in the Middle East. They have coordinated protests and other activist work with CAIR (Council on American Islamic Relations) and USCMO (United States Council of Muslim Organizations). In fact, CAIR has presented its annual humanitarian award to the Turkish government in 2017 "for its humanitarian efforts for Syrian and Iraqi refugees".[56] Just a few weeks ago, the USCMO leadership was in Ankara to congratulate President Erdogan on his recent sham of an electoral victory as guests of the Turkish regime. CAIR's Hussam Ayloush praised It is "democracy and the rule of Law" in 2016 and also congratulated Erdogan on his victory. They all did not seem to care about the fact that the Committee to Protect Journalists named Erdogan's Turkey "the worst jailer of journalists in 2017."[57] In fact, leaders of the Egyptian Americans for Freedom and Justice (EAFJ) like Mahmoud ElSharkawy with strong ties to the Muslim Brotherhood have also worked closely with these Turkish Islamist organizations in the U.S. They have all sought an aggressive activist role in downplaying the 1915 Armenian genocide that killed 1.5 million people. They all promoted a FactCheckArmenia.com anti-Armenian propaganda site.

## Conclusions and Recommendations

The importance of identifying the Muslim brotherhood as a terrorist organization could not be clearer to our national security and counterterrorism strategy. This will begin not only a necessary process of treating the cancer at its core before it metastasizes rather than its byproducts after it has already spread. But now we can also begin a much longer strategy of identifying other Islamist movements that are parallel to the Muslim Brotherhood and equally dangerous. I leave you with the following recommendations:

1.      Designate the Muslim Brotherhood (MB) a foreign terrorist organization beginning in Egypt and then on a country by country basis. Libya, Syria, Kuwait, Jordan, Iraq and Yemen branches of the MB are the most obvious follow-ons based on my testimony here. But I would recommend that the designation be taken on a country by country basis and not a blanket global one, and only be driven by a need to designate every group in the world which is either a self-identified actual Muslim Brotherhood organization or an obvious Islamist terror group. This designation is not only an ideological one but one related to material, social, and militant support of the Muslim Brotherhood's salafi-jihadi movement.

2.      Use this designation of the Muslim Brotherhood as a terror organization as a pilot strategic designation to be made country to country across the world, but do not dismiss the equal global threat of parallel militant Islamist groups like East Asia's Jamat-e-Islami, Iran's Khomeinists, or Turkey's AKP to name a few.

3.      Call out American Muslim leaders to take a position on the Muslim Brotherhood, the evidence provided here, and its overarching theo-political ideologies. Will my fellow Muslims be on the side of freedom?

4.      Develop foreign policy mechanisms to disincentivize Qatari and Turkish government facilitation of the Muslim Brotherhood and its global affiliates including those in the West. Considerations should include a move

to suspend Turkey from NATO (perhaps warranting a separate hearing on the very complex U.S.- Turkey relations).

5.      Lift up diverse pro-liberty, secular reformist Muslim voices beginning with our Muslim Reform Movement and its allies within the Muslim community who are anti-Islamist. Use that strategy and our Declaration of our Muslim Reform Movement to identify allies within Muslim communities across the world.

6.      Use the MB designation as a template to transition immediately from the currently useless non-ideological center of gravity that relies on "Countering Violent Extremism" (CVE) to a much more practical one centered on "Countering Islamism" (CI) or (CVI).

7.      Stop engaging Muslim Brotherhood legacy groups in government and media and NGO's and recognize their Islamist terror sympathies, misogyny, anti-Semitism, homophobia, and anti-American ideological underpinnings. We must recognize that they are not the only voice for American Muslims or any community of Muslims.

8.      Re-open investigation into CAIR's radical ties and into the extensive domestic and foreign network of foundations and poorly hidden branches. Also investigate the Syrian American Council, MUSAID USA and Islamic Relief USA to name a few organizations with concerning global Islamist ties. We are Muslims who live in the 21st century. We stand for a respectful, merciful and inclusive interpretation of Islam. We are in a battle for the soul of Islam, and an Islamic renewal must defeat the ideology of Islamism, or politicized Islam, which seeks to create Islamic states, as well as an Islamic caliphate. We seek to reclaim the progressive spirit with which Islam was born in the 7th century to fast forward it into the 21st century. We support the Universal Declaration of Human Rights, which was adopted by United Nations member states in 1948.

We reject interpretations of Islam that call for any violence, social injustice and politicized Islam. Facing the threat of terrorism, intolerance, and social injustice in the name of Islam, we have reflected on how we can transform our communities based on three principles: peace, human rights and secular governance. We are announcing today the formation of an international initiative: the Muslim Reform Movement. We have courageous reformers from around the world who have written our Declaration for Muslim

Reform, a living document that we will continue to enhance as our journey continues. We invite our fellow Muslims and neighbors to join us.

*Dr. M. Zuhdi Jasser, M.D. is the Founder and President of the American Islamic Forum for Democracy (AIFD) and Co-Founder of the Muslim Reform Movement. He is also the author of A Battle for the Soul of Islam: An American Muslim Patriot's Fight to Save His Faith (Simon & Schuster, June 2012). On March 20, 2012, Dr. Jasser was appointed by Senate Minority Leader Mitch McConnell (R-KY) to the United States Commission on International Religious Freedom (USCIRF) where he served two terms both as a Commissioner and Vice-Chair until May 2016. He hosts the new podcast REFORM THIS! On The Blaze Radio Network.*

## CHAPTER 4

# AIMS AND METHODS OF EUROPE'S MUSLIM BROTHERHOOD

### *Dr. Lorenzo Vidino*

In 1990 Yusuf al-Qaradawi, an influential Sunni scholar and the unofficial theological leader of the international Muslim Brotherhood (al Ikhwan al Muslimoun), published a book called Priorities of the Islamic Movement in the Coming Phase.[1] This 186-page treatise can be considered the most recent manifesto of the Islamist revivalist movement. As Qaradawi explains in the introduction, the "Islamic Movement" is meant to be the "organized, collective work, undertaken by the people, to restore Islam to the leadership of society" and to reinstate "the Islamic caliphate system to the leadership anew as required by sharia"

Qaradawi's treatise introduces a new agenda and modus operandi for the movement, signaling a clear break with many salafi groups and even with some past ideological elements of the Muslim Brotherhood. While the book does not rule out the use of violence to defend Muslim lands, it generally advocates the use of dawa, dialogue, and other peaceful means to achieve the movement's goals. This doctrine is commonly referred to as "wassatiyya," a sort of "middle way" between violent extremism and secularism, and Qaradawi is one of its key proponents.[2]

After examining the situation of the "Islamic Movement" throughout the Muslim world, the dissertation devotes significant attention to the situation of Muslims living in the West. Qaradawi explains how Muslim expatriates living in Europe, Australia and North America "are no longer few in numbers," and that their presence is both permanent and

114

destined to grow with new waves of immigration. While Qaradawi says that their presence is "necessary" for several reasons such as spreading the word of Allah globally and defending the Muslim Nation "against the antagonism and misinformation of anti-Islamic forces and trends" it is also problematic. Because the Muslim Nation, and there- fore Muslim minorities "scattered throughout the world," do not have a centralized leadership, "melting" poses a serious risk. Qaradawi warns, in other words, that a Muslim minority could lose its Islamic identity and be absorbed by the non-Muslim majority.

Qaradawi sees the lack of Muslim leadership not only as a problem, however. He also views it as an unprecedented opportunity for the Islamist movement to "play the role of the missing leadership of the Muslim Nation with all its trends and groups." While the revivalist movement can exercise only limited influence in Muslim countries, where hostile regimes keep it in check, Qaradawi realizes that it is able to operate freely in the democratic West. Muslim expatriates disoriented by life in non-Muslim communities and often lacking the most basic knowledge about Islam, moreover, represent an ideally receptive audience for the movement's propaganda. Qaradawi asserts that revivalists need to take on an activist role in the West, claiming that "it is the duty of [the] Islamic Movement not to leave these expatriates to be swept by the whirlpool of the materialistic trend that prevails in the West."

Having affirmed the necessity of the Islamist movement in the West, Qaradawi proceeds to present a plan of operation. The Egyptian-born scholar openly calls for the creation of a separate society for Muslims within the West. While he highlights the importance of keeping open a dialogue with non-Muslims, he advocates the establishment of Muslim communities with "their own religious, educational and recreational establishments." He urges his fellow revivalists to try "to have your small society within the larger society" and "your own 'Muslim ghetto.'"

Qaradawi clearly sees the Islamist movement playing a crucial role in creating these separated Muslim communities and thereby providing it with an unprecedented opportunity to implement its vision, at least partially. Its local affiliates will run the mosques, schools, and civic organizations that shape the daily life of the desired "Muslim ghettoes." And Qaradawi's ambitions go further still. Without saying so openly, he suggests that sharia law should govern the relations among inhabitants of these Muslim islands; Muslim minorities "should also have amongst them their own ulema and men of religion to answer their questions when they ask them, guide them when they lose the way and reconcile them when they differ among themselves."

What Qaradawi outlines in his treatise might, at first glance, appear to be nothing more than a fantasy. In reality, it corresponds to what the international network of the Muslim Brotherhood has been doing in the West for the past fifty years. Since the end of World War II, in fact, members of al Ikhwan al Muslimoun have settled in Europe and worked relentlessly to implement the goals stated by Qaradawi. In almost every European country, they founded student organizations that, having evolved into nationwide umbrella organizations, have become thanks to their activism and to the financial support from Arab Gulf countries the most prominent representatives of local Muslim communities. They established a web of mosques, research centers, think tanks, charities and schools that has been successful in spreading their heavily politicized interpretation of Islam. Finally, today, with the creation of a supranational jurisprudential body called the European Council for Fatwa and Research, the Ikhwan is taking its first, cautious steps toward Qaradawi's final goal: the introduction of sharia law within the Muslim communities of Europe.

Having been the focus of attention of authorities since its early days, the Muslim Brotherhood tends to be extremely secretive, and only if circumstances are favorable do its members reveal their affiliation. While most of the first Islamic activists in Europe were official members of the Brotherhood, moreover, formal links between the group's Middle Eastern base and its European followers have waned over time for various reasons. But the issue of formal affiliation to the Ikhwan is moot because the Muslim Brotherhood is more than a group; it is now better defined as a movement whose organization is far from monolithic and whose members are kept together mostly by ideological affinity.

Mohammed Akif, the current General Guide and supreme leader of the Brotherhood and a former head of its Islamic Center of Munich, explained the Ikhwan's transcendence of formalities in an interview with Xavier Ternisien, a French expert on religion.[3] He said, We do not have an international organization; we have an organization through our perception of things. We are present in every country. Everywhere there are people who believe in the message of the Muslim Brothers. In France, the Union of Islamic Organizations of France (UOIF) does not belong to the organization of the Brothers. They follow their own laws and rules. There are many organizations that do not belong to the Muslim Brothers. For example, Shaykh al-Qaradawi. He is not a Muslim Brother, but he was formed according to the doctrine of the Brothers. The doctrine of the Brothers is a written doctrine that has been translated in all languages. In a 2005 interview Akif elaborated further. European Ikhwan organizations have no direct link to the Egyptian branch, he insisted, but they nevertheless coordinate actions with them. He concluded the interview saying, tellingly, that "we [the Ikhwan] have the tendency not to make distinctions among us."[4]

Regardless of their official affiliation, many individuals and organizations that identify themselves with the message of the Ikhwan operate in Europe and have been actively working toward the goals outlined by Qaradawi in his above-mentioned dissertation. Driven by their firm belief in the superiority of Islam to any other religion or system of life, the European Brothers fight daily to achieve their goal, using all possible tools, including painful but necessary compromises with European authorities. "Islam will return to Europe as a conqueror and victor, after being expelled from it twice," Qaradawi says. But he adds, "I maintain that the conquest this time will not be by the sword but by preaching and ideology."[5] The European Ikhwan network, under the cover of various civil rights groups and Islamic organizations, is the vanguard of this peaceful conquest.

## Putting Down Roots in Europe

According to Mohammed Akif, "the Brotherhood established itself in Europe" in the 1950s.[6] At that time Nasser and other pan-Arabist regimes were cracking down on the organization, and many of its members had to flee their homelands. For various rea- sons most of the Muslim Brothers leaving the persecution of Middle Eastern regimes chose West Germany as their destination. Some had reportedly established links with Germany during World War II when the Grand Mufti of Jerusalem, Haj Amin al Husseini, moved to Berlin and aided the Nazi regime in its anti-Jewish propaganda.[7] Others benefited from the fact that the West German government, implementing what came to be known as the Hallstein doctrine, had opened its doors to dissidents persecuted by regimes that had recognized East Germany, which included Egypt and Syria.[8] Many were attracted, moreover, by the prestige of the country's technical faculties and decided to further their studies in Germany's engineering, architecture, and medical schools. Among this group of pioneers of revivalist Islam in Europe, Said Ramadan stands out.

Born in 1926 in a village north of Cairo, Ramadan joined the Muslim Brotherhood at age of 14 after attending a lecture by the organization's founder, Hassan al-Banna.[9] In 1946, upon obtaining his law license from the University of Cairo, Ramadan became al-Banna's personal secretary and began the publication of Al Shihab, the organization's official magazine. In 1948 he fought in Palestine among Arab volunteers and was briefly appointed the head of Jerusalem's military corps by King Abdallah of Jordan. He then traveled to the newly established state of Pakistan where, despite his young age, he competed for the chair of secretary general of the World Muslim Congress.

By December 1948 the Egyptian government had outlawed the Brotherhood, and the following year Egyptian police assassinated al-Banna. Given these developments, Ramadan decided to remain in Pakistan, where he worked as a "cultural ambassador" of the country to the Arab world. In 1950, as the ban on the Brotherhood was lifted, he returned to Egypt and began to publish Al Muslimoon, one of the most important magazines of revivalist thought. Nasser's sudden rise to power in 1953 shook Egyptian political life and after a short period of peaceful coexistence among the Brothers and Nasser's Free Officers government another clampdown on the Brotherhood ensued."

Realizing he could not continue his activities in Egypt, Ramadan left the country after his release. Following short sojourns in various Middle Eastern countries, he moved to Europe permanently with his wife Wafa, al-Banna's eldest daughter. They settled in Geneva, Switzerland, and Ramadan enrolled at the University of Cologne, where he obtained a graduate degree in law with a dissertation on Islamic law. In 1961 Ramadan founded the Islamic Center of Geneva, located first in a villa donated by an Arabian prince and then in an odd white and green building a stone's throw from Lake Leman. Other eminent Islamic scholars sat on the founding board of the center, including the Indian scholars Mohammed Hamidullah and Maulana Abdul Hassan Ali al Nadwi. It became one of the main headquarters of the Muslim Brotherhood in Europe, and was the first of a score that Ramadan worked to set up throughout Europe with the financial support of Saudi Arabia. The next year Ramadan was also instrumental in the Saudi kingdom's establishment of the Muslim World League, a government- funded transnational organization created to spread the Saudi interpretation of Islam. Ramadan was one of its main founders and even wrote its constitution.

With the ample financial backing of the Saudis, Ramadan began to establish the Brotherhood in other European countries. An early opportunity arose when a group of Arab students in Munich contacted him for help with the construction of a mosque in that city. The Arab students were competing for control of the Mosque Construction Commission, a body that was trying to raise funds for the new Munich mosque.[10] Their adversaries were a group of Muslim ex-soldiers who had fought with the Nazis during World War II and had stayed in Munich after the conflict. Originating from Central Asia and the Caucasus, these ex-soldiers embraced a moderate interpretation of Islam that clashed with the more militant views of the Arabs. By 1960 Ramadan, thanks to his Saudi funding, secured for himself the position of chairman of the commission, and by 1973, when the mosque was completed, the Brotherhood had completely overshadowed other influences over the mosque.

As Geneva was the launching pad for the European operations of the Brotherhood, Munich became its main headquarters in Germany. The Ramadan-dominated Mosque Construction Commission became a permanent organization, which later changed its name to the Islamic Society of Germany (IGD). Ramadan headed the organization for ten years until 1973, when one of the students who had originally contacted him, Syrian- born Ghaleb Himmat, took over at the helm.[11] Himmat, who kept his position until 2002, is a prominent member of the European Ikhwan network and co-founder of Bank al-Taqwa, a financial institution widely believed to have served as the Brotherhood's clearinghouse in the West. According to European and American authorities, Himmat and Youssef Nada, one of the Brotherhood's top financial minds, used al-Taqwa and an extensive network of companies to finance the construction and activities of dozens of Brotherhood-related projects throughout the West. Both men, whom the U.S. Treasury Department also accuses of having financed Hamas and al Qaeda,[12] have been designated terrorism financiers by various Western countries and by the United Nations.

After Himmat's retirement, the chairmanship of the IGD passed to Ibrahim El Zayat, a younger, German-born activist with a phenomenal talent for both public relations and, like his predecessor, murky financial transactions. In 2002 El Zayat, as a director of the Saudi-based NGO World Assembly of Muslim Youth (WAMY) that spreads Wahhabi literature worldwide, came under investigation in Germany for having funneled more than two million dollars to an al-Qaeda-linked charity and for his involvement in other money-laundering activities.[13] Yet thanks to its activism and good finances, the IGD is now Germany's most important Muslim organization, representing more than sixty Islamic centers nationwide. Together with Milli Görüş, the Turkish revivalist organization linked to the Refah party that has more than 25,000 members and an estimated 100,000 sympathizers in Germany, the IGD is the de facto voice of the German Muslim community.[14] The two organizations whose leaders are linked through marriage[15] have formally joined forces, creating the umbrella organization Zentralrat, and they monopolize the public debate about Islam in Germany and control the majority of German mosques.[16]

Various German security agencies have repeatedly highlighted the links between these groups and the Brotherhood, and warned about the ambiguity of their rhetoric. An official report from the Office for the Protection of the Constitution in Hessen, for example, stated that the threat of Islamism for Germany is posed … primarily by Milli Görüş and other affiliated groups. They try to spread Islamist views within the boundaries of the law. Then they try to implement … for all Muslims in Germany a strict interpretation of the Quran and of the sharia…. Their public support of tolerance and religious freedom should be treated with caution.[17] Yet, despite these warnings, German politicians consider the Ikhwan groups their primary partners in the dialogue over issues involving the Muslim community, thus granting them legitimacy and empowering them.

Flowering in France he Said Ramadan was active in developing organizations in Germany, another founding member of the Islamic Center of Geneva, Mohammed Hamidullah, created the first revivalist organization in France. An Indian-born intellectual, author of almost two hundred works on Islamic history, culture and law, Hamidullah headed the Paris-based Association of Islamic Students in France (AEIF). Even though Hamidullah was a moderate, more intent on his studies than on political activities, the AEIF soon became home base for a small group of radical foreign Muslim students who were attending Parisian universities. Among them was Hasan al Turabi, a young Sudanese law student destined to become one of the most important figures of Islamic revivalism of the last thirty years.[18] The son of a qadi (Islamic judge) from the southern part of Sudan, Turabi had joined the Muslim Brotherhood on the campus of the University College of Khartoum in the 1950s and continued his Islamic militancy while studying law at the Sorbonne.[19] Other well-known figures who orbited around the AEIF were Abolhassan Banisadr, the first President of the Islamic Republic of Iran; [20] Said Ramadan al Boutih, one of Syria's most prestigious legal scholars; and Issam al Attar, a top Muslim Brotherhood leader who fled Syria to escape the regime and finally settled in the German city of Aachen, where he founded the Bilal mosque.[21]

This select group came to debate the purpose of their sojourn in the West. The Syrian branch of the Brotherhood, headed in Europe by Attar, viewed its exile as instrumental to furthering its struggle in Syria. For them, at least in the beginning, Europe was just a convenient place from which they could operate against the Syrian regime, and the AEIF was little more than a club for foreign Muslim students who were planning to leave France at the end of their studies. It had no serious political mission beyond promoting revivalist ideas among its members. But others in the European Brotherhood, particularly the Egyptians, saw their hijra (forced migration, comparing it to the Prophet's time in Medina) as more long-term and Europe as a permanent base from which to expand the Ikhwan's struggle to impose God's word worldwide. The Brothers were in Europe to stay, they concluded, and the continent with its freedom, wealth and growing Muslim population was the ideal new front from which the Brotherhood could operate.

In 1979 a small group of AEIF members who embraced the long-term vision of the Egyptian branch of the European Brotherhood, and who wanted to extend the influence of the movement to the Muslim population of France, created a new organization the Islamic Group in France, which in 1983 became the Union of Islamic Organizations in France (UOIF).[22] While the official founders were two students, Iraqi national Zuhair Mahmood and Tunisian national Abdallah Ben Mansour, the UOIF had two important godfathers. The first was Faysal Mawlawi, a former member of the AEIF during his Parisian days who had returned to his native Lebanon to run the al Jamaa al Islamiya radical political party. The second was Rashid Ghannouchi, secretary of the AEIF between 1968 and 1969 and head of al Nahda, the Islamist movement that battled the Tunisian regime.[23]

Ghannouchi and Mawlawi, wise politicians with a tremendous ability to adapt their rhetoric to circumstances, understood that the Brothers needed a well-structured organization to be able to influence the political debate and, simultaneously, to radicalize the Muslim minority in the European country with the largest Muslim population.

Over the last twenty years the UOIF has developed into France's largest and most active Muslim organization, controlling a large number of mosques and attracting tens of thousands of attendees to its annual gathering in Le Bourget. Today the UOIF even boasts its own institution of Islamic knowledge, the European Institute of Human Sciences (IESH).[24] Located in a castle in rural Burgundy, IESH offers various degrees and diplomas in Islamic studies, and states that its goal is to educate imams who, in addition to having an adequate theological and scientific background, will demonstrate "good assimilation in the Western reality." Given the background of the individuals involved in IESH, however, "assimilation" is unlikely to be its primary goal. The institute was found- ed by key members of the UOIF, such as Ahmed Jaballah and Zuhair Mahmoud, and regularly hosts the most prominent figures of the international Ikhwan network.[25] Its scientific council is headed by Yussuf al-Qaradawi,[26] and Faysal Mawlawi, the spiritual guide of the UOIF, is a frequent visitor and lecturer.[27]

The French government has a schizophrenic attitude toward UOIF. On the one hand, the French Council of State significantly turned down the naturalization request of Ben Mansour, a founding member of UOIF, alleging that he headed "a federation to which are affiliated many extremist movements which reject the essential values of French society."[28] On the other hand, French Minister of Interior Nicolas Sarkozy publicly stated that he believes the UOIF has always held positions that "respected the Republic" and is a reliable partner in the delicate dialogue over the integration of the French Muslim community.[29]

UOIF representatives, most of them recipients of degrees from prestigious French universities, are involved in countless interfaith, anti-racism, and pro-integration partnerships with Christian, private, and government organizations. At the same time, how- ever, they have not abandoned their radical worldview and are occasionally caught making blatantly anti-Semitic remarks or defending the actions of Hamas.[30] Books such as The Protocols of the Elders of Zion and works of al-Banna and Qutb are regularly sold at UOIF's events. Tellingly, when UOIF was still a small entity and not under much media scrutiny, one of its representatives, Ahmed Djaballah, defined the launch of the organization as having two stages: "The first stage of the launch is democratic; the second will be putting the Islamic society in orbit."[31]

## Hoping to Rule Britannia

Arab members of the Muslim Brotherhood spurred the spread of revivalist Islam in continental Europe, Muslims from South Asia initially played this role in the United Kingdom, where the majority of Muslims were Pakistanis and Indians. In the 1950s and 1960s, followers of Jamaat-e-Islami founder Abul Ala Maududi began to establish the first revivalist organizations in Great Britain. In 1962 a small group of Muslim activists from East London founded the UK Islamic Mission, an organization with the stated goal of "bringing about a new spiritual awakening" and building a society "based on the ideals, values and principles of Islam."[32] The Mission sees Islam as an all-encompassing system that covers every aspect of life. Defining itself as an "ideological organization," the Mission states that "Islam is a comprehensive way of life which must be translated into action in all spheres of human life. The Mission, therefore, aims at molding the entire human life in accordance with Allah's will."[33]

The Mission also openly declares its desire to introduce sharia in Great Britain, at least in the areas of private and family law. The UK Islamic Mission advocates, in fact, a "continuous campaign for the establishment of Muslim family laws," and an "Islamic social order in the United Kingdom in order to seek the pleasure of Allah." While the stated goal of many Muslim organizations created at the time was to safeguard the Muslim identity of the South Asian immigrant population, the scholar Gilles Kepel has correctly noted that the Mission goes beyond such a protectionist aim in openly promoting the Islamization of British society. Following Maududi's teachings, it urges the Muslim community not to be satisfied with simply keeping its own social values; rather, it should proselytize and strive to impose "the Islamic social order" on all, as a "vanguard to spearhead a life-long struggle in the cause of Allah."[34]

In order to carry out its goal of creating an "Islamic social order," the Mission under- stood the importance of extending its teachings to the largest audience possible. Today the UK Islamic Mission has become a nationwide organization with thirty-nine branch- es, over thirty-five mosques and

Islamic schools in which about five thousand British Muslim children receive Islamic education.[35] It has a youth branch, Young Muslims UK, that attempts to attract the sons and daughters of Muslim immigrants through study groups, summer camps, and Quran competitions. To appeal to the most Westernized among them, Young Muslims UK even sponsors such activities as Go-Karting and Paintball, all conducted in religiously-oriented and sex-segregated environments.[36] In 1973 the Islamic Mission established a college and research center, the Islamic Foundation. First located in a small two-room office in central Leicester, the Islamic Foundation has grown to be one of Europe's largest institutions of Islamic studies and, by 1990, moved its headquarters to a sprawling mansion in rural Markfield, a few miles from Leicester.[37] The Foundation regularly organizes symposia and conferences and even runs its own institute of higher learning, the Markfield Institute of Higher Education, which issues diplomas in Islamic jurisprudence. It translates and publishes scores of Islamic texts, with a clear focus on revivalist authors in general and Maududi in particular.

The links between the UK Mission and Maududi go well beyond ideology, moreover. The level of coordination between the Mission and Jamaat-e-Islami is very high, though Mission officers in Leicester have publicly denied that the two organizations are formally linked. "We belong to the international Islamic movement," claims Dr. Manazir Ahsan, the director general of the Islamic Foundation, "neither to Jamaat [-e-Islami] nor to Ikhwan nor to the Refah Party in Turkey but all of them are our friends."[38] The evidence contradicts him, however, and indicates that the relationship resembles more a symbiosis than a friendship, at least in regard to Jamaat-e-Islami. The first directors of the Islamic Foundation were officers of Jamaat-e-Islami, including Khurram Murad, who became one of Jamaat's top leaders after leaving Leicester.[39] One of the Foundation's founders and its current chairman is Khurshid Ahmed, a world-renowned Islamic scholar and member of the Pakistani Senate who joined Jamaat-e-Islami in 1956 and currently serves as its vice president.[40]

But it is also true that, as members and sympathizers are increasingly British-born Muslims who feel limited affinity to Pakistani politics, the UK Mission and the Islamic Foundation have developed a life of their own.[41] While issues such as Kashmir remain important, the Mission has increasingly focused its attention on problems affecting the everyday life of British Muslims, with the stated goal of preventing their absorption into mainstream British society. Radicalizing the Muslim community is the Foundation's first priority, but it also emphasizes the importance of carrying out its dawa mission among the non-Muslim British population. The Foundation publishes several introductory books to Islam aimed at British Christians, and its director during the 1980s, the above-mentioned Murad, even published a handbook on how to convert non-Muslims.[42] The Mission's brochures boast of the organization's successes in proselytizing in order to impress, as Kepel notes, "their Arabian benefactors and confirm the latter's conviction that Islam, in its most intransigent version, would subjugate the whole world, with the Mission forming an avant-garde."[43]

Outreach toward non-Muslims goes beyond the religious duty of dawa, as the Mission attempts to increase its influence in the social and political life of Great Britain. The Islamic Foundation is involved in partnerships with several secular institutions of higher learning, for example, and has signed memoranda of understanding with various Christian organizations. It often works with city councils on issues involving the Muslim community, and it even conducts Islamic-awareness training for British police officers. Given that politicians from all parties attend its conferences, it is not surprising that even the Prince of Wales, sitting beside Khurshid Ahmad at a 2003 dinner in Markfield, praised the Islamic Foundation as "all that is to be admired about Islamic scholarship in the West" and "a fine example for others to follow."[44]

In 1997 the Arab component of the Muslim Brotherhood founded its own organization in Great Britain, the Muslim Association of Britain (MAB). MAB's leadership includes individuals such as Azzam Tamimi, a former activist in the Islamic Action Front (the Jordanian Brotherhood's political party); Mohammed Sawalha, a self-declared former Hamas member; and Osama al Tikriti, the son of the leader of the Iraqi branch of the Brotherhood.[45] MAB's founding president, Kamal al Helbawy, was formerly the official spokesman for the Egyptian Muslim Brotherhood in Europe.[46] Having gained notoriety thanks to its active role in the anti-war campaign during the first months of the U.S. invasion of Iraq, MAB has formed strong alliances with British civil rights and leftist organizations. Its role as a political player became apparent as it endorsed such anti-war politicians and close allies as London mayor Ken Livingstone and Respect Party candidate George Galloway.

Given their large Muslim populations, Great Britain, France, and Germany are naturally the three main centers of activity of the Ikhwan in Europe. But virtually every European country has witnessed some degree of intense activity by the Brothers. As Ikhwan members often mention, their vision of Islam as a social religion compels them to create organizations. Tariq Ramadan, the ubiquitous Swiss scholar and son of Said Ramadan whose affiliation with the Brotherhood is much debated has stated that the communitarian dimension of Islam is fundamental because "the Islamic faith cannot be reduced to a strictly private affair."[47] But other scholars mention more practical reasons for the Ikhwan's organized activism. Qaradawi asserts that the "organized collective work" characteristic of the Islamic Movement "is ordained by religion and necessitated by reality."[48] Only a well-structured network enables the Brothers to implement their goals, the first of which is preventing the integration or, even worse, the assimilation of Muslim minorities.

## Cozying Up to the Elite

In conversations with journalists and diplomats [Tunisian Islamist Rachid] Ghannouchi gives a moderate, democratic, pluralist image," confessed a follower of this very important player in Europe's Ikhwan network. "With us," he added, "he talks about driving out the American invaders and their allies (the regimes in power),... of saving the Holy Kaaba and the Tomb of the Noble Prophet from the plots of the enemies of the Arabs and Islam."[49] The Muslim Brothers have an unparalleled ability to employ different tactics to adapt their rhetoric and modus operandi according to the circumstances.

In the first years of their existence, Islamist revivalist organizations took very hard and confrontational positions on issues that involved the Muslim community. This stance was apparently dictated both by the leaders' radical views and by the desire to make them known and gain primacy within the Islamic community. In 1988, for example, the Islamic Foundation of Leicester fought vigorously to play a predominant role in organizing the protests against the publication of Salman Rushdie's Satanic Verses protests that swept the South Asian Muslim community in Great Britain. While its out- rage was unquestionably genuine, the Foundation appeared to be most concerned about making sure that other Islamic groups did not lead the protests.[50]

The following year, having witnessed how the Rushdie affair enhanced the status of the Foundation, the French Ikhwan decided to imitate the tactics of their British comrades when an opportunity presented itself in France. As the first nationwide controversy over the use of the hijab in public schools erupted in 1989, the then-relatively power- less UOIF became the most active defender of the right to wear the veil. Hoping to attract the sympathies of the Muslim community, the UOIF showed little interest in pursuing a constructive dialogue with the French government while it organized several protests against the ban and declared that "the Muslims of France could not accept such attacks on their dignity."[51]

Today, now that it has achieved a dominant position within France's organized Islamic community, the UOIF has completely changed its tactics and strives to gain the trust of the authorities. Believing it can gain more by working within the system than against it, the UOIF is avoiding head-on confrontations with the government that could set back its agenda. In March 2004, therefore, when the French Parliament passed a controversial new law banning all religious symbols and apparel in public schools, the UOIF kept incredibly quiet. It abstained from participating in the protests that were organized, not only in France, but also throughout the world. Azzam Tamimi, a leader of the Muslim Association of Britain who was harshly critical of this decision, explained that the UOIF is now "against any activity that could cause a confrontation with the public powers."[52] In its change of behavior, the UOIF provides a quintessential example of the Brother- hood's most effective quality: flexibility. If in 1989 the issue of the hijab constituted a perfect opportunity to make the UOIF known to the French Muslim community as a strenuous defender of the honor of Muslims, fifteen years later it constituted a dangerous trap to avoid. Because the law passed with overwhelming and bilateral support, the UOIF saw no practical advantage in challenging the establishment.

Challenging the establishment, in fact, is not the current policy of the European Brotherhood. Realizing they are still a relatively weak force; the Brothers have opted for a different tactic: befriending the establishment. They are taking advantage of the European elite's desperate desire to establish a dialogue with any representatives of the Muslim community, and they are putting themselves forward as the de facto voices of European Muslims. Thanks to the Europeans' naïveté and their own activism, the Brothers are now the closest partners that European political elites have in discussing the integration of the local Muslim communities. Nowhere is this more evident than in Brussels, where Ikhwan organizations have become the only officially recognized representatives of the European Muslim population, monopolizing the debate with the institutions of the European Union.

In 1989 the European Brothers founded the Federation of Islamic Organizations in Europe (FIOE), with the stated goal of "serving Muslims in European societies."[53] Even though it has gained prominence in Europe as a moderate Muslim organization, however, FIOE is nothing more than the umbrella organization for most Ikhwan groups in Europe. Its founders and main members are the French UOIF, the German IGD and the British MAB, and its headquarters are in Markfield, located in spaces leased from the Islamic Foundation. Serving on FIOE's board are such prominent European Ikhwan figures as UOIF's Ahmed Djaballah and IGD's Ibrahaim El Zayat. Its president, Ahmed al Rawi, has personally defended suicide bombings in Iraq and Israel, claiming that Muslims "have the right to defend themselves." And yet he is a habitué of the European circles of power, having testified before the European Parliament and attended John Paul II's funeral.[54]

In 1996 FIOE created the European Trust, a financial institution devoted to raising funds for its various activities, such as the sprawling European Institute of Human Sciences, the Association of Muslim Schools in Europe, and its glossy magazine Al Europiya. Also, in 1996, in cooperation with the Saudi WAMY, FIOE established a youth branch—the Forum of European Muslim Youth and Student Organizations (FEMYSO). Originally headed by the ubiquitous El Zayat and strategically headquartered in Brussels, FEMYSO has managed to become, in its own words, "the de facto voice of the Muslim youth of Europe." Today it oversees a network of thirty-seven member organizations, and it enjoys regular relations with the European Parliament, the Council of Europe, and the United Nations.[55]

## The Long March Toward Sharia in Europe

The success of organizations such as FIOE and FEMYSO is the crowning achievement of the Brothers' thirty years of hard work. The Ikhwan groups have managed to be- come part of the establishment, finding a small niche in the corridors of European power. The Brothers view this triumph as a mere starting point, however. Having gained the trust of large segments of both Europe's elites and its Muslim communities, the Brothers want to use their newly acquired power to create the "Muslim ghetto" envisioned by Qaradawi. An extensive network of mosques and educational facilities already exists; the next step toward the creation of what Reuven Paz refers to as "non-territorial Islamic states in Europe" is the implementation of Islamic law for Europe's Muslim population.[56] An article in a 2002 issue of Al Islam, the official publication of the European Brotherhood's historic Islamic Center of Munich, openly states that "In the long run, Muslims cannot be satisfied with the acceptance of German family, estate, and trial law.... Muslims should aim at an agreement between the Muslims and the German state with the goal of a separate jurisdiction for Muslims."[57]

The Brothers fully understand that the implementation of sharia in Europe is a very difficult task that currently seems quite far-fetched. But patience and long-term vision are two of the movement's strongest assets, and the Brothers are working to reap their fruits "in the long run." For now, the Ikhwan is generally refraining from officially asking for the implementation of sharia, despite hints that make its ultimate aim quite apparent. The Brothers have begun, for example, to create an Islamic legal framework that lays the foundation for imposing sharia in the West. In 1989 the UOIF, perhaps the most important of the various European Ikhwan groups, made a small but extremely significant change to its name. Previously known as the Union of Islamic Organizations in France, it now called itself the Union of Islamic Organizations of France a small semantic difference that had a huge meaning.[58]

By changing the name, the Brothers declared that they were in France, and in Europe, to stay. They realized that the presence of Muslims in Europe was a permanent and growing phenomenon, and that it required a new approach. The following year Ghannouchi, one of the historical spiritual leaders of the UOIF, gave a landmark speech at the organization's annual meeting in which he referred to France as dar al Islam (land of Islam), a place where the presence of Muslims is permanent.[59] A definitive new Ikhwan position on the juridical connotation of Europe was formalized two years later, at another seminar organized by the UOIF. There, scholars of the importance of Qaradawi, Mawlawi, and Djaballah agreed that the traditional distinction between dar al Islam and dar al Harb (land of war) did not currently reflect reality. While Europe could not be considered dar al Islam because sharia was not enforced there, it could not be considered dar al Harb because Muslims were allowed to practice Islam freely and were not persecuted. According to Mawlawi, the distinction was based only on ijtihad (interpretation, not coming directly from the text) and limited to a historic context that no longer exists. The Ikhwan scholars decided, therefore, that it was possible for them to create a new legal category. They concluded that Europe should be considered dar al dawa (land of preaching), a territory where Muslims live as a minority, are respected, and have the duty to spread their religion peacefully. Other definitions have followed: Qaradawi has spoken of dar al ahd (land of contact), for example, while Tariq Ramadan has adopted the term dar al shahada (land of testimony).[60]

By acknowledging that the presence of Muslims in the West is permanent, and by giving their status a new legal definition, the Ikhwan scholars set the stage for creating new rules to regulate this presence. While there is extensive jurisprudence that addresses the situation of non-Muslim minorities living in dar al Islam, very few provisions cover the relatively new situation of Muslims living permanently in non-Muslim countries. For most European Muslims, this has not been a major issue, either because religion does not play a large role in their lives or because they have found their own ways to reconcile their faith with their lives in the West. But many do many feel the need for guidance from the ulema about such everyday matters as marriage, divorce and relations with non-Muslims. These problems require the development of a new jurisprudence, which has come to be known as fiqh (Islamic jurisprudence) for minorities (fiqh al aqaliyyat).[61] Given the lack of intellectual Muslim leadership and structured Islamic clergy in Europe, the Brotherhood sees itself as the entity most able to fill this void and to create this new fiqh.[62] Mawlawi, one of the top Ikhwan thinkers on minority fiqh, has said, "It is obvious that when secular and Islamic laws collide, a Muslim is expected to honor his Islamic law whenever possible."[63]

But while affirming the superiority of Islamic law, he refers to the Quranic verse that states "Be observant of Allah to the best of your ability" ("faittaqu Allaha ma istata`tum").[64] According to Mawlawi, this verse allows a Muslim who is in the "legal bind" of having to choose between respecting sharia or European law to follow the "less detrimental" option.[65] Other European Brothers hold slightly more ambiguous positions, torn between their beliefs and their political instincts. Thus far, formal proposals to introduce Islamic law in Europe have been quite timid, in fact, and the reaction from most European politicians has been cold, to say the least. For the time being, then, officially sanctioned Islamic courts in Europe represent only a dream. The European Ikhwan have established an unofficial one, however the European Council for Fatwa and Research. This body currently limits itself to dispensing advice to Muslims living in Europe who have to juggle obedience to Quranic precepts with respect for the laws of their host countries.

## The European Council for Fatwa and Research

In March 1997 FIOE sponsored the first meeting of the European Council for Fatwa and Research, an organization that has become quite a feather in the European Brothers' cap. Held in London, the meeting was attended by more than fifteen well-known Islamic scholars who endorsed the Council's draft constitution. The Council is described as "an Islamic, specialized and independent entity" created to issue "collective fatwas which meet the needs of Muslims in Europe, solve their problems and regulate their interaction with the European communities, all within the regulations and objectives of sharia."[66] In practical terms the Council is a jurisprudential body that provides Muslims living in Europe with non-binding legal advice focusing on matters they face in their everyday lives as members of a minority community in non-Muslim countries.

The Council's headquarters are in Dublin, where it operates in conjunction with the local Islamic Cultural Centre. Both institutions have received generous financial backing from the Al-Maktoum Charity Organization, which is headed by Shaykh Hamdan Al Maktoum, the UAE Minister of Finance and Industry and the Deputy Ruler of Dubai.[67] The Council generally meets twice a year in different European venues and currently comprises thirty-two Islamic scholars from throughout the world, the majority of whom reside within the European Union. (The Council's bylaws specifically state that no more than 25 percent of its total membership should live outside Europe.) Its sessions take place behind closed doors, and the clerics deliberate on issues brought forward by either Council members or European Muslims who ask the Council for advice.

In reality the Council is a body created and dominated by the Muslim Brotherhood's global network. Its jurisprudence is aimed at guiding Muslims through a "program of perfect life for the individual, the family, society and the state" phrasing that echoes al-Banna.[68] Among its members are key figures of the European Ikhwan, such as UOIF's Djaballah and OunisQourqah, IESH's al Arabi al Bichri, FIOE's al Rawi, and the ever-present Ghannouchi. Several other members are high-profile scholars from Arab Gulf countries, most of whom hold positions very close to those of the Ikhwan. The Islamic Cultural Centre of Ireland's Hussein Mohammed Halawa is the Council's secretary general and oversees its day-to-day operations, while the Lebanese cleric Mawlawi is its vice president an honor given to him in recognition of his role in promoting the his- toric doctrinal change of Europe from dar al Harb to dar al dawa. As Ghannouchi observed, "Some members [of the Council] belong to the Brothers, some others do not. What is important is the ideology, not the movement."[69]

Most tellingly, the president of the Council is Qaradawi, whose position of prominence is widely accepted by the other members. Though the Council is technically a democratic body in which the majority rules, its scholars rarely vote, tending instead to avoid internal dissent and to follow the position of Qaradawi and the Council's most influential figures.[70] Qaradawi is not only the Council's best-known scholar, but also the real driving force behind it. He is a charismatic figure whose prestige is crucially important to the Council's relevance. A gifted speaker with an uncommon ability to deal with the media, Qaradawi disseminates his teachings through his own website and a popular weekly show on al Jazeera called "Al Sharia wal Hayat" ("Sharia and Life"). He should now be considered, according to an internal memo of the British Home Office, "the leading mainstream and influential Islamic authority in the Middle East and increasingly in Europe, with an extremely large popular following."[71]

While Qaradawi is indeed extremely popular and influential well beyond the under- world of the Ikhwan, his views, as the same memo acknowledges, are far from moderate. He has repeatedly defended suicide attacks against Israel and American forces in Iraq. He has repeatedly pledged his support to such organizations as Hamas and Palestinian Islamic jihad, labeled the Middle East peace process as "a conspiracy to stop the Palestinian Resistance," and decreed that "jihad is incumbent upon the entire Muslim nation in order to liberate Palestine, Jerusalem, and the Al Aqsa Mosque."[72] Similarly, in 2004 Qaradawi issued a fatwa justifying attacks against all American citizens in Iraq, including civilians, saying "there is no difference between U.S. military personnel and civilians in Iraq since both have come to invade the country" and since "civilians are actually there to serve the U.S. occupying forces."[73]

The European Council for Fatwa and Research reflects the dual personalities of Qaradawi and its leaders. Overall, its jurisprudence gives the impression of being quite moderate and innocuous, offering suggestions to individuals who want to follow the requirements of their religion in their new land. Many fatwas simply discuss how to per- form certain Islamic rituals in non-Muslim countries, solving mostly logistical problems. Some rulings, for example, address questions about praying in buildings in which facing Mecca poses difficulties.[74] Another fatwa deals with the timing of Muslim prayers in Scandinavian countries in relation to sunrise and sunset.[75] As most Muslims living in the West must deal with the banking system, many decrees attempt to reconcile the need to contract loans, use mortgages, and open bank accounts, with the Islamic ban of riba (usury), which the Muslim Brothers interpret to include interest.

On these matters the jurisprudence of the Council is quite liberal. Its fatwas urge Muslims to seek all possible "Islamic alternatives" and "Islamic organizations throughout Europe to enter into negotiations with European banks to find formulas that are accept- able," as many of them are already doing.[76] But, if no alternative is possible and the haram (forbidden) transaction is vitally important, the Council draws on the principle of accommodation to allow the European Muslim to carry out transactions with riba. In general, the Court tends to respect Western law as much as possible and espouses a relatively moderate interpretation of Islamic law. No fatwa touches issues of criminal law, where any intrusion of Muslim jurisprudence would be perceived very negatively by Europeans. In some cases, the Council explicitly decrees that European Muslims should follow the laws of European countries and the rulings of its judges, even if those contradict sharia. In cases of divorce, for example, the Council ruled that "it is imperative that a Muslim who conducted his Marriage by virtue of those countries' respective laws, to comply with the rulings of a non-Muslim judge in the event of a divorce."[77]

But not all the jurisprudence of the Council follows this moderate trend. Despite its professed focus on issues affecting everyday life, some of the Council's fatwas are extremely political and reveal the radical side of at least some of its clerics. In the July 2003 Council meeting held in Stockholm, for example, Qaradawi described five categories of terrorism, including "terror that is permitted by Islamic law" and "martyrdom operations." Ruling that Israel could be defined as "invaders" and thus legitimately target- ed, Qaradawi stated that "those who oppose martyrdom operations and claim that they are suicide are making a great mistake."[78] Mawlawi, the Council's vice president, holds similar views about terrorism. In issuing a fatwa that prohibited Arab countries from cooperating with the United States in the "War on Terror," Mawlawi noted that what is dubbed terrorism by Washington is in most cases "Jihad and legitimate right," such as resistance operations in Palestine, Iraq and Afghanistan.[79]

Even more troubling, for its potentially disruptive effects, is the Council's jurisprudence that deals with family matters. While many rulings uphold Islamic principles that are perfectly compatible with European legislation, some fatwas express opinions that are at odds with basic Western concepts, particularly with regard to domestic violence and equality between the sexes. And while some fatwas instruct Muslims to follow European marriage and divorce laws, other rulings on the same matters refer only to Islamic law, omitting any reference to respecting Western legislation. The relationship between husband and wife is an area where the incompatibility between the Council's jurisprudence and Western law is particularly manifested. Various Council rulings state that men should be good husbands and fair to their wives, but some fatwas clearly pay no heed to the concept of equality between men and women. A 1997 Council fatwa, for example, states that a wife needs her husband's permission to cut her hair, provided that the cut is significant and "completely change[s] the appearance of the woman."[80] By the same token, the Council authorizes a husband to prevent his wife from visiting another woman, even a Muslim woman, "if he felt that this relationship has an adverse effect on his wife, children or marital life in general."[81]

These rulings are not surprising, given the positions that Qaradawi holds on marriage and marital relations. In his hallmark treaty on Islamic law, The Licit and Illicit in Islam, Qaradawi openly states that "the man is the lord of the house and the head of the family." He asserts, moreover, that when a wife exhibits "signs of pride or insubordination," her husband is entitled to use violence against her, even though this has to be done with- out hitting hard and avoiding the face.[82] These teachings are clearly at odds with the criminal law and public sentiment of every European country. Significantly, the provisions regarding the treatment of women caused

The Licit and Illicit in Islam to be banned in France in 1995. Charles Pasqua, France's Minister of Interior at the time, com- mented that the book deserved the ban because of "its violently anti-Western tones and the theses contrary to the laws and values of the Republic that it contains."[83] Qaradawi has also repeatedly observed that polygamy is a right that all Muslim men should be able to enjoy, provided they respect certain rules.

Polygamy and domestic violence represent two extremes, which would be prosecuted by European criminal laws. But the Council holds other positions that contradict Western laws governing marriage and divorce. It promotes an openly ambiguous situation for Muslims who have contracted marriage under European law, as the Council urges them to respect both the European laws and the conflicting principles of sharia. Just as disturbing is the possible application of the Council's jurisprudence to nikah marriages. A small, yet significant, number of Muslims living in Europe do not officially register their marriages but simply get married in an Islamic rite (nikah). In these cases, where the marriage does not exist under European law, the only rules that could apply are those of sharia, and the Council could potentially become the body regulating such marital relationships.

## Conclusion

The Council's fatwas are not legally binding, as they are simply opinions of respected scholars rather than judgments delivered by qadis. Members of the European Ikhwan network are quick to point out that its role, comparable to that of the Vatican's, is purely consultative, intended only to advise Muslims about religious issues that arise in their daily lives.[84] Yet the Brothers' ambitions for the Council go beyond a merely advisory role. As stated in its bylaws, the Council is "designed to become an approved religious authority before local governments and private establishments, which will undoubtedly strengthen and reinforce local Islamic communities."[85] The Brothers see today's non-binding Council's jurisprudence as just a step toward their long-term goal of establishing sharia for Muslims in Europe.

Most Ikhwan groups operating in Europe have the stated goal of establishing Islamic law for local Muslim populations. The Brothers understand that the places where this is most likely to occur are in areas of high Islamic concentration in other words, in Qaradawi's "Muslim ghettoes." The Brothers believe that, once Muslims reach a majority in certain areas of various European countries, European governments will feel compelled to allow Islamic law to regulate the personal/civil relations among them. While the Ikhwan's intentions might appear to be nothing more than a dream, a disturbingly large number of European Muslims seem to favor introducing Islamic law into Europe. A 2005 poll revealed that four out of ten British Muslims want sharia introduced into parts of Britain.[86] Another poll conducted by a local Muslim institute reports that 21 per cent of Muslims living in Germany believe that the German constitution is incompatible with the teachings of the Quran.[87] But while salafi and other extremist organizations are already demanding the introduction of sharia in a confrontational and counterproductive way, the more politically savvy Brothers are using a different strategy to achieve the same goal.

The European Ikhwan has repeatedly compromised their strict observance of sharia in order to advance their cause. Every tactic that might help the movement is justified, even if it entails breaking some Quranic principle, because the higher goal of spreading Islam excuses all deviations. Mawlawi and other Ikhwan scholars have asserted, for example, that the creation of Islamic centers in the West is a priority for the Islamic Movement. Muslims should make every effort, therefore, to purchase buildings and turn them into mosques, even if they must resort to financial transactions forbidden by Islamic law to do so.[88] Similarly, asked whether Muslims could vote and participate in the political life of their European host countries, the Council responded that the issue "is to be decided by Islamic organizations and establishment," which should evaluate what position best serves the interests of the Movement.[89] At the moment the Brothers have embraced compromise as the best means of increasing their influence, which will allow them in turn to lobby more effectively for their goals—goals that include the establishment of sharia in Europe.

Now relatively weak in the West, the Brotherhood has concluded that engaging in dialogue and showing openness and moderation is their wisest strategy. But if the balance of power were to change over the next few decades, nothing guarantees that the Ikhwan would not change its approach and discard dialogue. A German government's analysis of the tactics of Islamist groups operating in Germany reveals a well-founded suspicion that the Ikhwan's desire for dialogue is far from sincere: "While in recent times, the Milli Görüş has increasingly emphasized the readiness of its members to be integrated into German society and asserts its adherence to the basic law, such statements stem from tactical calculation rather than from any inner change of the organization."[90]

To date European Brotherhood organizations have rarely been directly linked to specific cases of terrorism, but their contribution to the education and radicalization of violent extremists has already been significant. The Brotherhood's renunciation of violence seems more opportunistic than genuine, moreover, when its European members use fiery rhetoric to endorse terrorist operations in the Middle East. While they are quick to condemn violence in the West to avoid becoming political pariahs, they do not refrain from approving of it elsewhere, notably in the Middle East, because they believe they can get away with it. It is not unreasonable to assume, therefore, that should it become convenient for them to do so, the ever-flexible Brotherhood would embrace violent tactics in the West as well.

*Dr. Lorenzo Vidino is the Director of the Program on Extremism at George Washington University. An expert on Islamism in Europe and North America, his research over the past 20 years has focused on the mobilization dynamics of jihadist networks in the West; governmental counter-radicalization policies; and the activities of Muslim Brotherhood-inspired organizations in the West. A native of Italy who holds American citizenship, Dr. Vidino earned a law degree from the University of Milan Law School and a doctorate in international relations from Tufts University's Fletcher School of Law and Diplomacy. He has held positions at Harvard University's Belfer Center for Science and International Affairs at the Kennedy School of Government, the U.S. Institute of Peace, the RAND Corporation, and the Center for Security Studies (ETH Zurich). The author of several books and numerous articles, Dr. Vidino's most prominent work is The New Muslim Brotherhood in the West, a book published in 2010 by Columbia University Press, with an Arabic edition released the following year by the Al Mesbar Studies and Research Center. The book offers a comparative study of Islamist organizing in various Western countries as well as the wide-ranging public policy responses by Western leaders. His most recent book, The Closed Circle: Joining and Leaving the Muslim Brotherhood in the West, offers an unprecedented inside view into how one of the world's most influential Islamist groups operates, and how some individuals made the difficult decision to leave. Founded in 1961 by strategist Herman Kahn, Hudson Institute challenges conventional thinking and helps manage strategic transitions to the future through interdisciplinary studies in defense, international relations, economics, health care, technology, culture, and law. Hudson guides public policy makers and global leaders in government and business through a vigorous program of publications, conferences, policy briefings, and recommendations. Hudson Institute is a 501(c)(3) organization financed by tax deductible contributions from private individuals, corporations, foundations, and by government grants. Hudson Institute is in compliance with the Sarbanes Oxley Act of Congress.*

# PART 2

# ISLAMIC REVOLUTIONARY GUARD CORPS (IRGC)

## CHAPTER 5

# A REVIEW OF IRAN'S REVOLUTIONARY GUARDS AND QUDS FORCE: GROWING GLOBAL PRESENCE, LINKS TO CARTELS AND MOUNTING SOPHISTICATION

*Alma Keshavarz*

The Islamic Republic of Iran's sophisticated military unit, the Quds Force (also known as "Quds Force"), made headlines on September 29, 2011 with the arrest of Mansour Arbabsiar, a naturalized U.S. citizen behind the assassination attempt of the Saudi Ambassador to the United States in Washington, D.C. What has been largely overlooked, however, is the wealth of information prior to 2011 on the Quds Force's global presence. The Quds Force is responsible for bolstering Hezbollah over thirty years ago and they have been working together across the globe ever since. In 2008, former Homeland Security chief Michael Chertoff stated that "someone described Hezbollah like the A-team of terrorists in terms of capabilities, in terms of range of weapons they have, in terms of discipline. Hezbollah makes Al Qaeda look like a minor league team."[1]

The Quds Force has funded and supplied Hezbollah at the behest of Iran. Much of what the media ignores is the Iranian Revolutionary Guard Corps (IRGC) and Quds Force's direct connection with Hezbollah and countless nefarious activities occurring around the world. This essay explores the timeline of the available research on the Quds Force, its presence in the Western Hemisphere, and any associations with the global drug trade. The IRGC is responsible for the creation of the Quds Force, thus, a notable place to begin explaining its origins.

## History of the Islamic Revolutionary Guard Corps (IRGC)

The Islamic Revolutionary Guard Corps (IRGC) was established immediately after the 1979 revolution in Iran by Ayatollah Ruhollah Khomeini. They function as "both the primary internaland external security force" with land, air and sea forces.[2] The IRGC has five arms: air force, navy, army, Basij, and the Quds Force. The IRGC at the top of the hierarchy helped establish the Quds Force and trigger the rise of Hezbollah, all of which happen to have similar flags. The member figures are estimates since Iran does not officially reveal its numbers. Numbers for Unit 400 are currently unknown, but it is believed that the Quds Force outsources operatives to Unit 400 to conduct clandestine missions against Western targets, which will be discussed further in this essay. The 10,000 to 15,000 Quds Force personnel provide logistical support and weapons deliveries to pro-Iranian organizations in Lebanon, Iraq, Syria, Persian Gulf states, Gaza/West Bank, Afghanistan, and Central Asia.[3] Additionally, FARS, Iran's news agency, reported that Hezbollah has up to 65,000 fighters.

The terror group also received substantial financial support as well as training from the IRGC, so much so that in the terror group's 1985 founding manifesto, Hezbollah vowed loyalty to Iran's Supreme Leader.[4] Moreover, a 2015 Congressional Research report provides details on the substantial political influence the IRGC possesses. Since 2007, Mohammad Ali Jafari has been Commander in Chief of the IRGC and is considered a "hardliner against political dissent and a close ally of the Supreme Leader."[5] The report continues that in 2009, the Iranian regime attributed greater authority in intelligence gathering to the IRGC, possibly over the regime's Ministry of Intelligence.[6]

The Quds force was established shortly after the beginning of the Iran-Iraq war in 1980, operating Iran's asymmetric warfare as well as collaborating with proxies, such as Hezbollah. They have been known to train and supply other groups like Hamas, the Afghan Taliban, and other Shiite insurgents. The IRGC and the Quds Force have historically denied any opposition from rising in the country and benefit economically through a variety of practices, both licit and illicit. They currently "dominate most sectors of the economy, from energy to construction, telecommunication to auto making, and even banking and finance."[7]

Additionally, they have actually benefited from global sanctions by tapping "into state funds and its relatively vast independent resources have provided a decisive advantage."[8] In 2005 with the election of Mahmoud Ahmadinejad, the IRGC received increased governmental loans and contracts as well as control of Iran's "internal and national security organizations."[9] With current President Hassan Rouhani, the IRGC are continuing their relationship with the administration. Overall, the IRGC is committed to promoting the revolution and will defend the Supreme Leader and his policies.

Nonetheless, the Quds Force remains a powerful military unit in Iran, operating outside of the country's borders and having a strong influence where they go, "gaining experience, fighting insurgencies, waging asymmetrical war, and studying the United States and Israeli militaries."[10] The Quds Force can best be compared operationally to U.S. special forces. They are well equipped to carry out attacks if they are commanded to do so by Iran's Supreme Leader, simultaneously with proxies abroad. Ultimately, the Quds Force was established to have a global influence on behalf of Iranian policies and it has thus far been successful in the Middle East, such as in Syria and Iraq, but also in Latin America, particularly in Venezuela and Bolivia.

## The Quds Force

Though the IRGC is Iran's formal military, the Quds Force is tasked with duties abroad, commanded by Maj. Gen. Qasem Soleimani since 1998. Officially, the Quds Force is "an elite unit that conducts clandestine operations outside Iran; provides training, financial, and other support to Islamic militant groups; and collects strategic and military intelligence against Iran's enemies, especially the United States."[11] The U.S. Justice Department defines the unit as a "branch of the IRGC that conducts sensitive covert operations abroad, including terrorist attacks, assassinations, and kidnappings, and is believed to have sponsored attacks against coalition forces in Iraq."[12] Much like the IRGC, the Quds Force has "corps" of its own, such as the Lebanon Corps, the Iraq Corps and Ansar Corps, which are regional factions designated with duties based on their geographical positions.[13] Unit 400 is the most recent faction of the Quds Force with reports indicating their rise to prominence among the Force as early as 2012. In 2007, the Quds Force was designated as a terrorist supporter for "providing material support to the Taliban and other terrorist organizations."[14] According to Bunker and Hazim (2007), as "soldiers of the Last Days,"[15] they represent "holy warriors who do the bidding of Iran's Shia clerics."[16] As the previous authors suggest, the Quds Force can be described more as a non-state entity than a military force, which is the IRGC.[17]

Moreover, an unclassified Department of Defense (DOD) report on Iran's military power in 2010 noted that the IRGC and the Quds Force have been behind, in some capacity, a number of the deadliest terror attacks of the past two decades. These include the bombings of the U.S. Embassy, annex, and Marine barracks in Beirut in 1983 and 1984, the attack on the AMIA Jewish Community Center in Bueno Aires in 1994, the Khobar Towers bombing in Saudi Arabia in 1996, as well as many of the insurgent attacks on Coalition and Iraqi Security Forces in Iraq since 2003.[18] As the report explains, the Quds Force merely guides or supports other groups that execute attacks, "thereby, maintaining plausible deniability within the international community."[19]

## The Quds Force Mark on the Western Hemisphere

The Pentagon's 2010 report to Congress on Iran's military power disclosed that the Quds Force is active in Latin America, stationing "operatives in foreign embassies, charities and religious/cultural institutions to foster relationships with people, often building on existing socioeconomic ties with the well-established Shia Diaspora and even carrying out paramilitary operations to support extremists and destabilize unfriendly regimes."[20] The DOD report indicated that Quds Force agents were noticed in Venezuela and were focused on "intelligence operations, paramilitary training for the Revolutionary Armed Forces of Colombia and security assistance for the government of Venezuela."[21] Since former Iranian President Ahmadinejad's "Tour of Tyrants Trip" to Latin America in 2012, the Quds Force increased their presence in the region.[22]

Moreover, Bunker and Hazim (2007) refer to Quds Force operatives as blended "criminal-soldiers," because they represent pre-Westphalian soldiers, or "holy-warriors that exist somewhere within the blurring of crime and war that is taking place globally."[23] Such a place is Latin America, which is arguably the international capital for transnational organized crime. Criminal groups, like drug trafficking organizations or cartels, are increasingly cooperating with terror groups. For instance, Arbabsiar, a

Quds Force associate, plotted with whom he believed was a member of the Mexican Los Zetas cartel.

Latin America expert Luis Fleischman noted that "in April 2010, the Pentagon reported the presence of paramilitary Al Quds [Quds Force] operatives in Venezuela."[24] Though the Quds Force presence can be traced as far back as Hezbollah's presence in Latin America, their activities were observed more closely during Ahmadinejad's presidency. In Venezuela, for instance, the Quds Force strengthened the country's secret service and police.[25] Additionally, it is believed that "Venezuela is the gateway for Iran in the Western Hemisphere."[26] Something similar is occurring in Bolivia, but more rapidly. The defense school located in Warnes near the city of Santa Cruz was inaugurated in 2012 with a significant Quds Force presence, including the former Iranian defense minister, Ahmed Vahidi. Therefore, not only does a steady presence of Quds Force members benefit Iran's agenda in Latin America, but it also unsparingly serves the host country.

## Involvement with the Global Drug Trade

The IRGC and Quds Force have been linked to the drug trade operating both in the Middle East and Latin America. Kronenfield and Gorzansky (2013) sufficiently trace the link between the Quds Force and the international drug trade, which includes involvements with crime organizations in Latin America. They explain that "these ties create operational and logistical platforms that support and enhance the ability of the Revolutionary Guards and specifically the Quds Force to pose a threat to their enemies' territories and populations by forging documents, smuggling goods across borders, laundering money, supporting black banking, and so on."[27] Due to international sanctions, the IRGC and Quds Force have established a lucrative business out of the global drug trade. Over the years, they have managed to successfully forge alliances with regional drug trafficking organizations or cartels to move drugs across borders and launder money. In the Middle East, the border Iran shares with Pakistan and Afghanistan is "one of the world's busiest drug smuggling corridors."[28]

Most importantly, the IRGC and Quds Force partnership with Hezbollah continues the flow of illicit practices in the region, especially in Venezuela, Colombia, and Bolivia. Hezbollah members have the skills and experience to employ rewarding operations in Latin America. The overwhelmingly profitable drug trade in Latin America is only continuing to fund the Quds

Force, while the rise in the number of members present in the region through cultural centers and in the form of diplomats furthers Iran's policy strategy for the Western Hemisphere.

## The 2011 Arbabsiar Plot

The most widely recognized link between the Quds Force and a cartel is the 2011 Arbabsiar plot. Mansour Arbabsiar, a naturalized United States citizen, conspired with senior Quds Force members to assassinate the Saudi Ambassador to the United States, Adel al-Jubeir. Arbabsiar agreed to pay $1.5 million to a DEA informant posing as a Mexican Los Zetas member for the assassination. The plan was to bomb a popular Washington restaurant, which many U.S. Senate and Congressional members dine, where al-Jubeir was to attend. Reports indicate that Arbabsiar was acting "under the direction of the Quds Force external operations senior officer (who is also his cousin), Abdul Reza Shahlai, and his deputy, Gholam Shakuri."[29] Shahlai is of particular importance, having played a "central role in the Quds Force's covert operations against and targeting of U.S. forces in Iraq since the 2003 invasion, and in 2007, he oversaw the kidnapping and assassination of five American service members from a U.S. base in Karbala, Iraq."[30]

In 2008, the United States Treasury Department labeled him as a specially designated terrorist, which makes his link to the assassination attempt all the more noteworthy. Shakuri, a senior Quds Force official, met with Arbabsiar, approving of the plan. Arbabsiar admitted his involvement with the plot as well as his communication with Quds Force members, finally pleading guilty in New York City federal court on May 30, 2013.[31] According to the complaint and indictment, Arbabsiar was in contact with Iranian co-conspirators based in Iran. He wired about $100,000 to a U.S. bank account as a down payment for the assassination.

Latin America expert, Ilan Berman explained in his 2012 testimony that this foiled plot is "known to have been both orchestrated and facilitated via South America, suggesting that Iran increasingly finds the region to be an advantageous operational theater."[32] The Director of National Intelligence (DNI) James Clapper even stated in his Senate testimony that the "Iranian regime has formed alliances with Chavez, Ortega, Castro, and Correa that many believe can destabilize the Hemisphere. These alliances can pose an immediate threat by giving Iran-directly through the IRGC, the Quds Force, or its proxies like Hezbollah – a platform in the region to carry out attacks against the United States, our interests, and allies."[33] Given an understanding of the Quds Force commands and operations, this assassination attempt would not have been developed or carried out without Iranian leadership's knowledge. In some way, it appears that Iran wants the international community to be made aware of their clandestine capabilities. Even in a post-Chavez era, the region continues to harbor Quds Force members.

## "Unit 400"

Both the IRGC and Quds Force have been secretive and Iran keeps most, if not all, of their activities and resources well guarded. However, giving the military unit, it is an expansive operations and so they developed another section within the organization for more specialized operations. This section is known as Unit 400, which is believed to be a clandestine unit of the Quds Force under the direct command of the Supreme Leader of Iran. Specifically, this Unit is employed to seek out Western targets across the world. A 2012 report investigated the botched Bangkok plot to assassinate Israeli diplomats in Thailand, revealing that Majid Alavi, a former deputy Iranian intelligence minister, "shifted to the Quds Force [2012] and along with [Hamed] Abdollahi, a commander accused in the Washington plot,"[34] operates Unit 400, which is "known as the Special Operations Unit."[35] According to State Department cables, Alavi also spied on dissidents living in London and Los Angeles.[36] Additionally, the 2012 report obtained information from U.S. officials that Unit 400 "conducts sensitive covert operations abroad [that] include terrorist attacks, assassinations, kidnappings and sabotage."[37] They have also supplied Iraqi Shiite militants, as well as "weapons, equipment, training and money to Afghan insurgents...and also arranges the delivery of lethal aid into Syria and Lebanon and military training for Hezbollah and Palestinian militants."[38]

Hence, the Quds Force has expanded its network to include a tight unit for the sole purpose of targeting westerners. The Arbabsiar plot as well as those afterwards continue to show the IRGC and Quds Force ambitions, though also indicative of their limits.

## Recent Quds Force Activities

In 2012, the Quds Force reportedly assisted with supplying the Houthi rebels in Yemen with AK-47s, rocket-propelled grenades, and other arms.[39] Additionally, "the Yemeni coast guard intercepted a boat smuggling arms, explosives, and antiaircraft missiles suspected to have originated in Iran."[40] Moreover, in 2014, the Treasury Department designated three Quds Force operatives as individuals who "threaten to commit, or support terrorism,"[41] for their part in planning attacks in Afghanistan with an Afghan associate. The designation names Alireza Hemmati and Akbar Seyed Al-hosseini for providing logical support to the Afghan associate, and Mahmud Afkhami to "highlight his influence over Afghan political affairs and his efforts to advance Iranian interests with the Government of the Islamist Republic of Afghanistan."[42] Today, the Quds Force is actively involved in the fight against ISIS in Syria, with at least "sixty to seventy Quds Force commanders" present in Syria to assist Syrian President Bashar al-Assad and his forces.[43]

Other Shiite groups, such as Hezbollah and Iraqi Shiite militants are also active in the fight to preserve Assad's reign in the country, under the guidance and command of the Quds Force. In 2014, the Islamic State threatened Iraq's government and Iran responded almost immediately by sending Quds Force "advisers, intelligence drone surveillance, weapons shipments, and other assistance."[44] They are well funded considering Iran's military budget between 2001 to 2009 was less than 4 percent of its GDP, and there is no additional data for the years that follow. As one report explains, the budget for the Quds Force is classified, "directly controlled by Khamenei (the Supreme Leader), and is not reflected in the Iranian budget. It operates primarily outside Iran's borders."[45] Given that the budget remains undisclosed by the Iranian government and the available sources linking the IRGC to drug trafficking, they are relying to an unknown extent on the illicit economy to fund their operations as well as the operations of their proxies.

Nonetheless, the Quds Force is continuing to maintain a presence internationally, including in the opium poppy cultivation and opium and heroin production in Afghanistan. In 2012, the Treasury Department designated Quds Force General Gholamreza Baghbani as a Specially Designated Narcotics Trafficker pursuant to the Foreign Narcotics Kingpin Designation Act (Kingpin Act), the first against an Iranian official.[46] According to the Treasury report, Baghbani granted access to Afghan narcotics traffickers to smuggle opiates through Iran in return for assistance, such as moving weapons.[47] Baghbani is a part of the Ansar Corps, located in the Sistan and Baluchistan province on the Iran-Afghanistan border, which holds about 4,000 Ansar Quds Force agents who are responsible for Afghanistan and Pakistan.[48]

## Conclusion

Ultimately, the Quds Force has been a dominant military unit spreading Iran's revolution across the Middle East and to Latin America. They have been just as effective as any other comparable organization, such as drug trafficking groups like Los Zetas or terror groups like Hezbollah. The United States has a number of sanctions against the Quds Force and many of its members for international terrorism-related activities. *Table* 1:4 provides a list of individuals sanctioned by the United States put together by a 2015 Congressional Research Service report on Iran sanctions.

Table 1: Sanctions against IRGC-QF Officials

| Executive order/Resolution | Date | Names |
|---|---|---|
| Res. 1747 | 10/21/2007 | Qods Aeronautics Industries; Brig. Gen. Qasem Soleimani |
| E.O. 13382 | 12/12/2013 | Qods Aviation Industries |
| E.O. 13224 | 10/21/2007 | Qods Force; Bank Saderat |
|  | 8/3/2010 | Qods Senior Officers: Hushang Allahdad, Hosein Musavi, Hasan Mortezavi, Mohammad Reza Zahedi |
|  | 10/11/2011 | Qasem Soleimani; Hamed Abdollahi; Abdul Reza Shahlai; Ali Gholam Shakuri; Manssor Arbabsiar |
|  | 10/12/2011 | Mahan Air |
|  | 3/27/2012 | Qods Officers: Esmail Ghani, Sayyid Ali Tabatabaei, Hosein Aghajani |
|  | 2/6/14 | Related to Afghanistan: Sayyed Kamal Musavi; Alireza Hemmati; Akbar Seyed Alhosseini; Mahmud Afkhami Rashidi |
| E.O. 12938 | 5/23/2011 | Qods Force |
|  | 11/8/2012 | Mohammad Minai |
| E.O. 13438 | 1/8/2008 | Ahmad Forouzandeh (Qods Commander Ramazan HQ) |
| E.O. 13572 | 5/18/2011 | Qods Force; Qasem Soleimani; Mohsen Chizari (Commander, operations and training) |

Table 1: Sanctions against IRGC-QF officials. Data source: Kenneth Katzman, "Iran Sanctions." Washington, D.C.: Congressional Research Service, 21 April 2015, https://www.fas.org/sgp/crs/mideast/RS20871.pdf.

The United Nations Security Council implemented Resolution 1747 to further restrict Iran's nuclear ambitions. Executive Order 13382 froze assets of those proliferating weapons of mass destruction, similar to Executive Order 12938, which assisted with combatting the spread of unconventional weapons. Executive Order 13224, signed on September 23, 2001, ordered to freeze "U.S.-based assets of and a ban on U.S. transactions with entities determined to be supporting international terrorism."[50] The entities and groups listed above funneled "Iranian money to Hezbollah, Hamas, PIJ, and other Iranian supported terrorist groups," which also included the Afghan Taliban.[51] Finally, Executive Order's 13438 and 13572 are related to the war efforts in Iraq and now Syria. Forouzandeh, for instance, was sanctioned as an entity who threatened the stabilization efforts in Iraq. Specifically, Executive Order 13438 pertains to any entity or organization "fomenting sectarian violence in Iraq and of organization training in Iran for Iraqi militia fighters."[52] Under Executive Order 13572, the Quds Force and its members were sanctioned for repressing the Syrian people and being involved with human rights abuses in the country.

Overall, "more than twenty terror attacks by Hezbollah [Hezbollah] or Quds Force operatives were thwarted over the fifteen-month period between May 2011 and July 2012; by another count, nine plots were uncovered over the first nine months of 2012. The key to all these attacks, however, whether carried out by Hezbollah [Hezbollah] or the Quds Force, was deniability."[53] What is certain with the development of Unit 400 and the Quds Force global presence and influence, "Iranian leaders appear committed to a policy of targeting Western interests, not only in places where countermeasures may be comparatively underdeveloped (e.g., Azerbaijan, Bulgaria, India, Georgia, Thailand) but, if opportunities present themselves, even in world capitals like Washington, D.C."[54]

Additionally, "the IRGC, which is perhaps the most equipped and sophisticated terrorist group of our time, has the will and capability to build a worldwide illicit network,"[55] and continues to fund Iranian activities in the country and abroad. Many experts agree that the United State should not allow the international Quds Force presence to go unnoticed. The research available offers an exceptional outline of where the Quds Force, backed by the IRGC, has been operating, how it funds its operations and to what extent they have managed to forge unsavory alliances with criminal organizations, and what they are really capable of with the right resources and connections.

Further investigations are required, specifically in Latin America as the number of diplomats in the region continues to grow as well as the significant presence of Hezbollah members. The diplomatic presence is indicative of Quds Force members taking on those roles to keep a watchful eye on the designated region they are assigned to. Another point worth reiterating is that Hezbollah activity in Latin American has surged since the presidency of Ahmadinejad. The 2011 link between Iran and Los Zetas should be of greater concern, since it can be argued that there may be an Iranian or Hezbollah presence in Mexico given past associations, Diasporas in Central America, and drug trafficking activities. Retired four-start Marine General James Mattis, former head of U.S. Central Command, stated in 2013 that the Arbabsiar plot was orchestrated "at the highest levels."[56]

Former DEA Chief of Operations Michael Braun stated in his 2012 testimony before the House Committee on Homeland Security that the Quds Force learn from the "most sophisticated organized crime syndicates in the world: the Colombian and Mexican drug trafficking cartels, which include the FARC. And these relationships most likely provide the Quds Force and Hezbollah with opportunities to leverage the transportation, money laundering, arms trafficking, corruption, human trafficking and smuggling infrastructures of the Colombian and Mexican drug trafficking cartels, as well as other organized crime and terrorist groups around the world."[57] Additionally, Braun explained that there is evidence proving Hezbollah and Quds Force operatives have crossed over into the U.S. through the Southern border.[58] Given the rhetoric of experienced U.S. officials, this area certainly requires further exploration to expose the magnitude of IRGC and Quds Force presence not only across our Southern border, but in the Western Hemisphere in general.

*Small Wars Journal facilitates the exchange of information among practitioners, thought leaders, and students of Small Wars, in order to advance knowledge and capabilities in the field. We hope this, in turn, advances the practice and effectiveness of those forces prosecuting Small Wars in the interest of self-determination, freedom, and prosperity for the population in the area of operations. We believe that Small*

Wars are an enduring feature of modern politics. We do not believe that true effectiveness in Small Wars is a 'lesser included capability' of a force tailored for major theater war. And we never believed that 'bypass built-up areas' was a tenable position warranting the doctrinal primacy it has held for too long -- this site is an evolution of the MOUT Homepage, Urban Operations Journal, and urbanoperations.com, all formerly run by the Small Wars Journal's Editor-in-Chief. The characteristics of Small Wars have evolved since the Banana Wars and Gunboat Diplomacy. War is never purely military, but today's Small Wars are even less pure with the greater inter-connectedness of the 21st century. Their conduct typically involves the projection and employment of the full spectrum of national and coalition power by a broad community of practitioners. The military is still generally the biggest part of the pack, but there are a lot of other wolves. The strength of the pack is the wolf, and the strength of the wolf is the pack. The Small Wars Journal's founders come from the Marine Corps. Like Marines deserve to be, we are very proud of this; we are also conscious and cautious of it. This site seeks to transcend any viewpoint that is single service, and any that is purely military or naively U.S.-centric. We pursue a comprehensive approach to Small Wars, integrating the full joint, allied, and coalition military with their governments' federal or national agencies, non-governmental agencies, and private organizations. Small Wars are big undertakings, demanding a coordinated effort from a huge community of interest. We thank our contributors for sharing their knowledge and experience, and hope you will continue to join us as we build a resource for our community of interest to engage in a professional dialog on this painfully relevant topic. Share your thoughts, ideas, successes, and mistakes; make us all stronger."...I know it when I see it.""Small Wars" is an imperfect term used to describe a broad spectrum of spirited continuation of politics by other means, falling somewhere in the middle bit of the continuum between feisty diplomatic words and global thermonuclear war. The Small Wars Journal embraces that imperfection.Just as friendly fire isn't, there isn't necessarily anything small about a Small War. The term "Small War" either encompasses or overlaps with a number of familiar terms such as counterinsurgency, foreign internal defense, support and stability operations, peacemaking, peacekeeping, and many flavors of intervention. Operations such as noncombatant evacuation, disaster relief, and humanitarian assistance will often either be a part of a Small War, or have a Small Wars feel to them. Small Wars involve a wide spectrum of specialized tactical, technical, social, and cultural skills and expertise, requiring great ingenuity from their practitioners. The Small Wars Manual (a wonderful resource, unfortunately more often referred to than read) notes that: Small Wars demand the highest type of leadership directed by intelligence, resourcefulness, and ingenuity. Small Wars are conceived in uncertainty, *are conducted often with precarious responsibility and doubtful authority, under indeterminate orders lacking specific instructions. Small Wars Journal is NOT a government, official, or big corporate site. It is run by Small Wars Foundation, a non-profit corporation, for the benefit of the Small Wars community of interest. The site principals are Dave Dilegge (Editor-in-Chief) and Bill Nagle (Publisher), and it would not be possible without the support of myriad volunteers as well as authors who care about this field and contribute their original works to the community. We do this in our spare time, because we want to. McDonald's pays more. But we'd rather work to advance our noble profession than watch TV, try to super-size your order, or interest you in a delicious hot apple pie. If and when you're not flipping burgers, please join us. ©2005-2020.*

*Small Wars Journal is published by Small Wars Foundation - a 501(c)(3) non-profit corporation. Original content is published under a Creative Commons License per our Terms of Use. Creative Commons. © Copyright 2020 | Site by 3C Web Services. For correspondence, our mailing address is Small Wars Foundation, 1350 Beverly Rd, Ste 115-224, McLean, VA 22101-3633.*

CHAPTER 6

# REVOLUTIONARY INTELLIGENCE: THE EXPANDING INTELLIGENCE ROLE OF THE IRANIAN REVOLUTIONARY GUARD CORPS

*Udit Banerjea*

## Introduction

Prior to the Iranian Revolution in 1979, Iran's primary intelligence apparatus was an organization known as SAVAK, an acronym for Sazman-e Ettela'atva Amniat-e Keshvar (National Security and Intelligence Organization). The pre-revolutionary government of Iran, under the Shah Mohammad Reza Pahlavi, had been installed with the help of the U.S. Central Intelligence Agency and the British, and had aligned with the West in the Cold War.

SAVAK was created with the assistance of the United States and Israel in the interest of protecting the Western-friendly Shah's regime from potential communist threats, given Iran's shared northern border with the Soviet Union. SAVAK grew to be a military-dominated organization of expansive scope, with "15,000 full-time agents and thousands of part-time informants."[1] SAVAK developed a reputation for brutality, but up until the 1979 Revolution, it successfully suppressed dissenters to the Shah's regime. SAVAK's brutal repression was an integral factor in the growing unpopularity of the Shah, which culminated in the Islamic Revolution.

In 1979, an Islamic Revolution swept across the country, and a clerical regime led by Supreme Leader Ayatollah Ruhollah Khomeini took power. Shortly thereafter, the new Islamic government set up a number of small intelligence agencies with various mandates alongside an organization known as SAVAMA (Sazman Ettela'atva Amniat Melli Iran), which inherited the pre- revolutionary intelligence apparatus from SAVAK. However, SAVAMA was more interested in finding and eliminating the Revolution's opponents—at home and abroad—than in collecting information. At this time, the Palestine Liberation Organization (PLO) provided most of its foreign intelligence information. A few years after the revolution, the intelligence services were consolidated under the Ministry of Intelligence and Security (MOIS). MOIS was and remains under the nominal control of the president of Iran, who is elected by the people and is in charge of running the government bureaucracy.

Meanwhile, the Islamic Revolutionary Guard Corps (IRGC) was established as an independent security force—reporting directly to the Supreme Leader—to preserve the ideals of the revolution and to serve as a counterbalance to the regular military. The IRGC was created as a guarantor for the Islamic clerical regime that took power in Iran after the 1979 Revolution. The very existence of the IRGC affords the organization special status, as it stands deliberately separate from the country's regular armed forces. The head of the IRGC reports directly to the Supreme Leader, and under Iran's constitution the Supreme Leader alone reserves the right to undertake the "appointment, dismissal, and acceptance of resignation of" the chief commander of the IRGC.[2]

The IRGC was initially tasked with enforcing revolutionary mandates and eliminating counterrevolutionaries. The IRGC eventually assumed an intelligence role, a role which has since expanded greatly.[3] After an opposition movement coalesced in 2009 to protest fraudulent elections, the Supreme Leader, Ayatollah Ali Hosseini Khamenei, consolidated major intelligence agencies across various organizations under an expanded IRGC Intelligence Organization. The newly-empowered IRGC dismantled the opposition movement and has maintained greater influence in Iran's intelligence system relative to MOIS ever since. Khamenei retains direct control of the IRGC Intelligence Organization as a check on potentially dissenting forces within the government. Meanwhile, the IRGC has grown into a potent political force itself, using its intelligence capabilities to gain control over the internet, telecommunications, and key economic sectors. As a result, the IRGC is arguably the most powerful force in Iranian politics with its own interests, which are, for the time being, mostly aligned with those of the clerical regime and the Supreme Leader.

## Literature Review

Research for this paper uncovered a dearth of academic literature on the intelligence role of the IRGC, with most sources focusing on its military and paramilitary operations. Of course, the IRGC's intelligence activities have historically been in support of its military and paramilitary activities, and they are closely linked. But the recent expansion of the IRGC's intelligence role beyond its historic scope has not been adequately covered in academic literature. Moreover, the IRGC is usually treated as a secondary consideration in the exploration of broader topics of research, such as Iran's foreign policy and its nuclear program. Iran's nominally principal intelligence agency, the MOIS, has been covered—most thoroughly in the Library of Congress's Federal Research Division report entitled Iran's Ministry of Intelligence and Security: A Profile, which serves as a valuable source of background information on Iran's overall intelligence apparatus for this article. Similar in-depth, comprehensive, and current coverage of the IRGC's intelligence operations, however, remains lacking in the academic context.

Given that the IRGC has now supplanted MOIS as the most powerful intelligence organization in Iran, it deserves a greater degree of academic study. While academic sources have been scarce, journalistic sources on this topic have been relatively abundant. Major newspapers and news magazines have taken the lead on providing analysis of recent developments. Due to the geopolitical importance of Iran to the West, the Western news media has made coverage of Iranian intelligence issues a priority. As the IRGC has evolved rapidly over the past decade, news outlets have been better able to keep up with the changes in the system, while academic journals have lagged behind. While news outlets are excellent at providing great breadth of coverage, they are unable to provide much depth-one notable exception is Dexter Filkins's detailed and excellent profile of the Quds Force and its commander for The New Yorker, titled "The Shadow Commander." This exception notwithstanding, a more scholarly approach is required to address this need. Even beyond Iran's intelligence apparatus, the IRGC has grown into arguably the most powerful institution in Iranian politics today, and its intelligence activities are a key means of maintaining power and influence within the country. The IRGC's expanded stature necessitates additional research into this essential topic.

## Organization

The IRGC has historically been a martial organization, having spent its formative developmental years combating Iraqi forces during the Iran-Iraq War. Overall, the IRGC consists of an estimated 125,000 members across all of its divisions.[4] But in addition to its more traditional military forces, which include the IRGC Land Forces, the IRGC Air Force, and the IRGC Naval Forces, the IRGC houses Iran's key unconventional warfare, covert operations, and intelligence forces. These include the Quds Force, the Basij, and the IRGC Intelligence Organization (formerly the IRGC Intelligence Branch). This paper focuses on these non-military divisions, as they are responsible for conducting and coordinating the IRGC's intelligence operations.

## The Basij

The Basij is a volunteer paramilitary reserve force and the largest security organization in Iran by manpower. The Basij has about 90,000 active personnel and can draw upon a combined active and reserve strength of up to 300,000. When fully mobilized, the Basij is capable of commanding nearly 1,000,000 men.[5] Part of the Basij's mission is to help generate popular resistance against a potential U.S. invasion, with Basij battalions integrated into the IRGC's military forces. However, the main mission of the Basij is riot control and internal security. The Basij serves as a non-sophisticated, decentralized, popular force that can be mobilized across the country on short notice. Basij volunteers were called upon to disperse and arrest protesters after the 2009 Green Revolution, which they successfully did, destroying the momentum of the opposition movement.[6]

## The IRGC Intelligence Organization

Prior to 2009, the IRGC Intelligence Branch was the official intelligence arm of the IRGC and had about 2,000 personnel. This division was responsible for gathering and analyzing intelligence in the broader Muslim world and targeting domestic opposition groups and individuals. The IRGC Intelligence Branch was "a largely politicized force with a political mission," whose "conformity and loyalty to the regime are unquestionable."[7] Events in 2009, known as the Green Revolution, however, led to a major expansion in the scope and importance of the Intelligence Branch. Major protests erupted after claims of fraud in the June election, in which

157

Islamist hardliner President Mahmoud Ahmadinejad (an IRGC veteran) was officially declared to have won a second term against reformist Mir-Hossein Mousavi.

Khamenei and IRGC leaders became concerned that a united opposition movement could threaten the legitimacy of the clerical regime. In the wake of the post-election protests, Iran's intelligence apparatus underwent its largest reorganization since the death of Ayatollah Ruhollah Khomeini in 1989. Ali Khamenei expanded the IRGC Intelligence Branch to form a new intelligence and security division, the Intelligence Organization, within the IRGC that would report directly to his personal office.

The new organization vastly expanded the existing IRGC Intelligence Branch and comprises seven separate intelligence and security divisions, including Khamenei's personal intelligence office known as Department 101, the Internal Security Directorate within MOIS, the Security Directorate of the Basij paramilitary force, and other plainclothes and paramilitary police units.[8] The IRGC Intelligence Organization also includes the newly created Cyber Defense Command. Hojjatoleslam Hossein Taeb, a cleric who had been acting commander of the Basij since 2008, was named the head of the IRGC Intelligence Organization. Taeb, who has served in the IRGC since 1982, is an ardent Khamenei loyalist. He had been a student of Khamenei during the 1979 revolution and he is a friend of Khamenei's son.[9]

While it is evident that the reorganization was undertaken as an effort to more effectively quell internal dissent from protesters and politicians alike in the aftermath of the fraudulent elections, it is unclear where the decision originated or how it was finalized. The creation of the IRGC Intelligence Organization was not a standalone event. Simultaneously, the IRGC conducted a secret purge within MOIS, removing hundreds of intelligence agents and directors from their positions.[10] This solidified the IRGC's control of Iran's intelligence apparatus and weakened the government's ability to challenge the IRGC's authority and to impede its activities in cracking down on dissenters.

Khamenei and the clerical regime undoubtedly felt threatened by the protests and the public challenges to their legitimacy, and the reorganization provided greater protection for them. Khamenei suspected that key MOIS officials sympathized with the opposition and would present a dangerous internal threat. But arguably the even bigger beneficiary to this reorganization (and purge) is the IRGC itself, which was able to assume much greater influence and power once the dust settled. It is likely that Khamenei and IRGC leaders acted in concert, as they found their interests to be aligned, as they so often have been. Ultimately, the clerical regime was able to maintain its legitimacy through a show of force, which was provided by the IRGC. In turn, the IRGC reduced its oversight, removed rivals within MOIS from positions of power, and took over key MOIS functions.

Tensions over intelligence matters between Khamenei and the government have continued since the 2009 shake-up. In April 2011, Ahmadinejad had removed the intelligence minister, Heydar Moslehi, from his cabinet, as was his right as the elected head of the government. Only a month later, in May, Ahmadinejad was forced to accept the MOIS head back into his cabinet after Moslehi was publicly reinstated to his post by Khamenei. The move by Khamenei was less about Moslehi's value in intelligence and more about publicly demonstrating of the limits of the government's power in such matters. Moslehi was far from a competent intelligence minister—he had a history of inventing foreign plots, and he publicly denied the success of the U.S. raid that killed Osama bin Laden, claiming to have evidence proving bin Laden had long since died of illness.[11] In effect, Khamenei strong-armed Ahmadinejad into keeping an incompetent intelligence minister in his cabinet as a check on his authority over intelligence matters. This development further eroded the government's oversight and control over the country's intelligence system, to the benefit of the IRGC.

## The Quds Force

The third major intelligence organization within the IRGC is the Quds Force, which is the most difficult to delineate. The Quds Force is primarily responsible for all Iranian intelligence activities and covert operations conducted abroad. However, the Quds Force often works very closely with Iran's other intelligence organizations, including MOIS, which can blur the distinction in responsibilities.[12] The size of the Quds Force is estimated to be 15,000 personnel – though[13] the true size is hidden even from the Iranian Parliament-located[14] in bases both in and outside of Iran. In many of Iran's embassies abroad, the Quds Force has sections that are closed off to most of the embassy staff. Members are selected for both competency and their allegiance to the Islamic principles of the 1979 revolution. New recruits are trained in Shiraz and Tehran before being sent for indoctrination at the Jerusalem Operation College in Qom.[15]

The Quds Force is divided into units called directorates based on regional scope. There are at least five such directorates: 1) Iraq; 2) Lebanon, Palestine, and Jordan; 3) Afghanistan, Pakistan, and India; 4) Turkey and Arabia; 5) Central Asian former Soviet Republics, Europe, North America, and North Africa.[16] After receiving training, rookie Quds Force operatives are deployed for several months on missions to Afghanistan and Iraq to gain field experience.[17] The Quds Force maintains close relationships with Iranian client organizations like Hezbollah-active primarily in Lebanon-and Shia groups in Iraq. Within the Quds Force, a secret group known as Department 9000 was responsible for providing training and support to Shia insurgents in Iraq to combat U.S. forces during the U.S. occupation.[18]

The Quds Force has been led by a man named Brigadier General Qassem Suleimani since 1998. Suleimani has been described by one former CIA officer as "'the most powerful operative in the Middle East today.'"[19] Suleimani is a powerful figure within the Iranian intelligence community, and his influence has made the Quds Force an important stakeholder in determining Iran's foreign policy. At times, Suleimani has been personally involved in shaping political developments in the regions, as demonstrated when he negotiated a truce in 2008 between the Mahdi Army, the Shia militia, and Iraqi government forces-although the Quds Force itself had been propping up the Mahdi Army.[20] Furthermore, Suleimani has often communicated indirectly with senior U.S. officials, including General David Petraeus, the commander of coalition forces, and Ryan Cocker, the U.S. Ambassador to Iraq as a negotiating tactic in the Iran-U.S. proxy war in Iraq.[21] Evidently, Suleimani wields considerable autonomy in the deployment of Quds Force operatives and in communicating with foreign officials, and the influence of the Quds Force is closely tied to his political stature.

## Intelligence Operations and Capabilities

The IRGC's intelligence activities include both domestic and foreign operations. Domestic operations are focused on internal security issues and eliminating dissent. These are primarily conducted by the Basij paramilitary force and the IRGC Intelligence Organization's cyber intelligence divisions. Foreign operations are usually directed at the United States and its allies in the Middle East, principally Israel and Saudi Arabia, or to preserve or expand Iranian influence in the region. The IRGC supports and coordinates with foreign client organizations that serve as proxies for Iranian interests, principally through the Quds Force. The IRGC also has a history of conducting targeted killings of individuals seen as particularly harmful to the clerical regime. Underpinning all of these operations and capabilities are the vast economic resources of the IRGC, which it generates through its involvement in the Iranian public and private economy.

## Internal Security

During the 2009 post-election protests, the IRGC led the crackdown on opposition supporters, making arrests through the Basij paramilitary force. The Security Directorate of the Basij was moved under the newly expanded IRGC Intelligence Organization, and the head of Basij, Hassan Taeb, was named head of the IRGC Intelligence Organization—Taeb was thus likely personally leading the crackdown. The IRGC held political prisoners in Evin prison in Tehran, in the "2A" ward operated by the IRGC. This ward was off- limits to regular prison guards, judiciary officials, and even MOIS officials. In a sign of the open power struggle between the IRGC and the government bureaucracy, the information ministry warned journalists that the IRGC had taken control of security in the country and that their contacts at MOIS would not be able to help locate or release them if arrested.[22]

## Foreign Proxies

The IRGC has consistently supported foreign armed groups that further Iranian interests in the Middle East and beyond. After the 1982 Israeli invasion of Lebanon, the Quds Force played in integral role in the creation and development of Hezbollah. Qassem Suleimani, now the head of the Quds Force, has developed close ties with Hezbollah leaders and oversaw the delivery of Iranian rockets to Hezbollah for use against Israel in the 2006 war.[23] Suleimani and the IRGC are also suspected of being involved in the 2005 assassination of Rafik Hariri, the former prime minister of Lebanon.[24] The IRGC has also at times supported Hamas and the Palestinian Islamic Jihad in their operations in Palestine.[25]

During the U.S. invasion and occupation of Iraq, the Quds Force supplied Shia insurgent groups and, in some cases, even Sunni insurgents with training and materiel to conduct a proxy war against the United States and its coalition partners.[26] In December 2006, U.S. forces captured the head of operations for the Quds Force in Iraq, and a month later, another five Quds Force operatives were captured carrying diplomatic passports.[27] Over the past few years, the IRGC has also been shipping arms to Shia Houthi rebels in Yemen, including AK-47s and rocket-propelled grenades.[28] Iran has increased its involvement in Yemen as Saudi Arabia has begun conducting extensive air strikes, setting off a proxy war between the two regional rivals.

A similar rebellion with IRGC backing in Bahrain was put down through Saudi intervention.[29]

The IRGC has also been highly active in supporting Bashar al-Assad's regime in Syria against Sunni-dominated rebels. Iran views the Assad regime in Syria as a vital link to Hezbollah. In August 2012, Syrian rebels captured forty-eight Iranian nationals, suspected by Western intelligence agencies to be members of the Quds Force, within the country. Suleimani took personal control over Iran's involvement in Syria, coordinating efforts between the Syrian military, Hezbollah, Iraqi Shia militias, and other IRGC commanders. Quds Force members currently in Syria are estimated to be in the thousands.[30] Suleimani has invested a great deal of personal effort in supporting the Assad government, and consequently, the IRGC is likely to remain invested in that goal as well.

**Targeted Attacks**

Iran has a history of conducting targeted killings and mass bombings to eliminate key opponents of the regime or to send a political message. American and Argentine officials believe that the IRGC was involved in the 1992 bombing of the Israeli Embassy in Buenos Aires and the 1994 bombing of a Jewish Center in the same city, which combined to kill over 100 people.[31] Other attacks linked to the IRGC include the bombing of the Khobar Towers in Saudi Arabia in 1996 and the assassinations of Kurdish Iranian opposition figures in the early 1990s. The IRGC's Quds Force likely coordinated with MOIS to carry out these attacks. Under the presidency of Mohammad Khatami, beginning in 1997, such large-scale attacks were abandoned to prevent the increased international isolation of Iran.[32]

While the IRGC has not carried out a major attack on a similar scale in recent years, smaller operations have continued. The Quds Force attempted over thirty attacks on foreign soil between 2011 and 2013, including in Thailand,

India, Nigeria, and Kenya. Most prominently, the IRGC attempted to assassinate the Saudi Ambassador to the United States. A Quds Force agent approached a Mexican drug cartel to detonate a bomb at a Washington, D.C. restaurant where the Saudi ambassador would be eating. The plan was immediately uncovered, however, as the cartel member approached was an informant for the U.S. Drug Enforcement Administration.[33]

## Cyber Intelligence and Signals Intelligence

The IRGC has taken on a significant role in internet surveillance and censorship in recent years. The Iranian government formed the Supreme Council for Cyberspace in 2012 to consolidate oversight of the country's internet service providers. While Ahmadinejad was still president, he served as the head of the council at the behest of Supreme Leader Khamenei. Thus, the government wields significant statutory authority over the internet in Iran. But the IRGC maintains powerful channels of influence. First and foremost, the IRGC controls Iran's leading internet service provider. The internet sector was privatized in 2009, and the IRGC successfully bid for a controlling stake of the Telecommunication Company of Iran, the country's dominant service provider, through an affiliated shell corporation called the Mobin Trust Consortium.[34]

The IRGC has also launched its own official website, Gerdab, which it uses to track the activities of suspected dissenters and to post public denouncements of them. Moreover, the IRGC also controls the Center for the Surveillance of Organized Crime and the Working Group for Determining Criminal Content, powerful groups with broad powers to censor and track internet users, through the IRGC Intelligence Organization's Cyber Defense Command.[35] In addition to its internal surveillance activities, there is evidence that the IRGC's cyber espionage extends outside Iran's borders as well. According to translations by an Israeli blog that covers Iranian military issues, the IRGC posted on its Gerdab website in 2010 that It is "'cyber teams' had hacked 'twenty-nine websites affiliated with the U.S. espionage network.'"[36]

To date, Iran's signals intelligence (SIGINT) capabilities are limited. As of 2006, Iran was operating two SIGINT stations in northern Syria and in the Golan Heights in cooperation with the Syrian government, with two additional SIGINT stations expected in northern Syria by 2007. These SIGINT stations are funded and operated by the IRGC and are used mainly to provide intelligence support to Hezbollah forces in Lebanon.[37] The IRGC also has the capability of flying reconnaissance aircraft to collect intelligence, but this capacity is limited to minor missions using only a few purpose-built aircraft. It is likely, however, that the IRGC monitors and tracks internet activity to collect domestic signals intelligence through its control of Telecommunication Company of Iran, the Center for the Surveillance of Organized Crime, and the Working Group for Determining Criminal Content.

## Economic control

After the death of Ayatollah Khomeini in 1989, Iran began to privatize its economy under Khamenei and President Akbar Hashemi Rafsanjani in an effort to spur economic growth. Privatization has accelerated over the last decade, with $120 billion of Iran's public sector assets being sold off in that period. However, according to the Principal Vice President, only 17 percent of these assets are in the "true private sector," while the rest of the assets have been turned over to quasi-governmental organizations.[38] These quasi- governmental organizations include the IRGC and various IRGC-linked companies and associations, like the Mobin Trust Consortium which purchased the aforementioned Telecommunication Company of Iran, one of the largest publicly traded companies in Iran.

During this period of privatization, the IRGC has bought up controlling interests in various major economic ventures, most with some sort of security angle. Most of these purchases are conducted by nominally intermediate financial institutions, like the IRGC and Basij Cooperative Foundations, which are entirely controlled by the IRGC (and the Basij).[39] The IRGC controls pipelines, airports, illegal jetties, and a major bank. The IRGC- owned construction company Khatami Al Anbia regularly receives massive contracts for infrastructure projects, including $342 million in 2007 to develop the ChahBahar seaport and $850 million in 2010 for several no-bid contracts in oil and natural gas development.[40]

But the increased economic activity of the IRGC has been publicly criticized in some sectors of Iran. The vast network of IRGC-linked companies has led to significant embezzlement. In 2009, the government blocked the purchase of a mine by an IRGC-linked company because the purchase price was far lower than the market value. Other IRGC and military leaders have been publicly chastised for corruption, and in 2013, a prominent businessman with close ties to the IRGC leadership was arrested in Turkey on corruption charges.

Iranian President Hassan Rouhani has once opposed greater economic involvement from the IRGC, cancelling several government contracts with the IRGC and associated firms in response to accusations of corruption.[41] In 2013, Khamenei himself told the leaders of the IRGC "that protecting the revolution does not mean protecting the economic and political domains, hence expressing his displeasure with the IRGC's involvement in both politics and the economy."[42]

The IRGC's involvement in Iran's private sector economy has also made it vulnerable to international economic sanctions. Western intelligence agencies have become acutely aware of the IRGC's economic entrenchment, and they have attempted to use this to their advantage when devising sanctions. IRGC officers involved in the black market may actually be benefitting from the sanctions, as it drives a greater share of economic activity into their domain. But these IRGC officers are low- or mid-level officials with little political clout. High-level leaders of the IRGC have economic interests in larger companies that are negatively impacted by the sanctions.[43]

## Conclusion

Over the past decade, the IRGC has become the dominant intelligence organization within Iran, and arguably the dominant political organization as well. This is the result of several factors: a coordinated effort along with Khamenei to purge and weaken MOIS while consolidating power; the reputation and influence of individual IRGC leaders like Suleimani; and the gradual entrenchment of the IRGC in Iran's economy. Significant challenges to the IRGC's current position remain, however. Internal dissent remains the IRGC's greatest threat, and the danger of a Green Revolution coming to pass in full is ever-present. The IRGC was able to mobilize the Basij to disrupt the movement in 2009, but as social media and other potentially socially- disruptive technologies continue to evolve and as international economic sanctions continue to take their toll, it may be more difficult to contain it the next time. Economic sanctions are also hurting the economic interests of the IRGC itself, as the top leaders have a great deal of economic exposure through investments in large companies being targeted. Moreover, if the IRGC's participation in the Iranian economy continues to grow, it may contribute to more public resentment of corruption, eroding the legitimacy of the IRGC.

The stated mission of the IRGC is to defend the doctrine of the 1979 revolution. In theory, this is a vague enough mandate that could be interpreted in many different ways. But in practice, this translates to the preservation of the Iranian clerical regime, led by the Guardian Council and the Supreme Leader. Consequently, the fate of the IRGC is linked with the fate of the Iranian theocracy. The two forces have formed a symbiotic relationship that keeps the current system in place. But if that system is threatened, the IRGC's leadership will have to adapt to a rapidly evolving environment to preserve its position of dominance. The IRGC has to-date supported the government's nuclear talks with the United States and other world powers, with Qassem Suleimani even defending the chief negotiator and foreign minister Mohammad Javad Zarif against hardliners in the Iranian parliament.[44] Should Iran reach a deal with the United States and thereafter establish more normal relations, the political, social, and economic landscapes in which the IRGC operates are likely to change significantly. In such circumstances, the pragmatic voices in the IRGC may choose to reexamine the organization's role in and relationship with the political sphere.

*Banerjea, Udit. "Revolutionary Intelligence: The Expanding Intelligence Role of the Iranian Revolutionary Guard Corps." Journal of Strategic Security 8, no. 3 (2015)93-106. DOI: http://dx.doi.org/10.5038/1944-0472.8.3.1449Available.at: https://scholarcommons.usf.edu/jss/vol8/iss3/6This Article is brought to you for free and open access by the Open Access Journals at Scholar Commons. It has been accepted for inclusion in Journal of Strategic Security by an authorized editor of Scholar Commons. For more information, please contact scholarcommons@usf.edu. Volume 8 Number 3 Volume 8, No. 3, Special Issue Fall 2015: Intelligence: Analysis, Tradecraft, Training, Education, and Practical Application, Article 6. Revolutionary Intelligence: The Expanding Intelligence Role of the Iranian Revolutionary Guard Corps. Udit Banerjea, Johns Hopkins University, udit.banerjea@gmail.com*

CHAPTER 7

# THE TWO FACES OF THE FATEMIYUN: REVISITING THE MALE FIGHTERS

*Mohsen Hamidi*

Over the last eight years, thousands of Afghan men and some boys have fought on the side of the Iran supported Assad government in Syria as members of the Fatemiyun group. Although they are sent to Syria from Iran and supported by the Iranian government, Tehran describes the group as "self-motivated." This dispatch, which is the first in a two-part series, explores why so many Afghan men decided to join the group and what the consequences of this might be for Afghan society at large. Given the recent drawdown of Syria's armed conflict, many of these men are now returning home, either to Iran or Afghanistan. This return is fraught with complexities. AAN guest author Mohsen Hamidi* also examines the reports that warn of a Fatemiyun threat in Afghanistan and notes how the Syrian war has become a way of life for some of these men, for better or for worse.

A second dispatch will look at the women behind the Fatemiyun fighters, exploring their roles and experiences as their men go to war in Syria – and return home.

### Afghans in the Syrian War: The context

The Iranian government has been a major actor in the catastrophic war in Syria.[1] It has deployed or supported proxy forces there as part of its policy to maintain and strengthen what it calls the 'Axis of Resistance', which, in its eyes, stretches to Palestine through Iraq, Syria, Lebanon and, to a lesser extent, Yemen.[2] Iran denies any role in forming or supporting any proxy force. It calls those fighting in Syria, for example, 'self-motivated' and argues individuals went there of their own accord in order to 'defend their faith.' It sees its role in the region as legitimate and itself as acting in self-defence against threats faced from the United States and Israeli governments and the risks of regional instability that threaten its allies such as the regime of Bashar al-Assad in Syria (details in this RUSI paper).

One of the proxy forces deployed to Syria by the Iranian regime has been the Fatemiyun, a group of thousands of Afghan men who have fought on the side of the Syrian government since 2012/2013. The group has played a small, but not insignificant, role in the conflict in Syria.

The name 'Fatemiyun', meaning 'followers of Fatema', was chosen on religious grounds. According to a 9 Khordad/Jawza 1394 (30 May 2015) report by Kayhan, considered a hard-line Iranian newspaper, the group was named after Fatema Zahra, daughter of the Prophet Muhammad, because it was formed during her traditional annual commemoration days (year not specified in the report).

Drawing on official Iranian historiography and individual founder biographies, Tobias Schneider, research fellow at the Berlin-based Global Public Policy Institute (GPPi), presented the group's 'origin story' in an October 2018 paper.[3] These sources trace the roots of the Fatemiyun to "a small and fluctuating number of [Afghan] volunteers organised as the Muhammad Corps [Sepah-e Muhammad]" that fought in a series of wars, including the Afghan resistance against the Soviet invasion and the Iraq-Iran war in the 1980s, as well as against the Taleban regime in the 1990s.[4] According to this history, the fighters moved to Iran from post-2001 Afghanistan because of what Schneider calls "fear of prosecution by the new Afghan government and its American-led coalition backers." The history continues that in about 2011 (the exact year is not specified in the paper):

> ...when the Syrian conflict erupted, the group's commander Ali-Reza Tavassoli, known as Abu Hamed, and senior cleric Mohammad BaqirAlaoui [Alawi] petitioned the Iranian government for his then 22-25 fighters based around Mashhad to be sent to Syria to defend the shrine of Sayyeda Zeinab.[5] The request was swiftly approved in Tehran under the new umbrella of the "Fatemiyoun."

Checking for facts, Schneider writes, "Kayhan's historical account appears to correspond to the individual biographies of senior Fatemiyoun commanders who were killed in battle and whose exploits could be recounted." Of this founding generation of commanders that have all been killed in action in Syria, he names Ali Reza Tavassoli, Sayyed Hakim, Hossein Fedai Abdarchi, Reza Khavari and Sayyed Ibrahim. Their biographies indicate they fought for Iran in the Iran-Iraq war in the 1980s and against the Taleban in the 1990s, most probably as part of the Shia factions that made up Hezb-e Wahdat.

The picture on the ground seems far messier, in contrast to the coherent historical narrative presented above. According to this author's research, for instance, one senior Fatemiyun commander and several members of the group were working as part of the security forces of the US-backed Afghan government post-2001. The commander had even worked in a private security company for a while, offering protection to convoys transporting supplies for the US-led foreign troops. He then quit and left to join the Fatemiyun in Iran.

It was only after former fighters who had been captured by rebels in Syria or fled to seek asylum in Europe began to speak to journalists and researchers, from 2015 onwards, that information started to emerge about this "Afghan face to the Syrian conflict" (see AAN reporting in June 2015 and this April 2016 report from BBC Persian). This reporting indicated that because the Syrian government had been running out of soldiers, its allies such as Iran had started mobilising proxy groups like the Afghan Fatemiyun to bolster its forces.

## Mobilising fighters: differing perspectives

Within a couple of years after 2011, the year in or around which discussions about forming the group probably started, the Fatemiyun group grew dramatically from a small core composed of a handful of individuals to thousands of fighters. The sudden growth of the Fatemiyun was due, in large part, to a pervasive recruitment campaign in Iran since 2012/2013, described as "maddening" (in the sense of disabling one's rational thinking) by an Afghan man who wished to join the group, but was prevented from doing so by his family (he then returned to Herat where he spoke to AAN). According to recent reporting, out of the roughly three million Afghan refugees and migrants living in Iran, an estimated 50,000, entirely Shia

Hazaras and Sayyeds, joined the group. At its peak, there were an estimated 10,000-20,000 active Fatemiyun.[6]

In several reports, some of them based on original research, one question stood out: why had so many Afghans joined the Fatemiyun to fight a war in someone else's country? All in all, two main explanations have been offered – both of which have been rejected by the group and its Iranian backers.

The dominant explanation has focused on the circumstances under which Afghans live in Iran. It says that Iran was able to successfully mobilise Afghans, especially those without papers, by offering various benefits, such as better pay (than they were getting elsewhere), more permanent residence permits and the promise of 'social recognition' gained by going to war in Syria. For most Afghans who joined the Fatemiyun, life in Iran was so miserable that it seemed a good option. Writing for the Middle East Institute, researcher Lars Hauch sums up this point of view:

[The] underlying violence is more structural than direct. The authorities in Iran have put them [Afghans] in such a horrible situation that many of them actively decide to join the Fatemiyoun because It is the only thing they can do to address the devastating feeling of not being accepted as human beings, to feel power in their lives, and find some sense of meaning, however fleeting.

This perspective might clarify why Afghans were susceptible to joining the Fatemiyun when the Iranian government, in particular the Islamic Revolutionary Guard Corps (IRGC), launched its active recruitment campaign. In November 2015, The Guardian, for instance, reported regular recruitment by the Iranian regime particularly through mosques in cities such as Qom and Mashhad – which are holy places for Shia Muslims – where "the [Afghan] refugees, usually young men, sign up on a daily basis to go and fight for Iran in Syria." According to this report, Afghan men approached these mosques, queuing to get registered for joining the war in Syria, and conditions of recruitment were easy: "those interested have to prove they are Afghan, and singles or minors must have parental consent." According to this author's research, however, many youths joined the group without the consent of their families.

There were also cases of coerced enlisting of undocumented Afghans in Iran, as reported by Human Rights Watch in January 2016:

Iran has not just offered Afghan refugees and migrants incentives to fight in Syria, but several said they were threatened [by Iranian police] with deportation back to Afghanistan unless they did. Faced with this bleak choice, some of these Afghan men and boys fled Iran for Europe.

Afghan children have also been recruited into the Fatemiyun. In October 2017, Human Rights Watch presented cases of Afghans not yet 18, including a boy as young as 14, who had fought and died in Syria and had then been brought back to be buried in cemeteries across Iran.

While the vast majority of Fatemiyun members have been recruited in Iran, some men and boys in Afghanistan, again all Shia Hazaras and Sayyeds, were also attracted and joined the group, as has been reported from Bamyan, Herat, Mazar-e Sharif and through an "unofficial recruiting centre in west Kabul." In most cases, they either decided to join the group themselves or were encouraged by pro-Iran Afghan clerics to do so. These men and boys first went from Afghanistan into Iran through smuggling and from there were enlisted to fight in Syria.

The second explanation for why so many Afghans decided to join the Fatemiyun focuses not so much on external pressures and conditions, but rather on the individual fighters and their choices. There is some research that views the Syrian war as an arena in which diverse actors – ranging from states to individuals – have sought to maintain, transform or gain social, political and economic capital to pursue their interests in and through the conflict.[7] Seen from this perspective, different actors, including individuals, have been pursuing their different interests in and through the armed conflict in Syria.

Drawing on this second perspective, previous AAN research showed that some Afghan youths who had failed to integrate back into in their local communities in Afghanistan and then failed in their efforts to get to Europe opted instead to go to the Syrian battlefield. In their view – and of their peers and families – it was a means to show they had matured into 'responsible' men fighting a 'just' war, thereby achieving identity and status. By defending Shia shrines, as they viewed it, they won recognition for themselves, their families and Afghan communities in Iran. More importantly, their wages as Fatemiyun fighters meant they could support their parental families. Some even later married and established their own families in or moved them to Iran. They regarded Iran as a safer and better place to live than Afghanistan, given their improved, post-fighting in Syria status, at least for now.

Neither explanation tallies with the Iranian government's (and by extension Fatemiyun's) view of Afghan participation in the Syrian war, however. Both have justified the fighters' 'voluntary' participation as the need to defend Shia shrines and especially the shrine of Sayyeda Zeinab (one of the great grand-daughters of the Prophet) in southern Damascus, against assaults by the Islamic State (IS, also known as ISIS/ISIL/Daesh)–only an explanation after June 2014 when the group declared itself–and other 'takfiris' (who believe in killing Muslims of other sects and schools, especially Shias). The official explanations have thus focused on religious faith as the fighters' key and even sole motivating factor. As a staunch, long-time Fatemiyun member told AAN, "Nothing material can make someone sacrifice their life." Iranian officials have said they find the singling-out by reporters and observers of the Fatemiyun "bizarre," because, from their standpoint, "there is no reaction to the recruitment of Afghan citizens by the IS in West Asia [Middle East]."[8]

It is not clear how many or indeed whether Afghans have gone to Syria to fight against the Assad government. There seems to be some, suggested a 2015 AAN dispatch without giving more detail: Syria had turned, it said, into an "odd meeting place" for Afghans, with both Shia and Sunni Afghans pitted against one another there. Yet, given the relative lack of reporting on Sunni Afghan fighters, it seems doubtful that their numbers have in any way matched those of the Fatemiyun.

Some Fatemiyun fighters were certainly religiously motivated from the outset. Also, in many cases, what they say about why they fought changed– from saying they wanting to fight for Iran to get benefits, to defending a 'just' religious cause in Syria. This change in perception or self-justification appears to have come following their initial or subsequent deployments to the war and socialisation with comrades. The religious justification is very apparent in official Iranian and Fatemiyun narratives which fighters came to adopt, which references broader aims, such as defending Shia shrines and the faith as a whole, guarding defenceless people and securing not just Syria, but also the broader region, including Iran and Afghanistan against Islamic State incursions.

It also has to be stressed that, far from defending Shia shrines, the Fatemiyun have been deployed by Iran and the Syrian government far more widely: the photograph accompanying this piece, for example, is from Palmyra (Tadmur) which is a long way from any Shia religious sites which cluster around Damascus, with a couple more in the northern city of Aleppo. As Fullbright scholar Ahmad Shuja Jamal wrote:

> ... the Fatemiyoun has been deployed in most of the Syrian theater and used to spearhead operations to recapture territory, which then would be handed to Syrian troops to hold. The Fatemiyoun fighters either operate alone or, in some of the toughest battles like the recapture of Palmyra and Deir Ezzor, fight in conjunction with other so-called resistance forces, including the Lebanese Hezbollah, the Pakistani Shia mercenary force of Zeinabiyoun, and Russian forces...

Moreover, he writes that "[the] Fatemiyoun are sometimes referred to as "cannon fodder" for their deployment as an expendable force. Stories of high casualties in several Fatemiyoun operations appear to bear this out."

## Returning 'home': complexities

Given the very high casualty figures, large numbers of Fatemiyun fighters have returned to Iran injured or it is their remains that have been returned. One August 2015 study estimated there had been 121 deaths between January 2013 and August 2015 based on open-source data alone. A later paper in November 2018 put the dead and wounded in action rates respectively at 10 and 30-40 per cent in the period 2013-17, indicating 2,000 killed and 6,000-8,000 injured from among what the paper estimated was a peak strength of 20,000 active Fatemiyun members.

The Iranian authorities have glorified fallen fighters by naming streets after them, praising their sacrifices through state media and providing their families with livelihood support. They have also paraded their coffins and buried them in high-status cemeteries in Iran. This includes Behesht-e Zahra in Tehran where some fallen Fatemiyun fighters have been buried in a special section near the mausoleum of Ayatollah Khomeini, the architect of Iran's Islamic Revolution, and next to thousands of Iranian soldiers who died in the 1980s war with Iraq.

It seems the Iranian authorities might also fear that Fatemiyun returnees to Afghanistan could reveal details about the group's internal affairs. This author has heard from two families that Fatemiyun members who wanted to quit and return to Afghanistan were likely to run into troubles with their previous organisation and its Iranian patrons. A Herat-based sister of a Fatemiyun fighter said their family thought her brother's death in a traffic accident in Iran was a "conspiracy" because "the Iranians didn't want him to get back to Afghanistan and somehow disclose their secrets." She said her brother was a Fatemiyun commander and had been about to step down and come back home. In another instance, on a short visit back to Herat, a former Fatemiyun fighter said that Fatemiyun members were afraid of what the Iranians would do to them if they decided to abandon the group and return to Afghanistan. That is why they tended to hide their travel plans from both their Afghan and Iranian supervisors or lie to them about where they were going, as he had done himself (eg saying they were going on a pilgrimage to Mashhad city in Iran while actually visiting family in neighbouring Herat across the border). Although it is impossible to verify these statements, they at least indicate that some Fatemiyun men may be so entangled in the Syrian engagement that they cannot easily get out of it even if they wanted to.

As for coming back to Afghanistan, several sources have reported that thousands of Fatemiyun members have returned home. In April 2019, for instance, the Associated Press quoted an unnamed "senior official in Afghanistan's Interior Ministry who is familiar with government intelligence" as saying that "[roughly] 10,000 veterans of the [Fatemiyun] brigade have returned to Afghanistan." In his March 2019 study of the Fatemiyun, Jamal says that "[individual] Fatemiyun fighters are returning to Afghanistan in the thousands."[9]

However, these numbers are disputed and likely wrong. First, they are based on government intelligence (in the first source quoted above) and we do not know how this information is gathered or checked. Second, the vast majority of men joined the Fatemiyun in a bid to turn Iran into a more permanent 'home' for themselves and their families including by taking their families there. This casts doubt over their returning to Afghanistan in such high numbers.

Regardless of the number of Fatemiyun returnees, all existing reporting, including research, concurs that they struggle to return to civilian life and to find adequate and meaningful employment in order to make a decent living for themselves and their families. As Jamal writes, "Many fighters returned to the same kind of economic difficulties that they sought to escape by going to Syria."[10]

The returnees to Afghanistan face other serious concerns, too. First, they fear a possible crackdown by Afghan government security agencies for participating in a foreign war. According to Jamal, besides the Law on Crimes against Internal and External Security, the Penal Code of 2018 (which has been revised and went into effect in February 2019) provides a clue on how ex-fighters such as Fatemiyun returnees could be treated by the criminal justice system.[11] The code (article 245 (4)) stipulates "long-term imprisonment" for those taking part in "wars or internal armed conflicts of other countries."[12] As Jamal writes, however, Afghan government security agencies such as the Ministry of Interior and the National Directorate of Security are not actively looking for Fatemiyun returnees because "their hands are full with more pressing threats"[13] notably the ongoing full-scale insurgency across Afghanistan.

Second, Fatemiyun returnees are afraid of retaliation by the Islamic State-Khorasan Province (ISKP), the local IS franchise. Some potential links, for example, already exist between ISKP-claimed attacks against Shias in and around Herat city and the participation of some young men from Herat in the Syria war (see this previous AAN dispatch), to say the least.

Third, added to the above, is the recent designation in January 2019 by the US Treasury of the Fatemiyun Division (in Iranian military ranking) for 'terrorism' and 'human rights abuses' – charges that have been vehemently rejected by the Fatemiyun themselves. Some Afghan politicians, including Muhammad Mohaqqeq, former second deputy to the government's Chief Executive, also think they have done nothing wrong.

As Jamal says, there could be "better options" both for the returning fighters as well as to "keep similarly vulnerable young men out of foreign conflicts."[14] The Afghan government could clarify its stance on how it intends to deal with the returnees and, if prosecution is not its intended course of action, it could help assuage fears among ex-Fatemiyun fighters. This could be followed by reintegration, eg through the provision of employment opportunities, including within the security and defence forces. Jamal concludes: "Individual Fatemiyoun fighters who are returning to Afghanistan are struggling to build a life after giving up violence. Helping them reintegrate is thus primarily a humanitarian task."[15]

## Moving on: Contingencies

Speculation has arisen about future trajectories of the Fatemiyun group. Although some reporting has wondered if the group could be deployed by Iran to fight for its allies in Iraq and Yemen (see here, here, here and here), the focus in this section is entirely on Afghanistan.

Recent reporting has paid increasing attention to what Iran could or might want to do to with, as one report calls it, "tens of thousands of battle-hardened [Fatemiyun] fighters." This has sounded alarm bells among some Afghan officials who fear that the return of Fatemiyun fighters to the country could turn Afghanistan into "the next great sectarian battleground" (see here) between regional foes, in particular, Iran and Saudi Arabia. Some Afghan authorities and commentators have expressed concerns that Iran may be laying the groundwork for an organised presence of its Fatemiyun proxy in Bamyan, Kabul and the country at large (see here and here). Some reporting claims that the Fatemiyun as an organisation has already been implicated in recent violent disputes in Afghanistan, the central highlands of Hazarajat in particular (see here). For example, Antonio Giustozzi and Shoib Najafizada have claimed:

> [The] organization [Fatemiyun] got involved already in the conflict between Pashtun nomads and Hazara settlers in central Afghanistan. Alipur, in the past a commander linked to a local Hazara party, has joined hands with Fatimiyun and started recruiting veterans of Syria into his militia that has been blocking access to the pastures of Hazarajat in Behsud (Wardak) against armed nomads for years. The two communities accuse each other of aggression.

These reports on alleged organised Fatemiyun engagement in Afghanistan appear flawed on at least two grounds. First, it plays up the 'Fatemiyun threat' by relying mostly on statements from unnamed Afghan government officials who tend to blame Afghanistan's troubles on anyone but the government. Second, they do present no evidence for the involvement of the Fatemiyun as a group in recent violent clashes in Wardak (Behsud), Ghazni (Jaghuri and Malestan) or Uruzgan (Khas Uruzgan) provinces. Indeed on-the-ground monitoring has found no footprint of the Fatemiyun as a group in these clashes.

It is important to note that the Fatemiyun does have the potential to act, as a group, in places Iran sees as important to its interests. However, central

Afghanistan is not such a place, at least not yet (see also this Hasht-e-Sobh report). In fact, as AAN reported in November 2018 (see here and here), the violence in Jaghuri and Malestan districts in Ghazni province and Khas Uruzgan district in Uruzgan province in late October 2018 involved fighting between the Taleban on the one hand and government forces and pro-government militias on the other (although there was also an ethnic dimension with the Taleban pushing deep into predominantly Hazara-inhabited areas). Fatemiyun returnees might have joined the local militia groups but if they did, they did so as individuals; we have no indication that any fighting occurred on an organisational basis.

Conditions may, however, arise under which the Fatemiyun could be mobilised in Afghanistan as a group. Summing up the views of Afghan clerics and politicians, Jamal lists two such conditions:[16]

First, if the Afghan government continues its perceived prejudice against Hazaras, and continues to neglect development in Hazara areas, it could alienate the Hazara and Shia communities. Second, if the government fails to protect Hazara mosques and communities against IS- and Taleban-perpetrated violence, militia forces could form. Possible options for future mobilisation could be the self-organisation of Fatemiyun returnees, their co-opting by Shia political forces that could provide them with logistics in Afghanistan, or Iran keeping or raising a similar military formation when and where it needs to, including in Afghanistan. It is doubtful that Iran would disband the group in its entirety. It is instead most likely that Iran will maintain the current core of Fatemiyun, who could then mobilise from among the vulnerable Afghan refugee and migrant population residing in that country, when and if needed. But that time has not yet come, at least as far as Afghanistan is concerned. For the time being, reports from Iran indicate that, given the down scaling of the war in Syria, new recruitment into the Fatemiyun has stopped, the group is being downsized and its members are returning 'home,' mostly to Iran rather than Afghanistan.

## Afghan Government: A Passive Posture

So far, the Afghan government has responded to Iran's mobilisation of the Fatemiyun group in a reactive way. A few senior officials, most notably Mohaqqeq, praised "combatants" such as the Fatemiyun for their "victory against Daesh" in a November 2017 speech in Tehran. When his remarks created great controversy, he said his speech had been misinterpreted and that he had only mentioned them because they "had freely participated in the war against Daesh … But this is neither my policy nor our party's policy nor our government's policy [to uphold them]."

On other occasions, watchdog reports (such as the Human Rights Watch report on the recruitment of children into the Fatemiyun) prompted the Afghan government to respond, again in a reactive mode. In October 2017, for instance, the Afghan Ministry of Foreign Affairs asked Iran to stop "pressuring and enticing" Afghan migrants, and children in particular, to take part in "activities contravening international principles." In January 2018, the Afghan government asked Iran to dissolve the Fatemiyun group. In late March 2019, an Afghan presidential advisor responded to the Iranian leader's meeting with families of the Fatemiyun and his special praise for the group by saying that "Iran has abused Afghan migrants [living in that country]."

There are a variety of reasons why the Afghan government has failed to deal seriously with Iran on the Fatemiyun issue thus far. First of all, the Afghan government is in the weaker position, unable to hold it to account given the leverages Iran has over Afghanistan, notably on the issue of the refugee population and its trade advantage. Second, the Afghan government is partly responsible for the conditions that have led many to flee the country, including those who have ended up being enlisted in the Fatemiyun. Third, given the proxy nature of the group, Iranian officials have engaged in a politics of denial, stating repeatedly that those who have formed and joined the Fatemiyun have done so on a 'voluntary' basis without Tehran taking any part in it. The Fatemiyun do not accept the proxy label either.

How much the issue of the Fatemiyun is tied to the broader issue of Afghan refugees and migrants in Iran came to light most recently in May 2019. Then, Abbas Araqchi, an Iranian deputy minister of foreign affairs, said that Iran would ask the Afghans living in that country to leave if "[US] sanctions are effective and our oil sales get to zero" and that "it was up to them where to go." He was severely criticised, including by influential Iranians (see, for example, this media report) who reminded him of Iran's leader's praise for Afghans such as the Fatemiyun who "participated well and fought well in situations such as Syria." The Iranian official later retracted his statement and said his remarks had been addressed to Europeans (warning them that Afghan refugees would leave Iran for Europe), not Afghans.

Apart from an Afghan government response that Iran should behave "responsibly" with the Afghans who live in that country, Araqchi's statement caused harsh reactions even among some Fatemiyun members. One of them told AAN: If you [Iran] are in danger, you make us Fatemiyun and if you need labour for the construction of your country, you make us workers. If you have a budget deficit, you tax us more and now that you are under the pressure of sanctions, you use us like a tool.

Existing studies on the Fatemiyun have focused on the Afghan men fighting for the Iran-backed government in Syria. The women behind the fighters – wives, mothers and sisters – have remained invisible, despite the fact that many fighters decided to go to Syria with family concerns in mind. Based on interviews with ten women in the Afghan city of Herat and Iranian capital Tehran, AAN guest author Mohsen Hamidi* uncovers what the Syrian war has meant for these Afghan women. They reveal the crucial role women played encouraging or trying to discourage their men from going to fight in Syria, the struggle of surviving without their menfolk, and for some, the ordeal of getting a dead body back, and for others, coping with men who have returned injured or traumatised. The interviews show how a faraway conflict has put many families in dispute with each other – not everyone viewed the Syrian war as a 'jihad' or believed the Fatemiyun had gone there out of piety.

## Why focus on the women?

The first dispatch in this two-part series looked at the Fatemiyun from the perspective of the male fighters. It explored the reasons for many Afghan men deciding to fight in Syria–from wanting to improve life for themselves and their families through the benefits provided by Iran to Fatemiyun, to a desire to protect Shia shrines in Syria, to seeing war as a way to become men. It considered the role of Iran's heavy propaganda campaign in recruiting fighters to support its ally, the Assad government, in the increasingly sectarian Syrian civil war, and the very heavy casualties taken by the Fatemiyun as it was deployed across Syria in some of the toughest battles of the conflict.

This second dispatch differs in two significant ways: it takes families and their decision-making as its point of departure, rather than individuals, and views the conflict and its impact from the point of view of the women whose men opted, or were compelled, to fight away from home, rather than from the standpoint of the men.[17]

This is important because crucial decisions, such as whether to join or stay with the Fatemiyun, have typically been made within the family context – through lengthy talks with spouses, parents and siblings – taking into account family concerns, such as financial support or the option to move one's family from Afghanistan to Iran. The members of the all-male Fatemiyun fighter group were never just isolated individuals, free from family ties or considerations. This is reflected in the current study.

This dispatch reveals the daily struggles of the fighters' families. As such, it may inspire greater efforts to reduce the conflict, by (re)humanising the people involved. The dispatch also fills a research gap, breaking new ground, since, as far as the author is aware, this is the first research on the women behind Fatemiyun fighters. For detail about the methodology behind this research, including how interviewees were chosen, five living in Herat and five in Tehran, and how this sensitive subject was tackled [18].The rest of this dispatch is organised in three parts and a conclusion.

First, it examines the roles women played when men were deciding to go to war in Syria, whether trying to argue against or supporting or being bypassed.

Second, it explores women's struggles to survive while their men are away fighting, whether their troubles are financial or being left alone without a man's protection in a patriarchal society. It looks at the rituals and support groups which have helped ease absences.

Third, it hears some harrowing stories from women coping with bereavement (ten per cent of the Fatemiyun are estimated to have been killed at the peak of the group's involvement), or with men returning injured (30-40 per cent) or severely traumatised by the war. It also looks at how they have tried to counter jibes that their men were fighting for material benefits or in someone else's war, not a jihad.

A conclusion surveys the complicated feelings many women whose men have fought in Syria are left with.

## Men going to war

### Women's stances

The distant Syrian war became near and very real for many Afghan families when their men, or men they knew, started signing up to join the Fatemiyun group. A first trigger was often increasing exposure to the conflict. Friends and relatives living in Iran began leaving for Syria as a result of an active campaign, including by Afghan clerics and sympathisers among the Afghan diaspora there, from about 2013 on. In Afghanistan, social media was an important means through which many young men learned about the armed conflict in Syria and, more importantly, how to participate in it (see examples in this previous AAN dispatch). More traditional means such as sermons or conversations in mosques also made many men think about going. When they began weighing up the pros and cons of joining the war in Syria, they often did so within a family context or with family concerns in mind.

The women in the family most affected by these men's decisions were their wives and mothers; children, including daughters, were also affected, but might not have realised the seriousness of the decisions. Also, most of the men going were young, so if they had children, they would also usually still be too young to be fully aware of what was going on. More generally, making such a decision affected the whole family, both male and female members, with ripple effects extending far more widely, to extended families, local communities and beyond.

In most of the families within the purview of this research, women's opinions counted, relatively speaking. This meant that major issues, such as a man's departure to join the war in Syria, involved consultation and negotiation in which women took an active part. Few were families in which women had to comply with whatever decisions their men made. In a few cases, the women, only found out about their men's plans through extended family members after the men had already left. In these cases, the men went to fight in Syria from Iran, while the women were in Afghanistan, with the men seemingly not wanting to cause family disputes that they would be unable to manage easily from afar.

Many families, and in particular mothers and wives, initially tried to discourage their men (sons and husbands) from fighting in Syria –

although this discouragement was stronger in Afghanistan than in Iran, where the environment was far more supportive of and conducive to Afghans' participation in the Syrian war. In nearly all cases, mothers and wives felt torn: they felt a profound desire to keep sons and husbands with them safely at home, but also knew that the material benefits provided to the Fatemiyun would ease difficult living conditions.

### Making the decision together

Some women described how they had delayed or tried to string out discussions and decision-making in the hope of dissuading their men from going. After months and, in some cases, years of on-and-off negotiations within the family, these women finally agreed to the men's decisions. (There are also families where the women successfully managed to fully dissuade men from leaving, but this study focuses on families whose men went to Syria). For example, in one family, which is very devout, a then Herat-based mother described how she bargained with her then Tehran-based son through social media for a year and a half, until she ultimately acquiesced to his departure to Syria. It ended tragically for this family:

He said, "Mum let me go to Syria." He was just 16 then and had gone with his kaka [paternal uncle] to Iran through smuggling to find work there. I didn't let him go because of his young age. He was also my eldest son. I wanted to see him rather than to let him go to Syria. He insisted for one year and a half. Sometimes he would tease me by writing: "Bye mum, I'm going to Syria." Some other times he wouldn't reply to my calls and messages, leaving me concerned and not able to sleep at night. I said "No" when we were in touch. I said, "You should be at least 18 or reach an age that you can tolerate seeing someone die and not tremble." He kept raising the issue and telling me he really meant to go to defend the [Shia] shrines [in Syria]. There was lots of preaching in Iran about it and we're also strong believers. So, I finally let him go and gave him my halaliyat [forgave him for whatever wrong he might have committed in the past] …We said goodbye [in our last chat]. I never saw him again. I didn't even hear his voice again … He just went once and he was martyred.

Couples also discussed the husbands' possible participation in the Syrian war for months, thrashing out how their families would function in their absence, socially, financially and in other ways. What featured in these discussions, as well, were the wives' concerns and deep desire to have their husbands stay at home.

A good example is a Herat-based couple where the husband finally opted to go to Syria after years of intermittent discussions within the family, including with his wife and a brother who was already a Fatemiyun member in Tehran and who was encouraging him to sign up. As a religious couple, both are religious students, with two children, they had tried to earn a decent living in seminaries in both Kabul and Mazar-e Sharif and then back in Herat for several years, but in vain. As the recognition that they would not be able to support their family in Afghanistan in a dignified way sharpened, they saw the war in Syria as an opportunity. Since the wife's parental family lived in the same neighbourhood in Herat, he could go without her and the two children being left completely on their own. The couple agreed and the husband followed his brother's call to enlist as a Fatemiyun member and work as a cleric, preaching the 'Fatemiyun cause' and performing religious rituals for Fatemiyun fighters in Syria (for detail on how clerics such as this Afghan man motivated combatants including Fatemiyun to fight in Syria, see here).[19] The opportunity to pursue a non-combat role in Syria made it easier for the husband and wife to arrive at this decision in agreement. The wife and children stayed behind in Herat, supported by remittances sent by the husband – directly or through his brother and other relatives in Iran. They are currently planning to move to Tehran. The wife said:

It is of course difficult for us to be away from each other. It is hard for every wife and husband. It is more difficult for the wife. But as a family we should tolerate the distance patiently. Syria has helped him get to know himself better. It is also a religious duty to go and help the people there. He also found a job and an income and even got us a residence permit in Iran.

### Making the decision alone

By contrast, the cases in which the men did not consult the women on their decision to fight in Syria, for whatever reason, were markedly different. Their decisions led to family disputes, but also reveal, strikingly, the agency some women have been able to exercise to prevent or discontinue some men's involvement in the war. A Herat-based woman said her brother's friend's wife had successfully prevented her husband from joining her brother in Syria by convincing him, often in squabbles, that he could not leave her and their children entirely on their own in Kabul (the husband joined the Afghan police instead, but was killed in the war in Afghanistan). Another example is a Herat-based wife who went to great lengths to make her husband leave Syria where he was fighting. She put it bluntly:

He would gone to Iran to find a better job and a better income. I didn't hear from him for three months or so. I then learned from my da'i [also known as mama, maternal uncle] that he would gone to fight in Syria. When I received a call from him, I quarrelled with him, asking "Why have you gone there?" and telling him to come back immediately. He came back home after a while, when he could. He was always talking about Syria and he again wanted to go. I fought with him again and there was lots of jang o jedal [wrangling and bickering] between us. He didn't give in and neither did I. I said "You've got kids and you must think about them. What will happen to them if you were no more?" I eventually went to the house of my khosor [father-in-law] and demanded a divorce, just to put more pressure on him to change his mind. His parents and siblings were also against him going. Though he again went to Iran, he soon came back home without going to Iran or Syria again.

The same interviewee spoke about how another woman she knew had managed to stop her husband from departing for the Syrian battlefield by pleading with him not to leave her and the children on their own, persuading him that she was content with whatever work he did and whatever money he could make in Herat. Her husband is a plasterer engaged in informal construction work and looks for work anywhere in Afghanistan, including Herat city and recently in Lashkargah city in Helmand province.

In other cases, men who had wanted to join the war in Syria, especially younger ones, entirely bypassed their families and made their decisions in concert with their peers instead. This points to the important role of extra-familial ties, particularly friendship ties, in decision-making, but also does not exclude family connections altogether, since many of these men have been enabled by fighting in Syria to support their families back home. (For more background on the role of families and peers in the context of decision-making, see AAN's previous reporting on migration to Europe). A Herat-based woman whose brother is a Fatemiyun fighter described how he was influenced by his peers to go to war in Syria:

One of his close friends came back to Herat from Syria and whispered thoughts into his ears to go to Syria. We [his sister and parents] said, "You'd better not go, there's war and It is difficult," but he didn't listen to us. So, he went because his friends were going and he wanted to fight beside them. He first got smuggled from [Herat] to Iran, and then signed up for the Syrian war.

In some cases, women used all the influence they had to stop men from going but ultimately failed. "Zur-e zanhabamardhanamirasa [women's force is no match for men's]," said one woman living in Tehran whose sister's son joined the Fatemiyun, summing up how an entire family including a mother, a sister and herself failed to keep a young man, a drug addict heavily influenced by his gang of friends, away from the Syrian battlefield. A similar experience was reported by another Tehran-based woman who did all she could, but failed to prevent her husband, also a drug addict under enormous peer pressure, from going to fight in Syria. Their stories point to the fact that drug addicts and other 'problematic' youths (those who have troubled relationships with their parents and siblings) are not only in a far more precarious situation and at greater risk of being recruited into the Fatemiyun, but are also more difficult to dissuade.

### Changing minds because of war-related benefits

For almost all the women interviewed, the positions they took on whether to agree to men going or continuing to fight in Syria were not static, but changed over time as circumstances varied. In most cases, their stances gradually shifted from adamant resistance to increasing acceptance after the men's participation in the war began bringing both material and immaterial benefits to their families. These benefits included better pay than from most jobs available to them in Afghanistan and Iran, more regular or permanent residence permits in Iran or the possibility of taking their families there and increased recognition in Iran such as preferential treatment with Iranian government institutions. There was also a growing conviction that their men were fighting a 'just' cause. These benefits definitely came as a relief to families in living in difficult conditions in Iran, especially those lacking residence papers.

This change was especially observed in families that had moved from Afghanistan to Iran after they had been given residence permits because their men were fighting in Syria. For families that were already living in

Iran, their men's involvement in the Syrian war and the residence permits saved them from constantly worrying about being rounded up by the Iranian police for deportation. They also reported better access to public services such as education for their children and healthcare for the elderly and infirm members of their families. This change in attitude towards men's involvement in the Syrian war was thus far greater among the families of the Fatemiyun living in Tehran than those in Herat.

Other factors that changed Iran-based Fatemiyun families' perspectives included pervasive exposure to extensive propaganda, including from Afghan clerics and sympathisers. The propaganda justified going to fight in Syria as a highly religious act that was socially valued. Its aim was to motivate families to support and press for men to join up. Increased social respect for Fatemiyun fighters in Iran, the senior ones, in particular, was real, illustrated by the fact that they were easily able to get visiting relatives' Iranian visas extended or could, more importantly, intervene and get the release of undocumented relatives from deportation camps.

There were also other practical benefits. The women related to the two drug addicts quoted above increasingly approved of the men fighting in Syria once they realised it had helped them overcome their addiction and made them more religious and responsible. This, in turn, improved the prospects for their families back in Iran. In another example of a man recruited from a precarious situation, a Tehran-based mother said her son's participation in the Syrian war had helped him overcome a series of troubles such as separating from his fiancée, dropping out from university and joblessness. It had also enabled his parents and siblings to move to Iran:

The benefits have been very good, spiritually and otherwise. He was an immature and inexperienced youth. He's become mature and has travelled to see other people and a different place. He's seen a war and has taken part in it. He's really more experienced now. He's also become more religious. He pays more attention to saying his daily prayers and following religious rituals. I'm very happy about it. I'm even now happy with him going to Syria. There's no problem, even if he becomes a martyr in Syria. I now understand him much better. I was not happy then [when living in Herat], but I am now [after moving to Iran]. I understand that our children are no better and no more than the children of Hazrat Fatema Zahra[19] and the children of the martyrs of Islam.

186

There was an arc about how families, including the women, felt about their men going to fight in Syria. From initially discouraging the move, they increasingly accepted the situation. This was especially true for those who had left Afghanistan to live in Iran. The women were, in many cases, an active and integral part of the decision to be involved in the war, even those who had not been consulted beforehand or had been completely sidelined. In any case, deciding whether or not to take part in the Syrian war made this distant conflict more tangible for these families. However, in many cases, it also led to bitter disputes over what to do, not just in terms of their men going to war there but also the war's legitimacy, as will be discussed below.

## When men are away

### Women's struggles

The men's absence had more impact on families in Afghanistan than in Iran. None of the families had men at home, but those in Iran had more access to 'war-related' benefits than those in Afghanistan. However, Afghanistan-based families' lives also improved when they moved to Iran thanks to their men fighting in Syria. Of the ten families involved in this study, four were already in Iran when their men went to war in Syria, three left Afghanistan to live in Iran, one was preparing to move to Iran, one had their man back in Herat and he decided not to return and one had stopped their man returning to war in Syria.

The most heavily-impacted families were those left with no adult man at home, especially wives on their own with small children. Interviewees said the mere presence of a man provided protection, given the patriarchal social context in which these families live, whether in Afghanistan and Iran. In this context, the fact that some of the interviewees were living on their own without a closely-related adult man (eg father, husband, brother) was generally considered 'abnormal' and 'bad' (especially if there were unmarried women in the household). According to a Tehran-based woman, her cousin's departure to Syria was difficult because it deprived his mother and two sisters of male presence and support at home:

Though he usually used to hang out with his friends before he went [to Syria], It is difficult for his family that he's away now. They don't have any other men at home. His dad had passed away. His mum is frail and unwell because she's suffering from high blood pressure and asthma. He has two young [unmarried] sisters at home and an elder brother – he lives nearby, but has wife and children of his own. The elder brother visits them [mother and two sisters] sometimes. So, they've at least got him around. Wives were most affected by men's absence. A Herat-based wife who remained alone with her two small children after her husband went to Syria had to ask her father and male siblings who lived nearby to come and stay at her house, especially at night. This was seen to offer her protection in the male-dominated community she lived in and to guard against or prevent local community members from talking about her behind her back.

Some women who were living with their in-laws (khesh) felt their husbands' absence in Syria and the lack of their company and support keenly. This was especially so where wives and their in-laws were not on good terms. A Tehran-based wife described her difficulties:

I don't have my [parental] family here [in Iran] while my husband's relatives are all here and around. My [parental] family is in Afghanistan. It was difficult for me and my little kid to have him not with us while I was living in my in-law's place. I was not happy and always talked to my husband about it. So, I moved out four or five months ago. I now live on my own and receive money from my husband to keep life running.

Living a day-to-day life without a man was a struggle for the interviewees. Men's absence required these families, the wives, in particular, to carry out male family roles themselves, including buying necessities in the market, finding and moving home if rent agreements changed and arranging protection for themselves and their children when needed. As women became responsible for all the housework, some reported getting help from female and male relatives with whom they were on good terms (if available, and often more from their own side than their husband's). Seen from a different perspective, men's absence forced some women to develop new skills and deal with the world outside the home, as also implied in the quote above by the woman who decided to live independently in the wake of her husband going to Syria.

Managing family finances has been another struggle for women, especially wives after their men joined the Fatemiyun group. When the exchange rate was still favourable, there were not too many financial hassles for these families to worry about. The Iranian government provided a monthly income of three million tomans – roughly 50,000-60,000 afghanis (1,000-

1,100 US dollars) – for the first few years of the Syrian war. Things changed, however, when the Iranian currency, began to fall sharply; since early 2018; its value has fallen by over 60 per cent. That meant the monthly income came to be worth about 18,000 afghanis (because of the depreciation of the afghani, as well, that currently amounts to only about 225 US dollars). This severe financial blow was felt both by Afghan families in Iran and the families in Afghanistan that depended on remittances sent from Iran, including families of the Fatemiyun. Family purses had to be tightened, but how to do this was tough. Interviewees described the negotiations, carried out through social media and when men returned for visits back home, over how much and where to spend the money.

In some extreme cases, the unprecedented depreciation of the Iranian currency was one of the reasons why some men decided to stop fighting in Syria. A Herat-based woman, the sister of a Fatemiyun fighter, said: His friends didn't go [back] and neither did he. One reason was that their pay got less and less because the toman-to-afghani rate became very low. There was not much war or much recruitment, either. So, he and his friends decided it was not worth going any more.

### Women's rituals and gatherings

For all the interviewees, in particular mothers and wives, being apart from their men was a constant struggle. They were constantly anxious about their safety, justifiably so given the high levels of Fatemiyun casualties in the Syrian war. To allay their fears, family members and in particular women resorted to a host of religious rituals including performing prayers (namaz and dua) and nazr (cooking and hosting/distributing food for free). Through these rituals, they sought to invoke divine protection for their men on the Syrian battlefield. This is illustrated by the following three quotes:

*It was very hard for our parents to bear his absence. They were always praying for his protection. We, his sisters, were also praying for his safe-keeping. We all were worried about him. He was always in our thoughts and prayers.*

-A Herat-based sister of a Fatemiyun fighter

*After he left, we went to [a local shrine] and prayed to God to guard him in Syria. His mum cooked ash-e posht-e pa [literally "soup behind the footstep," a ritual dish served to pray for someone's safe return] in Mashhad [centre of Iran's Razavi Khorasan province neighbouring Herat]. His sister also cooked this food in Tehran to pray for his safety in his Syria [war] journey. His mum also did nazr for him to pray for his safety.*

-A Tehran-based maternal aunt of a Fatemiyun fighter

*Every morning I prayed for my husband. The day my son also went [to Syria], I began saying two prayers, one for him and one for his father. I didn't want to be lazy.*

– A Tehran-based wife and mother of two Fatemiyun fighters (husband and son).

While these rituals were important to individuals performing them, those enacted collectively also served a social function. For instance, the women behind the Fatemiyun fighters brought together many other women affiliated to the Fatemiyun or not, in a ritual called sofrehsalawat (literally 'tablecloth of salutation'). This is a special kind of nazr (the cooking/hosting ritual) for women only (with any small children). It is held quite frequently. Besides being an opportunity for praying for the safety of the Fatemiyun fighters and the fulfilment of other wishes, the sofrehsalawat serves as a venue for simply getting together and sharing a meal and as a means to relieve stress. Through such events, women socialise and are able to stay up-to-date about the goings-on in one another's families.

In these gatherings, women spoke about the men who were, in one way or another, related to them and had left or were leaving or thinking about whether to leave for the Syrian war (although they kept some information private, such as actual decisions and dates of departure, or shared them only with close confidantes). During these conversations, they discussed the advantages and disadvantages of joining the war for the families, including considering what had happened to those they knew who were already in Syria and to their families in Afghanistan and Iran. These events thus played a role in shaping family decision-making – to go to Syria, or to stay there. Discussions went far beyond just the perceived benefits of joining the war in Syria for the men and their families. There were many contrasting voices. Representing several other interviewees, a Herat-based woman, the sister of a Fatemiyun fighter, said:

From sofrehsalawat ceremonies [and elsewhere], we were learning that those who had gone to fight in Syria had gotten rich, were getting [good] sums of money and were buying themselves things [land, house]. But he [my brother] was not getting rich and not bringing money home. Then what was the use of [him going to] the war in Syria? Nesf-e-nan rahat-e jan [Better to eat half a piece of bread and be comfortable]. Working here or in Iran would be better.

This reveals that the Fatemiyun group and the group of women related to its members were never a monolithic collective with only one voice and one narrative. While some women defended their men's participation on religious grounds, others countered that these families had mainly been swayed by material benefits. Some women behind the Fatemiyun fighters were indeed very frank in acknowledging the pivotal role material benefits had played in their men's departure to Syria and in them consenting to these decisions. Several other interviewees, however, especially those living in Tehran, spoke about how difficult they found it when others did not accept their religious justification for their men's participation in the Syrian war. This is illustrated by the following two quotes:

> Our relatives who are really near and dear to us aren't happy about him [my son] going to Syria. They say it is a pity he does this thing. His youth is wasted. They are also worried that something bad will happen to him there. My sisters and brothers tell me these things. Those who are more distant relatives say he has gone there for the money, the document [Iranian residence permit] and to live in Iran. We keep hearing these things and feel very bad and offended.

– A Tehran-based mother of a Fatemiyun fighter

> Our own relatives were against him going to Syria. They asked why I sent my son. Some were even saying "You sent him to bring money for you from there." These words have really been hurting me. They did not understand what I was telling them about defending the shrine of namus-e khoda [God's honour].[20]

– A Tehran-based wife and mother of two Fatemiyun fighters (husband and son)

Several women indicated that it was a constant struggle to explain to other people, including their close relatives, why their men had gone to fight in

Syria. They found it difficult to tolerate perspectives, including from within the Fatemiyun, which countered their explanations in bitter ways. But the high instances of casualties (deaths and injuries) and traumatic events once the men were in Syria exposed these families to far tougher questions in terms of justifying their men's involvement, both internally and in their encounters with their wider communities.

## Men killed, injured or traumatised

### Women coping with loss

Casualties among the Fatemiyun have been unsettlingly high: ten per cent killed and 30 to 40 per cent wounded at the estimated peak of 20,000 personnel from 2013 to 2018 (see the first dispatch of this series). Of the ten women interviewed, three had suffered bereavement, three had had their men return injured and rest their men traumatised, including after witnessing close friends and other comrades die horrible deaths. For instance, a Herat-based woman who maintains regular contact with several Fatemiyun families in Herat and Tehran said, "So many men got martyred in Syria. For example, there are so many men from [an area in Tehran] who have been fighting in Syria. There are very few families without a martyr there."

Given the high number of casualties, the women also suffered from the catastrophic war in Syria in an indirect way. The biggest shock came when they, mothers, sisters and wives in particular, learned of the deaths of their sons, brothers or husbands. Their descriptions of these painful moments were moving. Representing the three women who lost their men in the Syrian war, a Tehran-based mother, who had already lost a brother fighting for the government security forces in Afghanistan and who had moved to Iran to meet her son coming back from the Syrian war, said:

After arriving in Tehran, I noticed many of our relatives came to our place at once. I had told my husband not to inform anyone about my arrival, though. I wanted to be on my own for some time and was impatiently waiting to see my son back... I thought our relatives were coming to express their condolence to me on the death of my martyred brother in Afghanistan. My paternal uncle talked about him, my martyred brother in Afghanistan, and said "You were khahar-e shahid [sister of a martyr] and now you have become madar-e shahid [mother of a martyr]. [Name of her son] has been martyred in Syria." I paused after hearing this. I did not shake, but felt I was going down as ice melts. I felt I was being levelled to the ground and going down and the earth was opening.

They [Iran's authorities] provide a place to live, such as apartments, to the families of the martyred. They can live in that place for as long as they wish and are alive. But they are not owners and cannot pass that on as property after their death. There are apartment complexes for these families where they can live during their lifetimes. This is what my mum told me after coming home [to Herat] for a visit. She will soon go back to Iran. If they did not want to live [in the apartment complex], they would be given [money for] their rent and it would be up to them how to spend it and where to live. They also get the monthly pay of their martyred son [paid by the Iranian government's Foundation of Martyrs and Veterans Affairs]. They used to get support from him from Syria and Iran while he was alive, and they were living here in Herat.

One Tehran-based interviewee who had lost a son in Syria about three years ago said Iranian financial support had been decreasing over time, from a peak of 2.2 million tomans per month in 2016 to 1.2 million tomans per month in early 2019, a fall of about 55 per cent (at the time of writing, one million tomans was about 5,500-6,000 afghanis or 70-77 US dollars). Before the interviewee's son went to Syria, her husband had been dying of cancer and she had to support a family of four children – one daughter and three sons – on her own. Her request for aid at the time had been rejected, nastily, by the relevant Iranian authorities:

Because we were having a tough life, I once approached the komite-ye emdad [Imam Khomeini Relief Committee, a major Iranian charity organisation] for help. An officer there told me, "Woman, go! We cannot even help our own Iranians, and Afghans come here." I said "My husband has cancer and is dying. I have children." The officer said, "Don't argue with me!" I said, "You are Muslims and following the religion of Islam. You should help me in this situation. Many had introduced you to us to go to and get some help." But the officer took our [temporary migration] registration cards and tore them up. So I even lost my cards. We had registered but didn't get the [refugee] documents [known in Iran as amayesh cards].

In addition to some money and a food stipend from the Iranian government because of the death of her son in Syria, she and her remaining children work to make a living in Iran. However, residence papers are no longer a concern for them, as this family received them after their son fought in Syria. They might now even get Iranian citizenship following the son's death.

There has also been support of a religious, psychological and social nature for bereaved families. Several interviewees spoke about collective pilgrimages to Shia shrines in Mashhad and Qom, considered Iran's two holiest cities, and Damascus in Syria, especially the shrine of Sayyeda Zeinab. These would obviously not have happened without Iranian support. The women said the pilgrimages helped them begin coping with their bereavement. There were also informal support groups for bereaved women, both on and offline either organised by the women themselves or the Iranian government (or a combination of the two). Online, women formed groups through social media platforms such as Telegram (before and even after its filtering in Iran) where they wrote and talked to one another about what they were going through and shared memories and pictures. In actual get-togethers, often once a week on Thursdays before the weekend, they gathered to pray, read the Quran and listen to religious sermons and other speeches, including by Iranian clerics who tend to portray their losses in highly favourable religious terms. For instance, they indicated that the dead men had attained, as a Tehran-based interviewee put it, "one of the highest degrees of martyrdom in the presence of Allah the Almighty." The women also visit the graves of their men and others in cemeteries in Iran, both individually and collectively.

These women's activities and the official support accorded by the Iranian government also served to make both the Fatemiyun-related women and other Afghan women in Iran aware of the recognition Iran has given to these families. This, in turn, has made other families think about or be more receptive to the idea of men going to fight in Syria.

### Women coping with controversy

From the outset, there were bitter controversies about Afghan men fighting in Syria, the benefits they and their families receive, the status of men who lost their lives fighting in Syria and whether the sacrifices were worth it. With men getting killed or injured at very high rates, disputes became even more prominent. This has been very disconcerting for family members including women, in particular mothers and wives.

However, these controversies were not often spoken about in public. Moreover, members of Fatemiyun-related families tended to maintain limited interaction with others who challenged them over their men's involvement in the Syrian war.

In some instances, nevertheless, the contentious issues were discussed among Fatemiyun-related families themselves. In a Thursday get-together of women who had lost men in Syria referred to above, a Tehran-based woman who lost a son in the Syrian war addressed this question to the 'Haj Agha' (Iranian cleric) leading the discussion that day:

It is upsetting that some people don't consider our martyrs as martyrs. They say they have been killed in a foreign war. This is even said by our close relatives, who tell us, "Your sons or husbands haven't been martyred. You sent them to get killed in Syria intentionally." Even a cleric said those who went and lost their lives in Syria had not been martyred but were killed. The Haj Agha's reply was that those who say these things are gomrah [misguided] who want to impose their beliefs on the people.

Although the Iranian cleric's answer was a conclusive one, whether she was convinced by his answer is a different matter.

In Herat and Afghanistan more broadly, Fatemiyun-related families faced an additional controversy: why should men chose to fight jihad in Syria and not, for instance, against insurgents in Afghanistan that have also attacked religious places like mosques? Fatemiyun families including women found this question disturbing, but they were themselves unable (or unwilling) to elaborate, apart from saying that Islam has no borders. Even if some families got involved in heated disputes over this and other questions, answers were never convincing for the other side.

The controversy not only affected the Fatemiyun families but also the wider communities in which they live, including in Iran. This was even reflected in a rare Iranian news report about a Fatemiyun woman who had lost her husband in Syria. It recounts her meeting on a train two Iranian women who were opposed to the Iranian government's intervention there. A degree of jealousy or unhappiness towards Fatemiyun's privileges appears to be mixed in their argument:[21]

Once the two Iranian women noticed my husband was a Fatemiyun martyr, they said "You got 8 million tomans because your husband went to fight [in Syria]." I said "Look at me and my child's conditions. With these conditions, did we get eight million tomans? We still live in a rented house." I...said "If they gave you eight million tomans, you would also go ahead and send your dear ones there to bring you money." They said "It is none of our business. That alien country has nothing to do with us." I said, "What you mean by 'alien country'. If there's war in a Muslim country, we must all help. It is related to all of us. There's no such thing as our country and their country." My daughter afterwards told her amma [paternal aunt] that [one of the two Iranian women] was an old woman who was very bi-hijab [unveiled].

Why Afghan men go to war in Syria, why their jihad should be waged in Syria and how those killed in Syria should be treated have been particularly unsettling questions for the Fatemiyun families, including women. There has been no convincing response for those who asked. Many women who have lost their men in the Syrian war and others continue to wonder at whether the entire involvement was ultimately worth it.

*Women coping after men return*

The Syrian war has also given the women behind the Fatemiyun other problems. Once wounded and no longer able to fight, men were sent back to Iran for hospital care provided by the Iranian government. Once discharged, however, they returned to their homes, where it was women, mothers and wives in particular, who provided essential care to help them return to normal life. This has been a tremendous ordeal for women. Three of the interviewees were responsible for dealing with men with various injuries, including hands and legs shattered by shrapnel and a jaw hit by a bullet. In many cases, it took months for these men to recover, if they recovered at all, during which the women provided constant care, as well as prayers and other supportive rituals they believed would hasten the healing. However, the physical and mental scars of war will long remain with the men and their families.

Besides their physical injuries, according to all ten women interviewed, the Fatemiyun men have been severely traumatised. Upon their return, some men confided in their mothers and wives in particular about their terrible experiences in the war, especially their witnessing friends and comrades whom they had come to know intimately dying terrifying deaths. In addition to signs resembling the symptoms of post-traumatic stress disorder (those affected were called mawjishoda – shell-shocked – by the interviewees), such as nightmares, flashbacks, waking visions and unaccountable anger, the men suffer high levels of survivor guilt. Three quotes below describe the trauma of war, one indicating the psychological consequences of witnessing war crimes:

*After he returned, he was not the previous man. He was aggressive. He had nightmares. Sometimes he cried loudly. He was depressed and often nervous. He was always saying he must return, he must go back to the war in Syria and he must be martyred… He was not talking about the benefits Iran was giving the combatants any longer, but was always saying he didn't deserve martyrdom and must go back to get martyred. This was very worrying for me. Some nights, he talked about his close friends who had been martyred there in frightening ways.*

– A Herat-based wife of a Fatemiyun fighter

*My son is now mentally unstable. If the TV volume is a bit high or the kids make some noise, he soon becomes angry. He becomes irritated. He cannot tolerate sound easily. These are the effects of the noise of war and explosions, I suppose. No one knows what he's going through. These things happen to him sometimes. He's no longer calm. He is not happy. He says he never feels happy anymore.*

– A Tehran-based mother of a Fatemiyun fighter

*He said he would certainly go back to Syria after I told him not to go for the sake of his wife and children. He had one child then. He talked about the severity of the war, about Daesh kidnapping young girls and slaughtering and decapitating men, even old men … They [Daesh] slaughtered mothers and fathers and little children in front of the rest of their families. He said he was not at rest even for a second after seeing these scenes in Syria. I told him not to go this time, but he said it was just the beginning of his work in Syria. My parents fell at his feet, begging him not to go, but it was no use in keeping him away from Syria. His wife asked me to intervene, but we all failed in stopping him from going to Syria again.*

– A Herat-based sister of a Fatemiyun fighter

War crimes were also perpetrated in Syria by pro-regime forces (details on the serious violations of human rights and international humanitarian law committed by all parties to the conflict can be read in this February 2018 report of the Independent International Commission of Inquiry on the Syrian Arab Republic). It is possible that the Fatemiyun were involved in these crimes. AAN received information about at least one such case, on 15 February 2015, reported by human rights activists in Syria. According to this information, the Fatemiyun were part of a fighting force comprised of "[Pakistani] Zainabyoun, [Lebanese] Hezbollah, [Syrian] Assad army and Assad militants [possibly militias]" that blocked and attacked various small towns in the countryside north of Aleppo, namely in the Al-Mallah, Retyan, Herdatnin and Bashkoy areas. While the Syrian forces attacked houses in the towns driving some inhabitants to flee, the Fatemiyun were reportedly stationed at checkposts outside the towns and were involved in shooting fleeing civilians in their cars. In total, 43 civilians were killed and 150 more were injured (along with nine members of the opposition Free Syrian Army who were also killed). It is not clear whether the number of victims included only those harmed at the checkposts or also those in town. AAN has been unable to independently verify this report.

If true, however, this and other possible similar cases could be another factor contributing to former Fatemiyun fighters' trauma, as it would be extremely difficult to speak about and cope with them, with potential judicial consequences, at least in Afghanistan.

## Conclusion

While it was often the men themselves who ultimately decided whether to go to fight in Syria and to continue fighting there, the women, wives and mothers in particular, played important roles in the decisions made. In some cases, women were consulted and some women, certainly, were able to prevent or put an end to their men's involvement, often, however, through bitter rows. Yet in other cases, they lacked any influence in their men's decision-making.

These women were torn between wanting their men to stay at home and the knowledge that living without them would be economically tough. Often it was difficult living conditions which drove their men to go to Syria in the first place, given the promise of material benefits if they went; some fighters also had a strong religious motivation. Over time, for many of the women, their positions gradually shifted from total resistance – which had often delayed, but in the case of our ten interviewees, not stopped their men from going – to increased acceptance, once the men's involvement brought benefits to their families. This was especially the case for family's already in Iran or for whom their men's decision to fight in Syria meant they could move there.

Whatever role women had in men's decision-making, these decisions have seriously affected their lives. After their men left, it fell to the women, and to wives, in particular, to carry on all the family work. This was a daily struggle, particularly when financial support received in Iran shrank due to the plummeting value of Iran's currency. In particular, men's absence created huge difficulties for families left with no man at home and for those wives who had to live with in-laws they did not get on with. Gravely concerned about the safety of their men, women resorted to a host of religious rituals. Those enacted collectively served a social function as well, allowing women to keep abreast of the goings-on of Fatemiyun in Syria.

Women have had to struggle to cope with their men returning injured or traumatised, or as corpses. Women related in the interviews how they have provided care to those injured and traumatised to help them get back to normal life. They have been helped by online and actual support groups, but the hurt and damage of the war will remain to haunt these families for a long time. Supported by the Iranian government, these same support groups have made Fatemiyun-related and other Afghan families aware of the recognition Iran has awarded the Fatemiyun fighters and their families. That recognition has also, in turn, helped ongoing recruitment.

The women have also faced criticism from relatives and others as to why their men went to fight in Syria in the first place. Sometimes, they have become embroiled in bitter disputes within their communities. This has been especially the case in Afghanistan, where perceptions of Afghans going to fight in Syria have been far more negative than in Iran. There, regime propaganda in favour of the Syrian war has had a strong impact. Some women had second thoughts about whether the sacrifices had been worth it, especially when their men were killed or severely injured in action. Many continue to wonder at what has happened and why.

These ordinary, down-to-earth families were struggling to cope with dire socio-economic circumstances when they felt the pull of the Syrian war.

Their men opted or were compelled, to pursue war as a way of life, for better or for worse. They could have instead lived lives in and through peace.

(1) This dispatch is based on interviews with ten women with close relatives among the Fatemiyun: three wives, two mothers, three sisters, one maternal aunt and one woman who was both wife and mother to Fatemiyun fighters (ie her husband and her son). Given their indirect involvement in and deep knowledge of the Fatemiyun group, these women are key informants. To capture the potential geographic and other variations in experiences of Fatemiyun women, the author decided to conduct interviews in Afghanistan, in Herat city, and Tehran – five in each. They were carried out in late 2018 and early 2019. Of the ten families studied through these women, four were already in Iran when their men went to war in Syria, three left Afghanistan to live in Iran, one was preparing to move, one's male relative was back in Herat and had stopped fighting in the war, and the interviewee from the last family had prevented her male relative from returning to Syria.

The women were approached by two female research assistants (one in Herat and one in Tehran) who had previous acquaintanceship and therefore already some rapport with them. This prior familiarity provided easier and safer access, both for the key informants and the research assistants, and contributed to a 'do-no-harm' research approach. The anonymity of both the key informants and the research assistants is maintained here to protect their privacy and the confidentiality of the conversations.

Having secured the consent of the interviewees to take part in this research (in a few cases, potential interviewees refused to do so, something which was fully respected), the research assistants used a rough list of general, open-ended questions to stimulate conversation. The questions were about family decision-making prior to the men joining the war in Syria, family life while the men were fighting away from home, family life if the men were killed, injured or affected otherwise and family life after Syria, at least at the time of the interviews. The interviews were largely unstructured and the interviewees were not interrupted to allow as natural flow as possible in the conversations. The conversations were either recorded (if permission was granted) or written down. The transcribed and handwritten conversations were analysed and form the basis of this dispatch.

AAN takes research security seriously. Without stressing that the topic was 'sensitive' and thus making it so beforehand, the author held several rounds of consultations with the research assistants over the course of a couple of months, talking through the need to make sure their research would pose no risk to them or their key informants and that both had the right to quit the research whenever they wanted to. Since the research assistants approached women they knew and relationships of trust already existed, they determined that the research was reasonably safe and therefore doable.

The ten key informant interviews are complemented by the author's intermittent observations, since 2014, of an extended family that has members in the Fatemiyun. Through on-and-off observations and informal conversations over the course of five years, it became possible to study several members of the Fatemiyun from within and over time, contrasting with research approaches that have so far looked at the group from without or only at one point in time.

Finally, this dispatch does not claim to be representative. The sample size is small (n = 10) and the interviewees were chosen through convenience sampling. However, given what was feasible, it is an exploratory study that is relevant to the topic under discussion (experiences of the Syrian war by women whose men have participated in it). Such subjects are often best captured through qualitative approaches.

(2) One of the things clerics including this Afghan one has done in Syria has been to recite religious songs such as nohas (lamentations) and maddahis (panegyrics) to reinforce fighters' morale. For example, to challenge the idea that individuals have gone to war in Syria just to get better pay than what they could find back in Iran, one noha quotes a child whose father was killed in the Syrian war as saying: "Love is priceless. To fight and to die has no price but for love [of defending Shia faith]." The clerics are mostly stationed in military bases or mosques that the Fatemiyun fighters visit in Syria.

(3) Hazrat Fatema is the daughter of the Prophet Muhammad and wife to Ali ibn Abi Taleb, the first imam for Shia Muslims and the fourth caliph for Sunni Muslims.

(4) In sofrehsalawat ceremonies that were held or attended by the interviewees, a woman usually hosted other women in her home to recite thousands of salawat (salutations to the Prophet Muhammad and his

progeny) with tasbih (prayer beads). The women also prayed to God to answer their praying, including entreaties for their men to be well and return from Syria safe and sound. They then ate food that was mostly ash (soup). These events were also opportunities for both hosting and participating women to meet and socialise.

(5) It refers to the shrine/mosque in southern Damascus, the Syrian capital, in which lies the Prophet Muhammad's granddaughter, Sayyeda Zeinab. Her tomb is an important Shia shrine. She is highly revered by Shia Muslims for her role in preserving and continuing the prophet's lineage through her grandparents, Fatema and Ali.

(6) The Office of Supreme Leader Ayatollah Ali Khamenei (aka Beit-e Rahbari or the House of Leadership) is reportedly one of Iran's wealthiest institutions with "holdings of about $95bn," according to this BBC report about recent United States sanctions targeting his assets. However, Iranian President Hassan Rouhani responded to these US sanctions by saying: "They [the Americans] say they want to confiscate the property of our leader. His property is just a hosseiniya [a place of worship] and a simple house. Our leaders are not like the leaders of other countries who have billions in their foreign accounts that they want to sanction and confiscate."

(7) There have been protests in Iran against the Iranian government spending billions of US dollars financing and supporting its regional allies including Syria, given deteriorating economic conditions for Iranians inside the country. There was also heated discussion in Iran when militia groups such as the Fatemiyun got involved in assisting people affected by recent destructive floods there. Regarded as an 'alien' involvement, some Iranians said they had been sent to suppress domestic protests.

The Two Faces of the Fatemiyun (I): Revisiting the male fighters. The Two Faces of the Fatemiyun (II): The women behind the fighters. Mohsen Hamidi. 08 July and 16 July 2019. The Afghanistan Analysts Network (AAN) is an independent non-profit policy research organisation. It aims to bring together the knowledge, experience and drive of a large number of experts to better inform policy and to increase the understanding of Afghan realities. It is driven by engagement and curiosity and is committed to producing analysis on Afghanistan and its region, which is independent, of high quality and research-based. Our aim is to be bi-taraf but not bi-tafawut – impartial, but not indifferent. Since its establishment in 2009 AAN's publications have informed and influenced the work of policymakers, journalists, academics and development workers working on Afghanistan. AAN's analysts are regularly asked to speak at conferences and briefings around the world, and frequently appear as commentators in the media. https://www.afghanistan-analysts.org/about-us/

So, what do we make of the Fatemiyun based on the above? Although it is clear that one's understanding of the group is mostly shaped by where one stands ideologically and with whom one interacts, some assertions are more plausible than others. When it comes to mobilising fighters, the Iranian government with its incentives and pressures has been a key motivator, aided in large part by the miserable conditions in which many Afghans there live. At the same time, the agency of fighters themselves – mostly young men seeking an identity in dire circumstances – cannot be ignored; however, this would not have led them to fight in Syria without the mobilisation and propaganda by the Iranian government.

Historical accounts of Fatemiyun fighters indicate that several have been involved in a series of successive wars in the region, mobilised by various state and non-state actors. In these accounts, fighting wars on behalf of others has turned into a lifestyle for many men. This is yet another version of the damaging cultural message that to be a man means to fight a war. In the recent Fatemiyun reincarnation, many Afghan youths have gone to war in Syria to establish their identity as men. As such, they have been able to support their parents and form their own families and have taken them to live in Iran. They have also won recognition for Afghan communities in that country. So, they feel they have become men through joining the Fatemiyun and fighting Iran's war in Syria.

As for returning 'home,' Fatemiyun ex-fighters, regardless of their disputed numbers, generally prefer to return to Iran and to turn it into a 'new home' for themselves and their families. This is possible thanks to residence permits and other benefits achieved through fighting in Syria. As for those who return to Afghanistan, they struggle to get back to civilian life. Many again end up in the bleak conditions they tried to escape by going to fight in Syria in the first instance. So far, there seems to be no community support for their future reintegration into society. The generally negative attitude towards them by the government threatens to alienate them instead. On the other hand, some will argue that providing them with reintegration support might set a negative precedent, encouraging others to go and fight outside the country and then return and be welcomed back.

Reports of the involvement of the Fatemiyun as an organisation in recent fighting and other violent disputes in Afghanistan should be taken with a large grain of salt. If Fatemiyun members were involved, it was on an individual, not organisational, basis, at least thus far – although conditions might arise in the future causing higher levels of mobilisation (for instance the Afghan government's failure to protect Shia communities and in particular mosques). As for the members who are still in Syria or who have returned to Iran, they are clearly under much greater Iranian influence than those now in Afghanistan, since Iran could cut Syria-related benefits to 'encourage' them to, for example, return to Syria or to fight elsewhere. As Hauch writes, although the Fatemiyun have found a place in Iran's narrative on Syria, "their place in [Iranian] society remains precarious."

*Edited by Sari Kouvo, Martine van Bijlert, Thomas Ruttig and Kate Clark. Mohsen Hamidi (pseudonym) is a local researcher with focus on western Afghanistan including Afghan-Iranian relations. The Afghanistan Analysts Network (AAN) is an independent non-profit policy research organisation. It aims to bring together the knowledge, experience and drive of a large number of experts to better inform policy and to increase the understanding of Afghan realities. It is driven by engagement and curiosity and is committed to producing analysis on Afghanistan and its region, which is independent, of high quality and research-based. Our aim is to be bi-taraf but not bi-tafawut–impartial, but not indifferent. Since its establishment in 2009 AAN's publications have informed and influenced the work of policymakers, journalists, academics and development workers working on Afghanistan. AAN's analysts are regularly asked to speak at conferences and briefings around the world, and frequently appear as commentators in the media. https://www.afghanistan-analysts.org/about-us/*

# PART 3

# HEZBOLLAH

## CHAPTER 8

# HEZBOLLAH, THE SECOND LEBANON WAR AND ITS REPERCUSSIONS

*Dr. Magnus Norell*

This study, translated from the original Swedish, examines the international community's long series of failures in Lebanon between the May 2000 Israeli withdrawal and the 2006 war with Hezbollah failures caused primarily by an inability to confront Lebanon's truly divisive issues. These problems have repeatedly led to new crises and pose a danger to the entire region. The conflict between Lebanon and Israel is no longer a conflict between two states. Since the end of Lebanon's fifteen-year civil war, Hezbollah has remained strong enough to drag the country into war against the will of the sovereign government. In tandem with its military operations, Hezbollah, or the "Party of God," has provided legal, social, and political services to many Lebanese. Hezbollah is thereby able to keep its conflict with Israel alive, making any attempt at a peaceful solution impossible.

At the same time, Syria and Iran are working both regionally and internationally to interfere with the various initiatives intended to strengthen the Lebanese government. This situation is an embarrassment for the international community. In the face of threats from Damascus and Tehran, the United Nations and, to some extent, the European Union have allowed themselves to be run over. The best example of this trend is the UN Interim Force in Lebanon (UNIFIL), whose presence in the South was supposedly bolstered with the passage of UN Security Council Resolution (UNSCR) 1701 near the end of the 2006 war. Shortly afterward, Syria made it clear that any attempt to patrol the Lebanese-Syrian frontier the main access route for arms from Iran to Hezbollah would be seen as a hostile act and met by force and closure of the border.

The threat had its intended effect. Even before the ink had dried on UNSCR 1701, the UN declared that it had no intention of patrolling the border it had been empowered to control. Today, three years after UNSCR 1701 expanded UNIFIL's authority and increased its size from 2,000 to 15,000 personnel, the force is still incomplete. This reluctance to seriously confront the basic problems of Lebanon and its neighborhood is rooted in a fear of placing the UN in conflict with Hezbollah, even if such a move would benefit the Lebanese government.

In contrast, Hezbollah has been able to reinforce its position in southern Lebanon at a time when the government is held hostage by an ineffective "national dialogue" process. Hezbollah has no interest in ending this dialogue; rather, continued discussion ensures the indefinite postponement of demands for disarmament and allows the party to keep the conflict with Israel alive, effectively hindering any breakthrough in Arab-Israeli negotiations. Since the armistice went into effect in August 2006, Hezbollah has received regular shipments of arms and other matériel from Syria, across the same border the UN has scrupulously avoided monitoring.

Although assistance to the Lebanese government has been the stated goal of a long series of generous UN resolutions, in the end they have become nothing more than rhetorical dust. The harsh reality is that when confronted with the prospect of conflict that may not be resolved through dialogue alone, the UN chooses to bow down to threats of force. For Lebanon, this amounts to a tragedy. The country has no chance of strengthening its tenuous democratic structure if Hezbollah is permitted to remain a state within the state, backed by its own militia.

## Repercussions for Lebanon

The political fallout of the 2006 war continues to be felt in Lebanon. In November 2006, Hezbollah suspended its participation in the Lebanese cabinet, paralyzing the government of Prime Minister Fouad Siniora. Simultaneously, the party erected a tent camp in central Beirut, bringing normal business to a standstill. Hezbollah and its supporters then laid siege to the parliament and the prime minister's headquarters, further undermining the state. Despite these actions, Siniora's rump government continued to function, albeit without Shiite ministers.

The crisis escalated in spring 2008 when the government demanded an investigation into Hezbollah's security cameras at Beirut airport and its autonomous telecommunications network. Tensions turned to violence in May of that year, when Hezbollah took over West Beirut by armed force. The government and opposition struck an agreement in Doha, Qatar, to defuse the crisis, and a coalition government was formed that once again included Hezbollah ministers. In fact, Hezbollah's position in the government was strengthened by the Doha Accord, which provided the opposition with a blocking third of ministers and essentially gave the Party of God veto power over all government decisions.

Hezbollah's increasingly obvious influence as a king- maker in Lebanese politics has allowed the party to emphasize its demands for a more Islamic society and perpetual war against Israel. Its success to date is based on a strategy of adapting to the local political structure while maintaining its long-term regional goals.

## Repercussions for Syria

The 2006 war provided Syrian president Bashar al- Asad with an opportunity to portray his nation as the leading regional force in the larger, strategic struggle against Israel. This, of course, was nothing new: such rhetoric dates to Israel's founding in 1948. The 2006 war instilled new life in the rhetoric, however, allowing Asad to claim that Hezbollah's victory was a new beginning on the path to total victory and Israel's destruction. Damascus was therefore able to demand increased influence in broader political processes that began as a result of the war.

The recurring political crises in Lebanon have underscored the country's importance in facilitating Syria's role as a regional actor. Through Lebanon, the regime in Damascus is able to influence the situation in the region and undermine any peace deal with Israel that does not also satisfy Syria's claim to the Golan Heights. Furthermore, by serving as a way station for all Iranian support to Hezbollah, Syria has considerable control over both Iran and Hezbollah's ability to act. This situation allows Damascus to keep its options open in the event of new, direct negotiations with Israel. The regime saw the outcome of the 2006 war as confirmation that its political approach had been successful. Its options open in the event of new, direct negotiations with Israel. The regime saw the outcome of the 2006 war as confirmation that its political approach had been successful.

## Repercussions for Iran

Iran has shown that it is not above supplying very sophisticated matériel to Hezbollah and other non-state players. Examples include the Chinese C-802 missile used in the near sinking of an Israeli ship in July 2006, and the more advanced rockets and missiles that Hezbollah provided to Hamas during its six-month ceasefire with Israel. Iranian support is visible all over Lebanon, with each Iranian ministry and department having a branch office in Beirut. In addition, several Tehran-funded institutions operate independent of direct government control, such as the Iranian Red Crescent; the Committee of Ayatollah Khomeini, which focuses on education and propaganda; and al-Alam, an Arabic-language television station that Tehran founded in 2004, with offices adjacent to the Iranian embassy in Beirut. These Iranian interests in Lebanon reach far beyond purely military factors or rhetoric against Israel. Tehran's financial support to various Lebanese social and charity organizations has had a significant impact on Hezbollah's popularity.

Today, Tehran has partially fulfilled many of its regional goals. While Iran's Arab neighbors have lost regional and international influence, Iran has increased its clout, making it practically impossible to ignore Iranian wishes when formulating regional policies. From its status as special observer at Gulf Cooperation Council meetings to the fact that the Obama administration has announced a willingness to engage it in dialogue, Iran has become the Middle East's only regional superpower. The country has significantly expanded its influence not only in Iraq, Lebanon, and the Palestinian territories, but also in Afghanistan. It has developed a close alliance with Syria to ensure that the conflict with Israel remains alive and that any serious peace initiatives in the foreseeable future will be destined to fail.

## Conclusion

Seen in the light of the wider Arab-Israeli conflict, the war in Lebanon is just one of many unfinished Middle Eastern conflicts. But the 2006 war did clarify an important point: the conflict is not primarily about occupation or Israeli settlements, although these factors are obviously significant. Hezbollah attacked Israel just as it has done on several occasions since 2000 because it could not imagine a future in which Israel exists. The conflict is about Hezbollah's active attempts to prevent any form of peace process that might potentially end in a long-term agreement with Israel. This point has regional significance as well. Israel and Hezbollah were not the only parties that clashed in summer 2006. Regional actors such as Iran, Syria, and Sunni-dominated Saudi Arabia and Egypt were active as well. In this respect, the tensions that are fragmenting the region today between Sunnis and Shiites, Arabs and Israelis, Islamists and moderates, not to mention Lebanon's own sectarian communities have deepened.

Therein lies one of the war's most tragic consequences: Hezbollah continues to proclaim the 2006 war as a victory for armed struggle. Indeed, the war represents a victory for the belief that there is no need to compromise or get involved in complicated political processes with uncertain outcomes in order to get results. It works just as well, perhaps even better, to defeat Israel on the battlefield and force it to make concessions. If a sufficient number of other Arab actors adopt this destructive analysis of the war, the foundation will be laid for a new series of armed con- flag rations and small-scale wars that could continue for many years to come.

## Preface

On August 31, 2006, three weeks after an armistice agreement ended the summer war between Israel and the Lebanese movement Hezbollah, the Swedish government hosted a donor's conference in Stockholm. The result of intensive lobbying initiated during the war itself, the summit came to be symptomatic of how the international community has dealt with "the Lebanese problem" for many years.

The decision to convene the conference was influenced heavily by domestic Swedish politics: national elections were only weeks away, and the incumbent administration was eager to gain popularity through a new policy initiative. In addition to coordinating financial aid for Lebanon's reconstruction, the summit aimed to strengthen the government in Beirut and help it reclaim authority over the South, particularly the Hezbollah-controlled areas below the Litani River. yet, despite this goal, the current situation in Lebanon is almost identical to that which existed before the war. To be sure, some of the reconstruction funds have reached the local populace, but this is due primarily to Hezbollah's continued control over the state's public works machinery. None of the fundamental issues plaguing the country have been resolved neither its internal divisions nor its conflicts with Israel, Syria, and Iran. Consequently, the risk of further violence still looms large, even amid the steady flow of rhetoric and dollars into Lebanon.

Part of the blame for this situation lies in the misguided political concern that motivated the donors conference in the first place. Far from altering Hezbollah's role as a "state within the state," the summit seemed to make things worse. Instead of subjecting the group to political pressure, the donor community permitted Hezbollah to strengthen its hold on the South, and arms shipments continued to arrive from Iran via Syria. Today, Hezbollah is stronger than it was in July 2006, when the war began.

Nor did the conference help Lebanon create a foundation for long-term peace on the domestic or Arab-Israeli front. The government now finds itself in a much more vulnerable position vis-à-vis Hezbollah than it has for some time. This was demonstrated in May 2008, when the group temporarily took control of Beirut and forced the administration to acquiesce to political demands that amounted to sweeping Hezbollah veto power.1 The most recent parliamentary elections did not alter this balance of power; following the June 2009 vote, the seats were distributed more or less as they had been in the 2005 elections. In short, Hezbollah's hegemony continues to pose a fundamental challenge to Lebanese society, and there is little to suggest that this will change in the near future.

The international treatment of the Lebanese issue before, during, and after the Stockholm conference reflected an inability to grasp the regional significance of the Israeli-Lebanese conflict. At its core, this conflict is not a face-off between two states, nor has it been for a long time. Nearly two decades following its fifteen-year civil war, Lebanon still houses an armed movement, Hezbollah, that is strong enough to drag the country into war against the government's will. At the same time, that movement has succeeded in providing legal, social, and political services to the Lebanese people. As a result of its efforts, Hezbollah has been able to keep its conflict with Israel alive and prevent any attempt at a peaceful solution.

This problem would be less serious if Hezbollah's goal of demolishing Israel and transforming Lebanon into a theocracy were mere rhetoric. Both Iran and Syria are involved, however practically as well as politically. These regimes actively support Hezbollah with matériel and money, partly in an effort to preserve the group's role as an armed actor vis-à-vis the Lebanese government. On the political level, Tehran and Damascus have interfered with the various regional and international initiatives aimed at strengthening the Lebanese government. This constitutes an embarrassment for the inter- national community, whose efforts in the region have been thwarted continually. But this tactic is entirely in keeping with the two countries' clearly stated political agendas and, regrettably, it has worked. The UN and, to some extent, the European Union (which often seeks to act as a geopolitical counterweight to the United States) have allowed themselves to be run over by Syria and Iran, often with very little resistance.

The UN Interim Force in Lebanon (UNIFIL), whose presence in southern Lebanon has been ramped up since the end of the 2006 war, is perhaps the most salient example of this state of affairs. Soon after the war, Syria made it clear that any attempt to patrol the Lebanese-Syrian frontier across which Hezbollah receives its arms would be seen as a hostile act and met by force and closure of the border. The threat had its intended effect: before the ink had dried on UN Security Council Resolution (UNSCR) 1701, which offered a political resolution to the war, the UN folded and declared that it had no intention of challenging Syria by patrolling the border. This decision was made despite the Lebanese government's request for assistance on that very issue. In fact, UNSCR 1701 had granted UNIFIL its expanded mandate and had clearly assigned the border patrols to the UN.[2] UNSCR 1701 also stated that only UNIFIL and the Lebanese army were permitted to carry arms in the area between the Litani River and the Israeli-Lebanese border; all other armed groups in Lebanon were to be disarmed. Since Hezbollah was the only group still fitting that description, there was hardly any doubt about the intended target of the demand one first expressed by the international community in UNSCR 1559, adopted in 2004.[3]

But shortly after the ceasefire, in August 2006, Lebanese minister of defense Elias Murr let it be known that there would be no disarmament. Instead, a compromise was worked out with Hezbollah, which promised not to openly display its arms. In return, there would be no attempts to confiscate or destroy the group's arms stockpiles. The question of Hezbollah's weapons which form the basis of the organization's power in Lebanon was again shunted aside in favor of a new "national dialogue." This longstanding dialogue initiative has attempted to resolve the predicament of Hezbollah arms since the end of the civil war in 1990, and nothing suggests that it will be any more productive this time. To the contrary, Hezbollah has been able to reinforce its position in the South unhindered, while the Lebanese government remains powerless to impose solutions, held hostage by the ineffective national dialogue process. Hezbollah has no interest in concluding this dialogue, since further talks ensure that the demand for disarmament will remain indefinitely postponed. In fact, Hezbollah's stronger position has led to an increase in arms shipments from Iran via Syria. Several observers have noted this problem, leading the UN to issue a formal protest against Syria for violating UNSCRs 1559 and 1701.[4]

The Lebanese army, along with UNIFIL, has deployed approximately 15,000 troops along the Israeli-Lebanese border in the South. But that presence does not amount to any real control over the area. Thus, even if the military wanted to disarm Hezbollah, it lacks the capability to do so. The poorly trained and inexperienced soldiers of the Lebanese army would be no match for Hezbollah's seasoned guerrilla fighters.

Another significant impediment to disarmament is the religious composition of the Lebanese army. When the Lebanese civil war broke out in 1975, the army quickly fractured along sectarian lines. Since 1990, several Lebanese administrations have tried to alleviate these points of friction. They are still present, of course, and Lebanese politicians have attempted to avoid situations that might cause the old divisions to resurface. Confronting Hezbollah in earnest would likely be one such situation. Approximately 70 percent of privates in the Lebanese army are Shiite, the sect from which Hezbollah recruits practically all of its members. Most officers, on the other hand, are Christian or Sunni. This too was the case before the civil war.

For its part, UNIFIL would be hampered in any dis- armament effort due to problems in its own governing mandate. UNSCR 1701, like so many other Security Council resolutions, is full of ambiguities that allow for a range of interpretations. As a result, there is no universally agreed on understanding of what it actually says.

These ambiguities would place UNIFIL in a pre- carious position should it ever decide to crack down on arms trafficking over the Lebanese-Syrian border. For example, the resolution explicitly states that UNIFIL is permitted to carry out operations only between the Litani River and the Israeli border. But Lebanon's border with Syria stretches north of that area. Although such ambiguities helped 1701 pass in the Security Council, they also ensured that the resolution lacks teeth (unless figures such as the UNIFIL commander choose to interpret it aggressively).

Today, several years after the Security Council expanded UNIFIL's authority and increased its size from approximately 2,000 to 15,000 troops, UNIFIL has still not fulfilled its mandate. This reluctance to seriously confront the basic problems of Lebanon and the surrounding region is rooted in a fear of placing the UN in conflict with Hezbollah, even if a more aggressive approach would benefit the Lebanese state. Such fears have been reflected in the decisions of individual member states as well. Sweden, for example, drastically reduced its contribution to UNIFIL following the 2006 war: it offered only a single corvette to patrol the Lebanese coastline, despite having committed ground troops in previous years. This maritime contribution was intended to prevent arms smuggling to unsanctioned groups in Lebanon, but in reality, it was mere tilting at windmills: Hezbollah receives virtually no weapons by sea, and other groups that might make use of this route are so insignificant as to have no practical impact.

The reality is that since the 2006 armistice, Hezbollah has been receiving regular shipments of arms and other matériel by land, from across a border that the UN scrupulously avoids monitoring. If the border were watched as the mandate allows[5] UNIFIL would run the risk of provoking a conflict with Hezbollah and perhaps even Syria. But monitoring the border would also provide an opportunity to lend practical assistance to the Lebanese government, in accordance with a long series of UN resolutions over a number of years. Unfortunately, UN resolutions regarding Lebanon tend to turn to rhetorical dust, and not merely because they are ambiguously phrased. When confronted with the prospect of a conflict that appears unsolvable through dialogue alone, the UN has bowed down to threats of force. For Lebanon, this amounts to a tragedy; the country has no chance of strengthening its tenuous democratic structure if Hezbollah is permitted to remain a state within the state, backed by its own militia.

Secretary-General Ban Ki-Moon himself has confirmed the UN's failure to live up to its commitments under UNSCR 1701. After a March 2007 visit to Lebanon, he described reports of continued arms smuggling from Syria and Iran to Hezbollah. Thus, it took a new secretary-general and almost a year to publicly acknowledge what everyone already knew: that neither UN resolutions nor additional UN forces have resulted in a real ability or willingness to stop the rearmament of Hezbollah. Probably without irony,

Ban called the smuggling a "blatant violation" of UN resolutions, and the United States, France, and the United Kingdom subsequently demanded that a UN special investigator be appointed to look into the matter.

Additional proof of the steady flow of weapons to Hezbollah has come from the movement itself.

In an April 2007 interview with the *Guardian*, Sheikh Naim Kassem, the group's deputy secretary-general, said that Hezbollah had rearmed in anticipation of its next war with Israel.[6] That Hezbollah's admission of its continued violation of UN resolutions would appear in a major foreign newspaper reveals the contempt with which the group regards the UN, and the total impunity under which it operates. The situation brings to mind the words of Lebanese historian Kamal Salibi regarding foreign involvement in the region: "Great powers should never get involved in the politics of small tribes."

The primary purpose of this book is to describe and analyze the international community's long series of self-inflicted failures between Israel's May 2000 withdrawal from Lebanon and the outbreak of the summer 2006 war. These failures were caused primarily by political cowardice in confronting truly divisive issues issues that have led to crises and wars time and time again, and which continue to pose a danger to the region at large. If the situation does not change significantly, it may only be a matter of time before a new conflict erupts in and around Lebanon.

## Introduction

The Situation juts before Israel May 2000 withdrawal from southern Lebanon was a chaotic one: a combination of Lebanese rocket fire on Israel, kidnappings, terror, Israeli counterattacks, and fears of a humanitarian disaster. As Israel pulled back from its so-called security zone in the South, the United Nations promised to support the Lebanese government and prevent Hezbollah from establishing a "state within the state." And in 2004, UN Security Council Resolution (UNSCR) 1559 called for Hezbollah's disarmament. This task was to be carried out in part by the UN Interim Force in Lebanon (UNIFIL), which had been stationed in the country since 1978. The flow of international assistance also included economic and political support for the Lebanese government. With it, national authorities were expected to assume control over southern Lebanon. All in all, Hezbollah's role as a well-armed militia operating completely outside government control was correctly identified as the primary obstacle to addressing Lebanon's problems.

As is now commonly known, the international community's efforts to support Lebanon were a profound failure. We have witnessed the same tragic sequence of events unfold over and over again. The ingredients and the actors are the same, standing ready to reenact the same scenario today.

As in years past, Israel's withdrawal following the 2006 war was met with another round of pledges for additional UN troops, donor conferences, and solemn speeches about the need to help Lebanon rebuild. Then, as now, there was talk about the importance of supporting the Lebanese government in reclaiming control over the South and countering Hezbollah. The UNIFIL presence there was already established in accordance with UNSCRs 425 and 426 of 1978, which formed the basis of the force's mandate to "assist the Government of Lebanon in ensuring the return of its effective authority in the area."

yet, despite this longstanding UN presence, Hezbollah had no difficulty establishing itself in southern Lebanon after the May 2000 words, confronting the group in any serious way was always out of the question. For its part, the Lebanese government had been too weak to confront the organization on its own in 2000. The author, along with colleague Magnus Ranstorp, participated in some of the processes that preceded the Israeli withdrawal at that time, and it was a strange feeling to experience a similar scenario after the 2006 war. Before May 2000, it was clear to both the Israeli and Lebanese governments that disarming Hezbollah and bringing the South under Beirut's control were necessary conditions for a peaceful solution that could stand the test of time. It was equally obvious that the Lebanese government would not be able to do this on its own. Despite its previous troubles with the UN, however, the Israeli government decided to "bet," as it was put at the time, that the international community would remain true to its word, especially since troops and a mandate from the Security Council were already in place.

The prospect of disarming Hezbollah has become even more difficult since 2000. The group has spent the intervening years greatly expanding its military capacity, to such a degree that it can now decide whether Lebanon goes to war. Not only has Hezbollah bolstered its military power and political influence, it has also strengthened its relations with Syria and Iran. Finally, it has kept its conflict with Israel at a level high enough to ensure that the question of peace remains moot, but not so high as to endanger its political and military position within Lebanon.

To be sure, the thirty-four-day war in summer 2006 came as a surprise to Hezbollah even the movement's leader, Secretary General Hassan Nasrallah, has admitted as much. And the group's losses, in terms of both matériel and manpower, were greater than has previously been acknowledged. Nevertheless, shipments of arms and other items from Iran and Syria have easily compensated for these losses. Meanwhile, the international community's various political and diplomatic initiatives since the end of the war have maintained the withdrawal in other status quo rather than advancing the prospects for a long-term solution. As mentioned previously, UNIFIL's current man- date already offers an opportunity to help the Lebanese government. The latest UN resolutions, including UNSCR 1701 (passed in 2006), appear to be stronger than UNSCR 1559, lending further weight to Hezbollah's disarmament. Specifically, the newer resolutions stipulate that the area south of the Litani River be free of non-state militias, while the expanded UNIFIL now has a mandate to halt any arms shipments to Hezbollah across the Lebanese-Syrian border (though see the Preface for a discussion of problems with the wording of these mandates).

Yet the international community, via UNIFIL, has tacitly abided by the internal agreement between Hezbollah and the Lebanese government that allows the group to keep its arms hidden in southern Lebanon. This agreement has undermined calls for the group's full disarmament and demilitarization. In addition, the question of what is to be done with arms stored in other parts of Lebanon has been postponed indefinitely. Lebanon's convalescent democracy will never fully recover as long as Hezbollah can maintain its current position, backed by its own militia. And the UN has failed to show that it has either the will or the ability to disarm the group. It was Hezbollah's role as a state within the state that caused the conflict to become "hot" in summer 2006. Because the conflict is still unresolved, the risk for new flare-ups will therefore remain high. At its core, this situation is a result of Hezbollah's position in Lebanon, its commitment to fighting Israel by any means possible, and its willingness to block any political deal that accepts the existence of a Jewish state. Therefore, the prospects for long-term peace are fairly poor.

## Background

The Middle East Today suffers from a severe lack of confidence-building efforts. Instead, suspicions, heightened tensions, and a general fear of renewed violence have replaced the hopeful climate that characterized the peace process of the 1990s, with Lebanon perhaps the most notable example of this trend.

Despite this climate, the Middle East will remain a key area of interest for the European Union for the foreseeable future. This is true on all levels: economically, politically, and militarily. But even from a strict security perspective, the region cannot be ignored. Although a large part of the Islamist terrorism that has struck Europe in recent years has been linked to Central and South Asia, the Middle East remains important as a recruiting center for Islamist militants devoted to an extremist version of political Islam.

Moreover, the EU's relationships with Middle Eastern countries have grown stronger in recent years, thanks to the Association Agreements that have been negotiated within the Barcelona Process and the Euro- pean Neighborhood Policy. The EU contributes a significant amount of aid to foster, among other things, human rights and democracy in the region. In several Middle Eastern countries, democratization processes have begun, though the outcomes are far from certain at the moment.[7] Many other regional countries, how- ever, have been moving in the opposite direction.[8] The Arab experts who produced the UN Development Program's *Arab Human Development Report* have identified three main obstacles to regional development: the scarcity of political rights and democratic governments, the lack of women's rights, and inadequate education. It should also be noted that the aid given to promote human rights and democratization has had its greatest impact in those countries where such processes were already underway.[9] In countries such as Syria and (pre-2003) Iraq, these investments produced no noticeable movements toward democracy.

Although conditions vary sharply within the region, commonalities such as poverty, rapid population growth, and rampant unemployment are shared across the board. Emigration from the Middle East to Europe has, at times, been extensive. And the fact that 8,000 Swedish citizens had to be evacuated from Lebanon during the summer 2006 war revealed how much migration binds the Middle East and Europe together. Not only do the region's conflicts cause waves of migration, they also erect barriers between countries that impede economic growth. Lebanon is a good example of this phenomenon, as well.

Many Middle Eastern countries have also witnessed a greater commitment to activist Islam. This is most obvious in the way that political Islam, or Islamism, has increasingly become a political force to be reckoned with throughout the region.[10] One of the most salient examples unfolded in Lebanon in May 2008, when Hezbollah instigated an armed confrontation with the government of Prime Minister Fouad Siniora. At that point, it became clear that the confrontation could spread rapidly throughout the region.[11] Although a solution was worked out with the help of mediation from Qatar, the result was a clear victory for Hezbollah, not a compromise that satisfied all parties.

The 2006 war and its aftereffects are also significant in this respect. As described in the Preface, the conflict between Israel and Hezbollah involves more than just these two parties alone it is intimately linked to several other regional problems, including Islamist terrorism. And the international community's some- times awkward inability to settle the conflict increases the likelihood of another war. Should one break out, it would be clear that what was once considered a locally confined conflict will have achieved regional significance, with considerably higher stakes to match. All the actors in the Lebanese drama have been sucked further into this now-regional conflict.[12] This means that Lebanon's problems are less likely to be solved in a way that would limit the risk of new "hot" conflicts.

The biggest losers in the 2006 war were the Lebanese people (whose homes and means of livelihood were largely destroyed in the fighting) and the Lebanese government (which suffered the ultimate humiliation of finding itself utterly irrelevant and ignored). The economic upturn that Lebanon had experienced in previous years came to an abrupt end. Its infrastructure took a long time to repair and, in some cases, has still not been restored to prewar standards. And the country is still far too weak to defend itself from external attacks or handle internal threats to its stability; the Lebanese people have concluded that their government is incapable of defending them from enemies foreign or domestic.[13]

The war's fallout also influenced Lebanon's domes- tic politics, culminating in the spring 2008 showdown in which Hezbollah took control of internal political developments once and for all. Officially, the Siniora government, supported by the March 14 coalition an alliance of anti-Syrian domestic political parties backed by the United States and France managed to remain in power. But as discussed previously, Hezbollah's campaign of political pressure and civil disobedience, along with the violence of May 2008, helped the group gain considerable influence over the government regardless of election results.

Of course, the 2006 war had come as a surprise to Hezbollah, as Secretary-General Hassan Nasrallah admitted shortly after the end of hostilities.[14] The organization lost approximately 500 men from its elite units and, at least in the short term, its members could no longer readily appear in public with arms in hand. Moreover, once UNIFIL was bolstered in the area south of the Litani River, Hezbollah found its access to the Israeli-Lebanese border which it could depend on before the war cut off.

Within a couple of years, however, Hezbollah managed to rebuild its capabilities and reclaim the initiative in the South. It replenished its supply of arms and rockets, half of which the Israelis had destroyed in the war. Although there may be fewer arms south of the Litani River, this is likely a result of new arms being moved north rather than an indication of diminished stockpiles. Similarly, new bunkers have been built to replace those targeted during the hostilities. And as recently as November 2008, Hezbollah carried out military drills south of the Litani River in violation of UNSCR 1701.[15] That Hezbollah knowing full well such activities would hardly go unnoticed carried out these drills without any attempt to conceal them speaks volumes about the status the group enjoys in Lebanon today. This status has only been bolstered during the reconstruction of southern Lebanon, given that Hezbollah has proven to be significantly more reliable than either the Lebanese government or the West.[16]

In light of these factors, Hezbollah now finds itself in a stronger position than it has for a long time. The victory it claimed in summer 2006 has been put to good use in its propaganda its victory in the increasingly important media war has been unequivocal. Although many Lebanese look at Hezbollah with great suspicion, most agree that it won the war.[17] In addition, the conflict and its aftermath have shown that the group is the most important and powerful actor in the country, one that continues to enjoy a surge in prestige domestically and beyond. Hezbollah's popularity is due in part to its ability to claim that it was the only Arab force that could stand up to Israel and win.

This does not necessarily mean that Hezbollah wishes to engage in another large-scale confrontation with Israel in the near future. yet, thanks to the changes it forced on the Lebanese government and the UN protection it enjoys, Hezbollah is guaranteed significant influence in all future government decisions, while also retaining its new and improved arsenal. Furthermore, the group has its own communications network that covers the country and provides intelligence from Bei- rut's airport to its harbor all completely independent from official channels.[18] Both the war and its political aftermath in Lebanon have also strengthened Hezbollah's long-term strategic vision namely, that of preventing any normalization of relations with Israel.

Another of the war's winners is Iran, Hezbollah's closest ally. The Iranian regime has long viewed Hezbollah as a successful example of its ability to export the Islamic Revolution. For Tehran, the war constituted further proof that it is possible to confront Israel without paying too high a cost. Supporting Hezbollah has been, and still is, a convenient way for Tehran to expand its regional influence.

There is no doubt, however, that Iran had nothing to do with the war's outbreak. Some have suggested that Iran initiated the conflict to pressure the United States in Iraq and divert attention from its nuclear weapons program, but this was hardly the case. When it comes to Iraq, Tehran has sought to influence the situation through various Iraqi Shiite groups rather than trying to influence the Americans directly. Furthermore, Nasrallah's postwar admission that he would not have kidnapped the two Israeli soldiers had he known the consequences also undermines any notion that Iran was somehow behind the war.

Of course, Iran was quick to replace Hezbollah's losses in arms and matériel in the wake of the war, and continuing such support makes good political sense in Tehran's eyes. By maintaining significant influence in Lebanon, Iran is in a good position to counter U.S. influence in the Middle East and become the most important regional actor opposing Israel. In that sense, Hezbollah's victory in the war was also Iran's victory. Furthermore, Iran has recently strengthened its ties with Syria, another of the war's winners.

For Damascus, the war marked a turning point: Syria had been pushed into a corner after Lebanon's March 14 movement forced it to withdraw its troops from the country. Moreover, the UN had released an unusually tough first report on the murder of former Lebanese prime minister Rafiq Hariri, identifying Syrian officials by name as being responsible. [The first report named members of the Syrian regime in the tracked changes of a version leaked to the press in the days following its announcement. Ed.][19] But the war and its aftermath changed the regional and intra-Lebanese dynamics, bringing Hezbollah's pre- eminence to the fore.

Today, it has become all too clear that those who dared to challenge Syria and Hezbollah prior to 2006 now find themselves on the losing side. The events of May 2008, along with the assassinations of anti-Syrian journalists and politicians in 2007, reinforced the view that confronting Hezbollah and Damascus exacts a heavy cost. As in the past, Hezbollah's dependence suits Syria well, giving the regime a useful tool in any future negotiations with Israel and the West. And although Damascus supports Iran and Hezbollah at the moment due to aligned interests, this could change. As for all other actors in the Middle East, the war and its aftermath continue to affect their stances toward Hezbollah. After initially criticizing Hezbollah, the more moderate Sunni-dominated countries quickly changed their tune as the war-ravaged Lebanon and public opposition to Israel grew. The quick war that Israel and, surely, the United States had envisioned became something else, and Hezbollah's strengthened position and rising popularity forced the moderate Arab states to take a more cautious approach.

Within Lebanon itself, the war illustrated how the conflicts that had divided the country for many years had not disappeared. What has changed since the war is that Hezbollah has boldly established itself as the country's dominant political and military force, and the roles of Syria and Iran have been strengthened. Meanwhile, the country's moderate forces, including advocates for democracy and reform, have lost ground. It is doubtful whether the Lebanese government can change this reality, but it certainly cannot do so with- out large-scale international support

It is unclear what form such support ought to take. As previously stated, the massive support Hezbollah gained during the war has made Lebanon's Arab neighbors leery of criticizing the group too strongly. They also want to avoid accusations of meddling in Lebanon's internal affairs, especially since the Doha Agreement (signed between the Lebanese government and the Hezbollah-led opposition) has gained political legitimacy.[20] Although this agreement was more or less forced on the government in the wake of armed clashes between Hezbollah and progovernment militias (the army remained on the sidelines), the outcome of the fighting has since been given official, political sanction.

The Doha Agreement also affects the options available to other outside parties. On one hand, the international community has committed itself to supporting the elected government. On the other hand, however, it is afraid to challenge Hezbollah, which still has troops in the South[21] and the capability to strike Israel with long-range rockets.[22] The UN's mandate (guided by UNSCRs 1559 and 1701) has more potency than ever before, but this authority has gone unused. The UN's role in Lebanon therefore remains largely symbolic, and UNIFIL's expanded presence will not change that fact. It is too early to tell what this will mean for the UN's credibility as a peacekeeper. But a larger and more expensive UN force financed and filled mostly by Europeans, doing little except driving around and flying the UNIFIL flag will not garner greater trust or respect.

For Israel, the war did not constitute the definitive showdown for which it had hoped. Israeli forces did not deal a serious enough blow to bring Hezbollah down, though they did inflict some significant damage.[23] Most important, Hezbollah was able to continue its rocket barrage against Israel even during the ground offensive. And the remains of the kidnapped soldiers, who had been killed at some point during the ambush or while in Hezbollah's custody, were not returned until much later, and only as the result of a prisoner exchange with Hezbollah.

The war's real turning point came after it became obvious that Israel could no longer achieve any kind of strategic victory specifically, when Israeli prime minister Ehud Olmert insisted, as a condition for a ceasefire, that the two kidnapped soldiers be returned and that Hezbollah leave southern Lebanon. To Hezbollah and many others, including members of the Israeli government, Olmert had set the bar too high. Hezbollah had been caught by surprise by Israel's powerful response, particularly the precision strikes targeting rocket launch pads that the group's leaders had believed to be safe. But Olmert's demand convinced Hezbollah that all it had to do was to hold on, refuse to agree to any of the terms, and declare itself the victor once the war was over.[24]

The last opportunity for Israel to agree to a ceasefire with favorable terms evaporated on July 30, when its forces bombed the southern village of Qana.[25] Shortly before that incident, U.S. efforts led by Secretary of State Condoleezza Rice had produced a ceasefire draft that all parties agreed to in principle.[26] After Qana, however, the agreement did not stand a chance, and Prime Minister Siniora was forced to bar Rice from returning to Lebanon for the next meeting.[27]

Nor has the aftermath of the war turned out in Israel's favor. The expanded international presence might make it harder for Hezbollah to strike across the Israeli border, but UNIFIL, regardless of its size, would not be much of an obstacle for the group if it were to attack Israel. The challenge for Israel's new government will be to internalize the conclusions of several official commissions of inquiry published after the war, the best known of which was the Winograd Commission.[28] The most important consequence of the second Lebanon war is that it may have ushered in a new phase of Israel's conflict with its neighbors, many of whom are still banking on a military solution to "the Israeli problem" and now view this course of action with renewed legitimacy. This does not mean, however, that negotiations are out of the question under any circumstances.

## A History of the Arab-Israeli Conflict

From a historical point of view, the Arab-Israeli conflict can be divided into three periods. The first stretched from Israel's 1948 declaration of independence to the October War of 1973. During this time, opposition to Israel was dressed in the garb of pan-Arabism. The goal of this ideology was to build coalitions based on Arab unity in order to isolate and destroy Israel militarily by waging war on multiple fronts.

The fundamental problem with this strategy was rooted in the very ideology of pan-Arabism. The Arab states, led by Egyptian president Gamal Abdul Nasser, found it impossible to unify their strategic goals, a weakness that led to defeats in the wars of 1948 and 1967. Ironically, it was Syria and Egypt's partially successful attack on Israel in October 1973 that caused Cairo to abandon the failed project of collective Arab strategic thinking and sue for a separate peace with Israel. This spelled the end of the "classic" period of the Arab-Israeli conflict.

In the second period, the Israeli-Palestinian conflict came to the foreground, pushing Israel's conflict with its Arab neighbors to the sidelines. Combining political initiatives with an armed struggle that included terrorism, the Palestine Liberation Organization (PLO) was able to open several fronts against Israel while also striking at Jewish targets around the world. Having portrayed its armed struggle as part of a worldwide revolutionary struggle against colonialism, the PLO was able to ally with a host of leftist groups, most notably in Europe. These groups provided political support that extended into the European mainstream.

As with the pan-Arab approach, however, the PLO's multifront tactics were hampered by the organization's inability to formulate a coherent strategy. Under Yasser Arafat, who dominated decision making to a significant degree, the PLO made a long series of tactical decisions that resulted in an equally large number of different policies. Despite some successes on the tactical level,[29] the PLO's broad approach to reaching a political solution amounted to a dead end. Arafat's death in 2004 marked the end of the period in which the Arab-Israeli conflict was defined primarily as an Israeli-Palestinian affair.

Today, the Arab-Israeli conflict has been trans- formed into a primarily religious clash between Israel and Islam. The beginnings of this transformation can be traced to Iran's Islamic Revolution of 1979, when Ayatollah Ruhollah Khomeini brought forth a new vision of Islam's role in the conflict with Israel. Unimpressed by Israel's military victories, Khomeini rejected the notion that the country's existence was a fait accompli. He viewed the conflict and the establishment of Israel as an affront to God, and the struggle against Israel as a test for Islam. If Muslims stayed true to their faith, he argued, Israel would be annihilated.

For that to become possible, Islamists could not remain content with a passive, supporting role. Instead, their stance amounted to a direct critique of countries such as Saudi Arabia, which supported the Palestinians financially without sacrificing its otherwise luxurious standard of living. In order to defeat Israel, a more activist role was necessary, and the 1982 war in Lebanon provided such an opportunity. After the Israeli invasion, Iran was presented with an opportunity to strengthen and expand its role there. Tehran already had a toehold in Lebanon thanks to its support of the country's Shiite population. The creation of Hezbollah allowed Iran to open a front against Israel that was entirely independent of other Arab states and the PLO, which Khomeini saw as incompetent and corrupt. Hezbollah's strategic aim was to resist Israel on all fronts, thereby hastening its final defeat.[30]

During the 1990s, various Islamist movements gained influence in the region and became increasingly important political actors. Hezbollah successfully struggled against the Israeli occupation of southern Lebanon. Israel's withdrawal in 2000 was viewed as a victory for Hezbollah and, more generally, as proof that armed struggle could achieve measurable results in the fight against Israel.[31] On the Palestinian front, Hamas gained power at the expense of the PLO, culminating in a victory over Fatah, the largest PLO party, in the 2006 Palestinian legislative elections. The victory was solidified when Hamas ousted Fatah from Gaza in June 2007.

The Islamists had never hidden their view that the only way to confront Israel was through armed struggle. But not until summer 2006 did the Islamists seriously challenge the strategic monopoly that the Arab states and the PLO had over choosing how to approach Israel. The type of struggle the Islamists favored was primarily a long-term war of attrition, which they believed would eventually lead to Israel's defeat. The 2006 war in Lebanon provided the Islamists with an opportunity to push their strategic vision of how the Arab world should deal with Israel.[32]

Several factors contributed to this rebirth of armed struggle as an overarching strategy. First, Hamas's 2006 electoral victory gave the Islamists a mandate to change the entire Palestinian strategy. From the Islamist perspective, the Oslo peace process was an unprecedented failure. The electoral victor and Hamas's military victory in Gaza a year later allowed the organization to shift its focus back to violent confrontation. To the Islamists, both the June 2006 kidnapping of Israeli soldier Gilad Shalit in Gaza and Hezbollah's attack the next month testified to the power of their strategy and its potential for success.

In May 2000, Israel withdrew its troops from Lebanon without a peace agreement,[33] and in August 2005, it disengaged unconditionally from Gaza. In Israeli decision-making circles, these actions were seen as a way of improving the prospects of a long-term peace agreement. But the Islamists perceived these events as pure capitulation, a result of their own armed struggle. Consequently, moves that had been intended to provide an opening for peace negotiations instead had the opposite effect, increasing the Islamists' political influence at the expense of those parties still working toward a negotiated settlement. In both cases, Israel's unconditional concessions worsened the overall security situation for all parties concerned: the Israelis, the Palestinians, and the Lebanese.[34] These events are excellent examples of what can happen when two fundamentally different negotiating traditions and strategic perspectives meet.

The other factor that has shifted the paradigm away from negotiation and toward armed struggle is Iran's desire to attain nuclear weapons.[35] A nuclear Iran would quickly change the balance of power in the region in an unprecedented way. Regardless of how long it will take the regime to obtain such weapons, the question itself has strengthened the Islamist argument that the best way to deal with Israel is to defeat it on the battlefield. Through the combination of Iran's nuclear ambitions, Hezbollah's rockets, and Hamas's takeover of Gaza, it has once again become part of legitimate political discourse to speak of the conflict with Israel as something that can be solved militarily, through a multifront attack led by Islamists.

During the 2006 war, this coalition of forces found itself at war with Israel for the first time. Iran was reluctant to be dragged into war at that point, but it made a virtue of necessity and managed to turn the conflict to its advantage, even though the military outcome did not amount to a clear victory for either side. That did not change the Islamists' view, however. Through their prism, the war was a decisive victory. Furthermore, the war revealed the source of the coalition's power: a basic and well-thought-out ideological foundation, complete with the "evidence" that, because they had won the war, God was on their side. From this viewpoint, armed struggle had forced Israel to leave both Lebanon and Gaza.

The coalition has been able to flex its military strength by combining various actors a state (Iran), a semi state actor (Hamas), and a non-state actor (Hezbollah), each with its own innovative tactics and weapons systems (e.g., rockets, long-range artillery, suicide bombings). Through these tactics, each has attempted to vitiate Israel's superiority in conventional warfare. The 2006 war testified to the strength of this coalition and the power of its ideological foundation. This new stage in the conflict between Israel and its neighbors is not entirely complete. On the one hand, the Islamists have achieved a number of victories that have caused a political shift in favor of armed struggle, confrontation, and a complete rejection of Israel's right to exist. On the other hand, there are weaknesses in the Islamic coalition, and it may not be able to change strategic thinking as much as it would like. After all, as a result of the 2006 war, the border with Israel is increasingly inaccessible to Hezbollah, and a rocket or artillery attack would give Israel an excuse to strike back. Furthermore, the coalition is dominated by Iran and Shiite Islam, which makes it difficult to reach Sunni- dominated areas of the Arab world.

Nevertheless, this coalition of radical Islamists is strong enough to block any new peace initiative, at least as long as the international community does not fully support it. The peace processes of the 1980s and 1990s made considerable gains and proved that there is support for a peaceful settlement. But without complete and consistent international backing, that goal will be impossible to reach.

In addition to demonstrating the risk of armed militant groups along Israel's border, the 2006 war showed that the region could become considerably less stable if no progress is made toward peace between Israel and its neighbors. The Arab-Israeli conflict is not the core problem of the Middle East. Radical Islamism is especially its ability to subvert the rather weak forces that advocate negotiation.

## Causes and Effects of the Second Lebanon War

Hezbollah's Attack on Israel on July 12, 2006, provided the immediate trigger for the month-long war. Under the cover of rocket fire aimed at several Israeli cities, Hezbollah militias crossed the border and attacked two Israeli vehicles. During the attack, which had been planned for several months, several soldiers were killed and two were kidnapped.[36] Kidnapping Israelis and using them as bargaining chips to secure the release of its own prisoners has been one of Hezbollah's longstanding goals. In this way, Hezbollah opened a new front against Israel, primarily to exploit Israel's embroilment in Gaza at the time. The attack may have been an attempt to directly support Hamas in Gaza, which would explain the timing: at that time, the Gaza Strip was subject to heavy pressure from Israeli forces, a situation that had arisen as a result of the kidnapping of an Israeli soldier a few days earlier.

A ceasefire came into effect on August 14, after the UN Security Council had passed UNSCR 1701 on August 11. The resolution was intended to restore full control over all parts of the country to the Lebanese government, as well as enforce the disarmament of all domestic and foreign groups operating in Lebanon, which UNSCR 1559 had called for in 2004. Thus, UNSCR 1701 outlawed all arms dealing not approved by the country's government. And to assist the Lebanese government, it expanded the existing UNIFIL force.[37]

Hezbollah and Hamas have no operational links, but Hezbollah has functioned as something of a role model to Hamas with regard to its political and military structure. Both movements receive support from Iran and want to eliminate Israel. Both are opposed to making peace with Israel and both employ a similar mix of political, social, and military activities, including terrorism, that characterize some Islamist movements in the Middle East.[38]

The stated aim of the attack was, as previously mentioned, to acquire prisoners who could be held hostage and used as bargaining chips in negotiations with Israel. Hezbollah's leader, Hassan Nasrallah, said that the only way for Israel to secure the release of its soldiers would be through a prisoner exchange. It was not the first time that Hezbollah had attempted such an endeavor. This time, however, the consequences would turn out to be significantly more serious than Nasrallah had anticipated.

Another motivating factor for Hezbollah might have been a desire to prevent a solution to the crisis in Gaza that did not benefit Hamas. Both Egyptian President Hosni Mubarak and his Palestinian counterpart, Mahmoud Abbas, have said that an agreement was all but complete but that the delicate negotiating game between Israel and Gilad Shalit's kidnappers, over whom the Palestinian government had no control, broke down after Hezbollah's attack.

Some have speculated that Iran was directly involved in the attack in order to thwart, or at least complicate, the UN Security Council's attempts to condemn Iran's nuclear program. There is, however, no hard evidence to support this theory. In any event, the war had no influence on the effort to force Iran into making con- cessions: on July 31, in the midst of the war, the Security Council issued a resolution demanding that Iran immediately cease its uranium enrichment. Hezbollah acted on its own, but it informed Iran that an attack was imminent.

While Iran does not control Hezbollah, the two parties have an understanding that Hezbollah must seek Iran's approval before engaging in operations that have international or regional consequences. Since Hezbollah's leadership was expecting the "usual" Israeli response limited artillery fire, possibly coupled with an air strike Iran was informed of the operation on July 12. The consequences turned out to be far more serious than what many in Lebanon, including Nasrallah, had expected.

But the war and its consequences for Lebanon are not undisputed, even among the Lebanese Shiites in Hezbollah: discussions about the wisdom of Nasrallah's aggressive tactics have been ongoing since the war began. Criticism of Nasrallah came from Hezbollah's political adversaries in the March 14 coalition which dominated the government at the time of the 2006 war, while Hezbollah was a minority coalition partner in the government as well as from other oppositional parties.

Most interesting and important to the future is the criticism that came from within Hezbollah. For example, Hezbollah's former secretary-general, Subhi al-Tufeili, has taken Hezbollah to task. In an interview with the Kuwaiti newspaper *al-Siyassa*, Tufeili, who out of loyalty stood behind Hezbollah during the war, accused Hezbollah of becoming a tool of Iran, and even its security service.[39] He also explicitly said that the policies of Hezbollah's leadership caused the war, laying the blame for dragging Lebanon into a costly war squarely with Hezbollah.

Tufeili also discussed Syria's desire to influence Hezbollah and even to use the organization to further its own interests even when the pursuit of those interests is harmful to Lebanon.[40] Another issue that sur- faced in the interview, and that several other Lebanese commentators have touched on, is the international tribunal investigating the murder of Rafiq Hariri. The UN's investigation identified leading Syrian politicians and military personnel, and even some Lebanese with connections to the Syrian security services, as responsible.[41] That the war came at an opportune moment for the Syrian regime is beyond doubt. The Lebanese government came under great pressure to resign and to reform, such that Hezbollah would gain a significantly larger role. Like Syria, Hezbollah demanded an end to the UN investigation into Hariri's murder. According to Tufeili's analysis, however, Iran's influence over Hezbollah is much greater than that of Syria.

Another important precursor to the war was UNSCR 1559, adopted on September 2, 2004, which called on the Lebanese government to disarm Hezbollah and place army forces in southern Lebanon. None of this happened, since the Lebanese government was far too weak to face down Hezbollah a fact that came as no surprise to anyone. But the resolution nevertheless gave Hezbollah a sense that it might be wise to anchor and consolidate its position in Lebanon. What Hezbollah along with every other actor in the region saw was that the international community was not interested in actually enforcing the resolution.

## Tactics and Strategy

The triggers of the war have been discussed above. The underlying cause of the conflict was that Hezbollah was never seriously confronted, nor was disarmament ever attempted. This reluctance and inability to handle Hezbollah allowed the organization to establish itself beyond its stronghold in southern Lebanon, in Beirut. Parts of the city remain outside the authority of the Lebanese government a legacy of the civil war, when Hezbollah established itself in the city. The government has little control over the neighborhood of Haret Hreik, where Hezbollah had its headquarters. From there, Hezbollah planned and directed all its operations.

Contributing factors to the war on the Israeli side have already been discussed above, but the actions of Hezbollah in and of themselves were a sufficient casus belli: Hezbollah launched an attack, penetrating the Israeli border, killing a number of soldiers, kidnapping two others (who were later killed), while also shooting rockets against various Israeli cities and villages with the aim of killing and injuring noncombatants. The attack was carried out with complete disregard for the Lebanese government, which included two Hezbollah members, who were not informed beforehand an indication of the strong position Hezbollah enjoys in the country.

According to international law, it is the Lebanese government that is responsible for activities in its territory. Thus, in principle, it is responsible for Hezbollah's attacks. In practice, however, the government in Beirut was powerless to prevent Hezbollah from acting, and it still would have been powerless had it known beforehand what Hezbollah was about to do. This is the core of the problem in Lebanon. Israel filed a com- plaint with the government in Beirut, which it knew full well was powerless to do anything. Meanwhile, the UN refused any responsibility by deferring to the same government, despite UNIFIL's mandate to prevent precisely those kinds of actions against Israel.

As has been pointed out before, it might never be entirely clear why Nasrallah chose to initiate his operation at that time. The disturbances in Gaza were undoubtedly an important factor. Attacks and kidnappings had been occurring for a long time and, as was shown above, Hezbollah has been openly propagating continued conflict with Israel and has publicized its intentions to kidnap and/or kill Israelis whenever possible. It was the fact that soldiers were not only killed, but also kidnapped, that limited the options of the Israeli government. A powerful response was necessary. And possibly, it was the extent of the response that surprised Hezbollah.

But the decision to answer quickly and forcefully also meant that the Israel Defense Forces (IDF) did not have sufficient time to prepare.[42] After having participated in various counterterrorism missions and small-scale operations on the West Bank and Gaza, the IDF's ground forces were more or less unprepared for a traditional ground war against a regular enemy.[43] Even though there were preexisting plans for an invasion of Lebanon to eliminate Hezbollah, the army was unprepared to act on such short notice. Instead, it was the navy and air force that provided the bulk of the forces initially. The navy erected a blockade of Lebanon, and during the first forty-eight hours the air force destroyed practically all of Hezbollah's medium and long-range rockets. What was not destroyed was forced underground and remained unusable for the rest of the conflict.

The air force was not able to knock out Hezbollah's short-range rockets, which Hezbollah continued to fire throughout the war 3,500 in total causing great damage to Israel's civilian infrastructure. In order to neutralize the threat, it became necessary to bring in ground forces. This is where Israel's failures became most apparent. Some reservist units, who had not trained together for many years, performed inadequately. Poorly organized logistical support left troops without important equipment, such as night vision goggles and bulletproof vests. And they mounted clumsy frontal attacks against an enemy that was well trained, motivated, and entrenched in good defensive positions.[44]

Ultimately, the IDF managed to reach most of its targets, but it never succeeded in ending the rocket fire entirely. Nor did the Israelis take many prisoners, a clear indication that they never succeeded in cut- ting off Hezbollah's reinforcement lines. This was all the more remarkable since there were ready-made plans to quickly airlift Israeli troops and deploy them along the Litani River, thereby cutting off Hezbollah's support lines and crushing militants through a two- front attack, from north and south. But it was not until the end of the war that troops were deployed in the north, and the plans to launch the operation were never initiated.

These problems were accentuated by internal dissension within the Israeli military staff. In the middle of the war, Army Chief of Staff Dan Halutz replaced the chief of northern command, Gen. Uzi Adam, with his own deputy, Moshe Kaplinsky.[45] This change did not lead to any noticeable improvements.[46] And Adam did not stay quiet: as soon as he was fired, he began to criticize the military leadership, especially Halutz, for having prevented him from implementing the plans that had been prepared for such a situation.

In the end, a commission was appointed, named after Eliyahu Winograd, the judge chosen to lead it. The conclusions, criticisms, and proposed reforms that the report laid out spurred a series of radical changes in the IDF. These changes could be seen during Israel's operation in Gaza from December 2008 to January 2009. Israel's tactical, operational, and logistical shortcomings were evident during the 2006 war and became the subject of expansive reform. Like other modern industrial nations, Israel had been charmed by the notion that wars could be won with advanced technology and that relying primarily on ground forces was a thing of the past.[47] This, of course, turned out not to be true. The war also emphasized the need to ensure that reservists receive sufficient, continual training.

Israel's greatest concern, however, is the rocket fire, a problem it had to deal with in the north and the south with Hamas in Gaza. When Israel decided to respond forcefully to the incidents in Lebanon and Gaza, the potentially serious effects of an increased threat of rockets and missiles launched by non-state actors played a large part in its decision.[48] Israel is also expending considerable effort to create a missile-defense system that is effective against short-range Katyusha rockets.[49]

Of course, another question is whether the long- term consequences of the war will prevent new conflicts from erupting or encourage them. Israel's forceful response in Lebanon and Gaza might work as a deterrent vis-à-vis Hezbollah and Hamas. At the same time, however, the 2006 war has not prevented Hezbollah from expanding its military capacity. Nor has the war made Hezbollah change its attitude toward Israel in any way. It remains to be seen whether the 2006 war will prove to be the last of its kind or merely another round in a far more extensive war. But considering the situation in Lebanon and the strengthened position of the Islamists in the region, new conflicts are likely. Even if there are no eruptions of regular warfare in the near future, it is likely that the conflict will continue in another form namely, as a war between intelligence agencies. This was already the case during the last war between Israel and Hezbollah.

Hezbollah's security service consists of three main parts: preventive security, which handles the protection of its leadership (including Nasrallah); counterespionage, which was very active during the war; and the investigations branch. This war between the intelligence agencies has continued after the war, and for Israel the main objective is to locate Nasrallah, who rarely appears in public, and other key leaders in the organization. The branches of Hezbollah's security service have been important in its contact with Palestinian groups such as Hamas and Islamic Jihad. In Lebanon, these branches strengthen Hezbollah's position within the country by, among other tactics, killing opponents and tracking political opposition.

The war showed why Hezbollah was so successful in resisting Israel. The extensive network of tunnels and bunkers that Hezbollah created in southern Lebanon and Beirut turned out to be extremely effective. These tunnels and bunkers, created by Hezbollah when Israel pulled out of Lebanon in May 2000, were intended to serve both offensive and defensive purposes. The IDF was planning to destroy as many of them as possible during the operation, but the war ended before there was time to implement the plan.[50] This network was rebuilt, and Hezbollah's ability to use it in waging asymmetrical warfare has been restored.

Due to the way the tunnel system was constructed, Lebanese civilians ended up in the line of fire. Tunnels and bunkers were often built near civilian homes or storage facilities, many of which were used to store weapons. As a result, they were targeted by the Israeli attacks. Hundreds of houses were destroyed and hundreds of Lebanese civilians were killed. For Hezbollah, this was a "victory," since it lent credence to the argument that Israeli attacks were killing and injuring Lebanese civilians.

Another variation on the same theme was Hezbollah's tactic of firing Katyusha rockets at Israel from locations close to UN observation posts. Israel, Hezbollah hoped, would not run the risk of hitting the UN stations, thus allowing Hezbollah to avoid drawing fire. And if the Israelis did decide to return fire, UN workers were liable to be killed or injured, which could then be used as Hezbollah propaganda.[51] The network of bunkers and tunnels that Hezbollah built from 2000 to 2006, which have now been repaired and expanded, was of little use to civilians. Their only option for avoiding the fighting was to flee, which, in turn, created a situation in which Israel could be accused of attacking civilians.[52]

Hezbollah's tactic of using residential areas to launch rockets was deliberately done to put civilians in harm's way, and it was used to turn popular opinion against Israel.[53] As a consequence of Hezbollah's tactics, the number of Lebanese civilians killed or injured was in the hundreds, whereas Israel's civilian losses were relatively small. This was because Israel, unlike Hezbollah or, for that matter, the Lebanese government provided civilians with bomb shelters and facilitated their relocation during the fighting. Israel never deliberately directed its attack against civilian targets, something that Hezbollah did without exception and as a matter of course.[54] Another issue that has been a part of this discussion is Israel's use of cluster bombs.[55] These weapons are not illegal, but they can easily kill and injure civilians since they are widely dispersed and may be hard to find.

Hezbollah's tactics, in short, were geared toward demoralizing the Israelis by turning international public opinion against them. This tactic had great success. Hezbollah never needed to win militarily; it was sufficient not to lose. And even when the Israelis won, it could be turned to Hezbollah's advantage, since those victories often resulted in civilian casualties.[56] Hezbollah's use of civilians as shields sometimes made it very difficult for Israel to target Hezbollah fighters without also injuring civilians.[57]

In conclusion, the 2006 war was fought between two forces with two very different conceptions of how war should and must be fought. At least since Operation Litani in 1978, when Israel first established its security zone in southern Lebanon, Israel has fought several low-intensity battles against its Palestinian and Lebanese adversaries. This kind of "post-heroic" warfare[58] is characteristic of the non-existential conflicts that some liberal democracies in the West, including Israel, have fought since World War II. These post-heroic wars have two main goals for the countries waging them: to avoid losses among their own combatants, and to avoid, or at least minimize, civilian losses.[59] For a long period, such warfare allowed Israel to combine operational efficiency with a high standard of ethics, in fighting battles against an enemy that fought "heroically"[60] an enemy, in other words, that had no compunction about sacrificing its own fighters and whose aims included killing as many of the enemy's civilian population as possible.

The Lebanon war, as well as the subsequent fighting with Hamas in Gaza, exposed the limitations and dilemmas inherent in these kinds of conflicts. For Israel, the dilemma lay in the fact that its ambitious political and military goals made it necessary to risk larger losses of its own troops and of Lebanese civilians. Initially, Israel adhered to the logic of post-heroic warfare. But this limited its ability to maneuver, and when it diverged from this doctrine, more Israeli soldiers and Lebanese civilians died.

This, in turn, suited Hezbollah perfectly. A non- state actor such as Hezbollah attacks the conventionally stronger enemy in part by limiting the fighting to small-scale conflagrations involving small units. Tactically, this was accomplished by engaging the IDF in guerrilla warfare and, whenever possible, avoiding larger battles.[61] Strategically, the aim of Hezbollah's rocket fire on northern Israel was to demoralize Israeli civilians. This continued throughout the war.

Israel in part because of its adherence to the post- heroic doctrine of warfare was reluctant to deploy large infantry forces in order to prevent Hezbollah from exploiting the terrain. It was thus impossible for Israel to stop the rocket fire. In turn, hundreds of thousands of people had to leave their homes in northern Israel, which, too, became a tool in Hezbollah's increasingly important propaganda war.

Another flaw in Israel's tactics was an overreliance on its high-tech air force at the expense of ground operations. During the first forty-eight hours of the war, the Israeli air force destroyed virtually all of Hezbollah's long and mid-range rockets with firing ramps. According to Israeli war plans, this initial success was to be followed by an immediate pincer movement by airborne infantry and commandos, whose task was to cut off Hezbollah's supply routes along the Litani River. But this only happened in the last days of the war, when it was already too late. Instead, Israel began with far slower and less effective frontal attacks. These played into the hands of Hezbollah, which made full use of its militants' defensive positions. The air force was unable to neutralize the short-range rockets that Hezbollah relied on throughout the war, a task that required ground troops.

The underlying problem was that Israel's military and political ranks expected the air force, in combination with smaller special units, to be sufficient. That attitude accorded with the post-heroic logic under which Israel was operating. When the predictions proved false, it quickly led to friction between the military and political leadership, indecision, and needlessly slow and costly deliberations.[62]

As the outcome of the war made abundantly clear, ignoring fundamental military principles and significant shortcomings in the political-civilian management of the war effort was bound to cause problems. None of the very ambitious goals that the Israeli government initially set out were ever met, making the failure all the more serious.[63]

Instead, Hezbollah was able to declare victory by dint of not having been defeated and not having been forced into making any concessions. Its tactics had been very successful, and Hezbollah could, with some merit, claim that it had repelled the Israeli attack. Overall, and for these reasons, the war was a success for Hezbollah, even though the criticism that surfaced even within its own Shiite community was never entirely silenced. Taking a longer view, the war also made it possible for Hezbollah to strengthen its position domestically in Lebanon.

## The Wars's Actors

**Lebanon:** The domestic components of Lebanon's problems have been well documented. Deep seated wounds were never allowed to heal entirely after the misery of the fifteen-year civil war. Lebanese society is deeply fragmented along clan, tribe, and family lines. Regional, social, and ideological differences continue to divide the country. As was made clear before, during, and after the second Lebanon war, the state lacks genuine authority, which harms its credibility as an institution capable of protecting its citizens and providing sufficient social services. In addition, there is a deeply entrenched system of corruption, through which various parties have a vested interest in keeping the state weak to benefit sectarian interests. A last addition to Lebanon's troubles is the assassination of anti-Syrian leaders such as former prime minister Rafiq Hariri in February 2005.[64]

These domestic conflicts and fissures are often exacerbated by foreign actors; Hezbollah's strong ties to Iran and Syria are the most notable example. The situation is worsened by the fact that the two political blocs competing for power in Lebanon are of equal strength. On the one hand, there is the moderate March 14 coalition. It won the most seats in parliament in the June 7, 2009, election and has the support of the more moderate Sunni-dominated countries, such as Egypt and Saudi Arabia, as well as the backing of the West. On the other side are Hezbollah and its allies including the March 8 coalition, which actually won more votes supported by Iran, Syria, and various Islamist movements in the region.

The tug of war between these two groups is based on a conflict that runs far deeper than mere politics. At least since the final years of the Lebanese civil war, two completely different visions of Lebanon have competed for influence in the country. The Lebanese scholar Nadim Shehadi refers to them as "the riviera" and "the citadel."[65] "The riviera" sees the country as built on tolerance and openness, whereas "the citadel" seeks to transform it into a bunker state and the front line in a war against the United States and the West, from which Israel is to be resisted by any means necessary.

Both these ideological projects have local and regional dimensions. They draw completely different conclusions from the 2006 war, and they enjoy support from all parts of Lebanon. Neither is entirely sectarian. The visions of Lebanon's reconstruction are radically different. Regionally, Saudi Arabia is the primary investor in the "riviera model"; Iran is the main sponsor of "the citadel."

The model advocated by the March 14 coalition envisions a future for Lebanon based on the way things were before the civil war a cosmopolitan country with an open and tolerant society, sustained by trade and a strong service industry. Support and protection come from the West, and it comes from the knowledge that the country is founded on free, democratic principles with the military playing a limited role.

The success of this vision for Lebanon was dependent on the Middle East peace process, which had the potential to make Beirut, and Lebanon, a hub of finance and trade in the new Middle East. For almost an entire decade, the main architect of this vision was Hariri, who, thanks to his close ties with Saudi Arabia, set out to transform Lebanon into a center of a new, peaceful Middle East. Countries such as Egypt and Jordan both of which have peace agreements with Israel and thus a vested interest in the success of this project were important allies.

The second vision looks completely different. To begin with, the supporters of this vision draw fundamentally different conclusions from history. As they see it, Lebanon descended into civil war because it was too weak, because it lacked a strong, coherent idea of what it should be, and, no less importantly, because it was too open to the world at large, and to the West in particular. To protect itself, the state needed a strong army and security service and control over the economy.

Furthermore, it was believed that the peace process especially if successful would drastically reduce Lebanon's ability to play a key role in the armed struggle against Israeli and Western influence. When Israel pulled out of the security zone in southern Lebanon in May 2000, it was seen as a victory, the result of an honorable struggle and an incentive to continue the armed struggle. In large part, it was then Lebanese President Émile Lahoud who, sympathetic to that ideological current, facilitated the process. In addition to the support from Iran, Syria, and Hezbollah, with his anti-Americanism, Lahoud was able to count on the support from such disparate countries as Venezuela and China.

The struggle between these two visions has characterized Lebanese politics ever since. During the years immediately before and after the war, this conflict paralyzed political life in Lebanon. Hezbollah and its supporters claimed that the struggle was by no means over. Pointing to the Sheba Farms dispute, over land they claimed was Lebanese territory still occupied by Israel even after the withdrawal in 2000, they argued that the whole country was not yet liberated. Only armed struggle, Hezbollah and its supporters claimed, could guarantee final victory over Israel, and Hezbollah was the only group that could guarantee Lebanon's security.

The opposition, for its part, claimed that Israel's withdrawal in 2000 made Hezbollah's demands to keep its arms untenable. The opposition also maintained that diplomacy was a better way to recover the Sheba Farms and solve other domestic issues. At that time, many Lebanese could not even identify the area on a map including Nabih Berrih, the speaker of the parliament.[66] There can be little doubt that for the proponents of "the citadel," the 2006 war and its aftermath was a partial victory, perhaps not because of the military outcome, but because of the political fallout from the war. What can be said for certain, however, is that this tug of war over Lebanon's soul will characterize future political struggles in Lebanon.

Another explanation of Lebanon's current political situation can be found in the developments that followed the Israeli withdrawal from the security zone in southern Lebanon.[67] Israel and Hezbollah had been fighting a low-intensity war in the area around the security zone, a situation that has been a constant since the mid-1980s. The evacuation was preceded by several years of backchannel negotiations, some of which involved the author.[68]

After the Israeli withdrawal, Hezbollah continued to build its military capacity, in spite of the international community's decision that all Lebanese militias would be disarmed in accordance with UNSCR 1559, which was adopted in 2004. Hezbollah's disarmament was also stipulated in the Taif Accord, the peace agreement that ended the Lebanese civil war. However, the Taif Accord also called for the liberation of the South by any available means. Because of Israel's continued presence in southern Lebanon, Hezbollah was considered a "resistance" group rather than a militia, and it was understood that, under the Taif Accord, it could keep its arms.

Hezbollah also continued its attacks against Israel. A stated aim of these attacks was to kidnap Israeli soldiers to use as bargaining chips in negotiations with Israel.[69] As Hezbollah's military capacity grew, so did its confidence. Kidnappings, along with sporadic rocket fire targeting Israeli cities and villages, yielded some results. The successful attacks resulted in the recovery of prisoners, and Hezbollah's were anticipating a similar result from the attack of June 12, 2006.

Since the ceasefire, Hezbollah Secretary-General Hassan Nasrallah has skillfully exploited the results of the 2006 summer war to strengthen Hezbollah's political position. Hezbollah's attempt to consolidate its power has not been limited to its military strength; its political ambition has grown, too. The relationship between Hezbollah and the government of Prime Minister Fouad Siniora deteriorated after the 2006 war, culminating in the resignation of Nasrallah and his allies from the cabinet, which paralyzed the government.[70]

But the remaining cabinet ministers did not resign as Hezbollah had hoped. With the support of a parliamentary majority, the government tried to push through reforms and fulfill UNSCRs 1559 and 1701. Hezbollah blocked this attempt by laying siege to downtown Beirut, making it impossible for the government to function,[71] and by delaying the election of a new president. In addition to preventing its disarmament, Hezbollah, along with its allies, also temporarily succeeded in preventing the implementation of the parts of the UN resolutions that regard the investigation into the assassination of Hariri. The UN's first investigation[72] identified representatives of the Syrian and Lebanese security services as responsible for his murder. The investigation also concluded that the Syrian regime deliberately misled the investigators. An important goal of the opposition was preventing the results of the investigation from leading to a trial.[73]

To help explain the current situation, it should also be noted that Michel Sulaiman, then chief of staff of Lebanon's army, said that the army would not try to disarm Hezbollah, or search for its weapons.[74] Nor has the army seriously attempted to patrol the Syrian border or prevent the smuggling of weapons to Hezbollah. It is doubtful that the army could stabilize southern Lebanon. With approximately 70,000 men in total, it has limited capabilities and, in some cases, antiquated equipment.[75] As has been pointed out before, the majority of its officers are Christians and Sunni Muslims, whereas the privates and junior officers are 70 percent Shiite.[76] It is very unlikely that today's army would survive a crisis, such as the one that preceded the breakout of the civil war in 1975. Tensions remain between the various confessional groups. If anything, they have grown since the May crisis in 2008, when the army proved unwilling to resist Hezbollah's invasion.

Thus, UNSCR 1701 has not been carried out in its entirety. In fact, its central tenets—the disarmament of Hezbollah and the establishment of control over the Lebanese-Syrian border—have yet to be implemented. Soon after the war, it became evident that UNSCR 1701 did not prevent Hezbollah from rearming and replacing destroyed and lost weapons. Only one month after the war ended, in September 2006, Nasrallah declared that Hezbollah had replaced all the weapons lost and had become stronger than it was before the war.[77] Paragraphs 14 and 15 of UNSCR 1701 give the Lebanese government, in cooperation with UNIFIL, a mandate to secure its border to prevent illegal arms deliveries. Nasrallah's statement was therefore an unabashed confession that Hezbollah had violated the resolution.

**The Lebanese Elections.** Hezbollah's leadership has repeatedly declared that the organization will not dis- arm. Instead, it argues that Hezbollah needs weapons to defend Lebanon in the absence of an effective Lebanese army.

The question of what it is, exactly, that is to be defended after Israel left the security zone in May 2000[78] has been raised many times, both before and after the 2006 war. Hezbollah has chosen to focus on a small patch of land on the border between Syria and Lebanon. The area is a part of the Syrian Golan Heights and, as such, should be of no relevance to Lebanon.[79] But the border between Lebanon and Syria has never been formally delineated,[80] and both Syria and Lebanon, not just Hezbollah, have in recent years claimed that the area really belongs to Lebanon. The area has remained uninhabited since 1967, when it was appropriated by Israel from Syria during the Six-Day War.

The area allows Hezbollah to claim that not all of Lebanon is liberated, justifying the organization's pos- session of arms.[81] Nasrallah has also said that whatever the UN has to say on the matter is irrelevant to Hezbollah.[82] The question is complicated further by the forces in both Lebanon and Syria that still consider these two countries as one. The two countries were, up until independence in 1943, twin protectorates under a French mandate from the League of Nations. After independence, some parties continued to propagate the idea of "one country," and no diplomatic relations were ever established.[83] The current ambiguity over ownership of the Sheba Farms is sure to remain, since it gives both Syria and Hezbollah space to maneuver in dealing with any future conflicts with Israel. As far as Hezbollah is concerned, nothing good can come out of a solution to its conflict with Israel before Israel has reached a peace agreement with Syria. The present situation plays right into Hezbollah's hands. Since the end of the war, the government in Beirut has launched new initiatives with regard to the area.[84] The idea that has been put forth is for the UN to assume jurisdiction over the area until Lebanon's claim can be met in full.[85] Naturally, the text glosses over Syria's and Hezbollah's lack of interest in resolving this issue.

It is possible, however, that Syria will become interested in resolving the issue as new peace negotiations with Israel over the Golan Heights unfold, but hardly before that. This makes it difficult for the UN, which considers the area as part of Syria,[86] to deploy there merely because the Lebanese government has asked it to. Hezbollah's popular support among the Shiite population is an aggravating factor for the Lebanese government in its attempts to reclaim control over southern Lebanon and disarm Hezbollah. When the army chief of staff is unwilling even to attempt to disarm Hezbollah, the government's task of reclaiming control over southern Lebanon becomes even harder. The resignation of the Hezbollah ministers in November 2006 should be understood in the light of this crisis. The ministers resigned in order to vitiate the government's attempts to constrain Hezbollah's ability to act unilaterally. The possibility of integrating the militia into Lebanon's regular army must be weighed against the potential risk of fanning the flames of sectarian strife in the process. Regardless, there is no reason to believe that Hezbollah would be willing to even entertain the idea of dissolving its militia by integrating it into the Lebanese army.

**The 2008 May Crisis.** The run-up to the crisis in May 2008 had its beginnings during the second half of 2004, when Prime Minister Hariri, with the support of the United States and France, began to push the Syrian occupation force out of Lebanon. This, in turn, was triggered by Syria's attempt, via its allies in Lebanon, to get the Lebanese parliament to extend Syrian-backed President Émile Lahoud's term in office in violation of the Lebanese constitution. In September 2004, the UN Security Council passed UNSCR 1559, which, among other things, demanded that all domestic and foreign militias be disarmed and that "all foreign forces withdraw from Lebanon" and cease their involvement in Lebanese domestic affairs a not so subtle allusion to Syria.[87]

The Syrian troops withdrew from Lebanon in April 2004. The withdrawal was the result of demonstrations in Lebanon, coupled with foreign protests and pressure against Syria after the assassination of Rafiq Hariri in February 2005, which many Lebanese blame on the Syrians. In the elections held in June, the anti-Syrian, West-oriented camp won a decisive victory. It was a triumph for those forces in Lebanon that nourished the vision of Lebanon as an open, democratic part of the Middle East. During the rest of 2005, a number of Lebanese journalists and politicians, all with anti-Syrian back- grounds, were assassinated. It was an obvious attempt to roll back the successes of the March 14 coalition. In June 2005, the parties compromised, and Hezbollah was given two cabinet posts. For the first time ever, Hezbollah had direct access to government power, and it had achieved it without winning an election.[88]

The political fallout in Lebanon from the war also proved significant in the long run. Beginning in November 2006, Hezbollah set out to paralyze Beirut and all government activity of importance. It employed radical activities, including civil disobedience campaigns. Among other things, Hezbollah erected a tent camp in central Beirut, which made it impossible to conduct any normal business in the area. The government offices were under siege, and parliament could not convene. Hezbollah's cabinet members resigned shortly after the war, when the government refused to meet a series of demands that Hezbollah put up as conditions for staying in the government. Although Hezbollah hoped the resignations would cause the government to fall, that did not happen. The crisis escalated, with the government and opposition trading accusations[89] until the spring of 2008, when the conflict finally ended in clashes between Hezbollah and various militia forces loyal to the government.

On Friday May 9, 2008, Hezbollah seized control over large parts of Beirut.[90] The immediate trigger was the government's decision on May 6, 2008, to dismiss the Hezbollah-friendly Beirut airport security chief, Gen. Wafiq Shuqeir, after he had allowed Hezbollah to set up its own surveillance cameras at the airport.[91] But the crisis was the culmination of a years-long conflict between the Siniora government and the opposition namely, Hezbollah.

On the same day that the government issued its decision to dismiss Shuqeir, it proposed to investigate the legality of Hezbollah's private telecommunications network. Hezbollah responded quickly with a series of countermeasures. At the initial stages, these were comprised of civil disobedience and attempts to take control over the infrastructure in Beirut. Hezbollah, in other words, was flexing its muscles in order to get what it wanted. By May 7, it had become clear that the situation had escalated and that Hezbollah was beginning to strengthen its grip on the country: the air- port was closed and media critical of Hezbollah were shut down. The opposition party Tiyar al-Mustaqbal (the Future Movement), led by the Saudi-born Saad Hariri, found itself under considerable pressure from Hezbollah's militia. Fighting in various parts of Lebanon between supporters of Hezbollah and supporters of the March 14 coalition—in which Hariri's Future Movement is the largest party started on May 7 and continued for a week.

It turned out to be an uneven fight since, by and large, Hezbollah's troops are better equipped, trained, and motivated than any other group in Lebanon today. Even the Lebanese army did not stand a chance against the movement. Since Hezbollah is the strongest military force in Lebanon, an unconventional military imbalance between the country's government and its opposition has arisen. The disparity became clear during the fighting, when the Lebanese Armed Forces remained on the sidelines as Hezbollah took control of Beirut, only to resume control when Hezbollah's leadership ordered its troops to hand power back to the army.

This show of strength proved effective and politically rewarding for Hezbollah and its allies. Following mediation efforts in Doha, Qatar, an agreement between the warring factions was reached on May 21, 2008. The Doha agreement required extensive diplomacy between the most influential actors in the region Iran, Syria, and Saudi Arabia and it was a decisive victory for Hezbollah. The government initiatives that triggered the crisis the dismissal of Shuqeir and the investigation into Hezbollah's telecommunications network were reversed unilaterally by the government, and Hezbollah ministers rejoined the cabinet.

The agreement also facilitated the election of a new president, which had not been possible since November 2007, when President Lahoud resigned at the end of his term. The elections on May 25, 2008, offered no surprises. Former Army Chief of Staff General Michel Sulaiman was elected president. A Christian, he was accepted by both the March 14 coalition and the Hezbollah-led opposition. The international community also welcomed Sulaiman's appointment. The crisis that took place in mid-May, which pushed Lebanon to the brink of another civil war, resulted in a new, seemingly more stable Lebanon. But in light of Hezbollah's strengthened position as the de facto kingmaker in Lebanese politics, stability is far from certain. The question remains, of course, how this will affect Lebanon's future development.

The chances that Lebanon can solve its present conflicts and achieve a workable political system unburdened by sectarianism have decreased. The events of the first weeks of May 2008 made it clear that Hezbollah is a force that any Lebanese government must take into consideration, regardless of whether the party has representation in the cabinet. With the May crisis, Hezbollah has, once again, shown that it is the most powerful actor in Lebanon today. The army, formally controlled by the government, refrained from intervening, except when it was formally "invited" by Hezbollah to resume control of certain areas. Hezbollah's demand for a coalition government that includes the opposition and gives it a right of veto over important decisions has now been met. And so Hezbollah and its allies may acquire ultimate control over the government, regardless of electoral outcomes. It should also be noted that Hezbollah does not seem to have the ambition to acquire absolute power in Lebanon and impose an Islamic state like the one in Iran. Lebanon's current electoral system, which invariably results in coalition governments, suits Hezbollah's purposes perfectly.

This illustrates another important ingredient in the political and social structure of Lebanon. Hezbollah's strength is a result of its self-definition, which is based on religion. Since Shiite Muslims comprise as much as 40 percent of Lebanon's population, Hezbollah has a large potential constituency. This demographic weight is particularly beneficial in outlining the political platform before elections. It also causes other sects, including the other large Shiite party, Amal, to band together to counter Hezbollah's influence. (Today they are closely allied with each other.) Hezbollah's leadership knows this, and it has tried, especially since the war ended, to emphasize its Lebanese identity and downplay its sectarian profile. The Lebanese flag, for instance, is becoming an increasingly common staple at Hezbollah gatherings, and spokesmen for Hezbollah repeatedly underscore the importance of "national unity" and working for the good of all of Lebanon. Nonetheless, other groups in Lebanon are still suspicious of Hezbollah. It is clear that without its formidable military capacity, Hezbollah would not be able to retain its influence, even with the support it enjoys from Syria and Iran. The elections in June 2009 underscored this reality: Hezbollah failed to expand its appeal to non-Shiite groups in Lebanon.

The events of May 2008 undermined Hezbollah's claim that it was a movement for all Lebanese. That Hezbollah was so quick to turn its weapons against other Lebanese to defend its foreign and particularistic interests heightened the tensions in the country, and the war and its aftermath have not done anything to soothe the conflicts. On the contrary, the political aftermath only made matters worse. All concerned parties in Lebanon have gambled with political capital and, in the series of political crises that has afflicted the country since the war, they have lost. Some groups, of course, have lost more than others.

Once again, the government has proved severely limited in its ability to seize the initiative and force Hezbollah into the political fold. The effort to deal with Hezbollah's military structure by investigating its telecommunications network and the attempt to stop its control over the airport were unmitigated failures. The army, formally under the control of the government and the ministry of defense, proved incapable of standing up to Hezbollah. This is due in part to the presidential ambitions of Michel Sulaiman, the chief of the army, and it is doubtful whether Sulaiman could have been president without Hezbollah's support.

The army is passive because it lacks sufficient equipment, training, and manpower to challenge Hezbollah in an open confrontation. Today, Hezbollah is much more than just a militia. It is a regular army, complete with its own uniforms, communications network, and arms stockpiles. It is completely beyond the control of any government institution. The Lebanese army's loss of credibility may prove difficult to repair. After the civil war, the army was hoped to be a symbol around which the Lebanese, irrespective of religion or ethnicity, could unite and build a *Lebanese* identity. Many Lebanese hoped that the army would provide the basis for national unity as a means of countering the built- in tensions of the political system. Although this hope is not altogether dead, the crisis in May 2008 showed how long a way there is to go.

Finally, although Hezbollah was strengthened by its latest confrontation with the government it forced it to back down from all its demands it might have to pay a significant price internally for the success. In turning its weapons on other Lebanese not an unprecedented move, though it has never before been done so openly many Lebanese came to regard Hezbollah as promoting a sectarian agenda, not a national one. Since the Israeli withdrawal and the war in 2006, Hezbollah has been at pains to underscore that it always puts Lebanese interests first. The events in May 2008, however, have shown that Hezbollah is not beyond using force to protect its independence from the government. A desire to fight the Israeli occupation is no longer a valid excuse for Hezbollah's retaining its own military structure outside the government's control.

It is obvious that this part of Hezbollah's activities is in line with the strategic interests of Iran and Syria in the tug of war with Israel and the Sunni-dominated countries such as Saudi Arabia. It is obvious that this part of Hezbollah's activities is in line with the strategic interests of Iran and Syria in the tug of war with Israel and the Sunni-dominated countries such as Saudi Arabia.

**Israel:** Israel has only one demand with regard to Lebanon, one it has voiced persistently ever since its May 2000 withdrawal: that Lebanon, with the help of the UN, stop the rocket fire, border incursions, and kidnappings. For a long time, Lebanon and the UN have failed to meet this demand.

When the Israeli government decided to go to war, it was the result of a hasty and ill-thought-out process.[92] As fate would have it, Israel's newly elected government was led by people with scant military experience. Neither Prime Minister Ehud Olmert nor Defense Minister Amir Peretz had much experience with defense issues.[93] Army Chief of Staff Dan Halutz, who was also new on the job, refused to launch a ground offensive for several weeks. There were even prepared plans for such an offensive that were modeled on scenarios almost identical to the actual situation Israel found itself in during the summer of 2006. Instead, Halutz relied almost exclusively on the air force. This turned out to be a grievous mistake, as several people within the IDF pointed out during the campaign.[94] During the first hour of the war, Israel took out several stationary rocket-launch pads made for Iranian-made Fajr ("dawn," in Persian) rockets, hidden in houses at various locations in southern Lebanon. This was Israel's greatest success in the war, and it took Hezbollah by complete surprise, because Hezbollah believed that these weapons were entirely unknown by the Israelis.

With regard to the short-range Katyusha rockets, the situation was different. These can be fired quickly, giving the Israeli air force little chance to neutralize the threat before the mobile launch pads were removed.

Only a ground offensive could deal with this issue. Even though there were preexisting plans for how such a ground offensive would be carried out, throughout the war Halutz refused to launch such an offensive. In this, he was supported by Olmert and, initially, by Peretz. And so Hezbollah was able to fire its rockets against Israel for the duration of the war, even from positions very close to the border. The air force, from which Halutz himself had emerged, failed to suppress the rocket fire.

When the ground offensive was finally launched, it was too late to make any real difference. A ceasefire had already been negotiated[95] and the date for its activation had already been decided when the offensive began. It lasted less than two days and failed to achieve its stated goals. Many of the Israeli casualties occurred during these forty-eight hours. Criticism of the military and political leaders was devastating.[96] They were accused of mishandling the offensive, stalling, only to then needlessly waste human life once the ground offensive was launched. In short, the discussion that preceded the offensive and the internal frictions within the military leadership made for a truncated and inefficient offensive, launched too late to be of any real use.

The criticisms voiced after the war revolved around several issues. First, none of the stated aims of the operation had been achieved. The kidnapped soldiers had not been freed; because Hezbollah refused to allow Red Cross representatives to visit them, at that time it was not known whether they were still alive. Hezbollah had not been taken out of commission or crushed, and the one-sided reliance on the air force had not significantly decreased the rocket fire. Second, neither the civilian population nor military was ready to handle the war. On the military side, there were logistical shortcomings: equipment was not delivered to the troops on time, and the wrong decisions were made in choosing between the air force and infantry. The military leadership remained internally fragmented throughout the war, and it under- estimated Hezbollah's capabilities.[97]

Another issue that was discussed after the war one that had its origins in the 2000 withdrawal from south- ern Lebanon was the character and focus of Israel's defense forces. These had changed since 2000, as a result of the intifada. As the Winograd Commission and other commissions found, insufficient and irregular training and an exaggerated reliance on the air force and unmanned aerial vehicles explained the military's poor performance. The war made it clear that a reliance on the air force and other technical solutions was not an adequate substitute for ground forces when it came to neutralizing the threat that Hezbollah's rocket and missile units posed.

Voices within the IDF and the government, such as former defense minister Shaul Mofaz, claimed from the start that, after the initial successes of the air force against the Fajr missiles, the government should have initiated negotiations and launched a ground offensive to put force behind its words.[98]

Following the ceasefire in August 2006, the significant political consequences of the wartime failures began to unfold. The defense minister and several leading military figures were forced to resign or chose to quit before being forced out. Several investigatory committees were appointed, the Winograd Commission among them, and their conclusions will likely be discussed for a long time.[99]

In the long run, the consequences in Israel of the second Lebanon war may extend beyond politics. Israel's withdrawal from Lebanon in 2000 and the disengagement from Gaza in August 2005 were both intended to renew the peace process. They represented a way to upset the status quo and improve the standing of those on the other side, be they Palestinian or Lebanese, who were interested in a peaceful solution, by allowing them to point to tangible benefits from peace processes. The problem, of course, was that these initiatives did not result in any real benefits for the Israelis. The disengagement from Gaza and Lebanon increased, not decreased, rocket fire. And civilians paid the highest price.

Furthermore, these initiatives were viewed as signs of weakness by both Hamas in Gaza and Hezbollah in Lebanon. For these organizations, the withdrawals amounted to Israeli surrenders, and they probably increased, rather than decreased, the risk of further military conflict. As a result, the Israeli population now looks far more suspiciously on unilateral peace initiatives like these. Political parties that choose to adopt such a strategy in their political platforms will find it difficult to win future elections. This, of course, will make it more difficult for Israel to find an opening in its relations with its Arab neighbors.

This brings us to Israel's most talked-about aims: deterrence. One of the most important reasons why the newly elected Israeli government's response to the kidnapping was so severe was that it wanted to send a signal to Hezbollah and other potential enemies that the price of continued raids into Israeli territory would be steep. That the kidnapping occurred only a couple of weeks after the kidnapping of a soldier in Gaza is likely to have been a contributing factor: it became necessary for the new government to resort to a more forceful response in light of two such attacks in close succession.[100] Similar incidents in the past, following the 2000 Israeli withdrawal, had not resulted in any major response from Israel. Hezbollah's "miscalculation," then, was based on previous experience. Nasrallah emphasized this when the UN representative in Lebanon confronted him with the question.[101] He assured the representative that Hezbollah was not seeking a large-scale conflagration, and that the incident would not escalate the conflict.

Israel's longstanding policy of a restrained response to Hezbollah's provocations had led Nasrallah to believe that another kidnapping was unlikely to lead to any major escalation, much less war. Israel had gone to great lengths to minimize the risk of new kidnappings. Accordingly, it maintained a state of alertness and conducted its patrols so that it would minimize the risk of confrontation as much as possible.[102]

But Israel's restraint was taken by Hezbollah as evidence that its strategy of constant rocket attacks and kidnappings worked, without provoking Israel too much. It was in Hezbollah's interest to maintain a state of conflict just short of full-scale war in order to stymie any serious peace process.

Furthermore, several years of trying to avoid con- fronting Hezbollah had made the IDF reluctant to patrol the border aggressively in order to "disturb" Hezbollah's preparations. This was a tactic that had been used successfully in the past as standard operating procedure in Lebanon and with regard to various Palestinian groups. When a host of factors coincided, a trio of Israeli leaders almost entirely lacking in defense experience decided that it was time to put their foot down. Hardly anyone had expected such a harsh Israeli response to the relatively minor incident, but it is possible to argue that the Israeli response in 2006 served as a warning. Furthermore, Israel's response was a reaction to six frustrating years of failed attempts to push the Lebanese government or the UN, preferably both, to deal with Hezbollah and implement UNSCR 1559.

Seen in this light, the lessons of the 2006 war might deter Hezbollah from launching future attacks. But it is equally possible to claim the opposite, that Hezbollah has been emboldened. None of the basic reasons for the war have been resolved. Hezbollah's position has strengthened. Lebanon's political situation is just as complicated, with the only difference that Hezbollah and its allies now have a stronger legal and constitutional position from which to control much of what happens in the country.

For Hezbollah, too, the basic issues remain the same: Israel is still viewed as an enemy that must be fought with all means necessary. In Lebanon, Hezbollah's clearly stated aim is, primarily, to act as a base for the movement's larger strategic and ideological struggle. Its dependence on Iran and, to a lesser extent, Syria plays a part here. If, say, the United States launches new initiatives with the intention of driving a wedge between Iran and Syria, or if Iran is pressured to stop its nuclear weapons program, Lebanon's security situation will worsen. Moreover, Israel's unilateral withdrawals from Gaza and Lebanon did not produce the intended opening toward a new peace process. On the contrary, these withdrawals are seen, not only by Hezbollah and Hamas, as victories in the armed struggle. These events probably did serious damage to the Israeli model of deterrence.[103]

Exactly how the war will affect Israel in the long term is hard to predict. There can be no doubt, how- ever, that the war led to some serious introspection. The soul-searching was not only about the core problem of the war the conflict with Hezbollah but also, more significantly, about Israel's future role in the Middle East. Since the unilateral steps Israel took to open up an opportunity for a new peace process with the Palestinians and Lebanon caused more, not less, violence, many have lost hope that a peace process will bring about any positive benefits. Perhaps it should come as no surprise that the very move meant to facilitate peace and fewer violent attacks instead resulted in the opposite. But for the long-term work toward peace, this development is bad news.

## Hezbollah:

No one can imagine the importance of our military potential as our military apparatus is not separate from our overall social fabric.

—Open letter from Hezbollah[104]

Today, Hezbollah is better equipped than it was at the outbreak of the war in 2006. Even though Israel's response to the kidnappings and murders was far more forceful than what Hezbollah's leadership had expected, the poor showing of the Israeli army gave Hezbollah little reason to fear a new confrontation. The buildup of arms stockpiles and the strengthening of defensive lines and communications networks both north and south of the Litani River are a clear indication that Hezbollah expects to be even better prepared if or when another war breaks out.[105] Hezbollah's strongholds are located north of the Litani River and in the Bekaa Val- ley, where large areas have been made off-limits to most Lebanese. In the area south of the Litani River, it has been more discreet, so as to avoid embarrassing the Lebanese soldiers stationed in the area. The basic principle, however, is to prevent UN resolutions or forces, such as UNIFIL, from standing in its way. On several occasions, Hezbollah has violently prevented UNIFIL from patrolling the areas over which it is formally responsible.[106] Another war with Israel is expected to happen sooner or later, and Hezbollah is not prepared to allow its preparations to be hampered, either to the north or south of the Litani River.[107]

Hezbollah's successes during the 2006 conflict were made possible by several years of preparation and depended on several different factors. During the six years that passed between the Israeli withdrawal in 2000 and the outbreak of the war, Hezbollah expended significant effort in building up its defensive capabilities in southern Lebanon. It created an extensive network of bunkers, gave its militiamen frequent training, expanded food and weapons supplies around the Litani River, and prepared plans for defending the area in a future battle with Israel. All these activities were carried out with large support from Iran and Syria.[108]

The extensive network of bunkers proved to be particularly effective in countering Israel's advance into Lebanon. In part, this was because, for a long time, Israel was reluctant to commit ground forces in the operation.[109] But even if the Israeli air force made it more difficult to move troops around, Hezbollah's order of battle was such that the various defensive systems, based on the bunker networks, were generally self-sufficient with regard to weapons and food. That, together with an intimate knowledge of the area and good communications, was sufficient to put up a more effective resistance to the IDF than had been expected. On several occasions, Hezbollah attempted to penetrate Israeli territory with small forces, but these were repelled every time.[110] Hezbollah was, however, able to continue its rocket fire on Israel throughout the war. Even though artillery or air force counterattacks were initiated only minutes after the initial attacks, on most occasions, Hezbollah's highly mobile rocket-firing crews were able to leave the area in time. This speaks volumes about the extent of Hezbollah's preparations and the effectiveness of its strategy of firing rockets.[111]

Iran's and Syria's support of Hezbollah in rebuilding its capabilities in southern Lebanon and in rebuilding the rest of Lebanon has already been mentioned. Iran's support is of particular interest. The country's current regime has contributed both the religious and ideological base for Hezbollah, but it has also, in an unconventional manner, financed a large part of Hezbollah's activities. Before the war, in early summer 2006, Iran had already changed the way it finances Hezbollah mainly in reaction to the increased pressure that the U.S. Treasury placed on Lebanese banks in its investigations of suspicious financial transfers to Hezbollah.[112] The unconventional, or possibly very *conventional*, way that Iran supported Hezbollah was by smuggling cash in diplomatic pouches between Tehran and Beirut. Unlike money transfers through banks, the method left behind no trace.

The branch of the Islamic Revolutionary Guard Corps (IRGC) that funded Hezbollah during and immediately after the war was led by Gen. Mir Faysal Baqer Zadah. During summer of 2006, in direct connection to the war and its immediate aftermath, a number of these transfers were carried out.[113] The money came from various religious centers that were not directly under the control of the government, primarily from one run by an imam called Reza in the city of Meshed.[114] Money was also sent from smaller centers in Qom, Shiraz, Kerman, and Isfahan. In doing so, the government in Tehran used an old and trusted and difficult to trace method of transferring money.[115] Consequently, the Iranian government could not be held directly responsible for its financial support, and it could avoid accusations of financing an organization labeled by many as a terrorist organization.

The support for Hezbollah thus comes from kindred organizations in Iran that back their coreligionists in Lebanon. Until the United States stepped up its efforts which have been redoubled after the war, for obvious reasons Iran transferred money primarily through Bank Saderat, an Iranian bank that maintains four offices in Lebanon. The money that flowed into Lebanon after the war was earmarked to aid the reconstruction effort, allowing Hezbollah to quickly help civilians rebuild their homes and infrastructure. The effort stood in stark contrast to the slowness with which the government in Beirut and the international community acted.

In Lebanon, it was primarily Hezbollah's chief of finances, Hassan al-Shami, who handled and distributed the funds.[116] Al-Shami used his two companies Beit al-Mal and yossr which control Hezbollah's welfare organizations and which also collect money from Shiite Muslims in North America and South America. This enables Hezbollah to mix the financial support it receives from various sources, making it even more difficult to trace its origins.[117] The basis for Hezbollah's activist politics can be traced back to the traditional division between activism and passivism in Shia Islam.[118] Both these ideas have had adherents in Lebanon, but as Hezbollah's influence has grown, the activist part has become dominant.

An example of the passive branch of Shia Islam is the Iraqi Shiite leader Ali Sistani.[119] The passivist tradition, of keeping out of the political sphere as much as possible, is based on the knowledge that political forces "come and go." Especially with Shia Islam which has always been the minority and which has often been the victim of oppression by the dominant Sunni forces this was a lesson for which the community has had to pay dearly. Since the dominant forces were often Sunni, the relationship between the two branches of Islam was, at best, one of disinterest; at worst, it was one of open hostility, with various forms of oppression as a result. The passivist philosophy is based on the notion that one should devote time to theological issues and leave the political arena entirely. With the exception of Iran and now Iraq, Shia Islam has been a minority religion in all the countries dominated by Islam.[120] For its entire existence, Shia Islam has been wholly dependent on the beneficence of the majority's culture and political power. The widespread victim mentality within Shiite tradition is largely explained by this his- tory, which also explains much of the passivist tradition within Shia Islam.[121]

Even though it grew out of the same religious roots and historical experiences, the second philosophy, the activist branch of Shia Islam, is much younger. The most notable representative of this tradition is Iran's supreme leader, Ayatollah Ruhollah Khomeini. His political activity has in great part overshadowed the religious changes he instigated after Iran's Islamic Revolution of 1979. The notion of a religious "high office" (the Guardianship of the Islamic Jurists)[122] directly involved in day-to-day politics and the importance of "guiding" politicians on the true religious path were, when Khomeini imposed them, completely alien traditions to most Shiite Muslims. This was the case even though Khomeini based the changes on existing religious traditions.

It is this activist tradition, aided by its strengthened position after the Islamic Revolution, that serves as the foundation for Hezbollah today. The links between Shiites in Iran and Lebanon and between Lebanon and the various religious sites of learning in Najaf and Karbala in Iraq have ancient roots, of course, and they were established long before Hezbollah. But as a result of the Islamic Revolution and the Lebanese civil war, the new regime in Iran was presented with an opportunity to exert influence over Lebanon much more directly. Hezbollah which, in turn, is an off- shoot of the older Shiite organization Amal[123] was modeled after its Iranian mother organization. Hezbollah, although not directly controlled by Iran, maintains links so strong that, with few exceptions, it is very unlikely that it would reach any important decision before consulting those branches of the Iranian government that are actively involved in its activities.[124]

In this way, the activist tradition was essential to the establishment of Hezbollah. Hezbollah's current secretary-general, Hassan Nasrallah, demonstrates the tradition's importance. His worldview is significantly influenced by the view of Shiites as victims of oppression by domestic and foreign enemies.[125] The Shiite view of the religious leadership's role "during the absence of the imam" and the conflict between religious, political and national interests thus had a crucial influence on Hezbollah and, by extension, on Lebanon. Since its founding, Hezbollah has evolved into perhaps the most talked-about Shiite political actor in the world, after Iran.

## Conclusion

Seen in the light of the broader Arab-Israeli conflict, the war in Lebanon was not decisive. Instead, it has fallen into the large category of unfinished conflicts that the Middle East has witnessed since the September 11 attacks. The war did, however, clarify the basic causes of the larger struggle looming in the background. The Arab-Israeli conflict is not primarily about occupation or settlement. These factors are significant, of course, and must be addressed in order to achieve peace. yet Hezbollah did not attack Israel because of the occupation of the Sheba Farms or the West Bank it attacked Israel because it is not interested in any sort of peace. Just as it has done on several occasions since 2000, Hezbollah attacked because it could not imagine a future in which Israel exists. The conflict is therefore shaped by the group's attempts to prevent any process that might end in a long-term peace agreement.

These factors necessarily have wider regional significance. Israel and Hezbollah were not the only par- ties that clashed in July 2006, after all; Iran, Syria, and Sunni-dominated Saudi Arabia and Egypt were active as well. In this respect, the tensions fragmenting the region today between Sunnis and Shiites, Arabs and Israelis, Islamists and moderates, not to mention Lebanon's own sectarian communities have deepened. This regional point illustrates how the 2006 war encompassed several different dimensions. The first was the Arab-Israeli conflict. Hezbollah attempted to dress the war in this garb, and although only some Arabs agreed with that interpretation, it was nevertheless an effective way for the group to garner support beyond its own sect. In this sense, the summer war constituted the sixth Arab-Israeli war.

Another dimension was Lebanon itself the war was yet another means of shaping the country's internal situation, which concerns nothing less than what form the state will eventually take.[126] The 1989 Taif Accord, which ended the Lebanese civil war, stipulated that all militias were to be disarmed. This mandate was enforced more or less on all groups except Hezbollah, which actually expanded its militia following the accord. The murder of former prime minister Rafiq Hariri in February 2005 and the Syrian military withdrawal from Lebanon two months later gave renewed strength to the domestic political forces demanding Hezbollah's disarmament. yet, because Hezbollah was the strongest military force in Lebanon (and the only real force in the South), such demands were easily buried under the so-called "national dialogue."[127]

The war had a global dimension as well. In particular, it highlighted the question of how best to handle radical Islam and its offshoot, militant Islamism. All of these dimensions are connected, but they can be viewed separately as well, and they have had different implications for various actors. One over- arching conclusion is that the 2006 war and its after-math amounted to a victory for those who favor continued conflict between the Arab-Islamic world and Israel. Indeed, it is difficult to imagine any concession from either side that would change the current state of affairs, at least in the short term. The Sheba Farms dispute or other territorial issues cannot hide the fact that the root of the Arab-Israeli conflict is a refusal to accept an Israeli state; if nothing else, the Lebanon war made that clear.[128] And Hezbollah has declared itself the representative of the Arab side of that conflict.

Herein lies one of the war's most tragic consequences: the notion that it was a victory for those who subscribe to armed struggle, those who believe they can achieve results without compromising or getting involved in complicated political processes with uncertain outcomes. From this perspective, it is just as effective, or even more so, to confront Israel on the battlefield and force it to make concessions. If a sufficient number of other Arab actors accept this destructive analysis of the war, the foundation will be laid for new armed conflagrations for a long time to come.

The fighting in Gaza supports this view Hezbollah and Hamas have used similar reasoning to justify armed conflict with Israel. And their efforts in recent years from the war in Lebanon to the Gaza hostilities that have continued ever since Israel evacuated its settlements there in 2005 have fostered greater mistrust between the respective populations. The end result is a hardening of attitudes and a decreasing willingness to compromise, which benefits those who are not interested in long-term peace.

Another key factor is that the Lebanon war ended in a ceasefire a far less stable solution than a proper peace agreement. This state of affairs has fomented expectations among Islamists of a second round. Furthermore, the position of strength Hezbollah has acquired since the war has made any full-fledged peace initiatives practically impossible.[129] By virtue of avoiding defeat and disarmament, Hezbollah has been able to claim, with some merit, that it did not lose the war. This "victory," along with the group's subsequent maneuvers to strengthen its position in Lebanon, has underscored the similarities between the Arab nationalist ideology of the past and the Islamist ideology of today. The old goals of the Arab nationalists to defeat Israel by force of arms, to fight deleterious Western influence, and to give Arab countries a common ideological base are different from current ideology in name alone. The only real differences are that Iran is now more influential, and that nationalism, having joined causes rhetorically with Islamism, now reaches more people.

More than thirty years after the Arab states and their military commanders concluded that it would be impossible to defeat Israel by military means, new leaders are making the opposite claim.[130] Since the 2006 war, Islamist representatives such as Hezbollah secretary general Hassan Nasrallah, Hamas leader Khaled Mashal, and Iranian president Mahmoud Ahmadi Nezhad have become more aggressive in predicting Israel's ultimate defeat. Prior to the war, this sentiment was limited mostly to individuals and organizations that had advocated violence as the only route all along. Afterward, however, these voices experienced something of a renaissance. The question of Israel's existence, which had been taken off the agenda in the past, once again became the subject of debate in the media and other circles. For example, one can find serious discussions of topics such as how long it would take one generation or several? to realize the vision of a Middle East without Israel. Without a doubt, individuals like Ahmadi Nezhad have been important catalysts for this development. But it is the putatively successful military actions of the Islamists that have played the most important part in changing this worldview.

The doctrine behind these views is commonly called muqawama. Sometimes translated as "resistance," a better rendering would be "constant struggle" or "constant war," which is certainly what Mashal and others mean by the word. Supporters of this doctrine have used the Lebanon war and the more recent 2008–2009 Hamas- Israel skirmishes to prove that theirs is the right path: that it is possible to confront Israel with force and win. Summarizing the ideologies underpinning this doctrine is important because it highlights the specific steps that Islamists believe Arab and Muslim countries should take in their dealings with Israel. First, long-term peace with Israel is considered out of the question, as is any form of recognition of Israel's right to exist. Temporary truces are acceptable if necessary, as was the case with Hamas in Gaza.[131]

Second, it is not necessary to delay action until the Arab world has reached military parity with Israel, as both Egyptian president Gamal Abdul Nasser and Syrian president Hafiz al-Asad sought. Instead, rocket fire, kidnappings, and other asymmetrical tactics can be used to achieve victory. Whatever the tactic used, the war must continue unless a temporary truce is in effect.

Third, it is not necessary to conquer territory; the more important goal is to systematically wear down Israel's morale. It follows, then, that targeting Israeli civilians is the best approach. The goal is to prevent the enemy from winning, not to achieve a quick military victory. In this way, Israel's conventional military strength is turned into a benefit for its opponents, who can shift their focus from military to civilian targets. The conflict in Gaza has revealed this tactic's effectiveness—Israel cannot entirely stop the rocket- fire from that territory unless it reoccupies the Strip, as the fighting in 2008–2009 made clear. Although Hamas seemed to take serious damage in that fighting, the organization nevertheless survived and continues to exert its influence over the area. In fact, the negotiated ceasefire was used as an opportunity to smuggle in new weapons and consolidate Hamas's role as the most important political force in Gaza.

Meanwhile, Hamas's strategy resulted in noticeable gains on both the intra-Palestinian and international fronts. For example, despite the June

2007 collapse of the Saudi-brokered agreement between Hamas and Fatah, the Palestinian Authority (PA) has continued to pay Hamas operatives in Gaza, including terrorists. In other words, taxpayers in those countries that contribute to the PA budget currently $120 million per month foot some of the bill for Hamas as well.[132] The massive criticism directed against Israel following its attacks in Gaza also benefited Hamas, which received considerably less flak for its role in the hostilities. And the political processes that followed the fighting have led to discussions in UN and European Union circles about whether to resume dialogue with Hamas. These discussions have taken place without Hamas fulfilling any of the conditions originally set for reengagement clearly a decisive victory for the organization.

*Dr Magnus Norell is a Senior Researcher for the Project for CHIIS at Islamic Theology of Counter Terrorism (ITCT), UK. He is an adjunct Scholar at the Washington Institute for Near East Policy, Washington DC, USA and also a Senior Fellow at the European Foundation for Democracy (EFD), Brussels, Belgium. He was a Senior Analyst at the Swedish Defence Research Agency (FOI), Stockholm, Kista, Sweden and Senior Analyst at the Swedish Institute for International Affairs, Stockholm, Sweden. Magnus served as a Senior Analyst at the Swedish Military Intelligence from 1993 – 1996. 1997 – 2000. Between 1997 and 2000 Dr. Norell created, together with colleague Dr. Magnus Ranstorp, a back-channel between the Lebanese Hizb'allah movement and the Israelis. The purpose of this endeavour was to find out the consequences of a unilateral Israeli withdrawal from the so-called security zone in the southern Lebanon. The Initiative came from Yossi Beilin who, within the Israeli Labour party, for many years had advocated such a scenario. The process was successful and based on the 'indirect' assurances given to Norell and Ranstorp by the leadership of the Hizb'allah, a swift and bloodless Israeli withdrawal took place in May 2000. Mr Norell obtained a PhD in Political Science from Stockholm University in 1998. Mr Norell has worked on many fields and projects related with counter terrorism, Islamist radicalisation and political Islam.*

CHAPTER 9

# IRAN AND HEZBOLLAH'S PRE-OPERATIONAL MODUS OPERANDI IN THE WEST

## *Ioan Pop & Mitchell D. Silber*

### Abstract

*Tensions between the United States and Iran/Hezbollah have been on the rise since 2018 when the U.S. administration withdrew from the 2015 nuclear deal. These tensions spiked in January 2020 when U.S. strikes killed Qassem Soleimani the leader of Iran's IRGC-Quds Force. Furthermore, there is mounting evidence that in recent years, Iran and Hezbollah have sought to create a sleeper network in the U.S. and Western Europe, which could be activated to launch attacks as part of a retaliatory attack. This paper assesses Iran and Hezbollah pre-operational modus operandi in the West derived from court documents and open source reporting of recent arrest of Hezbollah and Iranian agents in the US and abroad. It sheds lights on the recruitment, training, and placement of these agents and the intricacies of their past operations. While it is impossible to predict when, where or how Iran/ Hezbollah might retaliate as retribution for Soleimani's killing, this article argues that there is growing number of indicators and warning signs for a possible attack in the U.S. or against U.S. interests abroad.*

Tensions between the United States and Iran have been increasing since 2018 when the U.S. administration withdrew from the 2015 nuclear deal and reimposed comprehensive sanctions on Iran. In response, Iran and its proxies have committed a series of calibrated asymmetric regional escalations designed to pressure the United States and its regional allies. The January 3, 2020 U.S. strike that killed the IRGC-Quds Force leader,

262

Iranian General Qassem Soleimani, has the potential to be a dramatic step up the escalation ladder by the United States, which catalyzes formidable Iranian retaliation against American interests. From the authors' experience, as well as based on an assessment ofthe decade-long surge in Iran and Lebanese Hezbollah preoperational activities in both Western Europe and the United States, there is a high likelihood of a possible future attack on U.S. interests abroad and the possibility of an attack in the homeland. This article presents seven principles that underpin Iran and Hezbollah preoperational planning for a potential terrorist attack, ranging from surveillance, logistical planning, and front operations to disguise operatives to infiltration, recruitment, and targets election.

"They [U.S.] hit him [Soleimani] in a cowardly way, but with God's grace and through endeavors of freedom-seekers around the world who want vengeance over his blood, we will hit his enemy in a manly fashion," stated Esmail Qaani, the new leader of the IRGC-Quds Force following the death of his predecessor on January 3,2020 in a U.S. drone strike at Baghdad international airport.[1] Similarly, Iran's Supreme Leader, Ayatollah Ali Khamenei, called for "forceful revenge" to avenge Soleimani's death and; Hassan Nasrallah, the Secretary General of Hezbollah called on Hezbollah operatives globally to carry out "the appropriate punishment," stating that this "will be the responsibility and task of all resistance fighters worldwide."[2]

During the authors' time at the NYPD Intelligence Division (2005-2015), the threat from Iran and Hezbollah was always near and sometimes at the very top of the threat matrix for New York City based on Iran and Hezbollah's global reach,sophistication and lethality as well as particular features that made the city a uniquely attractive target.[3] Although the threat fluctuated depending on geopolitical tensions[4], given the killing of Qassem Soleimani, the commander of Iran's IRGC – Quds Force, amid a background of rising tensions between Iran and the United States,[5] the authors assess that the West is at an elevated risk for Iranian and, or Hezbollah retaliation. Therefore, it is important to analyze and assess Iran and Hezbollah's pre-operational[6] modus operandi for committing terrorist attacks in the West.

Based on recent history, the authors assess that it is likely that Soleimani's killing will trigger an Iranian/Hezbollah retaliatory response (or responses) similar to the reaction tothe assassinations of Hezbollah leaders Abbas Musawi (1992) and Imad Mugniyah (2008). Like those, the vengeance will likely be calibrated, sufficient to send a message, but not so extreme as to threaten the survival of the Iranian regime. While widespread COVID-19 transmissions rates in Iran[7] might delay Iranian plans for retaliation, based on past Iranian history[8], the regime is a patient actor and the IRGC is unlikely to be satisfied with anything less than a meaningful retaliatory response, delayed though it maybe.

If the past is prolog, analysts might look at the 1992 Israeli Embassy bombing in Buenos Aires, which according to Argentine officials, was committed by Iran/Hezbollah partially in response to the Israeli assassination of Secretary General of Hezbollah, Abbas Musawi.[9] Events that occurred in the wake of the February 2008 assassination of Hezbollah operations chief, Imad Mugniyah, by Israel and the United States may also be instructive.[10] Following his death in Damascus, Syria, Hezbollah plotted several attacks to avenge his death in Azerbaijan, Bulgaria, Cyprus, India, Kuwait and Turkey.[11] However, other than the 2012 suicide bombing attack on a bus carrying Israeli tourists in Burgas, Bulgaria, which killed six Israeli tourists and injured forty-two, all of the Hezbollah plots were thwarted.[12]

Iran is Hezbollah's closest ally and patron, providing money and weapons to the terrorist group often described as an "Iranian aircraft carrier parked north of Israel."[13] In addition to their ideological, political and military ties, Iran reportedly funds Hezbollah with an estimated $200[14]-700[15] million yearly.

Hezbollah and Iran's intelligence apparatus have a history of joint terrorist attacks globally, most notably, the attacks in 1992 and 1994 in Buenos Aires targeting the local Israeli Embassy[16] and AMIA[17], a Jewish cultural center respectively. Moreover, their joint mission over the past decade to keep Assad in power in Syria has led to significant augmentation of their cooperation. This makes it likely that any future external operations would entail joint operational planning and execution.

There is evidence Iran and Hezbollah have sought in recent years to create a sleeper network in the United States and Western Europe, which could be activated to launch attacks. The failed 2011 Iran-directed plot to target the Saudi Ambassador in Washington[18] illustrated an attack within the United States was not unthinkable.[19] Hezbollah operative, Ali Mohamed Kourani, told the FBI during his 2016-2017 interviews that "in the event that the

United States and Iran went to war, the U.S. sleeper cell would expect to be called upon to act."[20]

U.S. officials have made clear that Iran and Hezbollah continue to be a potential threat to the United States Homeland. In 2012, the then Director of National Intelligence (DNI), James Clapper stated that Iranian officials "are now more willing to conduct an attack in the United States in response to real or perceived U.S. actions that threaten the regime."[21] The director of the U.S. National Counterterrorism Center (NCTC), Nick Rasmussen, noted in October 2017, "It is our assessment that Hezbollah is determined to give itself a potential homeland option as a critical component of its terrorism playbook."[22]

Although decision-makers in Tehran will likely still think very carefully before striking the U.S. homeland to avenge the death of Soleimani, it is important for the analyst/ policymaker community to understand Iran and Hezbollah's efforts to create an infra- structure for potential attacks in the West. [23] In light of this and coupled with the recent history of Iran and Hezbollah terrorist activity outside the U.S., which this article will also outline, following the death of Soleimani, Iran may be less hesitant to authorize a retaliatory strike.

Based on the authors' analysis of Iran and Hezbollah's past operations, foiled plots, the recent U.S. arrests of Hezbollah operatives and their personal experience leading Iran and Hezbollah intelligence investigations for NYPD, seven principles[24] underpin the pre operational modus operandi of Iran and Hezbollah:

1. Intelligence gathering and surveillance activities;

2. Plausible diplomatic, business, education and other covers to conceal operational activities;

3. Infiltration of Iranian dissident groups;

4. Logistical planning for possible future attacks;

5. Preparing "human target packages" to enable assassinating dissidents and adversaries;

6. Counter-intelligence tradecraft, and operational security

7. Recruiting operatives with dual nationalities and Western passports from the Shia diaspora. Each of these are outlined in turn below.

## Modus Operandi 1: Intelligence Gathering and Surveillance Activities

One of the distinguishing characteristics of Iran and Hezbollah's modus operandi for operational planning in the West has been the sustained commitment to undertaking precise intelligence gathering and surveillance activities on targets that could support long term attack planning.

In some cases, Iranians have conducted intelligence gathering activities[25] and in other cases it has been Lebanese expatriates acting on behalf of Hezbollah[26], who have burrowed into diaspora communities overseas to disguise their efforts.

New York City has witnessed intelligence gathering activities by both Iranians and Hezbollah operatives that demonstrate methodology and possible targets. In the case of Iran, between 2002 and 2010, the NYPD and federal authorities detected at least six events involving Iranian diplomatic personnel that these authors (who were then serving in the police department) struggled to categorize as anything other than hostile reconnaissance of New York City.[27]

One of the most brazen incidents occurred at 2 a.m. on November 16, 2003 when uniformed NYPD officers riding a southbound 7 train observed two males filming the subway train tracks. The men, who initially claimed diplomatic immunity turned out to be guards at the Iranian Mission to the UN who had recently arrived in New York. "Despite two warnings from the State Department about this unacceptable behavior, in May 2004, two more Iranian Mission security guards were observed videotaping infrastructure, public transportation and New York City landmarks. One month later, the guards from the November 2003 subway incident were expelled by the United States for "engaging in activities that were not consistent with their duties" in other words, spying."[28].

Despite this official reprimand, suspicious activities by Iranian diplomatic personnel continued. "In May 2005, tips led the NYPD to six people on a sight-seeing cruise who were taking pictures and movies of city landmarks like the Brooklyn Bridge. In September 2008, police interviewed three people taking pictures of railroad tracks. And in September 2010, federal air marshals saw four people taking pictures and videos at a New York heliport."[29] During interviews by law enforcement, the four individuals disclosed that they were associated with the Iranian government. However, they were ultimately released and never charged.[30]

Iranian intelligence gathering and surveillance activities have extended beyond New York City. In November 2019, two men Ahmadreza Mohammadi-Doostdar, a dual U.S.-Iranian citizen and Majid Ghorbani, an Iranian citizen residing in California pleaded guilty to acting as illegal agents of the government of Iran on charges stemming from monitoring two Jewish facilities in Chicago and as well as American members of an exiled Iranian opposition group, Mujahideen-e-Khalq (MeK), an Iranian dissident group that seeks regime change in Iran.[31]

According to the criminal complaint, both men were accused of "acting on behalf of the Iranian government to gather information that could be used to identify and locate individuals and facilities."[32] Not only did they conduct physical surveillance on and collect information about Americans involved with MeK, but in July 2017, they also con- ducted hostile reconnaissance on the University of Chicago Hillel Center and a Rohr Chabad Center. "Doostdar was seen photographing the front and back of the Rohr Chabad Center, as well as the wrought iron fence surrounding the building. Doostdar also turned around to look at the building multiple times as he walked away."[33]

More recently, aggressive Iranian intelligence collection activities against Jewish targets have been detected in Europe. According to reporting from Israeli newspapers, German security forces raided various locations across Germany pursuing alleged members of Iran's Islamic Revolutionary Guard Corps - Quds Force for spying on Jewish and Israeli locations.[34] Raids were carried out in the German states of Baden Wurttemberg, North Rhine-Westphalia, Bavaria and Berlin, but no arrests were made.[35] Among the IRGC reconnaissance targets were Jewish kindergartens and the Israeli embassy in Berlin, Germany.[36]

Some of these activities were discussed in greater detail by the intelligence agency of the German state of North Rhine-Westphalia. In a report issued during the summer of 2019, it found that "a main focus [of Iran's regime] is spying on Israeli and pro-Israeli institutions, as well as citizens of the State of Israel living here [Germany] and persons of the Jewish faith."[37]

While more than twenty investigations related to Iranian espionage in Germany have been conducted,[38] the one[39] arrest and conviction in Germany linked to Iran dates back to 2017, when a Berlin court convicted Pakistani citizen, Haidar Syed-Naqfi, for being paid by the Quds Force to target Jewish and Israeli individuals and institutions. German prosecutors argued that Naqfi was told to identify, surveil and conduct reconnaissance on "Israeli and Jewish institutions and Israel advocates in Germany, France and other unnamed Western European countries for possible attacks."[40]

In recent years, more incidents of preoperational intelligence gathering, and surveil- lance activities have been detected, conducted by members of Hezbollah's Islamic Jihad Organization (IJO)[41] also known as Unit 910[42] than by Iranians. While New York City has figured prominently in these intelligence gathering efforts, Chicago, Washington DC and Boston have also registered as potential targets.[43]

Exhibit a for this concern was an Investigation by the NYPD and the FBI that led to the May 31, 2017 arrests[44] of two naturalized Americans from Lebanon who were recruited and trained by Hezbollah's unit 910 to conduct intelligence collection missions in the United States. While these two Lebanese expatriates, Ali Mohammed Kourani 32, and Samer El Debek, 37, at the time of their arrest, gave the outward appearance of leading ordinary lives in the U.S., in reality, they were conducting intelligence gathering missions for their Beirut based handlers. In fact, Kourani went as far to describe himself to the FBI as "an IJO 'sleeper' operative working undercover in the United States."[45] On December 3, 2019, Ali Kourani was sentenced to 40 years in prison for "covert terrorist activities on behalf of Hezbollah's Islamic Jihad Organization."[46] Samer El Debek's case is still pending in courts.[47]

In the wake of the arrest of these two IJO operatives, former New York City Police Department Commissioner James P. O'Neill noted, "preoperational surveillance is one of the hallmarks of [Hezbollah] in planning for future attacks."[48] The surveillance per- formed in New York City was done "in support of anticipated IJO terrorist attacks."[49]

The facts of the case, as laid out by the U.S. government, are worth recounting in detail. According to the Department of Justice "[f]rom at least in or about 2009, up to and including in or about September 2015, Kourani conducted surveillance of U.S. military and intelligence out posts in New York City, as well as airports in New York City and another country, in support of anticipated terrorist attacks by Hezbollah's Islamic Jihad Organization."[50] "Principally responsible for conducting IJO intelligence-gathering and surveillance activities, Kourani received taskings in Lebanon and executed his missions covertly."[51]

According to the Department of Justice, from Lebanon, Kourani was directed and "conducted physical surveillance of the following targets: FBI offices in Manhattan, New York; a U.S. Army National Guard facility in Manhattan, a U.S. Secret Service facility in Brooklyn, and a U.S. Army armory facility in Manhattan. Kourani used his phone to videotape activity around at least one of these surveillance targets, transferred the video footage to a memory card, and brought the memory card to his Lebanese-based handler[52] and other IJO personnel in Lebanon.[53]

When it came to airports, Kourani's intelligence collection, surveillance and reconnaissance were not limited to the United States and John F. Kennedy Airport in New York. The scholar Matthew Levitt, whose research has focused on Hezbollah, has written that Kourani was tasked to also focus on Toronto's Pearson International Airport, visiting Pearson seven times.[54]

According to Levitt, during his debriefings with the FBI, Kourani explained that "he provided Hezbollah with details about security procedures, the uniforms worn by security officers, and whether the officers were armed."[55] Kourani's surveillance "focused on exit points, security checkpoints, camera locations, baggage claim procedures, and what questions airport screeners asked passengers."[56]

Moreover, as Levitt notes, "aside from carrying out surveillance himself, Kourani also plied [Pearson] airport employees for information, some of whom understood they were providing information for Hezbollah while others were unwitting, in one case even smoking a hookah together with an airport employee who would "casually answer Kourani's questions about the locations of cameras and magnetometers. Kourani said he could ask the man to carry a bag onto an airplane for him, and he would do it. "According to a U.S. Prosecutor's statement during the trial, Hezbollah was 'thinking about how to get terrorists, and weapons, and contraband through airports, from Lebanon into Canada, from Lebanon into the United States."'[57]

Similarly, while prosecutors accused Samer El Debek of surveilling "potential targets in America, including military and law enforcement facilities in New York"[58], much of his intelligence collection activity occurred in Latin America. In Panama, he allegedly was tasked to locate the U.S. and Israeli embassies, "case and identify security procedures at the Canal and Israeli Embassy" and "to locate places where items such as acetone and battery acid, which are explosive precursors, could be purchased."[59]

Kourani and El Debek were not the only IJO/Unit 910 members conducting intelligence, surveillance and reconnaissance actives in the Americas. More recently, another Lebanese-born, Hezbollah trained IJO/Unit 910 member, Alexei Saab (AKA: "Ali Hassan Saab") 42, was arrested in September 2019, accused of providing Hezbollah with "intelligence and photographs concerning several locations Saab had surveilled in the New York City area, including the Port Authority Bus Terminal, Grand Central Terminal, the New York Stock Exchange, [NYC FBI Headquarters at] 26 Federal Plaza, and local airports."[60] Saab had been recruited into Hezbollah as a student in Beirut in 1996,[61] according to the Department of Justice, which is also the source of the allegations against Saab outlined in the paragraphs below.

For his surveillance training, besides classroom and field work in Beirut, Saab was allegedly taught sophisticated tradecraft to "start by recording an unrelated subject before panning the camera to the object of his surveillance" and "took videos from a high altitude and different zoom ranges to show perspective relevant to hezbollah".[62] For still photography, "Saab would also often pose people in front of the intended objects of his surveillance, to provide perspective and shield his true purpose from law enforcement."[63]

As part of his "intelligence collection" efforts, "Saab explained that IJO had trained Saab so that his mindset was that he should always be gathering intelligence and he was on 'autopilot' to collect intelligence at any opportunity, including while he was in New York City."[64] Admitting the purpose of his intelligence collection activities, "Saab understood that the information he provided to the IJO would be used to calculate the size of a bomb needed to target a particular structure and the ideal location in which to place explosive devices to maximize damage," so "Saab focused on structural weaknesses of the location he surveilled to determine how a future attack could cause the most destruction." Saab's information was allegedly prepared for the IJO in a seven to ten page report on New York City.[65]

New York City was allegedly not Saab's only target. According to court documents, he also admitted that as part of his reconnaissance and intelligence collection, he took photographs in Boston including Quincy Market, Fenway Park and the Prudential Center and in Washington DC including the Capitol Building and the White House.[66] His case is still pending in the courts.

## Modus Operandi 2: Plausible Diplomatic, Business, Cultural and Other Covers to Conceal Operational Activities

During a 2008 visit by an NYPD Intelligence Division team (including one of the authors) to Buenos Aires, Argentinian intelligence officials outlined how Hezbollah, in cooperation with various elements within the Iranian intelligence, was responsible for two separate terrorist attacks in Buenos Aires, the 1992 Israeli Embassy and the 1994 AMIA bombing. In both cases Iran leveraged a highly complex local intelligence net-work developed since the mid-1980s, which was run from Iranian Embassy in Buenos Aires and its Cultural Bureau. The local network for the 1994 AMIA attack, centered around a Shi'a Imam and Cultural Attaché to the Iranian Embassy and involved three front companies.[67] While the authors were told by Argentine intelligence officials that the decision to attack Argentina in 1994 was made at the highest levels of Iran's govern- mental structure, the Iranians used diplomatic cover, business cover and NGO/religious cover to mask their network on the ground in South America.[68]

A report by the AMIA Special Prosecutor, Alberto Nisman, illustrated the three elements – diplomatic cover, business cover and NGO/religious cover in Iran's robust spy network in Argentina. Mohsen Rabbani, who was both the Imam at At-Tauhid Mosque in Buenos Aires and later given the position of Cultural Attache to the Iranian Embassy in Buenos Aires benefited from both "religious cover" as an imam and later diplomatic cover. Nisman noted that both Rabbani and Ahmad Reza Asghari (Third Secretary of the Iranian Embassy in Buenos Aires) benefited from their diplomatic covers and "played key roles in the intelligence infrastructure that the Iranian government maintained in Buenos Air esat the timeof the attack."[69]

According to the report, Rabbani received his diplomatic cover (when he was named the Cultural Attaché to the Iranian Embassy in Buenos Aires) a few months before the attack. Nisman cited him as the "driving force" behind the Iranian intelligence collection efforts in Argentina and noted that he had received substantial amounts of money from Iran after the decision to carry out the attack was made.[70] Nisman noted that once the decision to attack had been made, "the information flow between Iran and its Argentinean embassy substantially increased, via functionaries and diplomatic couriers."[71] As part of the business cover for the Iranian spy network in Argentina, there were also three front companies, Government Trade Corporation (GTC), Imanco and South Beef SA, whose officials reportedly carried out various intelligence tasks.[72] GTC was established in Argentinain March 1985 and by mid-1993 moved its office in the same building as Iranian Embassy's Cultural Bureau.[73]

According to the Argentine intelligence officials, GTC "provided cover for Iranian intelligence operatives to enter Argentina," as it was alleged that its executive in Argentina, Seyed Jamal Youssefi, was an Iranian intelligence official.[74] According to Nisman's report, documentation showed that GTC and Imanco had not conducted commercial activities for extended periods of time and it believed that their main purpose was to provide support and cover for the Iranian intelligence network in Argentina.[75] Additionally, GTC interchanged personnel with Imanco and South Beef, all of which were in permanent contact with Mohsen Rabbani, the network's ring leader.[76] Similar to the organizations hiding under different types of cover in Buenos Aires, in New York City, Iran's presence included the Alavi Foundation, an on profit ostensibly devoted to charity works and promoting Persian and Islamic culture.

In December 2009, Preet Bharara, U.S. Attorney for the Southern District of New York, described Alavi a shaving "effectively been a front for the government to Iran."[77] The complaint filed by the Southern District of New York led to the seizure of Alavi's assets in colluding with the Islamic Institute of New York, the largest Shi'a mosque in the city and closely affiliated with Iran's UN mission. Although in August 2019 ,a federal appeals court which cited several errors by the trial judge, overturned the verdict that granted the seizure of Alavi assets[78], the reisun disputable evidence of Alavi links to the Iranian government.[79] The investigation of Alavi, which had begun with the NYPD Intelligence Division and the District Attorney's Office of New York, had been based on NYPD concerns that like in Argentina, Alavi could provide diplomatic and NGO cover to shield an Iranian spy net work in New York City. As in the case the Iranian net work in Argentina, several individuals with links with Alavi maintained close ties to Iranian government officials. They had traveled to Iran, had regular contact with Iranian government officials in New York City and participated as board members, executives or employees of Iranian governmental and non governmental entities in the U.S. such as the Iranian Mission to the UN, the Iranian Interest Section in Washington DC (located within the Pakistan's Embassy), and various Shi'a Islamic Centers funded by the Alavi Foundation.[80]

During the authors' time at NYPD Intelligence Division, they investigated Iran activities related to preoperational intelligence gathering and Iranian officials' associations and funding of local institutions. They also investigated how, through a sophisticated web of financial transactions and shell companies, millions from the rental income of a Manhattan skyscraper owned by Alavi Foundation and Assa Corporation, a shell company controlled by Bank Melli[81] (Iran), made its way to U.S. dollar strapped Iran, in violations of U.S. sanctions.[82]

## Modus Operandi 3: Infiltration of Iranian Dissident Groups

Iranian security agencies use a range of tactics to safeguard the regime, including infiltrating opposition groups. These agencies have "identified and eradicated opponents and defectors inside and outside of the country".[83] In the 1990s, elements within the Iranian Intelligence focused on targeting the opposition outside Iran and are believed to have been responsible for assassinating various dissidents, including Shahpour Bakhtiar, the last prime minister under the Shah.[84] In August 1991, Bakhtiar was stabbed and strangled to death at his home in France by three Iranian agents.[85]

The Iranian government infiltrates and collects intelligence on the Iranian diaspora communities in various ways. For example, a Paris-based organization named "Supporting Iranian Refugees" is alleged to be used by Iranian intelligence to recruit Iranian asylum seekers in France, in order to spy on Iranian nationals residing there.[86] A similar phenomenon of community monitoring was observed in NYC after the 2009 Iranian presidential election and the street demonstrations in support of the Green Movement[87] in Iran.[88]

Iranian intelligence has a history of infiltrating opposition groups such as the MeK, which in 2002 disclosed publicly that Iran has two covert nuclear facilities located in Natanz and Arak.[89] MeK also has had close ties to the U.S. intelligence agencies and it reportedly provided intelligence on Iran's nuclear program to the U.S. Government.[90] In 2018, two Iranians, Ahmadreza Mohammadi Doostdar and Majid Ghorbani, were indicted for reportedly spying on the MeK on behalf of the Iranian government. According to the Department of Justice, Doostdar and Ghorbani collected intelligence on "individuals considered by the government of Iran to be enemies of that regime, including Israeli and Jewish interests, and individuals associated with the MeK, a group that advocates the overthrow of the current Iranian government."[91] According to court documents, Doostdar was believed by U.S. investigators to be an Iranian agent who recruited Ghorbani to collect intelligence on MeK's activities in theU.S.[92]

According to the Department of Justice, in 2017 Majid Ghorbani attended a MeK rally in New York City, where he took photos of participants protesting against the Iranian government.[93] Court documents indicate that in December 2017, upon his return from Iran, Doostdar contacted and met with Ghorbani. He reportedly paid Ghorbani roughly $2,000 for 28 photographs that Ghorbani took at the MeK rally, "many of which contained hand- written annotations identifying the individuals who appeared in the photos."[94]

In March 2018, Ghorbani traveled to Iran, reportedly for an "in-person briefing."[95] Upon his return to the U.S., a document was titled "About the Organization" was found on Ghorbani which appeared to include specific instructions on how to target the MeK:

"More influence in order to find out secret information, people in the network and organization's decisions against Islamic Republic;"

"Attending the monthly gathering every last Sunday of the month at the church;"

"Evaluation of the workplace's independency and the possibility of using it for the gathering of the important people of the organization;"and "Introducing a second person who can be trained by uncle Sohrab[96] and can act like uncle Sohrab inside the organization."[97]

Subsequently, in May 2018, he attended Iran Freedom Convention for Human Rights in Washington, DC, which featured speakers and attendees which were members or supporters of the MeK. While in attendance at this conference, Ghorbani took several photos of various attendees and speakers. According to U.S. Department of Justice, shortly after, he was allegedly called by Doostdar to "discuss clandestine methods Ghorbani should use in order to provide this information to Iran."[98]

## Modus Operandi 4: Logistical Planning for Possible Future Attacks

Iran/Hezbollah's modus operandi is often characterized by advanced logistical planning for potential future attacks. In some recent cases, this preparation has focused on the secret accumulation and storage of explosive material for potential forthcoming attacks. According to Israeli intelligence sources, as reported in the Israeli press, the effort by Hezbollah's Unit 910[99] involves "long-term planning for immense, game-changing terror attacks."[100]

Hezbollah repeatedly and across different continents conducted this advanced logistical planning by establishing large stockpiles of harmless looking "First Aid" ice packs filled with ammonium nitrate. This characteristic Hezbollah tradecraft for pre-positioning explosives around the world has been evidenced by discoveries in Thailand, Cyprus and the U.K.[101] The first time Hezbollah's stockpiling of ammonium nitrate in First Aid ice packs was detected was in Thailand in 2012 and were linked to the efforts of previously mentioned Unit 910 member, Samer el Debek.[102]

According to el Debek's criminal complaint, in January 2012, Hussein Atris, a member of Unit 910 with dual Lebanese-Swedish citizenship was detained at a Bangkok airport, seeking to depart Thailand. He subsequently led Thai law enforcement to "a commercial building near Bangkok that housed a cache of 10,000 pounds of urea-based fertilizer and 10 gallons of ammonium nitrate which was stored in First Aid icepacks."[103]

Likely not unrelated, Samer el Debek, who had been trained in creating ammonium nitrate based explosives, went on his first mission for Hezbollah, years earlier, to Thailand in 2009 on behalf of Unit 910 and was tasked to dispose of the ammonium nitrate by moving it out of a house and pouring it down the drain because "they [Hezbollah] were under surveillance".[104] In Cyprus, a strikingly similar example of Hezbollah's advanced logistical planning was detected. A supply of First Aid ice packs consisting of more than eight metric tons of ammonium nitrate was found in the home of 26-year-old Hussein Bassam Abdallah, a dual Lebanese and Canadian national who admitted to being a member of Hezbollah. Abdullah "pleaded guilty and was given a six-year prison sentence in June 2015."[105]

Then, in September 2015, in the United Kingdom, multiple caches of tons of explosive materials were discovered as stockpiles on the outskirts of London, hidden at four properties in north-west London (three businesses and a home). The explosive ammonium nitrate was packaged in thousands of disposable First Aid ice packs which resembled those used for minor injuries. The clandestine hoard of what amounted to three metric tons of ammonium nitrate was discovered by MI5 and the Metropolitan Police in the autumn of 2015 and was believed to be directly linked to Hezbollah.[106]

This quantity exceeded the amount of ammonium nitrate that "was used in the [1995] Oklahoma City bombing that killed 168 people and damaged hundreds of buildings."[107] Despite the seriousness of this discovery in the United Kingdom, a suspect in his 40s who was arrested "was eventually released without charge". Reports suggest that the decision not to prosecute the suspect was done in order to protect sources and methods that derived from the covert intelligence.[108] Not only would a court trial of the suspect risked exposing human intelligence operations, British authorities had political considerations as well to factor in, with this discovery coming at a time when the U.K. had just signed on to the October 2015 JCPOA nuclear deal with Iran.[109]

In terms of targets, according to reports in the Israeli press, citing Israeli intelligence officials, police in Thailand, Cyprus and the U.K. determined that the stored explosives were to be directed against Israeli assets in those countries. Israeli newspaper *Yedioth Ahronoth* quoted an unnamed official, noting, "'Hezbollah is preparing for a situation in which it will decide to seek revenge, whether for something taking place between Israel and Lebanon or for an attack on Iran's nuclear sites, and has established a network of enormous caches of advanced explosive materials' for that purpose."[110]

Hezbollah advanced logistical planning for future attacks in the West was not only about ammonium nitrate in first-aid ice packs. For example, Ali Mohammed Kourani was tasked by his Hezbollah handler to "cultivate contacts in the New York City area who could provide firearms for use in potential future IJO operations in the United States."[111]

However, what has not previously been disclosed and may be a new element in Hezbollah's advanced logistical planning may be in the cyber realm. As part of the authors' research into Alexi Saab via his social media footprint, it was discovered that not only did he work as an information technology specialist, but he had been employed as a subcontractor for Microsoft with access to New York City's Domain Awareness System (DAS)[112]. The DAS is "one of the world's largest networks of cameras, license plate readers, and radiological censors, designed to detect and prevent terrorist acts, but also of great value in criminal investigations."[113] This system, which is operated by the NYPD's Counterterrorism Bureau, in coordination with the Intelligence Bureau, enables the department to track targets of surveillance and collect data on these targets in realtime.[114]

The system is connected to more than "18,000 CCTV cameras video cameras around New York City" and had access to data from more than "2[two] billion license plate readings, 100 million summonses[115], 54 million 911 calls, 15 million complaints, 12 million detective reports, 11 million arrests and [two] million warrants". While there is no public information to suggest that Saab utilized any malware or inserted any logic bombs into the system, the coincidence of his work on this counter terrorism system is suspicious, bordering on alarming, in the view of the authors.[116]

## Modus Operandi 5: Preparing "Human Target Packages" to Enable Assassinating Dissidents and Adversaries

"Target packages" are a file of information that "enable an intelligence or military unit to find, fix, track and neutralize a threat. A human target package includes information collected about an individual, such as the official position of the individual; an analysis of personal vulnerabilities or other opportunities to exploit the individual and confirmation of the identity and location of the individual."[117] A target package could include "capture/kill operations".[118] There is strong evidence that assembling human target packages has been a consistent element of Iran/Hezbollah's modus operandi in the West with examples in the Netherlands, France, Denmark, New York City and Washington DC.

For example, in Amsterdam, Iranian anti regime dissident, Ahmad Mola Nissi, was likely the victim of an Iran/Hezbollah liquidation operation in late

2017, when he was gunned down in front of his apartment. As the leader of the ASMLA, a movement that promotes the rights of the Ahwazi, an Arab people who feel oppressed in the oil-rich Iranian region of Khuzestan, he had sought refuge in the Netherlands since 2005. In the month leading up to his attack, Nissi had gone to the police expressing concerns about his safety. U.S. Secretary of State Pompeo appeared to refer to the alleged assassination in May 2018, when in a major statement he noted, "today, the Iranian Quds Force conducts covert assassination operations in the heart of Europe."[119]

While Dutch authorities did not officially charge anyone in connection with this crime, they did arrest and then release two Iranian embassy staff in the wake of the killing.[120] The Nissi assassination was likely not the first conducted on Dutch soil by Iranian/Hezbollah hit squads as, "the AIVD [Dutch General Intelligence and Security Service] has strong indications that Iran has been involved in the liquidation of two Dutch people of Iranian origin (in Almere in 2015 and in The Hague in 2017), both known as opponents of the Iranian regime."[121]

Meanwhile, another liquidation attempt in 2018 was very clearly Iran-related and involved a sophisticated "human target package" as well as TATP explosives in France. The target was a conference in Paris for the political arm of the MeK, called the National Council of Resistance of Iran (NCRI), with 25,000 visitors expected, including more than thirty former U.S. officials, among them, former House speaker Newt Gingrich and former New York City Mayor Rudy Giuliani.[122] However, coordinated intelligence operations in Europe thwarted the plot. In late June 2018 in Belgium, special police units stopped a Mercedes driven by an Iranian-Belgian couple on their way to Paris bringing with them a bag with 500 grams of TATP explosive and an ignition mechanism. The bomb was fully functional.[123]

Simultaneously, "an Iranian diplomat stationed in Vienna is arrested in a parking lot in Germany. According to the German authorities, the man works for the Iranian security service MOIS. During a meeting in Luxembourg, he [allegedly] handed over the explosives to the Belgian couple. The French government now says it is certain that Iran is behind the foiled bomb attack and announces targeted sanctions, including against a deputy minister who is seen as the mastermind behind the action."[124]

Similar to the Netherlands, but with a different outcome, in October 2018, Denmark announced it had foiled an operation to kill an Iranian dissident on its territory. Danish authorities arrested a Norwegian citizen of Iranian descent for allegedly planning the assassination of a Denmark based leader of ASMA the same ethnic Arab separatist group that Nissi in Amsterdam had been a member of according to Denmark's Security and Intelligence Service (PET). Danish Prime Minister, Lars Lokke Rasmussen pointed the finger at Iran noting, "It is totally unacceptable that Iran is planning liquidations on Danish soil."[125]

In yet additional preoperational Iran-linked espionage activity in Western Europe, Syed-Naqfi, a Pakistani national working as an operative for the Quds Force, collected intelligence for his targeting package on two known individuals. One was French-Israeli businessman and professor, "David Rouach, who teaches at thee lite Ecole Sup"erieure de Commerce de Paris and served as head of the French-Israeli Chamber of Commerce."[126] In Germany, Naqfi also monitored Reinhold Robbe, the former head of the German-Israel Friendship Society. According to German authorities, Naqfi actions were "a clear indication of an assassination attempt."[127]

Meanwhile during his time in New York City, Ali Mohammed Kourani was also tasked to complete human target packages, or as the criminal complaint notes, "to identify and collect intelligence regarding individuals in the United States affiliated with the IDF [Israeli Defense Forces]". Kourani told U.S. Law Enforcement officials that he believed that the IJO [Unit 910] "gave him this tasking to facilitate, among other things, assassinations of IDF personnel [living in the U.S.] in retaliation for the 2008 assassination of Imad Mugniyah, theformer leader of the IJO."[128]

Similarly, the two Iranian-linked individuals, Doostdar and Ghorbani, operating in Chicago, New York and Washington, D.C., focused on human targeting packages that could be used to identify and locate individuals related to the MeK and their supporters even if they were members of Congress. For example, Ghorbani traveled to New York City in September 2017 where he attended a MeK/NCRI rally that denounced the Iranian regime. "During this rally, Ghorbani conducted physical surveillance and photographed individuals participating in the rally."[129] In the wake of the rally, "during a court authorized physical search of Ghorbani's apartment, the FBI found several hand-written notes in Farsi regarding members of the MeK, including names, positions, and relations to other MeK members," according to the Justice Department.[130] "The FBI also found in a locked suitcase a manila envelope containing information, including biographical data and phone numbers, about several U.S. Congressmen who have overt ties to the MeK."[131]

## Modus Operandi 6: Counter-Intelligence Tradecraft and Operational Security

Another hallmark of Iranian/Hezbollah tradecraft is the employing counter-surveillance tradecraft and sophisticated operational security. A variety of modalities of this tradecraft has been utilized and observed in the United States. One example was the Doostdar case. The information outlined in the paragraphs below comes from details publicly released by the Justice Department. "From approximately July 25 through July 30, 2017, Doostdar was in Costa Mesa, California, where he met several times with Ghorbani. Doostdar employed intelligence tradecraft and ran surveillance detection routes before, during, and after his meetings with Ghorbani."[132] Doostdar also utilized tradecraft like "changing clothes before each meeting, visiting meeting locations prior to the actual meeting, and arriving and departing from each meeting in a circuitous manner." FBI surveillance teams also noted that "Doostdar walked slowly and was constantly looking around his surroundings" and looked at "the reflection of store windows as he passed by, consistent with checking for surveillance."[133] Consequently, the FBI assessed that Doostdar engaged in "intelligence tradecraft and counter- surveillance measures" that were "consistent with having received training from an Iranian intelligence service."[134]

The Iranians also observed secure communications protocols. Not only did they avoid speaking on open lines, but when Ghorbani asked if he could call Doostdar back on the same phone that he had been called from, Doostdar replied, "no, I call you from public phone … from Macy's public phone." Furthermore, Doostdar advised Ghorbani that despite turning their cell phones off, "they should wait until they got out of the car to talk, since phones could record even if they are turned off it is possible." After this particular call they then met at a Starbucks coffee shop for approximately forty-five minutes sitting in a more private area.[135]

When communicating back to Lebanon from the U.S., Unit 910 members also observed strict communications protocols. Ali Mohammed Kourani and his  handler, Fadi, used a marriage-related code, such as "bride," to signal to Kourani that he should return to Lebanon, according to the Justice Department.[136] After Kourani got married in real life, "Fadi communicated similar recall messages using coded references to a *job* or *employment prospect* in Lebanon."[137] Similarly, for Alexi Saab, "if Hezbollah ever needed him to return to Lebanon, Saab would receive an email to his personal email account that would appear to be spam. There would be a coded signal concealed in either or the subject or the body of the message that would alert Saab of the need to return to Lebanon."[138]

For regular communications back to Lebanon, "Kourani provided Fadi with the name of a particular childhood friend of Kourani, and Fadi established one or more email accounts using that name for purposes of operational communications." Also, "Kourani deleted electronic communications from Fadi immediately after reviewing them." Interestingly, "in approximately 2011 or 2012, Fadi instructed Kourani not to use existing operational email accounts or the IJO [Unit 910] Pager, as the IJO assessed that these communications selectors had been compromised. Kourani and Fadi did not use email to communicate regarding IJO operations after approximately 2012."[139]

However, coded email was also the means that both Samer el Debek and Alexi Saab used to communicate with Hezbollah members from overseas. El Debek said "[Hezbollah] gave him an email account to contact when he was away, and coded language to use in his emails to Hezbollah. He also said he was permitted to use any email account the wished to use to communicate with [Hezbollah] by email."[140]

Unit 910 members, like Ali Mohammed Kourani, observed elaborate communications protocols even when returning to Lebanon. He was advised that upon arrival in Beirut, he was to "call a telephone number associated with a pager (the "IJO Pager") and provide a code that he understood was specific to him. After Kourani called the IJO pager, Fadi [his handler] would contact Kourani to set up an in-person meeting by calling a phone belonging to one of Kourani's relatives."[141]

Meanwhile for Alexi Saab, when he returned to Lebanon, his handler utilized both a phone number and numeric code to inform his handler that he had returned to Lebanon, according to the Justice Department. After his handler received the code from Saab, he "would contact Saab on his personal cellphone or at his family home in Yaroun, Lebanon."[142]

As far as the means to provide the collected intelligence back to his Hezbollah handlers, "Kourani was instructed by IJO personnel abroad to use digital storage media, such as USB drives and memory cards, to transport pictures and data back to Lebanon relating to his external operations," according to the Justice Department.[143] Similarly, the Justice Department stated the Iranian, Doostdar also transported his information on two flash/USB drives,"one of which was concealed in a toy on a keychain."[144]

## Modus Operandi 7: Recruiting Operatives with Dual Nationalities and Western Passports

Iran and Hezbollah have a history of recruiting operatives globally from within Shi'a diasporas, preferably those who have Western passports. A representative example of this is Mansour Arbabsiar, a naturalized U.S. citizen of Iranian descent, who is October 2011 was arrested and charged with plotting to kill Adel al-Jubeir, the Saudi Ambassador to the United States.[145] According to the court documents, Arbabsiar claimed he had been recruited by a cousin in Iran who was a high-ranking member of IRGC's Quds Force.[146]

Similarly, the recent arrests of the reported Hezbollah Unit 910 operatives, Ali Kourani, Samer el-Debek and Alexei Saab in the U.S., reinforce the idea that Hezbollah focuses its external recruitment on individuals residing in the West, with dual nationalities and access to Western passports. For example, according to court documents, Kourani was recruited[147] mainly because his residence in the United States and "in connection with efforts by the IJO to develop "sleepers" who maintained ostensibly normal lives but could be activated and tasked with conducting IJO operations."[148] Moreover, one of his handler's "first instructions to Kourani, who was a lawful permanent resident at the time, was to obtain United States citizenship and a U.S. passport as soon as possible" and "to acquire a U.S. passport card "that could be used to reenter the United States if his U.S. passport was seized outside the U.S."[149] Similarly, Samer el-Debek, arrested for his links to Hezbollah, claims he was recruited because as a U.S. naturalized citizen, he was in possession of a U.S. passport.[150]

Although Alexei Saab was recruited in Lebanon before he spent time in the U.S. within five years of his lawful entrance, he applied for naturalized citizenship in the

U.S. Subsequently, according to court documents, Saab entered into a fraudulent marriage in order to gain U.S. citizenship.[151]

Many of the other Hezbollah Unit 910 operatives discussed earlier in this article similarly utilized dual citizenships to travel the world and operate on behalf of the unit. Hussein Atris, arrested in Thailand in January 2012 based on his links to the cache of thousands of pounds of urea-based fertilizer and gallons of ammonium nitrate, was a dual Lebanese–Swedish citizen.[152] Similarly, Mauhamad Hassan Mouhamad El Husseini, the Hezbollah suicide bomber who detonated explosives on a tourist bus carrying Israeli tourists in Burgas, Bulgaria, killing six in July 2012, had dual Lebanese – French citizenship. Also, Hussien Bassam Abdallah, the Hezbollah operative arrested in Cyprus with 8.2 tons of ammonium nitrate in his residence had Lebanese–Canadian citizenship.[153]

In New York, ownership of a Western passport was a key factor in Hezbollah's recruitment criteria for members of the Shi'a Lebanese diaspora as well based on the authors' experience investigating the group. From our observations, Hezbollah members in the city often traveled abroad to Lebanon, Latin America, Europe, China and Canada, using both, their U.S. and Lebanese passports.[154]

## The Ongoing Threat vs. the United States

Since the early 2000s New York City has been an active test bed for various preoperational activities conducted by both Iranian and Hezbollah agents. Although the city has not had, by any means, a monopoly on this preoperational activity, it has served as a unique observation post from which we could examine Iran and Hezbollah's hostile tradecraft, up close, virtually identical to what has been similarly observed in Western Europe, Latin America and even some other American cities.

Elements of this tradecraft have included: undertaking intelligence gathering and surveillance activities on possible targets; advanced logistical planning for future attacks; using sophisticated and plausible diplomatic, business, cultural and other covers to conceal operational activities; infiltrating Iranian dissident groups; preparing "human target packages" to enable assassinating dissidents and adversaries; employing counter-surveillance tradecraft, sophisticated operational security, including observing communications security; and recruiting operatives, especially those with dual nationalities and Western passports from the Shia diaspora.

They are all part of the Iran and Hezbollah's play book, or pre operational modus operandi in the West.

Even in the wake of Iran's ballistic missile attack on Al Asad Air Base in western Iraq in early January 2020, which injured more than fifty American soldiers and seemed like retaliation, President Hassan Rouhani of Iran told reporters on March 18, "Americans assassinated our great general, and we did not and will not leave this without a response," suggesting that there was more to come.[155]

While it is impossible to predict when, where or how Iran/Hezbollah might retaliate for the strike that killed IRGC General Qassem Soleimani, this article has made clear there is growing knowledge of the indicators and warning signs.

The authors' hope is that by illuminating these tactics, techniques, and procedures, allied law enforcement and intelligence agencies around the world might improve their odds in thwarting future Iranian/Hezbollah terrorist attacks in the future.

*Disclosure statement: No potential conflict of interest was reported by the author(s).*

*Notes on contributors: Ioan Pop is a former senior intelligence analyst at the NYPD Intelligence Division and currently an associate managing director at K2 Intelligence. Mitchell D. Silber is the former director of intelligence analysis at the NYPD Intelligence Division and an adjunct professor at Columbia University's School for Public and International Affairs. Mitchell D. Silber mitchsilber@protonmail.com Community Security Initiative, New York, New York, USA.* *To cite this article: Ioan Pop & Mitchell D. Silber (2020): Iran and Hezbollah's Pre- Operational Modus Operandi in the West, Studies in Conflict & Terrorism, DOI: 10.1080/1057610X.2020.1759487 To link to this article: https://doi.org/10.1080/1057610X.2020.1759487*

# NOTES TO CHAPTERS

## Introduction

1. https://www.encyclopedia.com/religion/encyclopedias-almanacs-transcripts-and-maps/ikhwan-al-muslimin.

2. Ibid

3. Brynjar, Lia. *The Society of the Muslim Brothers in Egypt: The rise of an Islamic Movement 1928 – 1942* (Reading, UK: Ithaca Press, 1998),55.

4. Ibid.

5. Muhammad Jeffery Hizwan Bin said, March 2018, Ikhwanul Muslimin, ResearchGate.

6. Ibid.

7. Grigsby, H, June 2014, "Sayyid Qutb's Penned war for Islamic Society", ResearchGate.

8. Calvert, John, (2012), Sayyid Qutb and the Origins of Radical Islamism, p 84

9. Ibid.

10. Charles Tripp, (1994), *"Sayyid Qutb, The Political Vision, in Pioneers of Islamic Revival,* (London Zed Books Ltd.)

11. Ibid.

12. Christopher Howarth, Sayyid Qutb, 2016,

13. Ibid.

14. Ibid.

15. *The Rise of Jihadist Extremism In the West,* Salah Publication, 2010.

16. John Calvert, 2018, *Sayyid Qutb and the Origins of Radical Islamism,* Chapter 1, page 28, C. Hurst & Co

17. Yusuf Unal, (2016), *Sayyid Qutb in Iran, Transnational the Islamist Ideology in the Islamic Republic,* (Indiana University Press).

18. Ibid (p 35).

19. https://www.brookings.edu/blog/order-from-chaos/2019/01/24/what-irans-1979-revolution-meant-for-the-muslim-brotherhood/.

20. Yusuf Unal, (2016), *Sayyid Qutb in Iran, Transnational the Islamist Ideology in the Islamic Republic*, (Indiana University Press).

21. Hamāyash-ibāz'khvānivabar'rasī-yididgāh'hā-yiSayyidQutb. The conference was organized by the Kanoon Youth Thought Center in collaboration with the University of Tehran, February 15–16, 2015.

22. William Shepard, Sayyid Qutb and Islamic Activism: A Translation and Critical Analysis of Social Justice in Islam (New York: Brill, 1996), 230–280.

23. Danny Dann, "who are Iran's 80,000 Shi'ites fighters" Jerusalem Post, April, 28, 2018.

24. Global Extremism Monitor 2017, Tony Blair Institute for Global Change, 13 September 2018.

25. The activity of 9,000 ideological- political coaches in the IRGC, Iranian students' News Agency (ISNA) 2018.

26. IntelligenceOnline.com, Tehran targets Mediterranean, March 10, 2006.

27. Ibid.

28. Anthony H. Cordesman, *"Iran's Revolutionary Guards, Al Quds Force and Other Intelligence and Paramilitary Forces"*, published by Centre for Strategic and International Studies, 16 August, 2007.

29. *Jamail, Dahr (20 July 2006). "Hezbollah's transformation". Asia Times.* Retrieved 23 October 2007.

30. *"Hezbollah (a.k.a. Hizbollah, Hizbu'llah)". Council on Foreign Relations. 13 September 2008. Archived from the original on 13 September 2008. Retrieved 15 September 2008.*

31. Levitt, Matthew *(2013). Hezbollah: The Global Footprint of Lebanon's Party of God. p. 15. ISBN: 9781849043335. ... the Jihad Council coordinates 'resistance activity'. Ghattas Saab, Antoine (15 May 2014).*

32. Dominique Avon, Anaïs-Trissa Khatchadourian, *Hezbollah: A History of the "Party of God"*, (Harvard University Press, 2012 ISBN: 978-0-674-07031-8) pp.21ff.

33. Mariam Farida, *Religion and Hezbollah: Political Ideology and Legitimacy*, (Routledge, 2019 ISBN: 978-1-000-45857-2) pp.1-3.

34. *Adam Shatz (29 April 2004). "In Search of Hezbollah". The New York Review of Books. Archived from the original on 22 August 2006. Retrieved 14 August 2006.*

35. Kali Robinson, "What is Hezbollah", *Council on Foreign Relations, 1 Sep 2020.*

## Chapter 1: The Muslim Brotherhood, A Failure in Political Evolution-Nawaf Obaid

1.  Lia (1998)

2.  Ibid.

3   Cameron (2015).

4   Emerson & Hoekstra (2015).

5   Baltacioglu-Brammer (2014).

6   Ibid.

7   Brown (2006).

8   Ibid.

9   Ibid.

10  The Tower Staff (2014).

11  Who Are Islamic Jihad? (2003).

12  Legge (2013).

13  Bechri (2014).

14  Wickham (2013).

15  Ibid.

16  Pargeter (2010).

17  Ibid.

18  Wickham (2013).

19  Pargeter (2010).

20  Roy (2012).

21. Noueihed & Warren (2012).

22  Hoffman & Jamal (2012).

23  Majzoub (2013).

24  Ibid.

25  Majzoub (2013).

26  Majzoub (2013).

27  Trager and Shalabi (2016).

28  Mauro (2014).

29  Dearden (2015). 30  Mauro (2014). 31  Younes (2014).

32  Teitelbaum (2011)

33. Weismann (2010).

34. Teitelbaum (2011). 35 Zisser (2005).

36  Wright (2008).

37  Zisser (2005).

38  Ibid.

39  Brown (2006).

40  Ibid.

41. Clark (201).

42  Brown (2006).

43. Ibid.

44  Ibid.

45  Euben& Zaman (2009). 46 Ziad (1993).

47  Robinson (2004).

48  Ibid.

49  Ziad (1993).

50  Ibid.

51  Ibid.

52  Ibid.

53  Jebnoun (2014).

54  Ibid.

55  Allani (2009).

56   Jebnoun (2014).

58   Marks (2015).

59   Stepan (2012)

61   Hamzawy (2008).

62   Hamzawy (2008).

63   Ibid.

64   Catusse& Zaki (2010).

65   El Sherif (2012)

66   Ibid.

67   Spiegel (2015).

68   Ibid.

69   Wickham (2013).

71   Ibid.

72   Pargeter (2010).

74   Ibid.

75   Zisser, E. (2005).

76   Ibid.

77   Ibid.

78   Ibid.

79   Porat (2010).

80   Brown (2006).

81   Ibid.

82   Bondokji (2015).

83   Brown (2006).

84   Roy (2003).

85   Robinson (2004).

86   Ziad (1993).

87   Ibid.

88    Roy (2003).

89    Ibid.

90    Election Guide.

91    Wirtschafter (2016).

92    Spiegel (2015).

93    Pellicer& Wegner (2012).

94    Catusse& Zaki (2010).

95    Marks (2015).

96    Stepan (2012).

97    Marks (2015).

98    Jebnoune (2014).

99    Ibid.

100   Ibid.

101   Zeghal (2013).

102   Sadiki (2016).

103   Ibid.

104   Al-Anani (2013).

105   Ibid.

106   Lynch (2012).

107   Kirkpatrick (2015).

108   Ibid.

109   Ibid.

110   Kholaif (2015)

111   Ibid.

112   Al Anani (2013).

113   Kirkpatrick (2012).

114   Al Anani (2013).

115   Ibid.

116 Giovanni and Elisson (2015).

117 Al Anani (2013).John F. Kennedy Street Cambridge, MA 02138. www. belfercenter.org

## Chapter 2: Muslim Brotherhood, Sayyid Qutb and Islamist Extremism-SakoAbou Bakr

1    Efraim Karsh, Islamic Imperialism: A History (New Haven and London: Yale University Press, 2006), 211.

2    Charles Tripp, "Sayyid Qutb: The Political Vision," in Pioneers of Islamic Revival ed. Ali Rahnema (London: Zed Books Ltd., 1994), 165. Signposts is also commonly translated into English as Milestones.

3    Emmanuel Sivan, Raddical Islam, Medieval Theology and Modern Politics (New Haven and London: Yale University Press, 1985), 48.

4    Elie Podeh and Onn Winckler, "Introduction: Nasserism as a Form of Populism," in Rethinking Nasserism: Revolution and Historical Memory in Modern Egypt ed. Elie Podeh and Onn Winckler (Gainesville: University Press of Florida, 2004), 17.

5    Sivan, 31-32.

6    Richard P. Mitchell, The Society of Muslim Brothers (Oxford: Oxford University Press, 1969), 152.

7    Ibid., 151-162.

8    Ibid., 212.

9    David Commins. "Hasan al-Banna (1906-1949)," in Pioneers of Islamic Revival ed. Ali Rahnema (London: Zed Books Ltd., 1994), 133-144.

10   Mithcell, 235.

11   Commins, 133-144.

12   Gilles Kepel, Muslim Extremism in Egypt: The Prophet and the Pharaoh (Berkley: University of California Press, 1985), 37, and Mitchell, 223.

13   Adnan Musallam, "Sayyid Qutb's View of Islam, Society and Militancy" (Journal of South Asian and Middle Eastern Studies, 1998), 71-74.

14   A.I. Dawisha, Arab Nationalism in the Twentieth Century: From Triumph to Despair (New Jersey: Princeton University Press, 2003), 161-213.

15   Podeh and Winckler, 18.

16  M. Riad El-Ghonemy, "An Assessment of Egypt's Development Strategy," in Rethinking Nasserism: Revolution and Historical Memory in Modern Egypt ed. Elie Podeh and Onn Winckler (Gainesville: University Press of Florida, 2004), 254-259.

17  Podeh and Winckler, 16.

18  Podeh and Winckler, 19. Karsh, 152.

19  Sayyid Qutb, Milestones, rev. translation with a foreword by Ahmad Zaki Hammad (Indianapolis: American Trust Publications, 1993), 8.

20  Gerald Hawting, The Idea of Idolatry and the Emergence of Islam: From Polemic to History (Cambridge: Cambridge University Press, 1999), 1-2.

21  Sivan, 22.

22  In Chapter 10 of his book Signposts, the term is used 52 times. Social justice in Islam, Introduction by Hamid Algar.

23  Sayed Khatab, "Hakimiyyah and Jahiliyyah in the Thought of Sayyid Qutb" (Middle Eastern Studies, 2002), 154.

24  Ibid., 155.

25  Qutb, Milestones, 49.

26  Ibid., 66.

27  Ibid., 69.

28  Ahmad Moussalli, Radical Islamic Fundamentalism: The Ideological and Political Discourse of Sayyid Qutb (Beirut: American University of Beirut, 1992), 20.

29  Commins, 135.

30  Tripp, 154.

31  Sayyid Qutb, Social Justice in Islam (Oneonta, NY: Islamic Publications International, 2000), 114

32  Moussalli, 25-30.

33  Sivan, 40.

34  Kepel, 27.

35  Kepel, 28. Moussalli, 36.

36  Sivan, 28-30.

37  Qutb, 40-41.

38   Mitchell, 267.

39   Qutb, Milestones, 102-103.

40   Mitchell, 265-266.

41   Musallam, 77.

42   Qutb, Milestones, 38.

43   Ibid., 15.

44   Musallam, 82. Kepel 61-67.

45   Kepel, 78-86.

46   Hrair J. Dekmejian, Islam in Revolution: Fundamentalism in the Arab World (Syracuse: Syracuse University Press, 1985), 91.

47   Tripp, 164.

48   Qutb, Milestones, 65.

49   Ibid., 112.

50   Nathan J. Brown, "Nasserism's Legal Legacy: Accessibility, Accountability, and Authoritarianism" in Rethinking Nasserism: Revolution and Historical Memory in Modern Egypt ed. Elie Podeh and Onn Winckler (Gainsville: University Press of Florida, 2004), 128, 136.

51   Dekmejian, 90.

52   Kepel, 35.

53   Tripp, 155.

## Bibliography:

Brown, Nathan J. "Nasserism's Legal Legacy: Accessibility, Accountability, and Authoritarianism." In Rethinking Nasserism: Revolution and Historical Memory in Modern Egypt, edited by Elie Podeh and Onn Winckler. Gainsville: University of Florida Press, 2004. 127-143.

Commins, David. "Hasan al-Banna (1906-1949)." In Pioneers of Islamic Revival, edited by Ali Rahnema. London: Zed Books Ltd., 1994. 125-153.

Dawisha, Adeed. Arab Nationalism in the Twentieth Century: From Triumph to Despair.New Jersey: Princeton University Press, 2003.

Dekmejian, Hrair J. Islam in Revolution: Fundamentalism in the Arab World. Syracuse: Syracuse University Press, 1985.

El-Ghonemy, M. Riad. "Egypt's Development Strategy, 1952-1970." In Rethinking Nasserism: Revolution and Historical Memory in Modern Egypt, edited by Elie Podeh and Onn Winckler. Gainsville: University of Florida Press, 2004. 253-263.

Hawting, G.R. The Idea of Idolatry and the Emergence of Islam: From Polemic to History. Cambridge: Cambridge University Press, 1999.

Karsh, Efraim. Islamic Imperialism: A History. New Haven and London: Yale University Press, 2006.

Kepel, Gilles. Muslim Extremism in Egypt: The Prophet and the Pharaoh. Berkley: University of California Press, 1985.

Khatab, Sayed. "HakimiyyahandJahiliyyahin the Thought of Sayyid Qutb." Middle Eastern Studies (2002): 145-170.

Mitchell, Richard P. The Society of Muslim Brothers. Oxford: Oxford University Press, 1969.

Moussalli, Ahmad. Radical Islamic Fundamentalism: The Ideological and Political Discourse of Sayyid Qutb. Beirut: American University of Beirut, 1992.

Musallam, Adnan. "Sayyid Qutb's View of Islam, Society and Militancy." Journal of South Asian and Middle Eastern Studies (1998): 64-85.

Podeh, Elie and Onn Winckler. "Introduction: Nasserism as a Form of Populism," In

Rethinking Nasserism: Revolution and Historical Memory in Modern Egypt, edited by Elie Podeh and Onn Winckler. Gainsville: University of Florida Press, 2004. 1-42.

Qutb, Sayyid. Social Justice in Islam. Oneonta, NY: Islamic Publications International, 2000 (reprint).

Qutb, Sayiyid. Milestones. Revised translation with a foreword by Ahmad Zaki Hammad (Indianopolis: American Trust Publications, 1993.)

Sivan, Emmanuel. Radical Islam, Medieval Theology and Modern Politics. New Haven and London: Yale University Press, 1985.

Tripp, Charles. "Sayyid Qutb: The Political Vision." In Pioneers of Islamic Revival, edited by Ali Rahnema. London: Zed Books Ltd., 1994. 154-183.

## Chapter 3: The Muslim Brotherhood's Global Threat Submitted- Dr. M. UHDI JASSER

1   Interim Report and Recommendations of the Homeland Security Advisory Council Countering Violent Extremism (CVE) Subcommittee of the US Department of Homeland Security. June 2016.

2   http://www.muslimreformmovement.org

3   Mustafa Mashhour, "Jihad is the Way" (AR) IkhwanWiki, http://www.ikhwanwiki.com/index.php?title=

4   MajmuatRasail Al-Imam al-shahid Hasan Al-banna. International Islamic Federation of Student Organizations. pp. 238 https://www.investigativeproject.org/documents/misc/837.pdf#page=239

5   Robert S. Leiken and Steven Brooke, "The Moderate Muslim Brotherhood," Foreign Affairs 86, no. 2 (March-April 2007), 108, 113.

6   Marc Lynch, "Assessing the MB Firewall" Abu Aardvark, May 13, 2008, (http://abuaardvark.typepad.com/abuaardvark/2008/05/assessing-the-m.html)

7   Eric Trager. Arab Fall: How the Muslim Brotherhood Won and Lost Egypt in 891 Days. Georgetown University Press. Washington, D.C. pp. 41.

8   Erick Trager. Arab Fall: How the Muslim Brotherhood Won and Lost Egypt in 891 Days. Georgetown University Press. Washington, D.C. pp. 44.

9   Eric Trager. Arab Fall: How the Muslim Brotherhood won and lost Egypt in 891 Days. Georgetown University Press. Washington, D.C. pp. 54.

10  Dispatch 3274. Muslim Brotherhood Supreme Guide: 'The U.S. is Now Experiencing the Beginning of Its End'; Improvement and Change in the Muslim World 'Can Only Be Attained through Jihad And Sacrifice. MEMRI. October 6, 2010.

11  Barry Rubin. The Region: The Declaration of War that went Unnoticed. JPost. 23:29. October 10, 2010

12  John Rossomondo. "Emails show Clinton was Told about MB-AQ Links". IPT News. May 2, 2016.

13  John Rossomondo. "Emails show Clinton was Told about MB-AQ Links". IPT News. May 2, 2016.

14  Adam Kredo. Open Jihad Declared in Egypt Following State Dept. Meeting with Muslim Brothhood-Aligned Leaders. Muslim Brotherhood call for 'long, uncompromising jihad'. January 30, 2015.

15  USCIRF Annual Report. Egypt: A Country of Particular Concern (CPC). May 2015.

16  Patrick Poole. Muslim Brotherhood Steps Up Terror in Egypt, While U.S. Provides Cover. PJ Media. June 2, 2015.

17  Leila Fadel. Egypt's Muslim Brotherhood Divides over Response to Killings. July 11, 2015.

18  Muslim Brotherhood supports call for retribution. Daily News Egypt. May 31, 2015.

19  Muslim Brotherhood Statement Reiterates Commitment to January 25 Revolution Goals. May 29, 2015.

20  John Rossomondo. "Emails show Clinton was Told about MB-AQ Links". IPT News. May 2, 2016.

21  Email (February 27, 2011) from Jake Sullivan to Hillary Clinton. Wikileaks. https://wikileaks.org/clinton- emails/emailid/28627

22  Al Arabiya Institute for Studies. Libyan Dawn: Map of allies and enemies. AlArabiya. August 25, 2014.

23  Top Tunisian Militant killed by U.S. Strike in Libya. AFP. July 3, 2015. https://tribune.com.pk/story/914209/top- tunisian-militant-killed-by-us-strike-in-libya-report/

24  U.S. Designates Bin Laden Loyalist. Department of Treasury Press Release. February 24, 2004. https://www.treasury.gov/press-center/press-releases/Pages/js1190.aspx

25  Abdul Majid Al-Zindani. The Global Muslim Brotherhood Daily Watch. https://www.globalmbwatch.com/abd-al- majid-al-zindani/ (accessed July 8, 2018).

26  Matthew Levitt. Untangling the Terror Web. Al Qaeda is not the only Element. Policy 672. October 28, 2002 http://www.washingtoninstitute.org/policy-analysis/view/untangling-the-terror-web-al-qaeda-is-not-the-only- element

27  Executive Order on Terrorist Financing. Blocking Property and Prohibiting Transactions with Persons Who Commit, Threaten to Commit, or Support Terrorism. White House Press Secretary. September 24, 2001.

28  The Charter of the Islamic Resistance Movement. August 18, 1988. https://fas.org/irp/world/para/docs/880818a.htm

29  Foreign Terrorist Organizations. U.S. Dept. of State. Hamas. October 8, 1997.

30  Noreen S. Ahmed-Ullah, Sam Roe and Laurie Cohen. Chicago Tribune. September 19, 2004. http://www.chicagotribune.com/news/watchdog/chi-0409190261sep19-story.html

31  John Rossomando. Islamist Activist Asks Obama to Support Libyan AQ Group. IPT News. March 18, 2016. https://www.investigativeproject.org/5217/islamist-activist-asks-obama-to-support-libyan-aq

32  John Rossomando. Libyan Security Committee calls U.S. Muslim Leader a Terrorist. IPT News. June 12, 2017. https://www.investigativeproject.org/6273/libyan-security-committee-calls-us-muslim-leader

33  M. ZuhdiJasser. Understanding the Cauldron that Brewed ISIS. Religious Freedom Institute. Georgetown University. July 12, 2016. https://www.religiousfreedominstitute.org/cornerstone/2016/7/12/understanding-the-cauldron-that-brewed-isis

34  Ravi Kumar. Syrian Brotherhood stands nearer to ISIS than to the U.S. IPT News. September 16, 2014.

35  Qatar-based cleric criticizes US role against Islamic State. Reuters. Middle East and North Africa. September 14, 2014.

36  John Rossomando, Syrian American Council Learns How to Pressure Washington. IPT News. April 3, 2018. https://www.investigativeproject.org/7393/syrian-american-council-learns-how-to-pressure

37  John Rossomando, Syrian American Council Learns How to Pressure Washington. IPT News. April 3, 2018. https://www.investigativeproject.org/7393/syrian-american-council-learns-how-to-pressure

38  Mohammed Al-Ghanem. Americans can trust Syrian rebels. The Hill. September 12, 2014. http://thehill.com/blogs/congress-blog/foreign-policy/217504-americans-can-trust-the-syrian-rebels

39  Mohammed Al-Ghanem. Taking Syria back from extremists. The Washington Post. December 27, 2012.

40  Kenneth Timmerman. Obama Administration let anti-gay Muslim leader into the U.S. NY Post. March 2, 2014. 43 John Rossomando. Photos show IRUSA Chairman's Muslim Brotherhood Support. IPT News. May 29, 2018. https://www.investigativeproject.org/7468/photos-show-irusa-chairman-muslim-brotherhood

41  John Rossomando. Photos show IRUSA Chairman's Muslim Brotherhood Support. IPT News. May 29, 2018. https://www.investigativeproject.org/7468/photos-show-irusa-chairman-muslim-brotherhood

42  Islamic Relief: Charity, Extremism, Terror. Middle East Forum. July 2018. https://www.meforum.org/MiddleEastForum/media/MEFLibrary/pdf/Islamic-Relief-FINAL-v3-Online-(002).pdf

43  CR No. 3:04-CR-240-P. Governnment's Amended Memorandum in Opposition to Petitioners Islamic Society of North America and North American Islamist Trust's Motion for Equitable Relief. USA vs. HLF et.al.

44  House Select Committee on Intelligence, "International Security Threats," C-SPAN, Feb. 10, 2011, http://c- spanvideo.org/program/InternationalSecuri

45  Glenn Simpson, "The U.S. Provides Details of Terror-Financing Web," Wall Street Journal, Sept. 15, 2003, http://online.wsj.com/news/articles/SB106358213631213600

46  John Rossomando. Explanatory Memorandum' Detractors Ignore Evidence about MB in America. IPT News. March 1, 2017. https://www.investigativeproject.org/5807/explanatory-memorandum-detractors-ignore-evidence

47  Ladan and Roya Boroumand. Terror, Islam, and Democracy. Journal of Democracy. 13.2 (2002) 5-20.

48  Egypt Bans Muslim Brotherhood. CBS News. October 8, 2013.

49  Reuters Staff. Saudi Arabai designates Muslim Brotherhood terrorist group. Reuters. March 7, 2014.

50  Reuters Staff. UAE lists Muslim Brotherhood as terrorist group. November

51  How Americans Feel About Religious Groups: Jews, Catholics and Evangelicals rated warmly, Atheists and Muslims more Coldly. Pew Research Center:Religion and Public Life. July 16, 2014.55 Weiss, Deborah Esq. The Organization of islamic Cooperation's Jihad on Free Speech. June 6, 2015

52  Eric Trager. The Muslim Brotherhood is the Root of the Qatar Crisis. The Atlantic. July 2, 2017.

53  Muslim Brotherhood thanks Turkey for Hosting 90th Anniversary Gala. Ikhwanweb. April 3, 2018.

54  Abha Shankar. Will Turkey's New Diplomatic Push Reduce its American MB Support? IPT News. July 7, 2016.

55  IPT News U.S. Islamists Ignore Erdogan's Authoritarianism, Celebrate Win. June 26, 2018.

## Chapter 4: Aims and Methods of Europe's Muslim Brotherhood- Dr. Lorenzo Vidino

1. Yusuf al-Qaradawi, Priorities of the Islamic Movement in the Coming Phase (Swansea, U.K.: Awakening Publications, 2000).

2. Eric Brown, "After the Ramadan Affair: New Trends in Islamism in the West," Current Trends in Islamist Ideology

(Hudson Institute), vol. 2, September 2005: 8.

3. Xavier Ternisien, Les Frères Musulmans (Paris: Fayard, 2005), pp. 110-11.

4. Sylvain Besson, "La Conquête de l'Occident: Le Projet Secret des Islamistes (Paris: Editions du Seuil, 2005), p. 100.

5. "Leading Sunni Sheikh Yousef al-Qaradhawi and Other Sheikhs Herald the Coming Conquest of Rome," Middle East Media and Research Institute (MEMRI), Special Dispatch #447, 6 December 2002.

6. Besson, La Conquête de l'Occident, p. 37.

7. See, for example, Kenneth R. Timmerman, "Preachers of Hate: Islam and the War on America (New York: Crown Forum, 2003).

8. Khalid Duran, "Jihadism in Europe," The Journal of Counterterrorism and Security International, Fall 2000: 12-15.

9. For the life of Said Ramadan, see: M. H. Faruqi, "Les Frères Musulmanes: Politique de 'Rabbaniyya,' les Prièresavant le Pouvoir," published on the website of the Islamic Center of Geneva (http://www.cige.org/historique.htm); and Tariq Ramadan, "Une Vie Entière," available at http://membres.lycos.fr/oasislam/personnages/tariq/tariq.html.

10. Ian Johnson, "The Beachhead: How a Mosque for Ex-Nazis Became Center of Radical Islam," The Wall Street Journal, 12 July 2005.

11. History of the IGD, available at IGD's website: http://www.i-g-d.com/uber percent20unss2.htm.

12. "Recent OFAC Actions," U.S. Department of the Treasury, Office of Foreign Assets Control, 7 November 2001.

13. Report on Ibrahim el-Zayat, Cologne police, 27 August 2003, and Ian Johnson, "How Islamic Group's Ties Reveal Europe's Challenge," Wall Street Journal, 29 December 2005.

14. Report on the Islamische Gemeinschaft Milli Görüs (IGMG), Innenministerium, Nordrhein-Westfalen land web- site: http://www.im.nrw.de/sch/582.htm.

15. Ibrahim El Zayat, chairman of the IGD, is married to Sabiha Erbakan, the sister of Milli Görüş's leader, Mehmet Sabri Erbakan.

16. For the activities of IGD, IGMG, and Zentralrat, see Udo Ulfkotte, Der Krieg in unserenStaedten (Frankfurt: Eichborn Publishing, 2003).

17. "Islamismus," report by the Landesamt fur Verfassungsschutz, Hessen, available at http://www.verfassungsschutz- hessen.de/downloads/islam.pdf.

18. Paul Landau, Le Sabre et le Coran (Monaco: Editions du Rocher, 2005), pp. 72-3.

19. Ahmed S. Moussalli, "Hasan al-Turabi's Islamist Discourse on Democracy and Shura," Middle Eastern Studies 30, issue 1 (January 1994).

20. Jean-Yves Camus, "Islam in France," paper published by the Interdisciplinary Center Herzliya (ICT), 10 May 2004, available at: http://www.ict.org.il/articles/articledet.cfm?articleid=514

21. Khalid Duran, "Jihadism in Europe," The Journal of Counterterrorism and Security International, Fall 2000. pp. 12-5.

22. Ternisien, pp. 254-5.

23. FiammettaVenner, "OPA sur l'Islam de France: Les Ambitions de l'UOIF," Paris: Calmann-Levy, 2005. pp. 11-14.

24. Website of the European Institute of Human Sciences: http://www.iesh.fr/Html/C_present.htm.

25. Hugh Schofield, "France's Islamic Heartland," BBC, 18 April 2003.

26. Website of the European Institute of Human Sciences: http://www.iesh.fr/Html/C_present.htm.

27. Venner, p. 102.

28. Decision of the French Conseil d'État, 7 June 1999, as quoted in Venner, p. 15.

29. Venner, p. 28.

30. For more information on the UOIF's double-talk, see Venner.

31. Mohamed Sifaoui, La France Malade de Islamisme (Paris: Le Cherche Midi, 2002), pp. 49-50.

32. UK Islamic Mission, "Introduction," 2004-2005 Annual Report.

33. UK Islamic Mission, "Introduction," as quoted in Gilles Kepel, "Allah in the West: Islamic Movements in America and Europe (Stanford, CA: Stanford University Press, 1997), p. 131.

34. Ibid., p. 132.

35. UK Islamic Mission, "Introduction," 2004-2005 Annual Report.

36. Website of Young Muslims UK: http://www.ymuk.net/.

37. Website of the Islamic Foundation: http://www.islamic-foundation.org.uk/.

38. Kepel, p. 133.

39. Ibid.

40. Biography of Khurshid Ahmed, website of the Jamaat e Islami: http://www.jamaat.org/leadership/pka.html.

41. Joergen S. Nielsen, "Transnational Islam and the Integration of Islam in Europe," in Stefano Allievi and Joergen S. Nielsen, "Muslim Networks and Transnational Communities in and across Europe" (Leiden/Boston: Brill, 2003), pp. 38-9.

42. Kepel, p. 132.

43. Ibid.

44. Speech by HRH The Prince of Wales during his visit to the Islamic Foundation, 24 January 2003, available at http://www.princeofwales.gov.uk/speeches/multiracial_24012003.html.

45. Michael Whine, "The Advance of the Muslim Brotherhood in the U.K.," in Current Trends in Islamist Ideology (Hudson Institute), vol. 2, September 2005: 30-38.

46. Ternisien, p. 124.

47. Tariq Ramadan, Les Musulmans dans la Laïcité (Lyon: Tawhid Editions, 1998), pp. 78-81.

48. al-Qaradawi.

49. Antoine Sfeir, Les Réseauxd'Allah: Les filièresIslamistesen France et en Europe (Paris: Plon, 2001), p. 51. 50. Kepel, pp. 126-35.

51. Ibid., p. 187.

52. Ternisien, p. 127.

53. Website of the FIOE: http://www.eu-islam.com/en/templates/Index_en.asp.

54. Ian Johnson, "How Islamic Group's Ties Reveal Europe's Challenge," Wall Street Journal, 29 December 2005.

55. Website of FEMYSO: http://www.femyso.net/about.html.

56. Reuven Paz, "The Non-Territorial Islamic States in Europe," paper published by the Project for the Research of Islamist Movements (PRISM), Herzliya, Israel.

57. Al Islam, issue 2, 2002: 14, as quoted in the 2003 report by the Baden Württenberg state Verfassungsschutzbericht, p. 48 58. Ternisien, p. 7.

59. Kepel, p.152.

60. Ternisien, pp. 190-2.

61. See Shammai Fishman, Fiqh Al-Aqaliyyat: A Legal Theory For Muslim Minorities. Hudson Institute: Research Monographs on the Muslim World. Series No. 1, paper No. 2. Accessed at: www.futureofmuslimworld.com

62. W. Shadid and P. S. van Koningsveld, "Religious Authorities of Muslims in the West: Their Views on Political Participation," Shadid, W. and P.S. van Koningsveld, eds. Intellectual Relations and Religious Authorities: Muslims in the European Union (Leuven: Peeters, 2002), pp, 149-70.

63. "Living Islam in the West: An Interview with Shaykh Faisal Mawlawi," Palestinian Times, Issue 98, Available at: http://www.palestinetimes.net/issue98/articles.html#7.

64. Quran, Surah at-Taghabun ayah 16

65. "Living Islam in the West: An Interview with Shaykh Faisal Mawlawi," Palestinian Times, issue 98, available at: http

//www.palestinetimes.net/issue98/articles.html#7.

66. Fatwas (First Collection), translated by Anas Osama Altikriti, European Council for Fatwa and Research, date unspecified.

67. Website of the Islamic Cultural Center of Ireland: http://islamireland.ie/enter-the-icci/about-us/.

68. Closing remarks at the Council session in Stockholm, July 2003, as quoted in Besson, p. 124.

69. Ternisien, pp. 197-8.

70. Alexandre Caeiro, "The European Council for Fatwa and Research," presentation at Fourth Mediterranean Social and Political Research Meeting, European University Institute, Montecatini Terme, 19-23 March 2003.

71. Memo on Shaykh Yusuf al-Qaradawi, Home Office, 14 July 2005.

72. "Sheikh Al-Qaradhawi on Hamas Jerusalem Day Online: 'We are a Nation of Jihad and Martyrdom'; 'The Resistance in Palestine, Iraq, and Lebanon Must Go On'; 'We Stand Alongside Our Brothers in Hamas and Islamic Jihad,'"

Middle East Media and Research Institute (MEMRI), Special Dispatch #1051, 18 December 2005.

73. Gihan Shahine, "Fatwa Fight," Al Ahram Weekly, 16-22 September 2004, issue 708.

74. "Fatwa 3," Resolutions and Fatwas (Second Collection), edited by Anas Osama Altikriti and Mohammed Adam Howard, European Council for Fatwa and Research, date unspecified.

75. "Fatwa 4," Resolutions and Fatwas (Second Collection), edited by Anas Osama Altikriti and Mohammed Adam Howard, European Council for Fatwa and Research, date unspecified.

76. "Fatwa 26," Resolutions and Fatwas (Second Collection), edited by Anas Osama Altikriti and Mohammed Adam Howard, European Council for Fatwa and Research, date unspecified.

77. "Fatwa 17," Resolutions and Fatwas (Second Collection), edited by Anas Osama Altikriti and Mohammed Adam Howard, European Council for Fatwa and Research, date unspecified.

78. "Al-Qaradhawi Speaks in Favor of Suicide Operations at an Islamic Conference in Sweden," Middle East Media and Research Institute (MEMRI), Special Dispatch #542, 24 July 2003.

79. Alaa Abu Elnin, "Tipping U.S. on Baathists Prohibited: Prominent Scholar," Islam Online, 30 May 2003, available at http://www.islam-online.net/english/News/2003-05/31/article07.shtml.

80. Fatwas (First Collection), translated by Anas Osama Altikriti, European Council for Fatwa and Research, date unspecified.

81. Fatwas (First Collection), translated by Anas Osama Altikriti, European Council for Fatwa and Research, date unspecified.

82. Yusuf al-Qaradawi, Le Licite et l'Illiciteen Islam (Paris: Editions al Qalam, 1992), p. 207.

83. Ternisien, p. 312.

84. Author's interview with Ali Abu Shwaima, editor of al Europiya (Milan), January 2006.

85. Fatwas (First Collection). translated by Anas Osama Altikriti, European Council for Fatwa and Research, date unspecified.

86. "Poll: Four in 10 Muslims want Sharia Law," Channel 4, 19 February 2006.

87. Data released by the Zentralinstituts Islam-Archiv-Deutschlandin; see debate on Deutschlandradio Kultur, 7 January 2006, available at http://www.dradio. de/dkultur/sendungen/tacheles/455731/.

88. Alexandre Caeiro, "The European Council for Fatwa and Research," presentation at Fourth Mediterranean Social and Political Research Meeting, European University Institute, Montecatini Terme, 19-23 March 2003.

89. Fatwas (First Collection), translated by Anas Osama Altikriti, European Council for Fatwa and Research, date unspecified.

90. Annual Report, Office for the Protection of the Constitution (Bundesverfassungsschutz), 2000, Cologne, p. 198.

## Chapter 5: A Review of Iran's Revolutionary Guards and Quds Force: Growing Global Presence, Links to Cartels and Mounting Sophistication - Alma Keshavarz

1. "Chertoff: Hezbollah Makes Al Qaeda Look 'Minor League.'" Fox News. 29 May 2008, http://www.foxnews.com/story/2008/05/29/chertoff-hezbollah-makes-al-qaeda-look-minor-league.html.

2. Ali Reza Nader, "The Revolutionary Guards." The Iran Primer. 2010 (August 2015 update), http://iranprimer.usip.org/resource/revolutionary-guards.

3. Kenneth Katzman, "Iran, Gulf Security, and U.S. Policy." Washington, D.C.: Congressional Research Service, 28 May 2015: 32.

4. Jonathan Masters. "CFR Backgrounders: Hezbollah." Washington, D.C.: Council on Foreign Relations, Updated 3 January 2014, http://www.cfr.org/lebanon/hezbollah-k-hizbollah-hizbullah/p9155.

5. Kenneth Katzman: 32.

6. Ibid.

7. Jonathan Masters: 3.

8. Ibid: 4.

9. Ibid: 5.

10. Michael Cummings and Eric Cummings, "The Costs of War with Iran: An Intelligence Preparation of the Battlefield." Small Wars Journal. 31 August 2012, http://smallwarsjournal.com/jrnl/art/the-costs-of-war-with-iran-an-intelligence-preparation-of-the-battlefield.

11. Michael McBride, "Evolution of the Immortals: The Future of Iranian Military Power." Small Wars Journal. 29 June 2014, http://smallwarsjournal.com/jrnl/art/evolution-of-the-immortals-the-future-of-iranian-military-power.

12. Department of Justice, "Manssor Arbabsiar Sentenced in New York City Federal Court to 25 Years in Prison for Conspiring with Iranian Military Officials to Assassinate the Saudi Arabian Ambassador to the United States." 30 May 2013. http://www.justice.gov/opa/pr/manssor-arbabsiar-sentenced-new-york-city-federal-court-25-years-prison-conspiring-iranian.

13. "The Quds Force, an elite unit of Iran's Islamic Revolutionary Guards Corps, spearheads Iran's global terrorist campaign." The Meir Amit Intelligence and Terrorism Information Center at the Israeli Intelligence and heritage Commemoration Center. 21 August 2012: 14, http://www.terrorism-info.org.il/en/article/20521.

14. Department of Justice, "Manssor Arbabsiar Sentenced in New York City Federal Court to 25 Years in Prison for Conspiring with Iranian Military Officials to Assassinate the Saudi Arabian Ambassador to the United States."

15. Robert J. Bunker and Hakim Hazim, "Are We Prematurely Designating Iran's Revolutionary Guards as Criminal-Soldiers?" Small Wars Journal. 5 September 2007, http://smallwarsjournal.com/blog/are-we-prematurely-designating-irans-revolutionary-guards-as-criminal-soldiers.

16. Ibid.

17. Ibid.

18. United States Department of Defense, "Unclassified Report on Military Power of Iran." April 2010, http://fas.org/man/eprint/dod_iran_2010.pdf.

19. Ibid.

20. Ilan Berman, "Iran's Influence and Activity in Latin America: Testimony before the United States Senate Committee on Foreign Relations Subcommittee on Western Hemisphere, Peace Corps, and Global Narcotics Affairs." 16 February 2012.

21. "Iran: Quds Force in Venezuela." STRATFOR Global Intelligence. 22 April 2010, https://www.stratfor.com/analysis/iran-quds-force-venezuela.

22. Sandra Warmoth, "Iran's Expanding Footprint in Latin America." Small Wars Journal. 29 May 2012, http://smallwarsjournal.com/jrnl/art/irans-expanding-footprint-in-latin-america.

23. Robert J. Bunker and Hakim Hazim, "Are We Prematurely Designating Iran's Revolutionary Guards as Criminal-Soldiers?"

24. Luis Fleischman. Latin America in the Post Chavez Era: The Security Threat to the United States. Potomac Books, 2013: 132.

25. Ibid: 131.

26. Author'sinterview with Michael Braun. 16 December 2015.

27. Sami Kronenfield and YoelGurzansky, "The Revolutionary Guards' International Drug Trade." American Center for Democracy. 1 November 2013, http://acdemocracy.org/the-revolutionary-guards-international-drug-trade/.

28. Saeed Ghasseminejad, "How Iran's Mafia-like Revolutionary Guard Rules the Country's Black Market." Business Insider. 10 December 2015, http://www.businessinsider.com/how-irans-mafia-like-revolutionary-guard-rules-the-countrys-black-market-2015-12.

29. Scott Modell and David Asher, "Pushback: Countering the Iran Action Network." Center for a New American Security. 5 September 2013, http://www.cnas.org/publications/pushback-countering-iran-action-network#.VnWjOktqrwI.

30. Ibid.

31. Department of Justice, "Manssor Arbabsiar Sentenced in New York City Federal Court to 25 Years in Prison for Conspiring with Iranian Military Officials to Assassinate the Saudi Arabian Ambassador to the United States."

32. Ilan Berman, "Iran's Influence and Activity in Latin America: Testimony before the United States Senate Committee on Foreign Relations Subcommittee on Western Hemisphere, Peace Corps, and Global Narcotics Affairs."

33. Ibid.

34. Sebastian Rotella, "Before Deadly Bulgaria Bombing, Tracks of a Resurgent Iran-Hezbollah Threat." ProPublica. 30 July 2012, http://www.propublica.org/article/before-deadly-bulgaria-bombing-tracks-of-a-resurgent-iran-hezbollah-threat.

35. Ibid.

36. Ibid.

37. Ibid.

38. Ibid.

39. Matthew Levitt. "Iran's Support for Terrorism Worldwide." Testimony submitted to the House Committee on Foreign Affairs Subcommittee on Terrorism, Nonproliferation, and Trade Subcommittee on the Middle East and North Africa, 4 March 2014, http://www.washingtoninstitute.org/uploads/Documents/testimony/LevittTestimony20140304.pdf.

40. Ibid.

41. Executive Order 13224: Executive Order 13224 blocking Terrorist Property and a summary of the Terrorism Sanctions Regulations (Title 31 Part 595 of the U.S. Code of Federal Regulations), Terrorism List Governments Sanctions Regulations (Title 31 Part 596 of the U.S. Code of Federal Regulations), and Foreign Terrorist Organizations Sanctions Regulations (Title 31 Part 597 of the U.S. Code of Federal Regulations). https://www.treasury.gov/resource-center/sanctions/Programs/Documents/terror.pdf.

42. Department of Treasury, "Treasury Targets Networks Linked to Iran." 6 February 2014, https://www.treasury.gov/press-center/press-releases/Pages/jl2287.aspx.

43. Matthew Levitt. "Iran's Support for Terrorism Worldwide."

44. Kenneth Katzman, "Iran, Gulf Security, and U.S. Policy": 34.

45. Anthony H. Cordesman and Khalid R. Al-Rodhan, "Iranian Nuclear Weapons? The Threat from Iran's WMD and Missile Programs." Center for Strategic and International Studies. 21 February 2006, http://csis.org/files/media/csis/pubs/060221_iran_wmd.pdf.

46. U.S. Department of the Treasury, "Treasury Designates Iranian Quds Force General Overseeing Afghan Heroin Trafficking Through Iran." 7 March 2012, https://www.treasury.gov/press-center/press-releases/Pages/tg1444.aspx.

47. Ibid.

48. Steven Hughes. "The Dirty Secret No One Talks About, Tehran's Heroin Drug Trade/Its Narco-War Against America." The Jerusalem Post. 11 March 2015, http://www.jpost.com/Blogs/The-Iran-Threat/The-Dirty-Secret-No-One-Talks-About-Tehrans-Heroin-Drug-Trade-its-Narco-War-Against-America-393542.

49. Kenneth Katzman, "Iran Sanctions." Washington, D.C.: Congressional Research Service, 21 April 2015, https://www.fas.org/sgp/crs/mideast/RS20871.pdf.

50. Ibid.

51. Ibid.

52. Ibid.

53. Matthew Levitt, "Hezbollah and the Quds Force in Iran's Shadow War with the West." Washington, D.C.: The Washington Institute for Near East Policy, January 2013: 9, https://www.washingtoninstitute.org/uploads/Documents/pubs/PolicyFocus123.pdf.

54. Ibid: 10.

55. Saeed Ghasseminejad, "How Iran's Mafia-like Revolutionary Guard Rules the Country's Black Market."

56. Ken Dilianian, "Retired General Criticizes U.S. Response to Alleged Iranian Plot." Los Angeles Times. 20 July 2013, http://articles.latimes.com/2013/jul/20/world/la-fg-wn-mattis-iran-obama-administration-20130720.

57. Michael Braun, "Iran, Hezbollah and the Threat to the Homeland." Testimony before the U.S. House of Representatives, Committee on Homeland Security. 21 March 2012, https://homeland.house.gov/files/Testimony-Braun.pdf.

58. Author interview with Michael Braun. 16 December 2015.

## Chapter 6: Revolutionary Intelligence: The Expanding Intelligence Role of the Iranian Revolutionary Guard Corps- Udit Banerjea

1   Federal Research Division, Iran's Ministry of Intelligence and Security: A Profile, (Washington, D.C.: Library of Congress, 2012), 6.

2   Constitution of the Islamic Republic of Iran, Article 110, Foundation for Iranian Studies, available at: http://fis-iran.org/en/resources/legaldoc/constitutionislamic.

3   Federal Research Division, Iran's Ministry of Intelligence and Security: A Profile, pp. 6-10.

4   Anthony H. Cordesman, Iran's Revolutionary Guards, the Al Quds Force, and Other Intelligence and Paramilitary Forces (Rough Working Draft) (Washington, D.C.: Center for Strategic and International Studies, August 16, 2007), 3-10, available at: http://csis.org/files/media/csis/pubs/070816_cordesman_report.pdf.

5   Cordesman, Iran's Revolutionary Guards, p. 10.

6   Marc Champion, "Revolutionary Guard Tightens Security Grip," Wall Street Journal, November 13, 2009, available at: http://www.wsj.com/articles/SB125797782460044139.

7   Cordesman, Iran's Revolutionary Guards, p. 13.

8   "Iran Exile Group Says Khamenei Tightens Intelligence Grip," Radio Free Europe/Radio Liberty, November 12, 2009, available at: http://www.rferl.org/content/Iran_Exile_Group_Khamenei_Tightens_Intelligence_Grip/1876444.html.

9   "Iran's new spymaster," Iran Focus, June 20, 2010, available at: http://www.iranfocus.com/en/index.php?option=com_content&view=article&id=20815: irans-new-spymaster & catid=29: exclusive-reports & Itemid=121.

10   "Iran's new spymaster," Iran Focus.

11  Thomas Erdbrink, "Iran's Ahmadinejad affirms Khamenei decision, tensions remain," The Washington Post, May 8, 2011, available at: http://www.washingtonpost.com/world/middle-east/irans-ahmadinejad-affirms-khamenei-decision-tensions-remain/2011/05/08/AFpK82QG_story.html.

12  Federal Research Division, Iran's Ministry of Intelligence and Security: A Profile, 16.

13  Cordesman, Iran's Revolutionary Guards, 8.

14  Scott Shane, "Iranian Force, Focus of U.S., Still a Mystery," New York Times, February 17, 2007, available at: http://www.nytimes.com/2007/02/17/world/middleeast/17quds.html.

15  Dexter Filkins, "The Shadow Commander," New Yorker 89, no. 30 (September 30, 2013): 10.

16  Cordesman, Iran's Revolutionary Guards, p. 9.

17  Filkins, "The Shadow Commander," p. 10.

18  Mark Hosenball, "Tehran's Secret 'Department 9000,'" Newsweek, June 4, 2007.

19  Filkins, "The Shadow Commander," p. 2.

20  "Iran's 'invisible man,'" Middle East no. 392 (August 2008): 28.

21  Filkins, "The Shadow Commander," pp. 1-23.

22  Champion, "Revolutionary Guard Tightens Security Grip."

23  Neil MacFarquhar, "Odd Twist for Elite Unit Guiding Iran's Proxy Wars," New York Times, October 12, 2011, available at: http://www.nytimes.com/2011/10/12/world/middleeast/new-plot-is-odd-twist-for-irans-elite-quds-force.html?_r=0.

24  Filkins, "The Shadow Commander," p. 18.

25  "Iran's 'invisible man,'" p. 31.

26  Hosenball, "Tehran's Secret 'Department 9000.'"

27  Filkins, "The Shadow Commander," p. 15.

28  Eric Schmitt and Robert F. Worth, "With Arms for Yemen Rebels, Iran Seeks Wider Mideast Role," New York Times, March 15, 2012, available at: http://www.nytimes.com/2012/03/15/world/middleeast/aiding-yemen-rebels-iran-seeks-wider-mideast-role.html?pagewanted=all.

29  MacFarquhar, "Odd Twist for Elite Unit Guiding Iran's Proxy Wars."

30   Filkins, "The Shadow Commander," pp. 4-5.

31   Filkins, "The Shadow Commander," p. 10.

32   MacFarquhar, "Odd Twist for Elite Unit Guiding Iran's Proxy Wars."

33   Filkins, "The Shadow Commander," p. 6.

34   Michael Slackman, "Elite Guard in Iran Tightens Grip with Media Move," New York Times, October 8, 2009.

35   Iran profile, "Special Edition: Surveillance," Reporters Without Borders website, available at: http://surveillance.rsf.org/en/iran/.

36   "IRGC on the web," Iran Military News website, available at: http://iranmilitarynews.org/irgc-on-the-web/.

37   Oliver Jones, Iran insights – Iran's intelligence and security apparatus, Newcastle: UK Defence Forum, 2011, available at: http://www.ukdf.org.uk/assets/downloads/RS84CIraninsights- Iran percentE2 percent80 percent99sintelligenceandsecurityapparatusx.pdf.

38   Akbar Ganji, "Iran: The High Cost of the IRGC's Economic Might," The National Interest, December 4, 2013, available at: http://nationalinterest.org/commentary/iran- the-high-cost-the-irgcs-economic-might-9495.

39   Ali Alfoneh, "All the Guard's Men: Iran's Silent Revolution," World Affairs 173, no. 3 (September/October 2010): 76.

40   Ganji, "Iran: The High Cost of the IRGC's Economic Might."

41   "Goon squad," The Economist, November 1, 2014.

42   Ganji, "Iran: The High Cost of the IRGC's Economic Might."

43   "Goon squad."

44   Ibid.

## Chapter 7: The Two Faces of the Fatemiyuon: Revisiting the Male Fighters Part-1and II- Mohsen Hamidi

1.   The Iranian government is not a unitary actor. Some have referred to a "deep state" consisting of the Supreme Leader, Ayatollah Ali Khamenei, and security and intelligence agencies in Iran that have the influence required to make key, but contentious, policy decisions, for example, on forming and supporting costly regional proxy forces. See: Alex Vatanka, Sanam Vakil and Hossein Rassam, "How Deep Is Iran's State? The Battle over Khamenei's Successor," July/August 2017, Foreign Affairs.

2. See, for instance: Ali Alfoneh, "Tehran's Shia Foreign Legions," 30 January 2018, Carnegie Endowment for International Peace; Payam Mohseni and Hussein Kalout, "Iran's Axis of Resistance Rises: How It is Forging a New Middle East," 24 January 2017, Foreign Affairs; W. Andrew Terrill (2015), "Iran's Strategy for Saving Assad," The Middle East Journal 69 (2): 222-36.

3. Tobias Schneider, "The Fatemiyoun Division: Afghan Fighters in the Syrian Civil War," October 2018, Policy Paper 2018-9, Middle East Institute: Washington, DC, pp 1-3.

4. Given some Afghan involvement through the then Iran-based Shia mujahedin factions including one by Muhammad Akbari in the Iraq-Iran war called Pasdaran-e Jihad-e Islami (founded in 1983; it joined Hezb-e Wahdat with seven other groups when it was established in 1989), it is possible that Sepah-e Muhammad emerged from this involvement.

5. Sayyeda Zeinab is the daughter of Hazrat Fatema and Ali ibn Abi Taleb and granddaughter of the Prophet Muhammad. She is highly revered by Shia Muslims for her role in preserving and continuing the prophet's lineage through Fatema and Ali.

6. The sources for the estimated 50,000 and 10,000-20,000 respectively are: Ahmad Shuja Jamal, "The Fatemiyoun Army: Reintegration into Afghan Society," March 2019, Special Report No 443, United States Institute of Peace: Washington, DC, p 3; Lars Hauch, "Understanding the Fatemiyoun Division: Life through the Eyes of a Militia Member," 22 May 2019, Middle East Institute. In October 2018, Schneider drew on an internal Fatemiyun source to put the range "at a more realistic peak of 12,000-14,000." See: Schneider, "The Fatemiyoun Division," p 5.

7. For instance, see: Adam Baczko, Gilles Dorronsoro and Arthur Quesnay (2018), Civil War in Syria: Mobilization and Competing Social Orders, translated by Louise Rosen and Henry Randolph, New York: Cambridge University Press. See also this review article: Daniel Neep (2018), "Civil War in Syria: Mobilization and Competing Social Orders by Adam Baczko, Gilles Dorronsoro and Arthur Quesnay (review)," The Middle East Journal 72 (4): 704-706.

8. In a recent reaction, which was a response to a 15 November 2018 event held in Kabul by the Afghan Institute for Strategic Studies (AISS) to present and discuss the Dari version of Schneider's above quoted paper, the Iranian embassy in Afghanistan rejected the paper as "incorrect propositions, contradictory arguments, doubts and ambiguities and, in numerous cases, exaggeration and hyperbole." In its obliquely-worded statement, the embassy described the paper as part of an "Iranophobia project in Afghanistan" by what it called "malevolent actors from outside the region" in which "a part of Afghanistan's society is unjustly subjected to accusation and criticism." It

finally emphasised the "continued constructive and close interaction" between Iran and Afghanistan based on "mutual interests and common threats."

9.  Ahmad Shuja Jamal, "The Fatemiyoun Army: Reintegration into Afghan Society," March 2019, Special Report No 443, United States Institute of Peace: Washington, DC, p 18.

10. Ibid.

11. Ibid, p 19.

12. Ibid.

13. Ibid.

14. Ibid, pp 20-21.

15. Ibid, p 21.

16. Ibid, pp 14-15.

17. This dispatch is based on interviews with ten women with close relatives among the Fatemiyun: three wives, two mothers, three sisters, one maternal aunt and one woman who was both wife and mother to Fatemiyun fighters (ie her husband and her son). Given their indirect involvement in and deep knowledge of the Fatemiyun group, these women are key informants. To capture the potential geographic and other variations in experiences of Fatemiyun women, the author decided to conduct interviews in Afghanistan, in Herat city, and Tehran – five in each. They were carried out in late 2018 and early 2019. Of the ten families studied through these women, four were already in Iran when their men went to war in Syria, three left Afghanistan to live in Iran, one was preparing to move, one's male relative was back in Herat and had stopped fighting in the war, and the interviewee from the last family had prevented her male relative from returning to Syria.

The women were approached by two female research assistants (one in Herat and one in Tehran) who had previous acquaintanceship and therefore already some rapport with them. This prior familiarity provided easier and safer access, both for the key informants and the research assistants, and contributed to a 'do-no-harm' research approach. The anonymity of both the key informants and the research assistants is maintained here to protect their privacy and the confidentiality of the conversations.

Having secured the consent of the interviewees to take part in this research (in a few cases, potential interviewees refused to do so, something which was fully respected), the research assistants used a rough list of general, open-ended questions to stimulate conversation. The questions were about family decision-making prior to the men joining the war in Syria, family life while the men were fighting away from home, family life if the men were killed, injured or affected otherwise and family life after Syria, at least at the time of the interviews. The interviews were largely unstructured and the interviewees were not interrupted to allow as natural flow as possible in the conversations. The conversations were either recorded (if permission was granted) or written down. The transcribed and handwritten conversations were analysed and form the basis of this dispatch.

AAN takes research security seriously. Without stressing that the topic was 'sensitive' and thus making it so beforehand, the author held several rounds of consultations with the research assistants over the course of a couple of months, talking through the need to make sure their research would pose no risk to them or their key informants and that both had the right to quit the research whenever they wanted to. Since the research assistants approached women they knew and relationships of trust already existed, they determined that the research was reasonably safe and therefore doable.

The ten key informant interviews are complemented by the author's intermittent observations, since 2014, of an extended family that has members in the Fatemiyun. Through on-and-off observations and informal conversations over the course of five years, it became possible to study several members of the Fatemiyun from within and over time, contrasting with research approaches that have so far looked at the group from without or only at one point in time.

Finally, this dispatch does not claim to be representative. The sample size is small (n = 10) and the interviewees were chosen through convenience sampling. However, given what was feasible, it is an exploratory study that is relevant to the topic under discussion (experiences of the Syrian war by women whose men have participated in it). Such subjects are often best captured through qualitative approaches.

18. One of the things clerics including this Afghan one have done in Syria has been to recite religious songs such as nohas (lamentations) and maddahis (panegyrics) to reinforce fighters' morale. For example, to challenge the idea that individuals have gone to war in Syria just to get better pay than what they could find back in Iran, one noha quotes a child whose father was killed in the Syrian war as saying: "Love is priceless. To fight and to die has no price but for love [of defending Shia faith]." The clerics are mostly stationed in military bases or mosques that the Fatemiyun fighters visit in Syria.

19. Hazrat Fatema is the daughter of the Prophet Muhammad and wife to Ali ibn Abi Taleb, the first imam for Shia Muslims and the fourth caliph for Sunni Muslims.

20. In sofrehsalawat ceremonies that were held or attended by the interviewees, a woman usually hosted other women in her home to recite thousands of salawat (salutations to the Prophet Muhammad and his progeny) with tasbih

(prayer beads). The women also prayed to God to answer their praying, including entreaties for their men to be well and return from Syria safe and sound. They then ate food that was mostly ash (soup). These events were also opportunities for both hosting and participating women to meet and socialise.

21. It refers to the shrine/mosque in southern Damascus, the Syrian capital, in which lies the Prophet Muhammad's granddaughter, Sayyeda Zeinab. Her tomb is an important Shia shrine. She is highly revered by Shia Muslims for her role in preserving and continuing the prophet's lineage through her grandparents, Fatema and Ali.

22. The Office of Supreme Leader Ayatollah Ali Khamenei (aka Beit-e Rahbari or the House of Leadership) is reportedly one of Iran's wealthiest institutions with "holdings of about $95bn," according to this BBC report about recent United States sanctions targeting his assets. However, Iranian President Hassan Rouhani responded to these US sanctions by saying: "They [the Americans] say they want to confiscate the property of our leader. His property is just a hosseiniya [a place of worship] and a simple house. Our leaders are not like the leaders of other countries who have billions in their foreign accounts that they want to sanction and confiscate."

23. There have been protests in Iran against the Iranian government spending billions of US dollars financing and supporting its regional allies including Syria, given deteriorating economic conditions for Iranians inside the country. There was also heated discussion in Iran when militia groups such as the Fatemiyun got involved in assisting people affected by recent destructive floods there. Regarded as an 'alien' involvement, some Iranians said they had been sent to suppress domestic protests.

## Chapter 8: The Second Lebanon War, Hezbollah and Its Repercussions- Megnus Lorell

1. Nima Damidez and Magnus Norell, "En ny början? Lebanon after president valet" [A new beginning? Lebanon after the presidential election], *FOI Memo 2435* (Swedish Defence Research Agency, May 2008).

2. United Nations Security Council, "Resolution 1701" (2006), http://www.un.org/News/Press/docs/2006/sc8808.doc.htm (accessed June 23, 2009).

3. United Nations Security Council, "Resolution 1559" (2004), http://www.un.org/News/Press/docs/2004/sc8181.doc.htm (accessed June 23, 2009).

4. Paragraph 14 in the text of UNSCR 1701 concerns the right of the UN force to assist the Lebanese government in its attempt to secure its borders.

5. Ban Ki-Moon, Reuters, May 8, 2007.

6. "US in Covert War against Hizbullah," *Guardian*, April 10 2007, http://www. guardian.co.uk/world/2007/apr/10/usa.syria.

7. For example, Lebanon, Iraq, and the Palestinian territories.

8. For example, Egypt and Iran.

9. For a more extensive discussion of these issues, see Magnus Norell, *Mellanöstern efter kriget i Irak-demokratisering med förhinder?* (Stockholm: SNS, 2004).

10. Damidez and Norell, 2008.

11. It should be noted, however, that according to several opinion polls, many Muslim Arabs see no inherent contradiction between Islam and democracy. See, for instance, G. Khouri in *The Daily Star*, November 16, 2005; and Massoud Derhally, "yearning for Change," Arabianbusiness.com, October 9, 2005, http://www.arabianbusiness.com/492075?ln=en (accessed June 23, 2009).

12. This is not the place to go over the many conflicts that have affected, and are still affecting, the relationship between Israel and its Arab neighbors. With regard to Lebanon, there are a number of longstanding issues that predate Hezbollah and its role in the country. The Palestine Liberation Organization, in its day, held a similar position, as "a state within the state." Another similarity between the two organizations is the Lebanese government's weakness and inability to neutralize the external and domestic groups that, at least in part, have acquired influence by force of arms.

13. See note 12.

14. Both Hassan Nasrallah and Mahmoud Koumati, the second-in-command of Hezbollah's political wing, have admitted in interviews that they were completely unprepared for the magnitude of the Israeli response to the kidnappings. Nasrallah has admitted that had he known what the Israeli response would be, he would not have launched the operation. See Daniel Byman and Steven Simon, "The No-Win Zone: An After-Action Report from Lebanon," *The National Interest*, November/December 2006, p. 56.

15. Barak Ravid, "Report: Hezbollah Carries Out Military Drills in South Lebanon," *Haaretz*, November 22, 2008, http://www.haaretz.com (accessed June 23, 2009). One example is the donors' conference that was held under the auspices of the Swedish government immediately after the war. See, for instance, Mag- nus Norell, "Regeringens givarkonferens förvärrar situationen i Libanon"

16. (The government's donor conference is worsening the situation in Lebanon), *DN.se*, August 30, 2006, http://www.dn.se/DNet/jsp/polopoly.jsp?a=568826 (accessed June 23, 2009).

17. "Majority of Lebanese Believe Hezbollah Won the War," *The Daily Star*, August 26, 2006, cited in Byman and Simon, p. 57.

18. This network is one of the issues that triggered the May 2008 face-off between Hezbollah and the Lebanese government. See Damidez and Norell, 2008.

19. The German prosecutor who led the investigation, Detlev Mehlis, proved able to resist pressure when he named individuals connected to the Syrian government as responsible for the murder. Mehlis was replaced by a significantly more pliant successor, who changed the original report and removed many of the more controversial parts. The new UN tribunal began its work in March 2009. For the mistakenly released report, see http://www. washing- tonpost.com/wp-srv/world/syria/mehlis.report.doc. For Mehlis's official report, see http://www.un.org/news/dh/docs/mehlisreport/ (accessed June 30, 2009).

20. By broadening the government, Hezbollah and its allies managed to acquire a "blocking third" of the ministerial portfolio seats in the Lebanese cabinet. r to its interests. This reflects the ambivalent attitude of Hezbollah to the state. On the one hand, it is part of the political structure in Lebanon. On the other hand, it is primarily interested in retaining its weapons and military structure independently of the state. The nation-state does not comprise an important part of Hezbollah's ideological foundation.

21. A "gentleman's agreement" of sorts can be said to govern the relationship between the UN and Hezbollah in the South: members of Hezbollah refrain from transporting or showing their weapons in the open, and the UN refrains from aggressively searching vehicles or buildings belonging to Hezbollah.

22. Byman and Simon, p. 60.

23. During the first days of the war, when Israel won its greatest successes (by taking out Hezbollah's medium-range Fajr missiles), the criticism directed at Hezbollah was the greatest. Even Arab countries such as Saudi Arabia, Egypt, and Jordan made it clear that they did not mind if Israel continued its operation until Hezbollah was broken. See, for example, Amos Harel and Avi Issacharoff, *34 Days: Israel, Hezbollah and the War in Lebanon* (New York: Palgrave Macmillan, 2008), pp. 98, 102–3.

24. Ibid., pp. 108–9.

25. Twenty-eight people were killed, including seventeen children. The strike was not conceived as an attack against civilian targets, of course, but it was a result of a tactic whereby the Israeli air force would bomb suspicious houses on the outskirts of villages, where Hezbollah may have hidden its short-range Katyusha rockets. It was a deliberate tactic of Hezbollah to use civilian structures as weapons storage (not just for rockets), mostly houses on the outskirts of the villages (Harel and Issacharoff, *34 Days*, pp. 158–61). These

short-range rockets were very hard to target for the Israeli air force. At the end of July, all the known targets were taken out; Israel carried out preemptive attacks against suspected targets. The house in Qana was one such target. The attack caused an even bigger stir because a similar attack had taken place in the same village in 1996 (during Operation Grapes of Wrath), when another house was fired upon by mistake, killing many civilians.

26. Harel and Issacharoff, 34 Days, pp. 175-158

27. Ibid, pp. 163

28. See *New York Times*, January 30, 2008. Preliminary results were presented in April 2007, and in January 2008 the full report was published.

29. A good example was the Palestine Liberation Organization's success in allying itself with a plethora of left-wing groups by portraying its cause as a post-colonial one in the 1970s and 1980s. This tactic has caused many left-wing observers today to see Israel as a purely colonial project. Especially in Europe, this has influenced the image of the Israeli-Palestinian conflict. There are examples of this in Sweden as well. When Sweden played a Davis Cup game against Israel in Malmö, Sweden, in March 2009, the left-wing majority in the Malmö municipality (led by Ilmar Reepalu) decided that the game would be played without an audience. The security reasons that were put forth did not fool anyone: the police had no difficulties controlling the protestors, and the decision to play the game without an audience divided the municipality along party lines. Reepalu himself claimed that the game would enrage the many voters of Middle Eastern extraction in the city. This demonization of Israel, deliberate or not, is an example of the significance this question has in Sweden. See also Per Gudmundson, editorial page, *SvD*, March 11, 2009.

30. Note that this was in regard to Israel as a state. Thus, it was not just the occupation of southern Lebanon that was the problem.

31. This interpretation, however, ignores a number of factors that played into Israel's decision to leave Lebanon unilaterally. In the long term, this may become dangerous, of course, since it might lead to a lowering of the bar for violent confrontation.

32. See, for instance, Omran Salman, "The Era of Iranian Hegemony in the Middle East Is upon Us," *Aafaq.org*, September 1, 2008, http://www.aafaq.org/ english/ Index.aspx (accessed June 23, 2009)

33. When the author (along with colleague Magnus Ranstorp, then working at St. Andrews University in Scotland), helped to create a channel for secret contacts between Hezbollah and Israel in 1997–2000, the question often surfaced "What would happen next?"—that is, after an Israeli withdrawal. It was rather obvious that in order for a withdrawal to be successful and not lead to future confrontation, it was absolutely necessary that the Lebanese government be

assisted in taking control of the South. That the power vacuum arising from an Israeli withdrawal would lead to a Hezbollah takeover was plain to see. At the time, however, Syrian forces still occupied parts of Lebanon, and it was equally obvious that the Lebanese government would not be able to reclaim the South while Damascus backed Hezbollah and worked against any initiatives that did not take Syrian interests into account. This was the message that the author and Dr. Ranstorp brought back from encounters with Lebanese interlocutors. These warnings were not heeded, however—although the withdrawal itself was carried out relatively quickly and painlessly, Hezbollah did in fact assume control over the South. The summer 2006 war was therefore expected, even if its timing was uncertain. As for the secret contacts preceding the 2000 withdrawal, their purpose had been to investigate the consequences of a unilateral move out of the Israeli security zone established in southern Lebanon in 1978. The initiative came from Israeli politician yossi Beilin, who for several years had argued within the Labor Party in favor of such a move.

34. For the Israelis, the rocket fire from Gaza has continued, as have the terrorist attacks coming from there. Israeli countermeasures, ranging from limited attacks and incursions to take out launch pads, to Operation Cast Lead in the winter of 2008–2009, have meant additional fighting and suffering for Palestinian civilians. For the Lebanese, the Israeli withdrawal resulted in a Hezbollah takeover, and a new brand of foreign soldiers controlling the area.

35. This controversial issue has dominated the relationship between Iran and the West for a long time. Iran's repeated assurances that it is only striving to develop nuclear power for peaceful use are contradicted by its own politics, as well as by the UN and International Atomic Energy Agency's repeated criticisms of Tehran's activities. Furthermore, there is no doubt that Iranian nuclear weapons would lead to a regional arms race. Several countries in the region— such as Egypt, Saudi Arabia, and the United Arab Emirates, which are already very critical of Iranian ambitions toward acquiring nuclear weapons and becoming a regional superpower—have stated that they would pursue nuclear weapons if Iran acquired nuclear technology. Interestingly, Israel's possession of nuclear weapons has never produced such a reaction. This underscores the fact that Iran is seen as a far more serious destabilizing factor than Israel. See also: Emily B. Landau, "New Nuclear Programs in the Middle East: What Do They Mean?" *INSS Insight* (edited by Mark Heller) no. 3 (December 11, 2006); Magnus Norell, "There Are Alternatives to Both War and Diplomacy," *Judisk Krönika*, vol. 75, no. 2, årgång 75, April 2007, pp. 33–37.

36. The attack clearly amounted to a casus belli (which obviously did not *force* Israel to strike back): Hezbollah crossed an international border and killed and kidnapped foreign soldiers of a country with which Lebanon was not at war. The interesting aspect, however, was not the obvious cause of the war but that Hezbollah was able to do this at all without having to take the Lebanese government into account whatsoever.

37. From approximately 2,500 men at the start of the war, the current number has reached about 12,700. The goal was for a force of 15,000 men.

38. See Magnus Norell, *Radical Islamist Movements in the Middle East* (Swedish Ministry of Foreign Affairs, March–June, 2006).

39. *Al-Siyassa*, December 14, 2006.

40. Tufeili is not the only one criticizing Hezbollah from within. Other important people of good standing in the Lebanese Shiite community have said similar things. These include Muhammad Hassan al-Amin, an Islamic thinker and judge in the Shia Islamic court in Lebanon; Sayed Ali al-Amin, the former mufti in Tyre and Jebel Amel, formerly of Amal (the other large Shiite movement in Lebanon, whose leader, Nabih Berri, is the speaker of parliament); and Hani Fahs, a scholar on Islam. He was also an apprentice of Ayatollah Khomeini.

41. See United Nations, *Report of the International Independent Investigation Commission Established Pursuant to Security Council Resolution 1595 (2005)*, http://www.un.org/news/dh/docs/mehlisreport (accessed June 23, 2009).

42. Martin van Creveld, "Israel's Lebanese War—A Preliminary Assessment," *RUSI Journal,* October 2006.

43. It merits pointing out that Hezbollah's firepower is more akin to that of a regular army than that of the more commonly used "militia." Hezbollah has a structure modeled on the Iranian pattern, such as the Islamic Revolutionary Guard Corps.

44. Van Creveld, "Israel's Lebanese War."

45. As a consequence of the war, Halutz, too, was forced to resign in January 2007.

46. Harel and Issacharoff, *34 Days.*

47. Perhaps the best-known example is former U.S. Secretary of Defense Donald Rumsfeld, whose doctrine of high-tech war was disproved through two wars. Though certainly effective in some aspects, it was not necessarily sufficient to win the war.

48. When it comes to Gaza, it is clear that Hamas has endeavored to expand its ability to fire on Israel with increasingly sophisticated long-range rockets. One of the things that came out as a result of the fighting in Gaza was the extent of Hamas success in smuggling sophisticated weaponry into Gaza.

49. Israel has one of the world's only operational missile -defence systems, called "Arrow" ("Chetz," in Hebrew).

50. The closest parallel is the Vietnam War, during which the Viet Cong's extensive system of tunnels, including in Saigon, made it possible for it to carry out attacks inside Saigon.

51. This happened on several occasions. One of the best-known incidents was the Canadian observer Maj. Paeta Hess–von Kruedener, who was killed at his post in the village of el-Khiam during the war. Only a couple of days before the incident, Hess–von Kruedener wrote an email to Canadian television saying that Hezbollah was using his UN post as a "shield" to launch rockets into Israel. Israel returned fire on several occasions to areas close to the UN position, before the final strike that killed Hess–von Kruedener and three other observers. According to Hess–von Kruedener, this was a common tactic employed by Hezbollah that occurred several times every day. See Joel Kom, with files from Steven Edwards, CanWest News Service, for *The Ottawa Citizen,* July 17, 2006.

52. It should be pointed out that this is not a position on the question of whether Israel really did carry out operations that could be classified as war crimes. According to Human Rights Watch this was indeed the case. See *Human Rights Watch*, vol. 18, no. 3, August 2006.

53. Ibid.

54. Nor is this a valid argument or excuse for any Israeli attacks that killed or injured Lebanese civilians. It does not mean, furthermore, that Israeli attacks against, say, convoys did not kill Lebanese civilians. Indeed, Human Rights Watch has brought out claims that that was the case. Ibid.

55. *Jerusalem Issue Brief*, vol. 6; and *Jerusalem Report*, November 13, 2006, pp. 20–21.

56. In part, Israel tried to avoid harming civilians by dropping leaflets, transmitting radio announcements, and sending out text messages encouraging the population to leave the area before the attacks took place, but this was not always sufficient to entirely avoid civilian casualties.

57. This was done in part by using civilian houses to store weapons and as entrances to tunnels and bunkers. In part, it was done by using civilian neighbor- hoods to launch rockets and missiles.

58. Avi Kober, "The Second Lebanon War," BESA Perspectives, Perspectives Paper 22, (September 28, 2006).

59. 59. Ibid.

60. Ibid.

61. Even when Hezbollah was forced to fight in large-scale battles, it often succeeded in inflicting significant losses on the Israel Defense Forces, since it fought effectively from the defensive positions it had built around southern Lebanon.

62. Harel and Issacharoff, *34 Days*.

63. This becomes even more obvious in light of the fact that the Israeli starting position was fairly advantageous: internal unity as to the justness of the war, international backing of its right to self-defense—including implicit support from several Arab countries that did not mind seeing Hezbollah and Iran suffering a defeat—and a feeling that time was on its side in carrying out its operation.

64. In addition to the murder of Rafiq Hariri, a dozen other politicians and journalists critical of Syrian influence and Hezbollah's role in Lebanon have been murdered.

65. Nadim Shehadi, "Riviera vs. Citadel: The Battle for Lebanon," *Open Democracy*, August 22, 2006, http://www.opendemocracy.net/conflict-middle_east_ politics/riviera_citadel_3841.jsp.

66. Harel and Issacharoff, *34 Days*, p. 38.

67. The Security Zone was created in 1978 after a short Israeli operation intended to prevent cross-border attacks. These attacks had been ongoing since the late 1960s.

68. See note 33.

69. The best-known case was an attack close to Mount Dov on October 7, 2000— that is, only four months after the Israeli withdrawal. Three soldiers were kidnapped, and their bodies were later exchanged for Lebanese prisoners in Israel. The scandalous part of the attack was that UN personnel, who did not intervene, filmed it. To make matters worse, they then refused to hand over the film for a long time.

70. His allies were the Shiite organization Amal and the Christian Free Patriotic movement.

71. From the fall of 2006 until May 2008, Hezbollah operated a tent camp in central Beirut. The camp was built as a protest against the government, and it resulted in large parts of Beirut being blocked.

72. United Nations, *Report of the International Independent Investigation Commission Established Pursuant to Security Council Resolution 1595 (2005)*.

73. In this, it has been relatively successful, since the UN has switched investigators and changed some of the most controversial conclusions, which clearly identified Syria as responsible. The court proceedings, however, began on schedule in March 2009.

74. During the period in which Israel maintained its security zone in southern Lebanon, it was even more difficult to try to disarm Hezbollah. Hezbollah's supporters had kept their guns when everyone else had relinquished theirs (at least largely). Nor is the conflict with the government in Beirut new; Hezbollah's

role in the country has given rise to a continual crisis for the government that—even when it was trying to decrease Hezbollah's influence—has proved incapable of disarming them. As Rafiq Hariri put it already in 1996, "We are unable to disarm Hezbollah, whether we agree with their political platform or not" (Harel and Issacharoff, *34 Days*, p. 37).

75. Congressional Research Service, "Lebanon: The Israel-Hamas-Hezbollah Conflict," Order Code: RL33566, September 15, 2006.

76. Ibid.

77. Ibid; Nicholas Blanford, "UN Resolution 1701: A View from Lebanon," Policy Watch 1414, Washington Institute for Near East Policy, October 21, 2008.

78. This process was formally concluded on June 16, 2000, when the secretary-general informed the Security Council that Israel was in compliance with the UN demands (UN Security Council Resolution 425), after having withdrawn from all Lebanese territory.

79. For the UN, the areas fall within the jurisdiction of the United Nations Disengagement Observer Force (UNDOF).

80. Congressional Research Service, "Lebanon: The Israel-Hamas-Hezbollah Conflict."

81. Since assuming office, Lebanon's president, Michel Sulaiman, a Syria loyalist, has claimed that the Sheba Farms area is Lebanese territory and needs to be liberated. See, for example, Sulaiman's speech from August 1, 2008 (Sana Abdallah, "Lebanon to Release Statement on National Resistance, Hezbollah Weapons," *Middle East Times*, August 1, 2008). The dispute is not likely to be resolved that easily, and even if the Syrian president said earlier this year that Syria and Lebanon are going to establish diplomatic ties, this has not yet happened. Nor has there been any progress on the work to settle the border. Lebanese military maps identify the area as belonging to Syria (see http://en.wikipedia.org/wiki/Image:Shebaafarms.png [accessed June 30, 2009]), as does the UN, which considers the area to belong to the Syrian Golan Heights. Meanwhile, other army maps identify the areas as being north of the border, i.e. inside Lebanon (see "Carte du Liban," Lebanese Army, http://www.lebarmy.gov.lb/Arabic/popup.htm?/images/pics/geographic/1sur100000. jpg [accessed June 17, 2007]).

82. Harel and Issacharoff, *34 Days*, p. 38.

83. At the beginning of 2009, Syria decided to appoint an ambassador to Lebanon.

84. Lebanese prime minister Fouad Siniora presented a seven-point plan at a conference in Rome on July 26, 2006. Nothing came of the conference, but the preface to UN Security Council Resolution 1701 references the plan, which included a stipulation to place the area under UN jurisdiction "until

border delineation and Lebanese sovereignty over them are fully settled" (Congressional Research Service, "Lebanon: The Israel-Hamas-Hezbollah Conflict," p. 9).

85. Ibid.

86. On several occasions after June 2000, the UN has confirmed that it regards the area as Syrian. See, for example, "Statement by the President of the Security Council," United Nations Security Council, June 18, 2000 (accessed September 29, 2006); and Gary C. Gambill, "Syria and the Shebaa Farms Dispute," *Middle East Intelligence Bulletin*, vol. 3, no. 5 (May 2001), http://www.meib.org/articles/0105_ll.htm (accessed September 29, 2006, and June 23, 2009).

87. United Nations Security Council, "Resolution 1559" (2004).

88. A close friend in Beirut put it thus, "Hezbollah has used arms to get itself into Government House!"

89. See, for example, H. Avraham, "Lebanon Faces Political Crisis in Aftermath of War," *Inquiry and Analysis*, no. 299, Middle East Media Research Institute, http://memri.org/bin/articles.cgi?Page=archives&Area=ia&ID=IA29906 (accessed June 23, 2009).

90. Hezbollah's military incursion was not limited only to Sunni-dominated western Beirut. The organization also seized other areas with a more mixed population (Shiite, Sunni, Christian, and Druze).

91. There were suspicions that Hezbollah was prepared to bring weapons and matériel in directly via the airport and not just through the Syrian-Lebanese border, as has so far been the case—this, in order to find alternative routes to bring in arms should the border with Syria be closed (for whatever reason). As early as a couple of weeks after the armistice in August 2006, the Turkish authorities announced that they had intercepted five Iranian planes and one Syrian plane with arms deliveries for Hezbollah (Blanford, Policy Watch 1414). In other words, only a few weeks after Resolution 1701 (which includes a complete arms embargo) had been passed, Iran and Syria were working to bring additional weapons into Lebanon.

92. Harel and Issacharoff, *34 Days*.

93. Peretz came up through the Israeli labor union Histadrut, for which he served as head for many years. He was forced to resign in June 2007 amid a wave of criticism, not least from other parts of the Labor Party. Furthermore, he lost the Labor chairmanship to Ehud Barak, who had led the withdrawal from Lebanon in 2000.

94. Harel and Issacharoff, 34 days

95. Ibid, 99. 201-8

96. Ibid

97. Ibid.; Congressional Research Service, "Lebanon: The Israel-Hamas-Hezbollah Conflict," pp. 11–13.

98. The plans that had been drawn up specifically for such a situation as the one that triggered the war in Lebanon predicted initial air strikes against specific targets (which did indeed occur) as well as a ground operation in which troops were deployed along the Litani River in order to cut off Hezbollah's transport and supply routes and then to proceed southward with the aim of capturing the Hezbollah forces between two shields. Indeed, this was what the overdue ground offensive intended to accomplish. But by that point it was already too late. Before the operation was even underway, operatives were told they had only sixty hours before the ceasefire would be in effect, which, Halutz promised the cabinet, would be enough time. It turned out, however, that this was far too little time. Most importantly, Hezbollah was likely to be saved by the bell from being rounded up and utterly defeated, the operation's coup de grace.

99. Van Creveld, "Israel's Lebanese War."

100. This becomes even more evident if seen in the light of similar cross-border attacks in the past, such as the one at Har Dov only a couple of weeks after the 2000 withdrawal. At that time, Israel limited its response to a few air strikes since it did not want to escalate the conflict. The result of this incident (and the Israeli response) was that Hezbollah and Hamas realized that this kind of attack could pay off and that Israel was not likely to react very strongly to relatively "small" incidents.

101. Hare and Issacharoff, 34 days, pp. 75-73

102. Ibid, pp. 39-50

103. 103. See, for instance, Martin Kramer, "The American Interest," *Wall Street Journal*, November 21, 2006.

104. From a somewhat expanded version of "Nass al-Risala al-Maftuha allati wajahaha Hezbollah ila-l-Mustad'afin fi Lubnan wa-l-Alam," first published as an open letter on February 16, 1985, in the Lebanese daily *al-Safir*. It was subsequently published as a brochure as well, in which the Hezbollah program was laid out and explained. This translation was published in *The Jerusalem Quarterly*, no. 48 (Fall 1988).

105. That Hezbollah has gone to great pains to prepare for another war—in which it has internalized the lessons of 2006—is made clear from a report that Hezbollah has laid fiber optic cables in the area south of the Litani River (see http://www.washingtoninstitute.org/templateC05.php?CID=2940). According to paragraph 8 of Resolution 1701, this area is to be kept free of

arms and armed personnel who do not belong to UNIFIL or the Lebanese Army. Furthermore, Hezbollah conducted a large training exercise in November 2008, again in the South. See *al-Akhbar*, November 5, 2008 (http://www.alakhbar.ca/pdf/numero percent20555.pdf ) and *al-Hayat*, November 6, 2008.

106. Blanford, Policy Watch 1414.

107. Civilian sources in Lebanon say that Hezbollah continues to maintain its bunkers and weapons storages in the South. It makes sure that material and supplies are kept in fresh supply and it pays local staff to see to this (Blanford, Policy Watch 1414).

108. Congressional Research Service, "Lebanon: The Israel-Hamas-Hezbollah Conflict," p. 10.

109. The larger offensive was not launched until a couple of days before the ceasefire went into effect (see the preceding section), but smaller operations with smaller units were launched throughout the war (mostly to hunt Katyusha batteries).

110. Congressional Research Service, "Lebanon: The Israel-Hamas-Hezbollah Conflict," p. 11.

111. This primarily concerns short-distance rockets (i.e., Katyushas). As was pointed out earlier, the Israeli air force destroyed almost all

112. Since Hezbollah is classified as a terrorist organization by the United States, all support for the organization is considered aiding terrorism and is there- fore illegal.

113. Interestingly enough, this altered image of how Iran supports Hezbollah financially can be traced to the end of June 2006, when the first large transport took place. It came along with the Iranian foreign minister, Manoucher Motaki, on his visit to Beirut, where he was meeting with his French counter- part, Philippe Douste-Blazy.

114. Intelligence Online, no. 532, October 6, 2006 (http://www.intelligenceonline. com).

115. Ayatollah Khomeini utilized these channels to fund his revolution in 1979.

116. Al-Shamil is from Nahariya in southern Lebanon and, furthermore, is Hassan Nasrallah's son-in-law.

117. As late as March 2009, Iran condemned Interpol's arrest orders for a number of Iranians (including former president Akbar Hashemi Rafsanjani) for involvement in the terrorist attacks on a Jewish center in Buenos Aires. Eighty- five people were killed in the attack. And Iran's new designated minister of

defense—Ahmad Vahidi—is wanted by Interpol for involvement in the same bombing.

118. These two branches or traditions within Shiism largely follow the two schools of jurisprudence that predominate within Shiism. *Akhbari* (the literalists) claimed that they were allowed to "hold off on Friday prayer" until the hidden imam returned, which led to a more passive attitude to the issue of religion and society. They also claimed that interpretations of religious texts could only be done with a basis in the Quran, the verbal traditions (Sunna), and the lives of imams. The second school is *Usuli* (the rationalists), who believed that they were in the position of successor in the absence of the imam. This led them to assume a far more activist position, of which Khomeini's revolution is a good example. Based on *Usuli*, there was a possibility to free interpretation within the framework of *Itjihad*.

119. Even if Sistani is influential in Iraq, it is mainly due to his religious standing, not as a politician. Sistani has never actively tried to gain political power or a political position. His role in Iraq does, however, illustrate the degree to which politics and religion are intertwined in Iraq.

120. In countries such as Iraq, Lebanon, and Bahrain, Shiites comprise the largest minority, and sometimes the majority, but the political and religious power has always rested with the Sunnis, with Iran as the sole exception.

121. For more on Shia and this "cult of victimization" especially, see Farha Khosrokhavar, *Suicide Bombers: Allah's New Martyrs*. (London: Pluto Press, 2005); and Heinz Halm, *Shiism* (New york: Columbia University Press, 1991).

122. *Wilayat al-faqih*. After the 1979 revolution, this effectively became the decision-making body in Iran.

123. *Afwaj al-Muqawamah al-Lubnaniya* (The Lebanese Resistance Detachments). "Amal" means "hope."

124. The decision to carry out the kidnappings that led to the outbreak of the war in 2006 was no exception to this principle. No one, neither the Hezbollah leadership nor Iran, had expected the nature of the Israeli response. Since similar events had taken place in the past, and Hezbollah for many years had attempted to kill and kidnap soldiers inside Israel, Iran was not informed of this particular event before it took place.

125. Hezbollah divides the world into two categories, *mustakbirun* (the oppressors) and *mustad'ifin* (the oppressed). Questions concerning society, the econ- omy, social justice, and the situation in the Middle East in general are fitted into Hezbollah's ideological worldview of good versus evil, which allows little room for compromise. Hezbollah follows the Iranian interpretation of *Usuli* and views the state as a necessity, the least bad alternative to achieve equality and liberty in anticipation of the hidden imam.

126. Ibid.

127. It should also be emphasized that this fact, of course, does not exclude the possibility of future changes with both Iran and Hezbollah, as well as with other Islamists.

128. There were critical voices even when the war was ongoing on the Arab side that claimed that Hezbollah was the guilty party and that the mere fact that it was not crushed is not sufficient to qualify as a victory. Abdel Monem Said Aly, "The Sixth Arab-Israeli War: An Arab Perspective," *Middle East Brief*, no. 11 (October 2006), Crown Center for Middle East Studies, Brandeis University.

129. See, for example, Ehud yaari, "The Muqawama Doctrine," *Jerusalem Report*, November 13, 2006, p. 60.

130. During the Gaza ceasefire discussions in January–February 2009, Hamas demanded that Israel open its border before it would agree to a cessation of fighting. In other words, the group made no attempt to move toward a permanent solution. And even as Hamas asked for this tangible concession (open borders), its only offer in return was to stop firing rockets—a powerful illustration of its strategy of extracting concessions through violence.

131. The relationship between Hamas and Fatah is exceedingly complex, of course, but the financial links are clear. See for example Dan Diker and Khaled Abu Toameh, "Can the Palestinian Authority's Fatah Forces Retake Gaza? Obstacles and Opportunities," *Jerusalem Viewpoints* no. 569 (January– February 2009).

132. See, for example, yoni Fighel and yael Shahar, "The al-Qaida–Hezbollah Connection," *ICT Report*, February 26, 2002; and Matt Levitt, "Ban Hizballah in Europe," PolicyWatch 958, Washington Institute for Near East Policy, February 16, 2005.

## Chapter 9: Iran and Hezbollah's Pre-Operational Modus Operandi in the West - Ioan Pop & Mitchell D. Silber

1. "Iran's New Quds Leader Vows 'Manly' Revenge for Soleimani Killing," *Aljazeera*, 20 January 2020, https://www.aljazeera.com/news/2020/01/iran-quds-force-leader-vows-manly- revenge-soleimani-200120144819073.html

2. Josie Ensor, "Hezbollah Chief Orders 'Resistance Fighters' around the World to Avenge Deathof Iranian Commander Soleimani," *The Telegraph*, 3 January 2020, https://www.telegraph.co. uk/news/2020/01/03/hizbollah-chief-orders-resistance-fighters-around-world-avenge/

3. New York City presents itself an iconic target for potential Iran/Hezbollah terrorist attacks. With its symbolic infrastructure, large Jewish population, Israeli diplomatic presence and     as the home to the Iranian mission to the UN it shares many of the attributes that made Buenos Aires an attractive

target twice. Not unlike Buenos Aires, the presence of an Iranian diplomatic mission in New York City allows officials from Iran's Ministry of Intelligence to live and operate in New York with official diplomatic cover. As stated by Mitch Silber during his 2012 congressional testimony, "Iran has a proven record of using its official presence in a foreign city to coordinate attacks, which are then carried out by Hezbollah agents from abroad, often leveraging the local community—whether wittingly or not—as facilitators," "http://www. homelandsecuritynewswire.com/dr20120323-u-s-congressman- hezbollah-greater-threat-than-al-qaeda" http://www.homelandsecuritynewswire.com/ dr20120323-u-s-congressman-hezbollah-greater-threat-than-al-qaeda

4.  The NYPD saw various degrees of severity of the Iran/Hezbollah threat in the past two decades. The 2006 Lebanon War and the 2008 assassination of Hezbollah head of external operations, Imad Mughniyeh were events that significantly increased the threat level and    led to increased efforts to collect actionable intelligence, create viable operational plans and further develop reliable sources with access to individuals linked to Hezbollah's external operations and / or Iranian spies. This observation is based on the authors' experience at   the NYPD during theseevents.

5.  Tensions between the United States and Iran/Hezbollah have been on the rise since 2018 when the U.S. administration withdrew from the 2015 nuclear deal and re-imposed comprehensive sanctions on Iran. In response, Iran and its proxies are believed responsible for a series of escalations, such as the attacks on oil tankers, the drone attack on oil facilities in Saudi Arabia and most recently, the attack on an Iraqi military base in December 2019. *Sources:* https://www.nytimes.com/2020/01/03/obituaries/qassem-soleimani-dead.html;    https://www.bloomberg.com/news/articles/2019-10-11/iran-oil-tanker-catches-fire-after-red-sea-explosion- irna; https://www.nytimes. com/2019/09/14/world/middleeast/saudi-arabia-refineries-drone-attack. html; https://www.economist.com/middle-east-and-africa/2020/01/03/iran-vows-vengeance- after-america-kills-qassem-suleimani

6.  Pre-operational planning is the process of preparing for a possible attack, including the surveillance of potential targets, target selection, recruitment of possible perpetrators and as upport network, explosiveor weapons procurementetc.

7.  Iran has been deemed a "Warning Level 3, Avoid Nonessential Travel" destination as a result of widespread ongoing transmission by the Centers on Disease Control, https:// wwwnc.cdc.gov/travel/destinations/traveler/none/ iran?s_cid=ncezid-dgmq-travel-single-001

8.  Following the death of Hezbollah operations chief, Imad Mugniyah in Damascus, Syria in 2008, Hezbollah plotted several failed attacks over four years to avenge his death in Azerbaijan, Bulgaria, Cyprus, India, Kuwait and Turkey, until the 2012 Hezbollah suicide bombing attack on a bus carrying

Israeli tourists in Burgas, Bulgaria, which killed six Israeli tourists and injured forty-two, Matthew Levitt, "Hezbollah and the Quds Force in Iran's Shadow War with the West," *The Washington Institute,* Policy Focus 123, January 2013,http://www.washingtoninstitute.org/uploads/Documents/pubs/PolicyFocus123.pdf

9. "Reverberations from Soleimani Death Requires Vigilance in NYC," *Atlantic Council,* 10 January 2020, https://www.atlanticcouncil.org/blogs/menasource/reverberations-from-soleimani- death-requires-vigilance-in-nyc/

10. Adam Goldman and Ellen Nakashima, "CIA and Mossad Killed Senior Hezbollah Figure in Car Bombing," *The Washington Post,* 30 January 2015, https://www.washingtonpost. com/world/national-security/cia-and-mossad-killed-senior-hezbollah-figure-in-car-bombing/ 2015/01/30/ebb88682-968a-11e4-8005-1924ede3e54a_story.html

11. Matthew Levitt, "Hezbollah and the Quds Force in Iran's Shadow War with the West," *The Washington Institute,* Policy Focus 123, January 2013, http://www.washingtoninstitute.org/ uploads/Documents/pubs/PolicyFocus123. pdf

12. Ibid.

13. Dexter Filkins, "After Syria: If the Assad Regime Falls, Can Hezbollah Survive?" *The New Yorker,* 25 February 2013,https://www.newyorker.com/magazine/2013/02/25/after-syria

14. Casey L. Addis and Christopher M. Blanchard, "Hezbollah: Background and Issues for Congress," *Congressional Research Service,* 3 January 2011, p. 19, https://fas.org/sgp/crs/mideast/R41446.pdf

15. Ariane Tabatabai and Colin P. Clarke, "Iran's Proxies Are More Powerful Than Ever," *Foreign Policy,* 16 October 2019, https://foreignpolicy.com/2019/10/16/irans-proxies-hezbollah-houthis-trump-maximum-pressure/

16. Matthew Levitt, "Hezbollah's 1992 Attack in Argentina Is a Warning for Modern-Day Europe," *The Atlantic,* 19 March, 2019, https://www.theatlantic. com/international/archive/ 2013/03/hezbollahs-1992-attack-in-argentina-is-a-warning-for-modern-day-europe/274160/

17. Daniel Politi, "Argentina Designates Hezbollah Terrorist Group on 25th Anniversary of Bombing," *The New York Times,* 18 July 2019, https://www.nytimes.com/2019/07/18/world/americas/argentina-hezbollah-terrorist-group.html

18. "Two Men Charged in Alleged Plot to Assassinate Saudi Arabian Ambassador to the United States," U.S. Department of Justice, 11 October 2011, https://www.justice.gov/opa/ pr/two-men-charged-alleged-plot-assassinate-saudi-arabian-ambassador-united-states

19. Former Assistant to President Barack Obama for Homeland Security and Counterterrorism Lisa Monaco stated in the October 2017 issue of this publication: "I think the case blew        the lid a little bit off the notion that there might be some sort of restraint being imposed        on the Quds force. At the very least, it was clear that whatever restraint was being imposed was not being heeded by the elements who were perpetrating this plot and who we named in the indictment." Paul Cruickshank, "A View from the CT Foxhole: Lisa Monaco, Former Assistant to President Barack Obama for Homeland Security andCounterterrorism," CTC Sentinel 10:9(2017).

20. Matthew Levitt, "Hezbollah Isn't Just in Beirut. It is in New York, Too," *Foreign Policy*, 14June 2019, https://foreignpolicy.com/2019/06/14/hezbollah-isnt-just-in-beirut-its-in-new-        york-too-canada-united-states-jfk-toronto-pearson-airports-ali-kourani-iran/

21. Eyder Peralta "Intelligence Chief: IranIsMoreWillingtoLaunchAttack OnU.S.," *NPR*, 31 January 2012, https://www.npr.org/sections/thetwo-way/2012/01/31/146144394/u-s-intelligence-chief-iran-is-more-willing-to-launch-attack-on-u-s

22. Elise Labott and Laura Koran, "US Officials Warn of Potential Hezbollah Threat to US Homeland," *CNN*, 11 October 2017, https://www.cnn.com/2017/10/10/politics/us-warn-hezbollah-threat/index.html

23. Acting Director of National Intelligence Joseph Maguire  stated  in  the September 2019 issue of this publication: "As for the threat  to  the homeland from  Iranian  proxies  right now in the U.S., I do not view that as a grave threat thanks to the work of our law enforcement, the Federal Bureau of Investigation, and the Department of Homeland Security." Paul Cruickshank and Brian Dodwell, "A View from the CT Foxhole: Joseph Maguire, Acting Director of National Intelligence," *CTC Sentinel*12, no. 8(2019):8–13.

24. As part of our research into this topic, we found that the U.K. based, Community Security Trust, in the wake of the July 2019 disclosure of the discovery of the ammonium nitratecaches linked to Hezbollah, conducted its own analysis on Iran/Hezbollah's modus operandi in a report issued in July 2019, "Iran & Hezbollah's Global Terrorism: Patterns & Methods," https://cst.org.uk/data/file/7/0/FINAL percent20Hizbollah percent20and percent20Iran percent20in percent 20the percent20UK percent20WEB.1563275831.pdf

25. In their report, they used a similar framework to assess and describe Iran/Hezbollah's tradecraft: "Undertaking intelligence, surveillance and reconnaissance (ISR) activities on targets; Long-term pre-attack planning over the course of several months or  years; Infiltrating Iranian dissident groups by using cover stories and coercive tactics; Using sophisticated and plausible diplomatic, business, education and other covers to disguise operatives' true intentions; Assembling "human target packages" for the

purposes of neutralizing adversaries; Employing counter-surveillance tradecraft and sophisticated operational security; Recruiting operatives worldwide, especially those with dualnationalitiesandWesternpassports. Thisarticlewillemulatetheirprinciples.

26. Warren Hoge, "Two Iranian Guards at U.N. Expelled for Filming New York Sites," *The New York Times*, 30 June2004. https://www.nytimes.com/2004/06/30/world/two-iranian-guards-at-un-expelled-for-filming-new-york-sites.html

27. Ed Shanahan, "Man Trained by Hezbollah Scouted Times Square as Target, Prosecutors Say," *The New York Times*, 19 September 2019, https://www.nytimes.com/2019/09/19/nyregion/new-jersey-terrorist-hezbollah-alexei-saab.html

28. Testimony by Mitchell D. Silber before the House Homeland Security Committee, "Iran and Hezbollah Threat Assessment", 21 March 2012, https://www.c-span.org/video/?305022-1/iran-hezbollah-threat-assessment&start=928 and Mitchell D. Silber, "The Iranian Threat to New York City," *The Wall Street Journal,* 14 February 2014, https://www.wsj.com/articles/SB10001424052970203824904577215592376556800

29. Ibid and Mitchell D. Silber, "The Iranian Threat to New York City," *Wall Street Journal*, 14 February 2014, https://www.wsj.com/articles/SB10001424052970203824904577215592376556800and Warren Hoge, "Two Iranian Guards Expelled for Filming New York Sites," *The New York Times*, 30 June 2004, https://www.nytimes.com/2004/06/30/world/two-iranian-guards-at-un-expelled-for-filming-new-york-sites.html

30. "NYPD Says Iran Has Conducted Surveillance in NYC," *Homeland Security Today*, 1 October 2012, https://www.hstoday.us/channels/federal-state-local/nypd-says-iran-has- conducted-surveillance-in-nyc-329/

31. Ibid and Mitchell D. Silber, "The Iranian Threat to New York City," *Wall Street Journal,* 14 February 2014,https://www.wsj.com/articles/SB10001424052970203824904577215592376556800

32. Spencer S. Hsu, "Two Men Plead Guilty to Acting as Illegal Agents for Iran in Surveilling Americans," *The Washington Post,* 5 November 2019, https://www.washingtonpost.com/local/legal-issues/two-men-plead-guilty-to-acting-as-illegal-agents-for-iran-in-surveilling- americans/2019/11/05/34af8cec-0025-11ea-8bab-0fc209e065a8_story.html

33. USA v. Doostdar, 8 August 2018, p. 18, https://www.justice.gov/opa/press-release/file/ 1088521/download

34. Ibid., p.6.

35. "Germany Seeks 10 Members of Iran's IRGC-Qods Force for Spying on Israeli, Jewish Targets," *The Tower*, 16 January 2018, http://www.thetower.org/5844-germany-seeks-10- members-of-irans-irgc-qods-force-for-spying-on-israeli-jewish-targets/ Benjamin Weinthal, "Germany Raids Iranian Regime Sites for Spying on Israel," *The Jerusalem Post*, 16 January 2018, https://www.jpost.com/International/Germany-raids-Iranian-regime-sites-for-spying-on-Israel-536897

36. Benjamin Weinthal, "Germany Raids Iranian Regime Sites for Spying on Israel," *The Jerusalem Post*, 16 January 2018, https://www.jpost.com/International/Germany-raids-     Iranian-regime-sites-for-spying-on-Israel-536897and

37. Christina Maza, "What is the Al-Quds Force? Iran Spies Targeted Kindergartens, Reports Warn," *Newsweek*, 17 January 2018, https://www.newsweek.com/what-al-quds-force-iran-     spies-targeted-jewish-kindergartens-reports-warn-784020

38. Benjamin Weinthal, "Iranian Terrorist Force spying on Israelis and Jews in Germany," *The Jerusalem Post*, 7 July 2019, https://www.jpost.com/Diaspora/Iranian-Terrorist-Force-     spying-on-Israelis-and-Jews-in-Germany-intel-594717

39. Benjamin Weinthal, "Germany is a Hotbed of Iranian Spy Activity That Targets Israel," *The Jerusalem Post*, 21 March 2019, https://www.jpost.com/Diaspora/Germany-is-a-hotbed-     of-Iranian-spy-activity-that-targets-Israel-488767

40. Benjamin Weinthal, "Germany Indicts Alleged Iranian Spy Accused of Targeting Israel Group," *The Jerusalem Post*, 4 January 2017, https://www.jpost.com/Diaspora/Germany-     indicts-alleged-Iranian-spy-accused-of-targeting-Israel-group-477447

41. Benjamin Weinthal, "Iranian Terrorist Force spying on Israelis and Jews in Germany," *The Jerusalem Post*, 7 July 2019, https://www.jpost.com/Diaspora/Iranian-Terrorist-Force-     spying-on-Israelis-and-Jews-in-Germany-intel-594717

42. IJO is a highly compartmentalized component of Hezbollah responsible for the planning, preparation, and execution of intelligence, counterintelligence, and terrorist activities outside ofLebanon.

43. The IJO uses multiple aliases, including "External Security Organization" and"910".

44. Jeffrey Martin, "New Jersey 'Hezbollah Scout' Assessed Targets in NYC, Boston And Washington, Feds Claim," *Newsweek*, 19 September 2019, https://

www.newsweek.com/new-    jersey-hezbollah-scout-assessed-targets-nyc-boston-washington-feds-claim-1460308

45. "Bronx Man and Michigan Man Arrested for Terrorist Activities On Behalf Of Hezbollah's Islamic Jihad Organization," Department of Justice, 8 June 2017, https://www.justice.gov/usao-sdny/pr/bronx-man-and-michigan-man-arrested-terrorist-activities-behalf-Hezbollah-s-islamic

46. USA v. Kourani, 31 May 2017, https://www.justice.gov/usao-sdny/press-release/file/972421/ download and USA v. El Debek, 31 May 2017, https:// www.justice.gov/opa/press-release/ file/972446/download

47. "Hezbollah Operative Sentenced to 40 Years in Prison for Covert Terrorist Activities   on   Behalf of Hezbollah's Islamic Jihad Organization," *US Department of Justice*, 3   December 2019, https://www.justice.gov/opa/pr/ Hezbollah-operative-sentenced-40-years-prison-covert-  terrorist-activities-behalf-Hezbollah-s

48. Judith Miller, "Taking No Chances in New York," *City Journal*, 7 January 2020, https:// www.city-journal.org/nypd-security-iran-threats

49. Jack More, "U.S. Foils Hezbollah Plot to Attack American, Israeli Targets in New York and Panama," *Newsweek*, 9 June 2017, https://www.newsweek. com/us-foils-hezbollah-plot- attack-american-israeli-targets-new-york-and-panama-623432

50. USA v. Kourani, 31 May 2017, p. 3, https://www.justice.gov/usao-sdny/press-release/file/ 972421/download

51. Ibid., p.3.

52. Ibid., p.7.

53. The IJO's "Operatives" Are Usually "Assigned a Lebanon-Based 'Handler,' Sometimes Referred to as a Mentor," and this person is "responsible for providing taskings, debriefing operatives, and arranging training." USA v. Kourani, 31 May 2017, p. 8, https://www. justice.gov/opa/press-release/ file/972446/download

54. Ibid.

55. Matthew Levitt, "Hezbollah Isn't Just in Beirut. It is in New York, Too, *Foreign Policy*, June   14, 2019, https://foreignpolicy.com/2019/06/14/hezbollah-isnt-just-in-beirut-its-in-new-   york-too-canada-united-states-jfk-toronto-pearson-airports-ali-kourani-iran/

56. Ibid.

57. Ibid.

58. Ibid.

59. "Bronx Man And Michigan Man Arrested For Terrorist Activities On Behalf Of Hezbollah's Islamic Jihad Organization," *Department of Justice*, 8 June 2017, https://www. justice.gov/usao-sdny/pr/bronx-man-and-michigan-man-arrested-terrorist-activities-behalf-Hezbollah-s-islamic

60. USA v. El Debek, p. 14, 31 May 2017,https://www.justice.gov/opa/press-release/file/ 972446/download

61. USA v Saab, p. 3 , 19 September 2019, https://www.justice.gov/opa/press-release/file/ 1203836/download

62. Ibid., p.7.

63. Ibid., p.13.

64. Ibid., p.13.

65. Ibid., p.16.

66. Ibid., p.16.

67. Ibid., p.20.

68. Investigations Unit of the Office of the Attorney General [Argentina], "AMIA Case" signed by District Attorney Marcelo Martinez Burgos, Attorney General Alberto Nisman, and Secretary of the Office of the Attorney General Herman Longo (25 October 2006), and Notes from NYPD Intelligence Division meeting with Argentine Secretariat of Intelligence, June2018.

69. Ibid.

70. Investigations Unit of the Office of the Attorney General [Argentina], "AMIA Case" signed by District Attorney Marcelo Martinez Burgos, Attorney General Alberto Nisman, and Secretary of the Office of the Attorney General Herman Longo, (October25,2006):22.

71. Investigations Unit of the Office of the Attorney General (2006), 23–4. Allegedly, both Rabbani and Asghari attended the August 14, 1993 meeting in Mashhad, Iran, when the decision to carry out the AMIA attack was made by Iran's "Committee for Special Operations."

72. Investigations Unit of the Office of the Attorney General [Argentina], (2006), 24.72. Ibid.,137.

73. Ibid.,310.

74. Ibid.,311.

75. Ibid.,315.

76. Ibid., 317–26.

77. "US Prosecutors to Seize Mosques and Skyscraper Suspected of Funding Iran," *The Telegraph*, 13 November 2009, https://www.telegraph.co.uk/news/ worldnews/northamerica/ usa/6558658/US-prosecutors-to-seize-mosques- and-skyscraper-suspected-of-funding-Iran.html

78. Jonathan Stempel, "U.S. verdict allowing seizure of Iran-linked Manhattan skyscraper is overturned, *Reuters*, 9 August 2019 https://www.reuters.com/ article/us-usa-iran-650-fifth-avenue/ u-s-verdict-allowing-seizure-of-iran- linked-manhattan-skyscraper-is-overturned-idUSKCN1UZ1YL

79. AuthorsexperienceworkingonNYPDIntelligenceDivision'Iran/ Hezbollahinvestigations.

80. Ibid.

81. Vivian Wang, "Manhattan Skyscraper Linked to Iran Can Be Seized by U.S., Jury Finds," *New York Times*, 29 June 2017, https://www.nytimes.com/2017/06/29/ nyregion/650-fifth- avenue-iran-terrorism.html; and Brendan Pierson, "Jury finds United States may seize Iran-linked office tower," *Reuters*, 29 June 2017, https://www.reuters.com/article/us-usa- iran-lawsuit/jury-finds-united- states-may-seize-iran-linked-office-tower-idUSKBN19K2NB

82. Authors' experience working on NYPD Intelligence Division' Iran/Hezbollah investigations.

83. "Iran's Ministry of Intelligence and Security: A Profile," *Library of Congress*, December 2012, p. 7,https://fas.org/irp/world/iran/mois-loc.pdf

84. "Iran's Ministry of Intelligence and Security: A Profile," *Library of Congress*, December 2012, p.1.

85. Leela Jacinto, "Ali Vakili Rad: The perfect murder and an imperfect getaway," *France 24,* 18 May 2010, https://www.france24.com/en/20100518-ali-vakili- rad-perfect-murder-imperfect-getaway-shapour-bakhtiar

86. "Iran's Ministry of Intelligence and Security: A Profile," *Library of Congress,* December 2012, p.30.

87. The Green protest movement came to prominence after the contentious 2009 Iranian presidential election, which was marked by irregularities. It sparked nation-wide protests, against the re-election of Mahmoud Ahmadinejad to the detriment of at Mir-Hossein Mousavi. – Hamid Dabashi "What Happened to the Green Movement in Iran?," *Al Jazeera*, 12 June 2013,https://www. aljazeera.com/indepth/opinion/2013/05/201351661225981675.html

88. Authors experience working on NYPD Intelligence Division 'Iran/Hezbollah investigations.

89. "Chronology of Iran's Nuclear Program," *The New York Times,* 8 August 2005, https:// www.nytimes.com/2005/08/08/international/chronology-of-irans-nuclear-program.html

90. "Iran's Ministry of Intelligence and Security: A Profile," *Library of Congress,* December 2012, p.35.

91. "Two Individuals Charged for Acting as Illegal Agents of the Government of Iran," *Department of Justice,* 20 August 2018, https://www.justice.gov/opa/pr/two-individuals- charged-acting-illegal-agents-government-iran

92. USA v. Doostdar, 8 August 2018, https://www.justice.gov/opa/press-release/file/ 1088521/download

93. "Two charged in US with spying for Iran," *BBC,* 21 August 2018, https://www.bbc.com/ news/world-us-canada-45261181

94. "Two Individuals Charged for Acting as Illegal Agents of the Government of Iran," *Department of Justice,* 20 August 2018, https://www.justice.gov/opa/pr/two-individuals- charged-acting-illegal-agents-government-iran

95. "Two Individuals Charged for Acting as Illegal Agents of the Government of Iran," *Department of Justice,* 20 August 2018, https://www.justice.gov/opa/pr/two-individuals- charged-acting-illegal-agents-government-iran

96. "Sohrab" is the alias used bye Majid Ghorbani.

97. https://www.justice.gov/opa/press-release/file/1088516/download, p.14.

98. "Two Individuals Charged for Acting as Illegal Agents of the Government of Iran," *Department of Justice,* 20 August 2018, https://www.justice.gov/opa/pr/two-individuals- charged-acting-illegal-agents-government-iran

99. Unit 910 or Islamic Jihad Organization (IJO), is Hezbollah's External Security Organization (ESO) responsible for intelligence gathering, surveillance, planning, coordination and execution of terrorist attacks outside Lebanon as per USA v. Kourani, 31May 2017,https://www.justice.gov/usao-sdny/press-release/file/972421/download

100. Times of Israel Staff, "Report: Hezbollah planned huge, game-changing attacks on Israel targets globally," *Times of Israel,* 12 June 2019, https://www.timesofisrael.com/hezbollah-    planned-immense-game-changing-terror-attacks-report/

101. Ibid.

102. Thomas Joscelyn, "Analysis: 2 US cases provide unique window into Iran's global terror network," *Long War Journal,* 23 June 2017, https://www.longwarjournal.org/archives/2017/ 06/analysis-2-us-cases-provide-unique-window-into-irans-global-terror-network.php

103. USA v. El Debek, 31 May 2017, https://www.justice.gov/opa/press-release/ file/ 972446/download

104. Ibid.

105. Matt Levitt, "Hezbollah's Criminal and Terrorist Operations in Europe," *AJC Global Voice*, 2 September, 2018 https://www.ajc.org/news/hezbollahs-criminal-and-terrorist-operations-in-europe#_ftn6 and MenelaosHadjicostis, "Hezbollah member pleads guilty to 8 charges in Cyprus," *AP*, 29 June 2015, http://bigstory.ap.org/article/9b2fba18477b4f9098dd3da95fb0ff2b/ hezbollah-member-pleads-guilty-8-chargescyprus

106. Riley-Smith, Ben, "Iran-Linked Terrorists Caught Stockpiling Explosives in North-West London," *The Telegraph*, 9 June 2019, https://www.telegraph. co.uk/news/2019/06/09/iran-           linked-terrorists-caught-stockpiling-explosives-north-west/ and Times of Israel Staff, "Report: Hezbollah planned huge, game-changing attacks on Israel targets globally," *Times   of Israel*, 12 June2019,

107. Ibid.

108. Ibid.

109. Ibid.

110. Times of Israel Staff, "Report: Hezbollah Planned Huge, Game-Changing Attacks on Israel TargetsGlobally," *Times o fIsrael*,12 June,2019.

111. USA v. Kourani, 31 May 2017, https://www.justice.gov/usao-sdny/press-release/file/ 972421/download

112. https://www.linkedin.com/in/ahsaab/

113. https://www1.nyc.gov/site/nypd/about/about-nypd/equipment-tech/ technology.page

114. Authors' personal experience and Neal Ungerleider, "NYPD, Microsoft Launch All-Seeing "Domain Awareness System" With Real-Time CCTV, License Plate Monitoring," *Fast Company Magazine*, at https://www. fastcompany.com/3000272/nypd-microsoft-launch-all-          seeing-domain-awareness-system-real-time-cctv-license-plate-monito

115. Summonses are citations by law enforcement for minor offenses or a notice to appear incourt.

116. Rocco Parascandola, "New NYPD Surveillance Cameras to Cover  Stretch of Upper East Side not Easily Reached by Patrol Cars, *New York Daily News*, 24 October, 2018, https:// www.nydailynews.com/new-york/nyc-crime/ny-metro-argus-cameras-east-20181024-story. html and E. S. Levine; Jessica Tisch; Anthony Tasso; Michael Joy, "The New York City Police

Department's Domain Awareness System," *Interfaces*, 47, no. 1: 70–84, February 2017,doi:10.1287/inte.2016.0860

117. USA v. Monica Elfriede Witt, 9 July 2018, https://www.studentpost.org/wp-content/ uploads/2019/02/Indictment-of-Monica-Witts.pdf

118. USA v. Doostdar, 8 August 2018,https://www.justice.gov/opa/press-release/ file/1088521/download

119. Borger, Julian, "Mike Pompeo claims Iran carrying out 'assassination operations' in Europe," *The Guardian*, 22 May 2018, https://www. theguardian.com/us-news/2018/may/22/ mike-pompeo-iran-assassination-operations-europe

120. 120 Hendrickx, Frank, "Nissi's Death Is Still Covered in Thick Fog," *deVolkskrant*, 9 November 2018, https://www.volkskrant.nl/nieuws-achtergrond/nog-altijd-is-nissi-s-dood- in-dichte-mist-gehuld b25158ed/. For more on the role of Iranian diplomats see Levitt, "Iran's Deadly Diplomats, CTC Sentinel,August 2018, 11, no. 7, https://ctc.usma.edu/ august-2018/

121. "The EU is Taking Measures Following the Liquidation in BezuidhoutWest," *Bezuidenhout.nl*, 8 January 2019, https://bezuidenhout.nl/blog/tag/ahmad-mola-nissi/

122. Adam Plowright, "What Do We Know about ALLEGED IRANIAN PLOT to Bomb Opposition Groups in Paris?," *Times of Israel*, 3 July 2018, https:// www.timesofisrael.com/ what-do-we-know-about-alleged-iranian-plot-to-bomb-opposition-groups-in-paris/

123. Hendrickx, Frank, "Nissi's Death Is Still Covered in Thick Fog," *deVolkskrant*, 9 November 2018, https://www.volkskrant.nl/nieuws-achtergrond/nog-altijd-is-nissi-s-dood- in-dichte-mist-gehuldb25158ed/

124. Ibid.

125. Norman, Lawrence, "Denmark Says It Foiled Iranian Assassination Plot," *Wall Street Journal*, 30 October 2018, https://www.wsj.com/articles/ denmark-says-it-foiled-iranian- assassination-plot-1540927533?mod=searc hresults&page=1&pos=1&mod=article_inline

126. Weinthal, Benjamin, "Iranian Terrorist Force Spying on Israelis and Jews in Germany," *The Jerusalem Post*, 7 July 2019, https://www.jpost. com/Diaspora/Iranian-Terrorist-Force- spying-on-Israelis-and-Jews-in-Germany-intel-594717

127. Ibid.

128. USA v. Kourani, 31 May 2017, https://www.justice.gov/usao-sdny/press-release/file/ 972421/download

129. USA v. Doostdar, 8 August 2018, https://www.justice.gov/opa/press-release/file/1088521/download

130. Ibid.

131. Ibid.

132. Ibid.

133. Ibid.

134. Ibid.

135. Ibid.

136. USA v. Kourani, 31 May 2017, https://www.justice.gov/usao-sdny/press-release/file/ 972421/download

137. Ibid.

138. USA v. Saab, 19 September 2019, https://www.justice.gov/opa/press-release/file/ 1203796/download

139. USA v. Kourani, 31 May 2017, https://www.justice.gov/usao-sdny/press-release/file/ 972421/download

140. USA v. El Debek, 31 May 2017, https://www.justice.gov/opa/press-release/file/ 972446/download

141. USA v. Kourani, 31 May 2017, https://www.justice.gov/usao-sdny/press-release/file/ 972421/download

142. USA v Saab, 19 September 2019, https://www.justice.gov/opa/press-release/file/ 1203796/download

143. USA v. Kourani, 31 May 2017, https://www.justice.gov/usao-sdny/press-rclcasc/filc/ 972421/download

144. USA v. Doostdar, 8 August 2018, https://www.justice.gov/opa/press-release/file/1088521/download

145. It is alleged that Arbabsiar, directed by the Iranian Revolutionary Guard Corps, hired, what he believed to be a member of a Mexican drug cartel to assassinate al-Jubeir. The plan involved bombing a Washington, DC restaurant, frequented by the Saudi ambassador, potentially killing many in the process.

146. USA v. Arbabsiar and Shakuri, 11 October, 2011, https://www.justice.gov/ archive/opa/ documents/us-v-arbabsiar-shakuri-complaint.pdf

147. According to court documents, "In approximately 2008, KOURANI was recruited by Sheikh Hussein Kourani in Lebanon to Join the IJO." From USA v. Kourani

148. USA v. Kourani, May 31, 2017, https://www.justice.gov/usao-sdny/press-release/file/ 972421/download

149. Ibid.

150. USA v. El Debek, 31 May 2017, https://www.justice.gov/opa/press-release/file/ 972446/download

151. USA v. Saab, 19 September 2019, https://www.justice.gov/opa/press-release/file/ 1203796/download

152. Ibid.

153. USA v. Saab, 19 September 2019, https://www.justice.gov/opa/press-release/file/ 1203796/download

154. Authors' experience working on NYPD Intelligence Division' Iran/Hezbollah investigations

155. Mark Mazzetti, Helene Cooper, Julian E. Barnes, Alissa J. Rubin and EricSchmitt, "As Iran Reels, Trump Aides Clash Over Escalating Military Showdown," *New York Times*, 21 March 2020, https://www.nytimes.com/2020/03/21/world/middleeast/trump-iran-iraq-coronavirus-militas.html

# INDEX

# About Editor

Mr. Noor Dahri is the Founder and Executive Director of Islamic Theology of Counter Terrorism- ITCT, a UK based Counter Islamist Terrorism Think Tank. Noor is also a contributing writer at US Homeland Security Magazine. He was an active member of Lahskar -e-Taibah (LeT), a Jihadist organisation in Pakistan. Mr Dahri has studied masters of science MSc in Terrorism, Security and Policing from Leicester University. Noor Dahri has also worked with the London Police department for the last seven years. He has studied diploma in Forensics and Criminal Psychology from Oxford – UK, Counter Terrorism from the University of Maryland – U.S.A and also online studied Counter Terrorism from International Institute for Counter Terrorism ICT- Israel. He is an independent researcher in Counter Islamist Terrorism and Radicalisation.

Mr Dahri is an advisor of three reputable organisations, Indian based security and defence company COVINTS and The World Hindu Struggle Committee as well as the US based Council of Muslims Against Anti-Semitism (CMAA). He is also a member of the UK based academic organisation, British Association for Islamic Studies (BRAIS).

He has written many research articles on the hot issues such as Counter Terrorism, Violent Extremism, De-Radicalisation and Israel-Palestine conflict which have been published in various newspapers. Noor has attended many events, conferences on the threat of Counter Terrorism and also visited many institutes and libraries. Mr Dahri is a Middle East Analyst at The Great Middle East and a regular contributor at the Times of Israel (Israel) and The Daily Times (Pak). He has appeared on numerous TV and Radio shows for his interviews.

Noor is a first Pakistani, who has been officially invited to deliver his speeches at the International Institute for Counter Terrorism -ICT in Israel on the topic of "From Daw'ah To Jihad: Breaking the Radicalization and Violent Cycle". Mr. Noor is the fellow member of the Intelligence Community USA and a member of the security think tank Henry Jackson society UK. He regularly attends discussion-based events in the House of Commons and the House of Lords (UK Parliaments). He has visited many countries for his research work.

Noor Dahri has received a "Life Achievement Award Certificate" by Lord Frank Judd at The House of Lords- London in 2017.

He has authored two books: "Global Jihad, Islamic Radicalisation and Counter Strategy" and "Terra Nullius: The Rebirth of a Land Without Peace" that were published from India in 2019 and also edited "Marketing Terrorism: The Continental Fear from Middle East & Asia to Africa" which was published from India in 2020.

www.ingramcontent.com/pod-product-compliance
Lightning Source LLC
Chambersburg PA
CBHW021113270326
41929CB00009B/862